Corporate Strategies in the Pacific Rim

Following a major international conference held in Sapporo, Japan, in 1992, on the impact of globalization and regionalization on corporate strategy and structure among Pacific Rim firms, this volume brings together the most important papers presented.

As part of the successful *International Business Series*, this book is highly topical in a number of ways. The Pacific Rim focus highlights an area which is playing an increasingly relevant and important role in today's global economy; the potential conflict between global and regional factors in this part of the world is analyzed; and contributors, including political scientists, relate trends in International Business to current literature on international affairs and political economy to give the volume an added dimension.

This is a book which provides a broad perspective on Pacific Rim corporate strategies vis-à-vis globalization issues, as well as providing excellent case studies on Fujitsu and Samsung.

Denis Fred Simon is Associate Professor of International Business and Technology and directs the Center for Technology and International Affairs at the Fletcher School of Law and Diplomacy, Tufts University.

International Business Series
Academic Editor: Alan M. Rugman, *University of Toronto*

Multinationals: The Swedish Case
Erick Hörnell and Jan Erik Vahlne

Japanese Participation in British Industry
John H. Dunning

Managing the Multinational Subsidiary
Hamid Etemad and Louise Séguin Dulude

Multinationals, Governments and International Technology Transfer
A. E. Safarian and Gilles Y. Bertin

Trade among Multinationals: Intra-industry Trade and National Competitiveness
D. C. MacCharles

Doing Business in Korea
Arthur M. Whitehill

Administered Protection in America
Alan M. Rugman and Andrew Anderson

The Italian Multinationals
Edited by Fabrizio Onida and Gianfranco Viesti

Multinational Joint Ventures in Developing Countries
Paul W. Beamish

Global Business: Asia–Pacific Dimensions
Edited by E. Kaynak and K. H. Lee

Government Export Promotion
F. H. Rolf Seringhaus and Philip J. Rossen

Multinationals in Latin America
Robert Grosse

Multinational Enterprises in India
Nagesh Kumar

Global Corporate Strategy
Alan M. Rugman and Alain Verbeke

Multinationals and Europe 1992
Edited by B. Burgenmeier and J.-L. Muchielli

International Business in China
Edited by Lane Kelley and Oded Shenkar

Corporate Strategies in the Pacific Rim

Global Versus Regional Trends

Edited by Denis Fred Simon

London and New York

First published 1995
by Routledge
11 New Fetter Lane, London EC4P 4EE

Simultaneously published in the USA and Canada
by Routledge
29 West 35th Street, New York, NY 10001

Phototypeset in Times by Intype, London
Printed and bound in Great Britain by
Mackays of Chatham PLC, Chatham, Kent

British Library Cataloguing in Publication Data
A catalogue record for this book is available from the British Library

Library of Congress Cataloging in Publication Data
A catalogue record for this book has been requested

ISBN 0–415–10455–6

Contents

Part III Pacrim firms: structure and strategy

Figures

Tables

Contributors

Denis Fred Simon is Associate Professor of International Business and Technology and directs the Center for Technology and International Affairs at the Fletcher School of Law and Diplomacy, Tufts University.

Takeshi Aoki is Professor of Economics in the Faculty of Social Sciences at Kyorin University in Tokyo, Japan.

Joseph R. D'Cruz is an Associate Professor of Strategic Management at the University of Toronto in Canada.

Richard Drobnick is Vice Provost for International Affairs and is Director of the Center for International Business Education and Research at the University of Southern California.

William Fischer is the Dalton L. McMichael Senior Chair and Professor of Business Administration at the Graduate School of Business Administration, University of North Carolina at Chapel Hill.

David Gold is Chief, Microeconomic Issues and Policies Unit, United Nations Department for Economic and Social Information and Policy Analysis, New York City.

Azizul Islam is Chief, Development Planning Division, United Nations Economic and Social Commission for Asia and the Pacific, Bangkok, Thailand.

Yongwook Jun is a Professor of International Business in the College of Business Administration at Chung Ang University in Seoul, Korea.

Katsuto Kondo is a Senior Researcher in Business and Technology at the Fujitsu Research Institute, which is located outside of Tokyo.

Bruce Koppel is Vice President for Research and Education at the East-West Center in Honolulu, Hawaii.

Stephen D. Krasner is Professor of Political Science at Stanford University, Stanford, California.

Chol Lee is a member of the faculty in the Department of International Trade of the College of Business at Hong Ik University in Seoul, Korea.

David C. Mowery is a Professor at the Haas School of Business at the University of California, Berkeley.

Terutomo Ozawa is a Professor of Economics at Colorado State University, in Fort Collins, Colorado.

Alan M. Rugman is a member of the Faculty of Management at the University of Toronto in Canada.

Chi Schive is Vice-Chairman of the Council for Economic Planning and Development under the Executive Yuan on Taiwan. He was formerly Professor of Economics at National Taiwan University.

George S. Yip is Visiting Associate Professor at the Anderson Graduate School of Management at the University of California at Los Angeles (UCLA).

Acknowledgements

The editor would like to express his appreciation to both the East–West Center in Hawaii and to NORPAC in Hokkaido, Japan for their support of this project. Special gratitude is owed to Dr. Bruce Koppel, Vice-President of the East–West Center for his willingness to help open up new vistas of scholarly inquiry for his institution as well as for the business and academic communities interested in contemporary Asian affairs. Last, but most important, I want to thank all of the people who participated in the meeting, some of whose papers were not included in this volume. Together, our gathering in Sapporo gave us a chance to break some new ground in terms of the evolving discourse between the traditional social sciences and the emerging field of international business.

DEDICATION

This book is dedicated to my wife Fredda, my daughter Melissa, and my son Mitchell – all three of whom have learned the growing importance of having a 'global outlook' as part of their personal evolution and maturation.

Introduction

Denis Fred Simon

Few phenomena have attracted as much attention as the impact of globalization. Along with having an important shaping effect on international business transactions and world production structures, globalization has also made itself felt in the realm of culture and political affairs.[1] As the constraints of space and time have become more and more manageable, the pressures for fundamental change in both the socio-political and economic spheres have steadily increased. Somewhat akin to the type of transformation that occurs in the midst of a scientific revolution, world affairs seem to be experiencing a type of paradigmatic change, engendered in large part by globalization. The only real question is how quickly and completely the world will move towards acceptance of this new paradigm, including all its new rules and norms.

Globalization has been driven by a number of critical factors. A significant one has been the spread of liberalization, privatization and de-regulation throughout the world. Simply stated, state control and ownership are steadily, albeit gradually, giving way to market dominance. Barriers to trade and investment have been falling for much of the postwar period, even taking into account the continuation of a number of bilateral trade frictions, e.g. US–Japan trade. As barriers to the movement of products, services, and capital have declined, globalization also has been facilitated by the technological revolution taking place in transportation and communication. A new information infrastructure has been created around the world linking markets and expediting the flow of data, statistics, and related information across borders. Seasonal differences for the purchase of fruits and vegetables do not seem to make much of a difference for consumers in most major markets as levels of demand can not only be assessed, but products can be delivered without significant delays or fear of spoilage. Discussions about the development of a so-called hypersonic airplane capable of moving people from New York to Tokyo in several hours further underlies the spread of globalization.

A third factor that has helped to enhance the momentum of the globalization process deals with the changing nature and structure of markets. Aided by the steady breakdown of political and even cultural barriers to the movement of people, products, and information, the purchasing patterns of various consumer groups have begun to converge. The idea of market globalization was early discussed by Ted Levitt in his seminal article in the *Harvard Business Review*. Today, globalization has been fostered by the vast similarities that exist in terms of tastes and wants across the international system. Superstars in sports such as Michael Jordan, in the music world such as Michael Jackson, and in the world of cinema such as Sharon Stone and Sylvester Stallone have a global following and the products they represent respectively in magazine or television advertising are usually marketed using similar rather than distinctive themes.

While most companies have tried to be highly responsive to the pull from new markets, there also has been a certain "push" factor underlying the movement into markets beyond the Western industrialized world. Faced with the growing problems of market saturation in their own national economies, the corporate leaders of world-class companies such as AT&T and General Electric have indicated that in the future approximately 50 percent of the revenues of their firms will have to come from beyond the US market; according to the new accepted wisdom, the so-called mega-markets of the future will be China, India, and Mexico. Based on the rapid pace of economic development and industrialization occurring in these economies, there certainly is good reason to anticipate a tremendous surge in demand, especially in the early part of the twenty-first century. This search for new markets abroad has also engendered a change in the nature of competition as home markets are no longer guaranteed profit sanctuaries; nor do they offer the security that they once did when local firms could count on a blend of government subsidies, tariff and non-tariff barriers, etc. Moreover, the intensity of competition continues to increase as new, dynamic players from emerging markets strive to play the global game and sell their products beyond their own borders – globally and regionally.

In the sphere of economic and business affairs, it is already clear that few industries have escaped the impact of globalization, even if that impact has been felt in different ways both within and across these respective industries. Moreover, as suggested, few markets have been able to cushion, let alone insulate, themselves from the effects of globalization. With world merchandise trade growing over 12 percent in 1994 and world exports increasing to over US$4.06 trillion in 1994 – an increase of about 9 percent from 1993 – it is indeed rare not to encounter many similar products and converging demand patterns in the world's major markets irrespective of geographic location or predominant cultural orientation. In fact, world trade in 1994 grew at a faster rate than world output – which grew only 3.5 percent. With the establishment of the World Trade Organization promising even greater liberalization and tariff reductions, barring a major global recession, the trend toward greater economic integration is likely to continue.

Adding further intensity to the impact of globalization has been the related growth in foreign investment by the world's leading multinational corporations (MNCs). According to the *World Investment Report – 1994* published by the United Nations, total flows of foreign direct investment reached US$195 billion, up from US$171 billion in 1992. While the level of foreign investment in 1993–4 did not reach the peak level of US$232 billion in 1990, the generally rising level of flows over the last several years has indicated a new reality in the world economy, namely the recognition and acceptance of the importance of direct foreign investment as an engine of growth and development throughout the globe. Today, there are approximately 37,000 MNCs operating worldwide, controlling more than 200,000 manufacturing and R&D subsidiaries as well as sales affiliates. The top 100 MNCs in the world own and control over 60 percent of the US$2.1 trillion in worldwide assets garnered through previous investments.[2]

As part of the globalization imperative, more and more of the world foreign investment flows are moving into the so-called developing world. According to a recent World Bank report, countries best placed to benefit from the new opportunities offered by globalization are those that are successfully transforming their policies and structures to support outward-oriented development; the fact is simply that some of the poorest countries in the world are the least integrated internationally.[3] Two games continue to be played on the international scene, one being the game of global competition and the other being the game of international development. In recent years, however, the paramount game has become global competition, with development taking a back seat in terms of attention and resources. To succeed in economic terms within today's globalizing world, most countries and the firms within them recognize that they have to join the mainstream of global competition. Otherwise, they, in all likelihood, will remain on the periphery of the global economy and are destined to become increasingly marginalized.

Of the US$195 billion invested in 1994, about US$80 billion went to the developing world, with the Asian economies accounting for US$44 billion or 55 percent of these flows.[4] It is no surprise, therefore, to find the Pacific Rim to be the most dynamic and fastest growing part of the world economy. In addition, if we scan the list of the Fortune Global 500, we can see 150 Asian companies, including 135 Japanese firms, and 12 Korean companies. Among Fortune Global Service 500 list, the results are similar, with 149 Asian firms, including 140 from Japan, three from South Korea, two from Hong Kong, two from China, one from Taiwan and one from Singapore. According to Singapore's former Prime Minister, Lee Kwan-Yew, the world should not be surprised if within the next fifty years, half of the Fortune 500 companies are headquartered in Asia, even if they are not owned totally by Asians.[5]

As globalization has made itself felt throughout the world, it has become clearer to both corporate decision-makers and government policymakers that the process itself has not been very homogeneous in terms of impact as well as spread. As indicated above, different industries have been affected in different ways by globalization, with some industries moving very quickly to adapt and adjust to the imperatives of globalization, and other industries seemingly responding with less concern in terms of time and speed. While expert observers of global trends such as Kenichi Ohmae continue to "preach" about the onset of a borderless world, the reality is that the globalization process has been characterized by a higher degree of heterogeneity than is generally acknowledged. This degree of unevenness in impact and differential responses to globalization trends underlies the core theme that ties together the various chapters in this volume.

The chapter by Simon and Koppel provides an overview of the impact of globalization on the prevailing paradigms of international relations. They raise a number of critical questions, arguing that the so-called "interdependence" paradigm is no longer comprehensive or properly focussed enough to capture the essential aspects of the globalization process, including the new relationships among non-state actors as well as the altered relations between nation-states and multinational corporations (MNCs). In trying to identify the core elements of a possible new paradigm, however, they are careful to indicate that the incompleteness of the globalization process itself leaves the shape and thrust of any new or competing paradigm still indeterminant.

According to Stephen Krasner, in the aftermath of the collapse of the former Soviet Union, the 1990s have been characterized by increasing levels of uncertainty and disquiet regarding the emerging shape of the post-Cold War international economy. Like Simon and Koppel, Krasner sees the current period characterized more by turbulence and indecision than by clear guidelines, especially in terms of the multilateral trading system. As a political scientist, Krasner's chapter is not specifically focussed on the international business environment; globalization has only recently begun to make itself felt in the thinking and writing on the global political economy. And, as Krasner's chapter indicates, incorporating the elements of globalization into an international relations framework where there appears to be a growing divergence in interests and behavior between private sector and state actors is a task not easily accomplished.

The "fuzzy" quality of the emerging picture of the international business environment is further discussed in the chapter by Gold and Islam, which deals with the role of the multinational corporation as both cause and effect of globalization. Reiterating the point made by Simon and Koppel regarding the fact that the globalization process is proceeding along different dimensions of economic activity at different rates, they nonetheless argue, implicitly at times, that the world is about to cross a critical threshold where policy makers, to be effective, must be prepared to rely on a new series of instruments and mechanisms to manage the significant changes engendered by the globalization process. Underlying their argument is the notion that the essence of the MNC itself has undergone some significant changes, including a new focus on networks and related strategies for orchestrating and organizing globally-integrated manufacturing and R&D activities.

If Gold and Islam are indeed correct in their suggestion that the MNCs of the 1990s have changed in behavioral, organizational, and strategic terms from those of the 1960s and 1970s, this may help to explain, in part, why the disdain that was once held for these large firms has been transformed into a new respect and a willingness to cooperate among most host countries. The chapter by Fischer suggests that there is indeed an effort underway, in terms of the technical activities of the firm, to adjust to the changing dynamics of international competition. Fischer's analysis highlights a variety of examples that show how the entire "business system" within various large, internationally-oriented companies is undergoing restructuring and re-engineering in response to global market changes. More to the point, however, is his finding that most of these efforts at adjustment and re-orientation are anything but elegant or coherent. Most of the initiatives at the micro-level discussed by Fischer reflect the same lack of symmetry across industries and markets pointed out by Simon and Koppel. Moreover, at times the responses lack appreciable consistency even inside the same firms.

These same themes about the unevenness of the globalization process in terms of impact and response are echoed by George Yip in his chapter dealing with the strategic challenges facing global companies. Taking the heterogeneous character of globalization as his starting point, Yip points to the existence of a range of so-called critical "globalization drivers." These drivers are composed of a series of market, government, and competition-related factors that influence the pace of globalization in each industry. Within Yip's scheme, the challenge facing each firm that aspires to be a global company is to understand the dynamics of change within their particular industry. In industries such as computers and aerospace, the bulk of the globalization drivers tend to be fairly consistent in terms of impact; in more "localized" sectors, these same factors, such as the role of government, may act to constrain the process of globalization, e.g. food industry or pharmaceuticals.

The analysis in Yip's chapter is based on an extensive interview study of eighteen worldwide businesses belonging to major American MNCs. In fact, with a few exceptions, the majority of the initial studies of globalization have been focussed on the experiences of US and European MNCs. As indicated above, with the further opening up of the world economy and the spread of industrialization to new parts of the globe, a significant number of new players have entered the international business scene as key actors in industries ranging from semiconductors to automobiles. As a result of the global diffusion of technology, new centers of technical excellence have emerged outside of the traditional bases of innovation and high productivity in the world economy. This is especially true with respect to the Asia-Pacific region, which continues to be the fastest growing part of the international economy system.[6] The rapid emergence of the Pacific Rim portends a possible shift in the locus of economic dynamism and technological leadership in the world. It is already clear that Japanese firms such as Hitachi, Toshiba, NEC,

Fujitsu, and Matsushita have altered prevailing patterns of competition and collaboration in traditional as well as high-technology industries.[7] Now, these firms are joined by companies such as Acer from Taiwan, Samsung and Goldstar from Korea, Singapore Technologies from Singapore, and Legend and Stone from China, all of whom have begun to make their competitive influence felt in both production and R&D terms.

The emergence of the Pacific Rim has had a number of important consequences in terms of the course of the globalization process. Most significant, the growing economic and technological power of the region has raised questions about the role of regionalization within the context of globalization. Unlike globalization, which has been largely driven by the actions of private sector – even taking into account the general liberalizing trends among governments around the world – regionalization in its European (EU) and North American (NAFTA) versions has been predominantly government driven. One merely has to read the voluminous materials coming out of the EU Secretariat in Brussels to appreciate the extensive role played by the various European governments in orchestrating the competitive and trade policies of this regional grouping. Similarly, in the North American case, the same type of government engineering has been responsible for the formalization of the regional cooperation between the US, Mexico and Canada.

Of course, this does not necessarily mean that governments can effectively carry the entire burden of creating and sustaining national competitiveness. In the Canadian case, for example, as the chapter by D'Cruz and Rugman points out, the issue of national competitiveness has assumed a high priority, particularly as Canada looks toward the twenty-first century. D'Cruz and Rugman argue for a more aggressive, dynamic role for the Canadian private sector. Using the concept of networks and industry clusters, they advocate the creation of an economic structure that explicitly does not place government in the vanguard in Canada's drive for competitiveness. Underlying their recommendation is an apparent belief not only in the efficacy of markets in response to globalization pressures and influences, but also a serious concern about the huge potential costs in efficiency terms associated with excessive reliance on government intervention and supports.

Interestingly, the situation regarding regionalization in the Pacific Rim differs quite substantially from the conditions which have characterized the European and North American regionalization experiences. Regionalization in the Pacific Rim has been largely private sector driven. In addition, even within the context of regional integration discussions within such organizations as APEC (Asia Pacific Economic Cooperation) and PECC (Pacific Economic Cooperation Council), the general thrust has been in the direction of "open regionalism."[8] While it is true that intra-regional trade and investment in the Asia Pacific region have been growing at a sustained pace since the mid-1980s, the economies within the Pacific Rim and the firms within these economies have expanded and matured utilizing an externally-oriented strategy that has taken advantage of the open, liberal world economic situation. Fragmentation of the world economy into three so-called regional blocs, a prospect that has been given added impetus in the context of some of the trade frictions discussed by Krasner and also in the chapter by Drobnick, would, in all likelihood, be an anathema to the interests of the Asia-Pacific region as a whole.

It also is clear in the case of the Asia-Pacific economies that the role of the MNC as an engine of development has long been recognized. The desire for continued openness of markets around the world does not obscure the fact that the economic development of the Asian newly industrialized economies (NIEs) and the ASEAN economies (Association of South East Asian Nations) has been closely tied to the processes of industrialization and structural upgrading occurring in Japan. The role of Japan as both an economic and technological power is one of the most significant forces effecting the thrust and character of both globalization and regionalization. Japan's global and regional impacts are likely to be felt even more in the years ahead; estimates are that the share of overseas production by Japanese companies will jump from 16.1 percent in 1993 to 21.6 percent in 1997.[9] Ozawa uses the lens of the economics of concatenation to explain the processes of growth and structural change among the Pacific Rim economies. He refers to the linkages that have developed among these economies as a form of concatenated integration, thus highlighting the linkages and sequential nature of the processes of economic development and growing competitiveness. According to Ozawa, Japanese production has become increasingly regionalized, while the marketing and technological efforts of Japanese firms are more and more globalized – a pattern being followed by several other economies in the Asia-Pacific region.

The evolving character of the emerging Japanese production system in the Pacific Rim is described by Takeshi Aoki, who sees the formation of manufacturing networks as a force *for* as well as a response *to* regionalization in the Pacific Rim. It is Aoki's view that the dynamism of the Japanese economy has manifested itself in the creation of an entirely new production architecture in Asia. He refers to this new architecture as a "core strategic network," whereby exports, imports and foreign investment form a type of trinity in terms of greater regional integration. The remarkable aspect of the proliferation of such networks by Japanese firms in the region is that they have steadily taken on a less hierarchical character over time.[10] There is a high degree of technological complementarity rather than hierarchy that seems to underlie the manufacturing relationships that are being forged.[11] While some US firms, for example Apple, also have been engaged in network type development, the Japanese efforts in this regard are far more pronounced.

Even in the midst of an expanding regional presence, however, Japanese firms, like their counterparts in the other Asia-Pacific economies, recognize that they also must have an appreciable global presence. From a global perspective, while the shift of Japanese production overseas usually incurs the most attention, the reality is that Japanese companies also have been quietly setting up and expanding R&D facilities in the US and Europe as well as in Asia (see Table In.1).[12] Globalization, Japanese style, however, seems to have presented a number of unique challenges to Japanese firms, particularly in terms of personnel policy and decision-making. Katsuto Kondo takes a close look at one such globalization effort inside of Fujitsu, one of the world's leading computer corporations. In the 1980s, Fujitsu began to follow the so-called "global path" through the promotion of offshore production and the formation of strategic alliances with partners in the US and Europe as well as the Asia-Pacific region. One of the hallmarks of Fujitsu's global strategy is the effort to take advantage of the imperatives of regionalization as a means to establish a competitive global presence. From Kondo's perspective, the atmosphere inside of Fujitsu is filled with discussions about partnerships, cross-cultural management, and trans-border R&D based on some sort of "tripolar" model for globalization.

As suggested earlier, the activities of Japanese firms are being complemented by the movement of companies from Korea and Taiwan in similar directions. Chi Schive indicates how Taiwan's numerous small and medium firms are expanding into both China and the ASEAN economies as part of their efforts to take advantage of lower operating costs as well as the increasing prosperity in these countries. The combination of Taiwan's unique political situation and the fact that its industrial structure is dominated by small and

Table In.1 Expansion of Japanese R&D Overseas

Company	*Est. Date*	*Location*	*Focus*
Mitsubishi Electric	Summer 95 Summer 95 Summer 95	Rennes France London, UK Massachusetts	Telecommunications Digital broadcasting Digital TV
Sharp	July 1995	Washington	Digital-image technology
Matsushita Electric	Summer 95	California	Image-compression technology
Toppan Printing	April 95	California	Image-compression technology
Olympus Optical	October 94	New York	Image-processing systems
Casio Computer	October 94	California	Mobile telecommunications
NEC	July 94	Bonn, Germany	Parallel processing
Sony	April 94	California New Jersey	Integrated circuit, image, and telecomm

Source: *Nikkei Weekly* (June 12, 1995), p. 1.

medium-sized enterprises, however, has created the impetus for a more activist government policy regarding both inward and outward investment. In terms of outward investment, the government on Taiwan has viewed the regional and global expansion of local firms as a tool of commercial diplomacy. On the inward side, the government has attempted to establish the island as a regional headquarters center, hoping to take advantage of the shift away from multi-domestic strategies towards more regional strategies among the world's leading MNCs.

The Korean case is more consistent with the Japanese experience, perhaps because there is a closer resemblance in terms of industrial structure and corporate orientation. While Taiwan companies seek to avail themselves of the overseas Chinese networks in operation in the Asia-Pacific region as their primary channel for market access and investment, neither Korean or Japanese firms have such channels readily available to them. Using examples drawn from the Korean electronics industry, Yongwook Jun examines the ways in which Korean companies have responded to the dual imperatives of globalization and regionalization. His analysis leads him to conclude that large Korean electronics companies such as Samsung and

Goldstar have become much more tied into the prevailing patterns of global competition in terms of R&D, manufacturing, and marketing. This has led them to place a high premium on global networking and strategic alliance formation. As Jun suggests, strategic alliances in the globalizing world economy are no longer simply the monopoly of the American, US or Japanese MNCs.

Jun's argument receives a further airing in the chapter by Chol Lee, which is focussed on a case study of Samsung, Korea's largest and most dynamic industrial conglomerate. With its roots in Korea, Lee argues that Samsung has had to overcome a variety of obstacles stemming from Korea's own historical and cultural circumstances. As a result, the globalization of Samsung has been neither easy nor smooth. For Samsung, the process of globalization is not so much measured in the number of overseas projects or cooperative ventures, but by the need for a dramatic sea-change in the mentality of Samsung personnel. To be truly successful at playing the game of global competition, Samsung managers and workers will have to get beyond their parochialism and embrace a new, more cosmopolitan approach to business. Perhaps this explains why Chairman Lee Kun-hee of Samsung has issued his own treatise on Samsung's new management, which is designed to prepare Samsung personnel for operating outside of the traditionally insular channels of Korea. As Chairman Lee has properly recognized in his so-called Frankfurt declaration, to be number one in Korea does not necessarily mean that Samsung possesses the right attributes to be number one around the world.[13]

The Fujitsu and Samsung cases point to one of the central features tying together the various Pacific Rim companies discussed in this volume, namely the heightened interest in strategic alliances and other forms of cross-border collaboration. David Mowery focusses on the formation and operation of collaborative ventures between US and Pacific Rim firms, highlighting the centrality of US–Japanese cooperative activities. His analysis suggests that within the growing number of technology-centered collaborative ventures, complementary capabilities are a greater source of strength and stability than are strong similarities among the partners. He argues that this should lead to an expansion of the number of alliances between US companies and firms from the Asian NIEs because of the complementary nature of their respective capabilities. In particular, the increasingly skilled labor force within Pacific Rim economies such as Taiwan and Korea should provide excellent assets that can be harnessed to enhance the globally competitive position of the respective partners.

While Mowery's data base does not include the expanding number of alliances between Japanese companies and firms from the Asian NIEs, e.g. the new Komatsu-Formosa Plastics alliance in integrated circuits,[14] the fact that these types of collaborative ventures are also increasing in number only serves to strengthen his argument about how the Asia-Pacific economies are being drawn into the mainstream of global competition.[15]

In assessing the drivers and the precise thrust of various corporate strategies toward the Pacific Rim in an era of both globalization and regionalization, it is important to recognize that many things remain in flux. The chapter by Drobnick suggests that the character of regionalization in the Pacific Rim is anything but certain. Expanded conflict and cooperation are both distinct possibilities – and not necessarily mutually exclusive. Drobnick argues that the size of the Japanese and American economies in both production and market terms means that they clearly are the dominant players on the Pacific Rim. Accordingly, it is incumbent upon them to settle their differences over trade and market access to provide support for the type of open regionalism that should theoretically mean a win–win outcome for everyone. Drobnick, however, does not give enough attention to the role of China, which conceivably could replace Japan on a regional, if not global, basis as a major economic and technological force. In 1994, China was the second largest recipient of direct foreign investment after the United States, with investment flows amounting to US$26 billion; it also became the eleventh largest trading nation in the world, up from the twenty-sixth spot in 1980.[16] It was once thought that to be a true global player, a firm had to have a significant presence in Japan as well as in the US and EU. Today it is probably the case that a truly global firm will also have to have a significant presence in China. More importantly, the bilateral sources of uncertainty highlighted by Drobnick are merely another indicator that the full impact of globalization has not yet been felt in all quarters. Strategic planners within corporations seeking to identify their options and opportunities would do well to recognize this simple but important fact.

Viewed from the perspective of the Pacific Rim, the majority of chapters in this volume share the view that the impact of globalization on corporate strategies remains non-linear, especially as the forces of regionalization seem to have created a type of counterforce, constraining at times, the drivers of globalization across a number of domains. The case studies of Fujitsu and Samsung as well as the overviews of Korean, Canadian, and Taiwan firms highlight the diversity in response in strategic and organizational terms among firms across the region. The same thing can be said about most governments as they attempt to formulate appropriate social and economic policies in this era of globalization; governments are increasingly constrained about what they can do. Moreover, there is no clear sense about what they ought to be doing. This obviously poses some new challenges for managing business–government relations in the Pacific Rim, as well as in other parts of the globe. It is a particularly vexing problem in the context of the Pacific Rim since most of the economic success stories can point to the dynamic role played by government in helping to drive the processes of industrialization and technological upgrading.

One thing does seem clear, however. In the midst of bilateral and multilateral discussions about appropriate policy and strategic responses to the new issues on the agenda, firms from all around the Pacific Rim are continuing to expand both their intra-regional and global interactions and cooperative alliances. There is a sense that these relationships will only continue to proliferate in the future, raising all sorts of new questions about the meaning of concepts such as "techno-security" in an age of globalization. Moreover, as the processes of technology exploration and commercialization become increasingly regionalized, if not globalized, one may ask whether or not it is useful to talk any longer about so-called national systems of innovation. The stark reality that governments have already lost a great deal of control over mainstream economic and technological affairs and are destined to lose even more may become an impetus to reassert government prerogatives and thereby slow down the spread of globalization. While this may not happen because of the inherent difficulties in ideological, political and logistical terms, the fact remains that there is no predetermined course that globalization and regionalization must follow. The chapters in this volume, while attesting to the ever increasing momentum of trans-border flows of products, capital, technology, and people *and* the growing efforts among managers and corporate planners to identify synergies and linkages among these flows, have suggested, in general, that companies, small and large, differ in how they assess the opportunities and challenges. Therefore, it is no surprise to find out that they differ in what they believe to be an appropriate response.[17] While there may be no doubt in the minds of many that the emergence of the Pacific Rim requires a new way of thinking about business and technology in the twenty-first century – the so-called Pacific Century – it is a sobering thought to recognize that there continues to be little consensus on what that new vision ought to be, let alone how it can be implemented.

NOTES

1 Malcom Waters, *Globalization* (London: Routledge, 1995).
2 United Nations, *World Investment Report – 1994* (New York: United Nations, 1994) [E94.II.A.14].
3 The World Bank, *Global Economic Prospects and the Developing Countries* (Washington, D.C.: The World Bank, 1995).
4 United Nations, *World Investment Report – 1994* (New York: United Nations, 1994) [E94.II.A.14].
5 Lee Kwan Yew, "Success in Asia needs the fusion of business cultures," *The Straits Times* (March 12, 1995), p. 6.
6 Denis Fred Simon, (ed.) *The Emerging Technological Trajectory of the Pacific Rim* (Armonk: M. E. Sharpe, 1995).
7 Laura Tyson, *Who's Bashing Whom?* (Washington, D.C.: Institute of International Economics, 1992).
8 Barbara K. Bundy et al., *The Future of the Pacific Rim: scenarios for regional cooperation* (Westport, Connecticut: Praeger, 1994).
9 Henny Sender, "Nippon's Choice," *Far Eastern Economic Review* (June 8, 1995), p. 39.
10 Maya Maruko, "Joint projects on the rise: high-technology firms re-focus on Asia," *The Japan Times Weekly*, International Edition (May 15–21, 1995), p. 13.
11 Edward K. Y. Chen and Peter Drysdale (eds), *Corporate Links and Foreign Direct Investment in Asia and the Pacific* (Pymble, Australia: Harper Educational, 1995).
12 For an analysis of the overseas R&D initiatives of Japanese firms see Hisayuki Mitsusada, "R&D goes abroad for a fresh twist on the future," *The Nikkei Weekly* (June 12, 1995), p. 1.
13 Denis Fred Simon, Yongwook Jun, and Junghwa Han, *Globalization, Korean-style: Samsung's emergence as a world-class company* (Boston: Harvard Business School Press, forthcoming).
14 Kelly Herr, "Japanese firm signs joint contract," *The Free China Journal* (May 12, 1995), p. 8.
15 For an overview of strategic alliances see Michael Yoshino and U.S. Rangan, *Strategic Alliances: an entrepreneurial approach to globalization* (Boston: Harvard Business School Press, 1995).
16 Amy Chew, "China second to the US in luring investment," *South China Morning Post* (September 1, 1994), p. 1.
17 Harvard Business Review, *Global Strategies: insights from the world's leading thinkers* (Boston: Harvard Business School Press, 1994).

Part I

The evolving global economy: macro versus micro forces

1 From interdependence to globalization

Changing perspectives and the changing international political economy

Denis Fred Simon and Bruce Koppel

Governments and Corporations are having to come to terms with a vastly altered international environment in which the location of the world's economic activities and the terms on which foreign direct investment take place have become of vital importance.
(Robert Gilpin, *The Political Economy of International Relations*, 1992: 262)

The strategic thrust of investing firms is to build plants whose output will be internationally competitive in cost and quality. In the era of globalization, plants tend to be focused in terms of product, robotized in terms of technology, and diversified in terms of markets served.
(Paul Beamish, et al., *International Management*, 1990: 94)

We must not fall into the mistake of thinking that it is America that trades with Taiwan, or Europe that trades with Asia. The truth is that it is American companies that trade with Taiwanese companies, and European companies that trade with Asian companies.
(Margaret Thatcher, *Far Eastern Economic Review*, September 2, 1993: 23)

INTRODUCTION

There is little question that conditions in and of the global economy have moved to the center-stage of corporate, government, and public attention. The financial pages of even regional newspapers in the United States now regularly carry summaries of stock market results and exchange rate movements from Europe and Asia. In the last few years, American investors have poured billions of dollars into internationally-oriented mutual equity funds. Companies historically conceived as national firms with global reach are today engaging actively and openly with "national" companies from other countries, even those who are their competitors in their home markets, in forms of cooperation that go beyond the usual characterizations of multinational corporate behavior. The politics of bilateral and multilateral international trade conflict remain central themes in American politics, and calls for sanctions and protectionism are frequently heard, often at the behest of major US corporations, yet these same corporations have already gone very far in internationalizing their R&D, production networks, and management structure. And finally, to underline all the above, international tourism, once the province of the affluent in the US and Europe, has become the world's largest single industry. Along with a rapidly unfolding international telecommunications revolution, the results are a globalizing of values and tastes – with implications that range from the internationalization of many product markets to reassertions of diversity and national uniqueness.

Not surprisingly, the last decade of the twentieth century is becoming known as the "age of globalization." But what is really happening? Are we witnessing the further evolution of an interdependent global economic system or are we seeing the emergence of new principles for the organization of international economic activities? According to some, the world economy has entered a new phase, characterized by the integration of markets across countries and by the growth of sophisticated international business networks around the world. These networks, which have been formed through the investment and technology transfer activities of large, transnational companies (TNCs), have become a principal mechanism through which various national economies, in whole or in part, are being linked together. One result is that, unlike the 1960s and 1970s, when transnational corporations were frequently viewed as agents of "distorted" and often undesired forms of development, TNCs and their associated networks are today increasingly courted by governments around the world as potential engines of economic and technological progress.

The onset of this era of globalization has multiple origins, with no single cataclysmic or epiphenomenal event precipitating a period of proliferating global business and technology links. The origins are partly technological, partly economic, and somewhat political. We say "somewhat" because political change, especially in terms of how international economic policies are conceived and managed, has generally lagged behind the consequences of the economic and technological changes usually associated with globalization.[1]

Pivotal aspects of the international business environment are changing in fundamental ways. Economic interdependence – a concept that compellingly described and even explained some of the major changes in the world economic system in the 1970s and 1980s – seems unable to capture the multiple dimensions of globalization as a force for change. Trade and investment were viewed as key factors driving greater global interdependence. The roles of TNCs were acknowledged, but were viewed as important only as agents for mushrooming trade and investment flows. It is increasingly clear, however, that the significance of TNC activities extends beyond these roles. Many firms are reconfiguring their operating strategies, organizations, and overall management objectives in fundamental ways.[2] One implication for how we understand international relations is that analysis needs to shift focus away from previous concerns with competition and cooperation over trade and investment flows and the so-called "negative" dimensions of interdependence (e.g. loss of state control), and toward more emphasis on the dynamics of selected industries which are globalizing through R&D networks, strategic alliances, mergers and acquisitions, etc.[3] This point is illustrated by Figure 1.1 which shows how different industries are responding to the cross-pressures for globalization and localization.

Susan Strange makes this point quite clearly in an article dealing with transformation in international relations.[4] She describes four emerging features in the world production system. First, the part of the international economy responding directly to political command is the smaller part and is shrinking. This process accelerated with the formal collapse of communism in the former USSR and Eastern Europe. Second, however, the part of the world economy that responds entirely to market signals without the interference of governments is *also* shrinking. New forms of state intervention are appearing with different aims and goals from those associated with socialist and centrally planned regimes. Third, production structures geared to purely national markets (which can be severely impacted by national policies and politics) are also shrinking. And fourth, the largest parts of the global production structures for raw materials, manufacturing, and service industries are dominated by large transnational corporations. Strange concludes that "the technological imperative to sell on a world market reduces the area common to

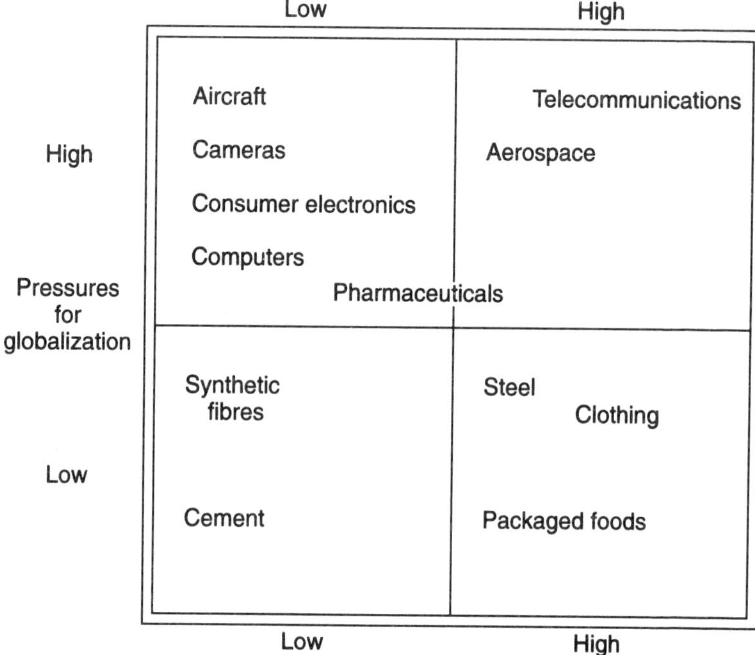

Figure 1.1 Industrial competition: pressures for localization versus globalization

Source: Derived from Paul Blanish, et al., *International Management: Text and Cases* (Homewood: Irwin, 1991)

all states over which national governments are able to exercise exclusive regulatory power."[5]

Another good indicator of changes in the international business environment can be found by reconsidering some of our traditional assumptions about national security.[6] As Klaus Knorr reminded us two decades ago, in his seminal book *Power and Wealth: the political economy of international power*, national security rests on a strong economic and technological base.[7] The United States, which has been the predominant military and economic power in the world for most of the last five decades, has been the best example of a country where the imperatives of economic strength and military power have converged; the former USSR is perhaps the best counter-example. Still, there is something different in the discourse about economic and technological dimensions of national security today that sets it apart from many of the things Knorr and others were discussing during the height of the US–USSR bipolar competition.

Today, national competitiveness in economic terms is viewed increasingly as the essential foundation of national security. The success of Japan in the postwar period, especially in terms of its ability to challenge the economic and technological leadership position of the United States has, however, established a new national security model for many countries. This model places greater primacy on achieving higher capabilities to develop and maintain competitive positions in R&D, export trading, and market access. With the general diminution of military tensions in several areas of the globe, many countries are less constrained in their abilities to focus significant attention and resources to what was once considered to be in the realm of "low politics."

There has not been a universal declaration among all countries that they will beat their swords into plowshares. Traditional threats to national security still exist, and there are disturbing new trends in arms expenditures and trade involving both low and middle income countries. However, the paramount and even unchallenged positions once occupied by defense matters and military interests in the affairs of nation-states are being altered (or at least challenged, as in Thailand) in basic ways. It is therefore not surprising to find that in many countries, there is increased emphasis on economic matters generally, and on forging strong relationships with some of the world's leading transnational companies specifically.

In suggesting that the forces of globalization mandate a re-examination of both structure *and* process in the international business environment, we are not suggesting that the existing major paradigms of international relations have become obsolete. Indeed, the issue of paradigmatic change in the field of international relations has long occupied the attention of scholars and foreign policy practitioners. Over the course of the last two hundred years, various transformations have taken place in the international system, some of which have extended the life of the so-called "state-centric" paradigm, while others have called into question the continued value of relying on any paradigm that maintains the nation-state as the central actor.

The aims of this chapter are far less bold than trying to undertake a dramatic reconceptualization of international relations or to suggest, as James Rosenau has done elsewhere, that there is some "unimaginable scheme" underlying world affairs today.[8] Rather, our aim is to highlight some of the qualitative changes that have taken place in the international business environment, commenting on how recent changes in the nature, aim, and intent of various international business transactions reflected the appearance of a new, though clearly not the only, core organizing concept in international relations. In this regard, we build upon the suggestion by John Ruggie that it is important to consider what Durkheim labeled the concept of "dynamic density" when contemplating the role of qualitative change within a system.[9] By calculating the level of dynamic density, i.e. the quantity, velocity, and diversity of international transactions as a determinant of change, we can assess how globalization might affect the nature of international affairs.

Second, we will give special emphasis to comparing and contrasting the relationships between the so-called interdependence paradigm, especially as developed by proponents such as Keohane and Nye, and the new globalization paradigm as discussed and developed by persons such as Porter, Ohmae, and Yip. We hope to show that from several perspectives, the interdependence paradigm no longer captures, if it ever did, the essential aspects of the globalization process – including the new relationships among non-state actors as well as the altered relations between nation-states and transnational corporations.

THE INTERDEPENDENCE PARADIGM

The notion that the so-called "state-centric" model of international relations is inadequate to explain the growing importance of such phenomenon as the global roles and impacts of transnational corporations was first expressed in the early 1970s in a book entitled *Transnational Relations and World Politics*.[10] The book was important because it tried to show that non-state actors were having an important effect on the conduct of international relations, and that the existing analytic framework for understanding the workings of the international system did not seem conceptually capable of incorporating non-state actors. The interdependence paradigm received its greatest boost, however, with the publication of another volume by Keohane and Nye, entitled *Power and Interdependence*.[11] Building on some of the work of middle-range and regional integration theorists in international affairs, Keohane and Nye attempted to show that military affairs were no longer the predominant international issue, and that economic, technology, and environmental issues – which traditionally had not been considered as critical as defense matters – were now within the once sacrosanct realm of so-called "high politics." They also set out to show that national power and interest were no longer simply defined in terms of military strength, but that on various non-defense issues, smaller, and perhaps militarily weaker, states could assert a great deal of influence depending on which types of "power assets" were deemed important in a specific issue area. The assumption in this case is that, for some issues, military strength is not the sole or even a principal determinant of political or economic outcomes.

What made the Keohane and Nye book especially important, however, was its central theme – the greater sensitivity of almost all nation-states to the actions and, at times, non-actions of other nation-states. The main transmission belt for this increased sensitivity was the expanded number of contacts and linkages – formal and informal, government and non-government – among nation-states. As a result, suggested Keohane and Nye, governments could not simply act unilaterally, nor could they expect their respective economies and socio-political systems to be immune from unplanned, and at times, undesirable external influences.

Other analysts pursued the argument that under the pressures of growing interdependence, policy autonomy would become increasingly constrained. Monetary, fiscal, and trade policies enacted in one country frequently reverberated in several other countries.[12] At the private sector level, one of the principal mechanisms for transmitting cross-border sensitivities was the transnational corporation. A variety of books appeared, many of which were extremely critical of the almost unparalleled power and influence of the TNCs on nation-states. From the radical *Global Reach*,[13] written by Barnet and Muller, to the more balanced *Sovereignty-at-Bay*,[14] by Raymond Vernon, it was argued that TNCs constituted a major threat to national sovereignty and control.

While some observers, such as George Ball, spoke in positive terms about such ideas as a world "cosmo-corp,"[15] others were raising questions about whether the economic futures of nation-states were actually being determined more within the boardrooms of the world's largest corporations than in the corridors of government economic ministries, especially in the Third World. In some cases, because of the extent of American power and influence at the time, including the fact that many of the Fortune Global 500 were based in the United States, TNCs were simply viewed as extensions of America's power.[16]

While interdependence was apparently growing, there were different assessments of what this growth meant. Authors on the left tended to see TNCs as a new form of neo-imperialism, while some of the more traditional students of international relations, such as Robert Gilpin, suggested that TNCs were instruments of a modern form of neo-mercantilism. For example, some analysts suggested that TNCs were serving as instruments to create and maintain dependent links between the more developed North and the still comparatively underdeveloped South.[17] This dependency perspective saw the world capitalist system as expanding by incorporating the Third World into permanently subordinate relationships with developed capitalist nations. Building on Lenin's "theory of imperialism," TNCs were viewed as an expression of the highest form of capitalist expansion. Unlike neo-mercantilists, who saw "the flag driving the dollar," dependency proponents believed that "the dollar drove the flag."[18] Countries such as China stressed the virtues of self-reliance and independent development as they sought to avoid the apparent political, economic, and social costs of linkage with the TNCs.

Thus, while interdependence advocates were thinking in terms of mutual costs and vulnerabilities, proponents of the dependency perspective saw costs and vulnerabilities as disproportionate burdens on the South. More specifically, three main consequences of excessive involvement with TNCs were cited: (1) local economic distortions, including preemption of host country entrepreneurship; (2) local political distortion, including excessive meddling in domestic affairs and efforts to subvert existing political and socio-economic institutions; and (3) socio-cultural distortion, including efforts to impose Western cultural and social values on the host society through advertising and the media.[19] The case of ITT in Chile was often cited as the best example of how the imperatives of capitalist expansion could distort the national priorities of the home country (the US) and result in continued exploitation of a host country (Chile) through foreign investment.

How interesting it is to see that today – among analysts of international relations as well as among many political leaders in the developing world – the dependency perspective has been largely discredited and the global spread of TNCs is being heralded as the principal catalyst driving the formation of a new world order. TNC investment is credited as having promoted the rapid and sustained development of the newly industrialized economies of Asia – the so-called four dragons of Taiwan, Hong Kong, South Korea, and Singapore – and is considered to be the impetus behind the rapid emergence of the leading ASEAN economies – Thailand, Malaysia, and Indonesia. Foreign investment is also being credited for the rapid growth of the economy of south China, a development which is all the more remarkable given the fact that many Chinese political leaders as recently as ten years ago eschewed the benefits of foreign capital and technology for greater national control. An absence of foreign investment is also viewed as one of the main liabilities of the former USSR and Eastern bloc countries.

THE GLOBALIZATION PARADIGM

What accounts for the changed attitudes toward the spread of TNCs in the world economy as well as the move toward globalization? Moreover, what distinguishes the period in which interdependence was the predominant concern of policy makers and business executives from the present period, where globalization appears to have assumed center-stage? And finally, what explains the ongoing changes in the behavior of TNCs, especially with respect to their internal structures and external strategies?

Between 1970–90, worldwide foreign investment outflows increased over 14 percent per year. Between 1985–90, in particular, the rate of increase was more than twice the twenty year average (see Figure 1.2). Compared to the 1960s when foreign direct investment grew at twice the growth rate of GNP for the OECD nations, by the 1980s it was growing almost four times as fast.[20] Exchange rate adjustments, including the Plaza Accords, had much to do with this increase, especially in the case of Japan. During the latter half of the 1980s, world economic recovery provided a powerful stimulus to foreign investment as did the opening up of the service sectors in various countries.[21] More important, however, underlying this rapid increase was a qualitative change in the treatment of overseas business activities within the firms themselves. This is exemplified by the rapid growth in intra-firm trade over the decade of the 1980s among Japanese TNCs in particular.[22] As one author has suggested in a discussion of the growth in foreign investment among the OECD industrialized nations, the "quantitative increases in FDI flows have reached the threshold where they create a qualitatively different set of linkages among advanced economies."[23]

To begin with, it is useful to spell out what is meant by the term globalization – since it is now a commonplace to talk about global firms, global markets, and global industries.[24] In the current literature, the term "globalization" appears to be used three ways: as

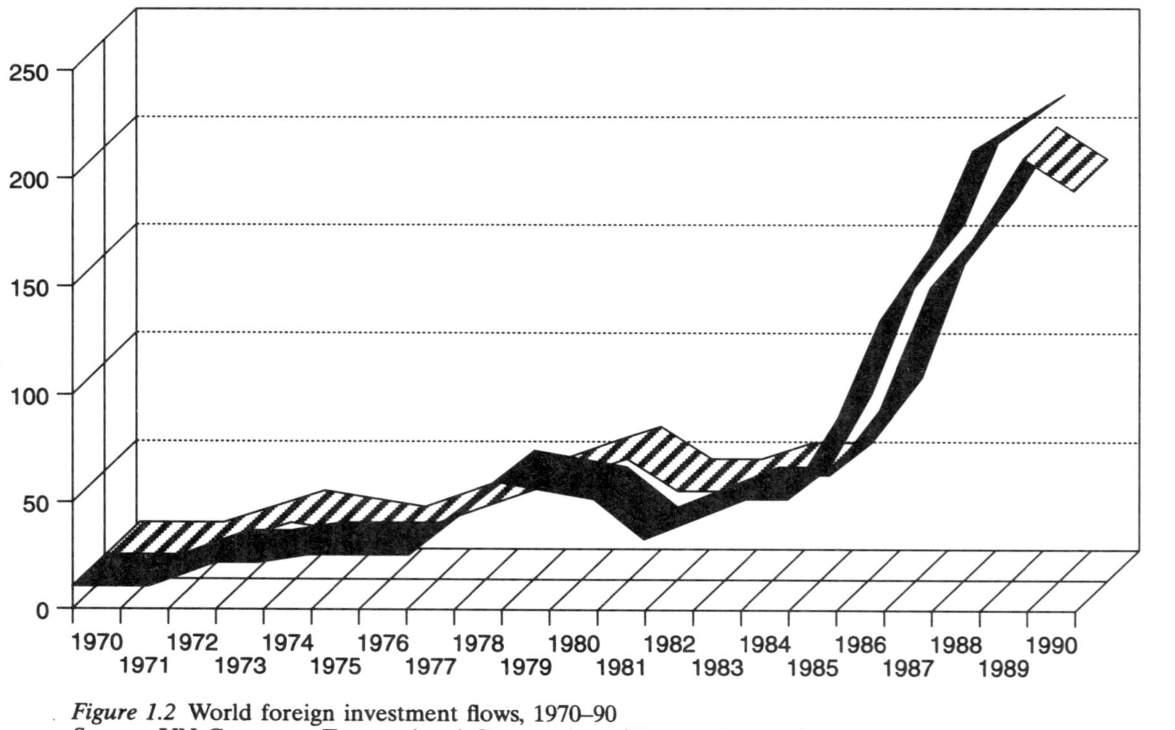

Figure 1.2 World foreign investment flows, 1970–90
Source: UN Center on Transnational Corporations (New York, 1992)

macroeconomics, as industry-level analyses, and as firm-level analyses.

Globalization as macroeconomics

Globalization is often used as a macro-level economic/business concept to describe the international business environment, if not also the overall structure of international relations itself. When Kenichi Ohmae writes about the "borderless" world, he is implicitly suggesting that structural changes are at work within the international system which are making national political boundaries largely irrelevant for *cross-border* business activities. Similarly, Robert Reich suggests in two major articles, "Who is Us?"[25] and "Who is Them?"[26] that national ownership means very little in a world in which cross-border linkages are growing by leaps and bounds. While Reich is responding to a somewhat different problem from Ohmae, i.e. concerns about excessive Japanese foreign investment in the United States, and thus does not go as far as Ohmae in postulating a borderless world, his point about the ever-expanding web of transnational partnerships, alliances, and joint ventures leads us to the hypothesis that globalization has recast the significance of political boundaries for the forms and strategies of economic and business organization.

Globalization as a macro-level concept has also been used to delineate processes of incorporation of more parts of the globe into a single world economic system. This can be connected to the dependency critique of interdependence. However, there are questions about whether, in fact, the world is becoming more interconnected in terms of unbroken international markets and commodity chains. There is evidence, for example, to suggest that the world is becoming increasingly bifurcated between those economies which have something to offer in the way of strategic assets vis-à-vis global competition, and those which do not.[27] In a recent book entitled *Dispelling the Myth of Globalization*,[28] Hazel Johnson challenges the notion that world markets as a whole are becoming more globally integrated. According to Johnson, regionalization is a better concept for capturing the direction of change in the world economic system. Johnson's challenge raises questions about the validity of the globalization concept as a macroeconomic concept insofar as the concept refers to the presumed homogeneous and uniform spread effects of international capital flows, technology transfer, etc.

Along with these two macroeconomic perspectives on globalization – a decline in the efficacy of politically-defined national markets and the more uniform diffusion of capital and technology – globalization as a macro-term has also been used to refer to the next stage of interdependence. In this context, globalization is viewed as the highest stage of a liberal world economy, where national governments have retreated, in large part, from their explicit efforts to dull the thrust of interdependence and have decided, de facto if not de jure, to allow the market to guide the character and direction of international business transactions.

The spread effects of the globalization process appear to have had their greatest impact within and across the international financial system. According to Masayoshi Tsurumi, who has led a project on financial globalization at Hosei University in Japan, there are five elements to financial globalization: (1) the formation of a global network of branch banking, led first by the American banks, and later followed by European and Japanese banks; (2) the development of a global information network and payments system (e.g. the SWIFT system for interbank telecommunications); (3) the emergence of a global trading system supported by satellites and computer technology that provides access to virtually any market from virtually any trading desk; (4) the homogenization of financial markets across countries; and (5) the maintenance of international dialogue to promote cooperative management of financial policy.[29] One only needs to be reminded of the October 1987 stock market crash in the United States and the extent to which its vibrations were felt around the world to appreciate the actual and potential consequences of Tsurumi's depiction.

Globalization as industry-level analyses

A second way that the globalization concept has been used has been to refer to processes of transformation at the level of an industry, including the markets for the sale of products within that industry. Ted Levitt, former editor of the *Harvard Business Review*, first identified the parameters of these new global industries when he suggested in 1983 that "the world's needs and desires have been irrevocably homogenized."[30] The driver behind globalization, for Levitt, is technology, which he asserted "drives consumers relentlessly towards the same common goals – alleviation of life's burdens and the expansion of discretionary time and spending power."[31]

Michael Porter took the globalization construct one step further and identified what he believed was the core defining feature of so-called global industries: "a global industry is one in which a firm's competitive position in one country is significantly affected by its position in other countries and vice versa."[32] Global industries are to be contrasted with so-called "multi-domestic industries," where all, if not a significant number of country-level subsidiaries, operate fairly independently of one another. As Daniels and Radebaugh suggest, "the underlying assumptions of this approach are that there are unique country situations that necessitate operational differences, and that a corporation's global performance will be best maximized by having each subsidiary do what is best for its own market."[33]

According to Porter's analysis, there are clear indicators that can be analyzed to determine whether or not an industry has indeed begun its march toward globalization. One characteristic has to do with the importance of scale economies. In globalizing industries (e.g. aircraft, computers, and microelectronics) the dynamics of business rivalry all suggest that standardization of design as well as parts and materials are important competitive elements. Another characteristic is the growing similarity in customer tastes and preferences across countries described by Levitt. Finally, globalization can be said to be occurring if the aggregate behavior of the firms in that industry reflects a greater emphasis on cross-border linkages and integration of activities. Under such circumstances, it is not surprising for one TNC to find itself competing against the same firms in different markets simultaneously, nor is it surprising for a TNC to find that its home country market is no longer a safe sanctuary in terms of market share or profitability.[34]

Globalization and the analysis of firms

The third way that globalization has been used has been at the level of the firm to refer to the new strategic and organizational posture that must be adopted for various firms to survive and prosper in their respective industries. We must be careful not to reify industries when looking at firm-level behavior; industries do not become globalized by themselves. The competitive dynamics – manifested in the mode of industrial organization, technological change and even political interventions – must somehow shift. In some important respects, the existing literature regarding globalization in both international business and international relations is very confusing because at times it appears that the world's largest firms are acting as both cause and effect of globalization. The sense of urgency present in the writings on global strategy by such authors as Porter, Kogut, Yip, Levitt, etc., in admonishing or encouraging firms to adopt a more global perspective on organizational structure leaves one with the sense that the bulk of the Fortune 500 or Business Week 1000 have yet to make substantial progress in either thinking or acting globally. Yet, if this is the case, then what is driving globalization?

What drives globalization?

George Yip, in his recent book, *Total Global Strategy*, highlights five different types of "drivers." (1) *market drivers*, such as convergence in per capita incomes and convergence in life-styles and tastes, and increased world travel promote greater awareness of one another; (2) *cost drivers*, such as accelerating technological innovation combined with shorter product life cycles and rising R&D costs, advances in transportation that expand coverage and reduce costs, and the rise of the NIEs with rapidly improving manufacturing and research capabilities; (3) *government drivers*, including reductions in tariff and non-tariff barriers, the spread of privatization, and the decline of socialism as an effective form of economic organization; (4) *competitive drivers*, manifested most clearly in continuing increases in the level of world trade and investment and the rise of new competitors with "global" ambitions; and (5) *other drivers*, such as the revolution in information and communication technologies.[35]

The essence of Yip's analysis is that there are some significant forces outside of the firm and its behavior that are driving the globalization process. While his main concern is to assist companies in understanding whether or not the conditions within their respective industries warrant a reorientation toward a more global strategic posture, he does help us understand those trends that are working to alter both the structure of the international business system and the processes underlying the dynamics of competition that might be operating in specific industries. Yip's assessment does depend heavily on what he believes is a significant degree of openness in the external environment.

It is interesting, for example, to contrast those factors cited by Yip as contributing to the spread of globalization with some of the analysis presented by Robert Gilpin in his book, *The Political Economy of International Relations*. Gilpin's book is relevant to this discussion because he specifically questions the continued staying power of the post-World War II liberal economic order that Yip and others contend has given rise to greater economic interdependence in the 1970s and globalization in the late 1980s and early 1990s. In particular, Gilpin cites several factors that indicate to him that "the liberal international economic order is rapidly receding." First, he suggests that the world is actually experiencing increasing levels of mercantilist-type competition. This competiton is manifested in more aggressive behavior by states to establish higher levels of national competitiveness in world markets. There is intensification in the struggle for world markets, says Gilpin, as countries believe that state-guided export-oriented growth is the only way to achieve desired levels of economic development. This reassertion of the state, stresses Gilpin, could gradually lead to a diminution in the primacy of the market as a means of organizing global economic relations.

Second, Gilpin suggests that there is movement toward regionalization rather than toward a more open liberal world trade and investment regime. The coalescing of the EC 1992 and NAFTA, combined with growing intra-regional trade within the Pacific Basin, reflect one form of response to the growth in competition. Moreover, while some see regionalization as part of the globalization process, perhaps even a necessary first step, it can also be suggested that it is merely a form of supra-nationalism designed to combat globalization trends. And third, sectoral protectionism is growing. Between 1980–8, for example, the overall percentage of US imports covered under some form of non-tariff barrier actually rose from 8.0 percent to 24 percent.[36] According to Gilpin, this form of "new protectionism" is resulting in the negotiation of market shares on a sector-by-sector basis, thus undermining the philosophical underpinnings of the GATT-oriented trade regime that has been in existence for over three decades.

Of course, it is by no means unique in the social sciences to have two observers view the same phenomenon and come up with radically different interpretations of what is happening and why. In this instance, what is most likely is that Yip and Gilpin are both correct to some extent, which then suggests that we need to re-think our tendency to view globalization merely as an outgrowth of the liberal economic order. Relatedly, as Porter has indicated, globalization is just as tied to slowing growth rates and eroding types of comparative advantage as it is to falling tariff barriers and market convergence.[37] Moreover, globalization also is not simply a manifestation of interdependence, although as we shall suggest below, it may be one form of response to the problem of managing interdependence.

DO STATES MATTER?

As interdependence began to make itself felt during the 1970s, reflected most vividly in the multidimensional "shocks and sensitivities" that were transmitted across national economies, it ignited a reassertion of national sovereignty and prerogative. As the literature on international relations trends at the time clearly stressed, faced with growing political pressures from a broad assortment of domestic interests, the nation-state was not made irrelevant. Instead, its job became more complex. In essence, while the discussions about interdependence were highlighting the growing difficulties of maintaining national economic and political autonomy, the expectation was that existing government structures would rise to the occasion to ensure that damage from lost autonomy would be minimal.

In the era of what we now call globalization, however, this newfound interest in the role of the state as a central economic actor is being seriously challenged. There is a strong counter focus now on the firm as a primary actor. In effect, it is the firm or series of firms that are the embodiment of industrial policy. States are in more of a reactive mode. This can be seen for example in the growing attention to deregulation and privatization.

Confronted by the consequences of interdependence – some of which were often unanticipated or unintended – the key objective of government was to regulate trade and cross-border activity to minimize the direct and indirect impacts from increased economic integration. In the current phase of globalization, the movement is clearly away from regulation and toward greater use of industrial policy to promote integration – though obviously on desired terms and conditions. The main instrument of power in the 1970s was "negative access," that is, an attempt to limit exposure to those forces promoting interdependence. In the 1990s, there is now a stress on "positive access." In other words, there is an immense emphasis on fostering a greater degree of articulation between the domestic economy and the external world economy.

Compare this to the principle concerns of policy makers as they confronted a more interdependent world in the 1970s and early 1980s. The major concern was "sovereignty." Any actual or perceived loss of control increased the sense of national vulnerability. In the 1990s, the term most often heard in conjunction with globalization is "competitiveness." Nation-states today seem willing to sacrifice a certain degree of national control in order to reap the benefits of foreign investment and trade. Moreover, as suggested earlier, rather than seeking to thwart the push or pull toward greater global integration, they are seeking new ways to encourage it. The result is that the central organizing principle underlying the orientation of the economic system has been changed. In the past, the chief organizing structure was "the national production system." Today, it is the case that "exchange" has become the most important organizing tenet.[38] The nature of the production endeavor has shifted away from its former emphasis on national systems. Industries form the primary unit of analysis rather than national economies. And, while a certain degree of national self-sufficiency remains important, it increasingly lacks the emphasis that was present during the earlier period of growing global interdependence.

WHITHER INTERDEPENDENCE?

There is little doubt that interdependence still remains a prominent shaping element in the international system, but it is important to recognize that we may now be witnessing some meaningful changes in the nature of interdependence and how it is managed. At the heart of this change in the nature of interdependence are some fundamental alterations in the fabric of the international division of labor. As Beamish, et al., have argued, under globalization, the issue is not simply where the firm can make its products cheaper, but where it can achieve the best combination of cost, quality and technology.[39]

This shift from variable cost to fixed cost competition has given additional weight to the role of innovation in maintaining competitiveness. The principal purveyors of innovation are the firms, especially TNCs. They are driving technology development and shaping industry structure. Nation-states may fashion the environment in which firms – large and small, domestic and foreign – operate, but it is far from clear that they can achieve, even if they desire to do so, the degree of control that they seek. The drive to plug into the technological assets of actual or potential competitors, to identify and take advantage of dynamic technological complementarities, and the growing technological openness of the world system, especially as the reach and breadth of COCOM has diminished with its collapse, all lend themselves to a re-configuration of the R&D, manufacturing, and related aspects of the value chain.

Of course, as Stephen Krasner has indicated in his book *Structural Conflict: the third world against global liberalism*,[40] nation-states still possess the ultimate form of control over firms, namely they control access, whether it be to markets, production sites, or natural resources. Nonetheless, if we consider what held the world economic system together in the 1970s and early 1980s, the cement came in the form of foreign aid, GATT, and intergovernmental agreements, mostly of the multilateral type. It also came in the form of calls for a "new international economic order," including a formalized code of conduct for managing the activities of TNCs. Today, the evolving system is tied together by a complex web of foreign investments, contractual joint ventures, licensing agreements, and production and R&D networks – the bulk of which are designed to faciliate technology exchange, expand information flows, and promote innovation.

Of course, these forms of cross-border interaction are not new. What is new, however, is the degree to which *both* horizontal and vertical integration are simultaneously driving the process of globalization. However, it would be wrong to delimit the spread of globalization simply to the behavior of TNCs. Globalization has as much to do with the industries in which firms are operating as with the firms themselves. As some authors have argued in the past, in many ways, TNCs are merely manifestations of the evolution of particular industries. If we take extractive industries as a starting point for understanding the rise of globalization, then we must begin with the reality that the critical sources of value in such industries are tied to the country or countries in which they are found. Still, when we see Saudi Arabia investing in the building of oil refineries in Japan, there is something taking place that seems to defy the traditional constraints – political and economic as well as physical – that once seemed to preclude such reverse linkages.

In the case of manufacturing in general, and high technology products in particular, neither production nor related R&D activities are tied to a specific site. Various activities could conceivably be located anywhere in the world that is appropriate – with "appropriate" here referring to the laws of specialization, location, etc. The advent of the so-called "R&D toss" that allows one research project to be worked on for 24 hours straight by combining the shift in time zones with the growing capabilities of computers and telecommunications, represents the mobility of such activities. Today, the growing complexity of most high technology industries, along with the high costs associated with sustaining them, are such that self-reliant approaches mean very little from the perspective of the firms operating in these industries.

The aerospace industry is one example where such complexity argues for close, sustained collaboration and cooperation – even if sometimes the terms are arrived at through delicate political negotiation between a company such as Boeing, its potential foreign partners, and the host government. McDonnell Douglas's decision to seek out a partner in Taiwan because of its own financial situation was made possible by the fact that there was a strong belief inside the company that an appreciable level of technical competence was available on the island. The very fact that McDonnell Douglas – which was one of the key producers of military aircraft for the US Department of Defense – could entertain such a provocative move further reinforced the notion that this industry may have reached a point where it is simply too big for one country to retain sole control. While "national security" concerns were expressed in the US Congress and certain portions of the Department of Defense, the deal seemed all too logical and desirable for McDonnell Douglas officials to ignore.

A similar argument can be made in the case of high definition television (HDTV). Here again, while governments in the US, Japan, and Europe argue over standards and technological rights, the reality is that cross-border agreements for sharing technology are occurring at a rapid pace as firms such as Fujitsu and Hitachi on the Japanese side and Texas Instruments on the US side recognize that only through technological sharing can they survive the huge risks and financial demands associated with such mega-projects.

WHITHER GLOBALIZATION?

If globalization is not simply an industry-linked phenomenon, i.e. if globalization expresses itself in distinct ways and at different stages in different industries, and it is not driven purely by firm behavior except as a second-order phenomenon, and it is more than just a response to the maturation of the "liberal" international economic order, then what can we say about globalization and its impact? One of the most likely explanations for the emergence of globalization is that it represents a response to interdependence rather than a consequence of it. Moreover, since globalization can be interpreted as influencing the "dynamic density" of transactions between countries, then it can be viewed as a determinant of changes in the nature of interdependence. These points can be seen in Table 1.1

Table 1.1 Interdependence and globalization perspectives: contrasting characteristics

Issue	*Interdependence*	*Globalization*
Key actors	Nation-states	Transnational firms
Objectives	Regulating trade and other external transactions	Network building and globalization
Most desired outcome	Minimize sensitivity and vulnerability	Achieve closer articulation W/TNCs and industries
Instruments of power (govts)	Negative access	Positive access
Chief concerns	Sovereignty	Competitiveness issues
Central organizing principle	Comparative advantage (focus on trade)	Competitive advantage (focus on FDI)
Central organizing structure	National production systems	Exchange and collaboration mechanisms (e.g. networks)
Unit of analysis	National industries and economies	Global industries and economy

which offers a stylized comparison of the interdependence and globalization perspectives.

In this regard, we must distinguish globalization as structure and globalization as process. In the case of the former, globalization refers to the new structure of the international business environment. This new structure is characterized by four main features: (1) a mixed system in which activist states are pursuing aggressive industrial policies complemented by trends toward greater privatization and deregulation; (2) a proliferation of trans-regional production and R&D networks managed and coordinated by TNCs with the gradual, albeit uncertain and uneven, coalescing of three major regional trading blocs; (3) the emergence of new and ever more complex technologies with continued efforts by political and economic interest groups to protect ageing and even obsolete industries; and (4) greater market openness in countries that were once considered to have closed markets, combined with an increase in the demand for foreign capital, technology and managerial know-how with new forms of protectionism, including non-tariff barriers and greater reliance on voluntary export restraints and orderly marketing agreements. Within each of these four areas, there is a dialectical process at work that seems to exacerbate the tensions at the level of the nation-state between more or less state intervention.

What becomes obvious when we evaluate the international business environment in terms of these four features is that it is filled with a great number of critical uncertainties. These uncertainties are compounded by the fact that the US, which was once the main source of stability and leadership – economically and politically – in the international system, is no longer capable of playing the role nor does it apparently desire to play such a role because the domestic costs are too high. As Gilpin has suggested, "the relative decline of American hegemony has seriously undermined the stable political framework that sustained the expansion of a liberal world economy in the postwar era, and increasing protectionism, instability, and economic crisis have developed."[41]

At the level of process, there seem to be two games transpiring at the same time. One game involves the nation-states competing with one another. This old game has certainly not disappeared, but it is changing. The bilateral conflict between the US and the USSR that dominated the entire postwar period has given way to new security issues (e.g. new sources of nuclear proliferation, resurgence of old ethnic conflicts, transnational environmental issues). Security is still a problem for nation-states. However, security issues dealing with technology, economics, and business sit at the top of the issue agenda for most policy makers in the developed world, and to some extent in the developing world. This shift in issues does not necessarily mean that interstate competition will be any less intense, nor that the state-centric paradigm has somehow outlived its utility as an analytic construct.

At the same time, there is a second game taking place, namely the game that we have been referring to as the *process* of globalization. This game is characterized by a tendency of the key actors, TNCs, to ignore many of the traditional themes that have been central to the process of international relations in the postwar period. This has been combined with an almost total lack of concern with the nation-state as a meaningful form of economic organization in the emerging world system, except insofar as government policies have proven a constraint to the achievement of TNC goals. The central actors are transnational corporations who, along with focussing on such traditional business goals as profitability and market share, seem to be engaged in a total reconceptualization of their approach to ownership. The principal characteristics of this reconceptualization consist of: (1) *ownership*: less emphasis on equity stake; (2) *technology transfer*: more emphasis on sharing; (3) *manufacturing and R&D strategy*: stress on network-type architecture; (4) *organizational structure*: trend toward decentralization; and (5) *personnel policy*: added emphasis on creating a truly multicultural workforce. Perhaps the most revealing aspect of change among TNCs has been the de-emphasis on control – which was achieved primarily through ownership structures – and the new stress on coordination. With the expanded use of information technologies, the nature of corporate governance structures are changing, allowing for management of all sorts of non-equity based relationships that better respond to the current requirements for agility, quick responsiveness, and adaptability in today's globally competitive environment.

While government officials, especially among the OECD nations, talk about the specter of trade wars, the spread of protectionism, techno-nationalism, and restricting immigration of cheap labor, TNCs are focussing on developing and managing strategic alliances, conducting collaborative R&D, achieving greater multinationalism, and reducing hierarchy in their relations with their counterparts around the world. With the future of the liberal order in question, and great anxiety about the ability of nation-states to successfully manage the transition to the post-Cold War era, globalization may be no more than a response to the inherent tensions between a world economic system based on loosely defined market principles and unmanageable interdependence *and* complex domestic economies where state intervention is very much alive. To succeed in such a world, TNCs must put together a strategy that responds to and yet hedges against the imperatives of Adam Smith's comparative advantage and Michael Porter's competitive advantage on one hand, and Karl Marx's world capitalist system and Ken Waltz's anarchical system on the other hand.

The reality is that while there are clear tendencies present in the world economy toward increased globalization, the picture remains incomplete. Perhaps this incompleteness is a reflection of the difficulty firms are having moving towards a more globally oriented structure for operations and decision making. It may also be a reflection, however, of the degree to which nation-states remain a vital part of the economic picture. We do not subscribe to the idea put forth by Rosenau that there has been a bifurcation of macro-global structures into "two worlds" of international affairs – a state centric and a non-state centric paradigm.[42] Rather we see three avenues of inquiry that remain very viable: (1) a macro-level approach that focusses on the relationship between states and growing interdependence in the overall world economy; (2) a micro-level approach that focusses on the relationships between TNCs and patterns of increasing interdependence in specific industries; and (3) a meso-level approach that looks at the relationship between these two levels. The first two of these approaches we seem to know and understand fairly well. It is the third – the relationships between processes of globalization in specific industries and in the overall global economy – which remains relatively unexplored.

In a recent book entitled *The Multinational Mission: balancing local demands and global vision*,[43] Yves Doz and C. K. Prahalad highlight the need for combining the imperatives of both globalization and localization. Their argument is based not merely on a recognition that we live in a multi-cultural world, but also that the degree to which states will attempt to defend and even extend their prerogatives in the economic realm remains highly uncertain. It is no wonder, then, that terms such as "think global, act local" have emerged and can be associated with policy responses as divergent as technosecurity policies to limit technology exports and international cooperation on greenhouse gas emissions. This divergence reflects the ambiguity that remains in a world where Michael Porter's *Competitive Advantage of Nations* can be read alongside Kenichi Ohmae's *The Borderless World* – and no-one is certain which is a more apt description of the future.

NOTES

1 Kenichi Ohmae, perhaps the leading exponent of what he calls "the borderless world," has suggested that the rigidity of political barriers constitutes the biggest obstacle to the imperatives of globalization. See Kenichi Ohmae, *The Borderless World: power and strategy in the interlinked economy* (New York: Harper Business, 1990).

2 See C. A. Bartlett, Y. Doz and G. Hedlund (eds), *Managing the Global Firm* (London: Routledge, 1990).

3 See Michael Porter (ed.), *Competition in Global Industries* (Boston: Harvard Business School Press, 1986).

4 Susan Strange, "Toward a theory of transnational empire," in Ernst Otto-Czempiel and James Rosenau (eds), *Global Changes and Theoretical Challenges* (Lexington: Lexington Books, 1989).

5 Ibid., p. 167.

6 Many of the issues regarding the changing security environment were first discussed in the early 1980s. The fall of the Berlin Wall and subsequent international political changes have only reinforced points now accepted about the demise of bipolarity and the likelihood that a post-Cold War security environment would not look much like the multipolar

structures envisioned during much of the Cold War period. See R. Magrhroori and B. Ramberg (eds), *Globalism versus Realism: IR's third debate* (Boulder, Colo.: Westview Press, 1982).

7 Klaus Knorr, *Power and Wealth: The political economy of international power* (New York: Basic Books, 1973).

8 James Rosenau, *Turbulence in World Politics: a theory of change and continuity* (Princeton: Princeton University Press, 1990), pp. 1–5.

9 See the article by Ruggie in Robert Keohane (ed.), *Neorealism and Its Critics* (New York: Columbia University Press, 1986).

10 Robert Keohane and Joseph Nye (eds), *Transnational Relations and World Politics* (Cambridge: Harvard University Press, 1972).

11 Robert Keohane and Joseph Nye, *Power and Interdependence: world politics in transition* (Boston: Little Brown, 1977).

12 Richard Cooper, *The Economics of Interdependence* (New York: McGraw Hill, 1968).

13 Richard Barnet and Ronald Muller, *Global Reach: the power of multinational corporations* (New York: Simon & Schuster, 1974).

14 Raymond Vernon, *Sovereignty-at-Bay* (New York: Basic Books, 1971).

15 George Ball, "The promise of the multinational corporation," *Fortuna* (June 1, 1967), p. 80.

16 This same view is still present. For example, Susan Strange argues that the US government still exerts a tremendous influence over the world economic system through its "alleged" dominance over credit, knowledge, and production. Moreover, the US position is enhanced by its predominant position in the national security sphere. See Strange, op. cit.

17 For example, see Jose Villamil (ed.), *Transnational Capitalism and National Development* (Sussex: Harvester Press, 1979).

18 Robert Gilpin, *US Power and the Multinational Corporation* (New York: Basic Books, 1975).

19 See the special issue on dependency in *International Organization* (Winter, 1978).

20 DeAnne Julius, *Global Companies and Public Policy: the growing challenge of foreign direct investment* (London: Royal Institute of International Affairs, 1990), p. 6.

21 United Nations Center for Transnational Corporations (UNCTC), *World Investment Report 1991: The Triad in Foreign Direct Investment* (New York: United Nations, 1992).

22 Ibid.

23 DeAnne Julius, op. cit., p. 40.

24 For example, "Stateless Corporation," *Business Week* (May 4, 1990).

25 *Harvard Business Review* (January–February 1990).

26 *Harvard Business Review* (March–April, 1991).

27 According to Mark Casson, "the statistical evidence shows that while there are substantial cross-flows of trade and investment, the world economy is still not fully integrated in the sense that some groups of countries have far stronger links with some partners than they do with others." In particular, Casson is referring to the close relationship that exists among the members of the so-called "Triad" – the US, Europe and Japan. See Mark Casson (ed.), *International Business and Global Integration: empirical studies* (London: Macmillan, 1992), pp. 1–24.

28 Hazel Johnson, *Dispelling the Myth of Globalization: the case for regionalization* (New York: Praeger Books, 1991).
29 Masayoshi Tsurumi (ed.), "The Japanese response to the challenges of financial globalization," *Journal of International Economic Studies* (March, 1989), p. iii.
30 Theodore Levitt, "The Globalization of Markets," *Harvard Business Review* (May–June, 1983).
31 Not all observers of the international business scene agree with Levitt's assertions about globalization. See Susan Douglas and Yoram Wind, "The myth of globalization," *Columbia Journal of World Business* (Winter, 1987), pp. 19–29.
32 Michael Porter (ed.), *Competition in Global Industries* (Boston: Harvard Business School Press, 1986).
33 John Daniels and Lee Radebaugh, *International Dimensions of Contemporary Business* (Boston: PWS Kent, 1993), p. 111.
34 See Robert Buzzell, John-Quelch, and Christopher Bartlett (eds), *Global Marketing Management: cases and readings*, 2nd edn (Reading: Addison-Wesley, 1992), pp. 2–9.
35 See George Yip, *Total Global Strategy* (Englewood Cliffs, N.J.: Prentice-Hall, 1992). Included in Yip's analysis of the five drivers of globalization are also a number of firm-related factors, such as establishment of world brands (market drivers), push for economies of scale (cost drivers), growth of global networks, and greater international orientation among companies (competitive drivers), etc. These firm-level factors appear to be more of a "response" to globalization than a cause, though in certain areas, follow-the-leader strategies adopted by some firms do have a cumulative impact that further reinforces the other tendencies cited by Yip.
36 Paul Beamish, J. Peter Killing, Donald Lecraw, and Allen J. Morrison, *International Management: Text and Cases* (Homewood: Irwin Publishers, 1991), p. 19.
37 One comment made by a senior American corporate executive is enlightening in his regard. Speaking about what drove his firm to consider adopting a more global perspective, he stated that "we would not have done anything had it not been for growing market saturation in our backyard [home economy] and the relative decline in the international position of the US economy." See also Michael Porter, op. cit.
38 This emphasis on exchange is best reflected by the fact that the level of output traded (internationally) as a share of total product – whether on an inter- or intra-firm basis – seems to be growing within most so-called "global industries."
39 Paul Beamish, et al., op. cit., p. 105.
40 Stephen Krasner, *Structural Conflict: the third world against global liberalism* (Berkeley: University of California Press, 1985).
41 Gilpin, *The Political Economy of International Relations* (Princeton: Princeton University Press, 1992), p. 351.
42 See Rosenau, op. cit., p. 105.
43 Yves Dos and C. K. Prahalad, *The Multinational Mission: balancing local demands and global vision* (New York: The Free Press, 1987).

2 The parameters of the evolving global political economy

Stephen D. Krasner

INTRODUCTION

In the late 1940s and 1950s the major concern of political leaders in the West was economic recovery and (especially for Americans) resistance to communism. By the early 1960s economic recovery had been accomplished in Western Europe and to some extent in Japan, and managing the international economy became almost a technical issue – trade barriers were falling, exchange rates were fixed, national governments could pursue autonomous monetary policies.

The 1970s and 1980s were more confusing. The United States unilaterally abandoned the Bretton Woods system by detaching the dollar from gold in August 1971. At the same time, however, the robustness of the international economic system was vindicated by the successful transition to flexible exchange rates, higher levels of macroeconomic coordination, and effective management of the first and second oil crises, at least for the advanced industrialized countries. The Third World did not fare so well with petro-dollar recycling and Reagan's monetary policy.

The basic parameters of the global political economy, at least the non-communist world's political economy, remained relatively stable through the late 1980s. The shared policy objective was liberalization of the movement of goods and capital. The mechanism was multilateral negotiations. The outcomes in terms of international economic flows were positive for the industrialized world and parts of the developing world as well, especially East Asia: trade, direct foreign investment, and other capital flows grew more quickly than aggregate economic output. The effort by the Third World to create a new international economic order had foundered.

The 1990s have been characterized by higher levels of disquiet and uncertainty. The Soviet empire has collapsed, but the transition to capitalism is troubled. The Cold War is over, but parts of Eastern Europe are descending into internecine ethnic strife. Market oriented economic policies have been embraced by Third World governments, but efficient markets have not emerged. International trade has continued to grow among the advanced countries, but macroeconomic performance has faltered. The leaders of the richest nations continue to profess commitment to global cooperation and liberalization, but the Uruguay Round has been highly problematic. Fears about regional closure have increased. Direct foreign investment has expanded leading to the view that the international economy is now characterized by globalization in which productive activities can be located at many different sites by integrated multinational corporations, but anxiety about nationalistic and closed economic policies has increased.

These conflicting trends, and the confusion that they have spawned, reflect the fact that the factors influencing the level and direction of international economic activity do not all point in the same direction. There are many variables that impact on how the global economic system functions. Among the most important are changing technologies related especially to communication and transportation, the impact and robustness of international institutions, academic ideas that influence policy makers, the nature of domestic political and economic institutions, the distribution of power among states, and the interests of various societal groups. Some of these factors have remained relatively constant, such as domestic political and economic institutions in the advanced industrialized countries. Others have changed in directions that would appear to support the persistence and even the enhancement of an open, liberal, multilateral system, such as the prevalence of liberal ideas, the delegitimation of communism, the weakening of socialist economic analyses, and the expanding scope of activities of international institutions committed to liberal policies.

Advocates of the notion that the world is moving not just toward greater interdependence but toward true globalization, in which economic activity around the world is not just interactive but truly integrated, point especially to the importance of continuing technological change.[1] Reduction in the cost of transportation and communication, coupled with more sophisticated workers in some poorer countries, have made it possible for multinational corporations to operate at a truly global level. As Simon and Koppel point out in Chapter 1, these enterprises now account for a major share of international trade and investment. The concept of a borderless world implies that these corporations can effectively organize global economic activity.

This vision underplays the fact that private economic actors cannot operate efficiently unless they have stable property rights and open borders for the transfer of capital and commodities. Multinationals cannot by themselves provide a firm underpinning for global economic exchange. Secure property rights and open borders are impossible without stable political institutions. While property rights in advanced market economy countries are secure, such security is hardly evidenced in many parts of Africa, Latin America, Asia, and the former Soviet empire where uncertainty, corruption, and regime changes undermine confidence in long-term commitments.

Moreover, even if property rights are stable this does not necessarily imply that domestic and foreign firms will be dealt with symmetrically. There has been considerable variation among advanced market economy countries in their treatment of direct foreign investment. Some countries have treated foreign and domestic firms in the same way; others have differentiated between national and nonnational firms; and still others have established or tolerated barriers to such investment.[2]

Even if property rights are stable domestically, the conditions under which capital, labor, and commodities move across national boundaries are inevitably affected by the policies of national governments. Multinational corporations may alter the incentives confronting political decision makers with regard to international trade and investment, but corporations cannot themselves establish rules that facilitate rather than impede cross-border movements. Open international regimes require state support.

The analysis of this chapter focusses on two factors which indicate that globalization is not foreordained:

1 the changing distribution of power among states;
2 the interests of various private economic actors which, in turn, influences national economic policies.

The changing distribution of power in the international system has created a more problematic environment. The global distribution of power has changed from bipolarity, in which the United States enjoyed hegemonic influence over some geographic regions and the Soviet Union over others, to flat unipolarity in which the United States is the only state which can plausibly make a claim to global preeminence, but at the same time American capabilities in some issue areas have substantially eroded. Because of this change in the distribution of power, the United States is less willing to support diffuse reciprocity and multilateralism than it was in the past when its position in the West was uncontested and when the threat of Soviet communism provided a political/security rationale for economic policies. The decline of American power in comparison to other advanced market economy countries does not doom the global system to closure, but it does mean that management of the international economic system will require sacrifice and cooperation among a number of states. Without the willingness of the United States to absorb some costs for the system as a whole, there is greater likelihood that some areas, especially Europe, could focus more on regional economic integration rather than global multilateralism.

The economic interests of various societal groups is a second major factor influencing the prospects for continued openness and multilateralism. The past forty years of growing international trade and investment have increased the influence and commitment of private economic actors in many countries to global openness. The ratio of trade to aggregate economic activity has increased for almost all major developed countries; export oriented sectors will have a strong interest in maintaining an open global order.

Changes in technology, the declining cost of transportation and communication, have led not just to increased trade but also to dramatic increases in the level of direct foreign investment. Globalization refers to the fact that many large firms now feel compelled to operate at a global level in terms of both production and sales. Multinational corporations act as integrated units across many different countries. The managers of these companies have a clear stake in expanding the opportunities for investment, production, and trade. The increased options for exit available to the managers of both manufacturing and financial capital have increased the potential political leverage that these actors can apply.[3] These private actors must, however, still rely on minimal levels of domestic political stability (direct foreign investment has hardly exploded in Somalia or Liberia), and on rules that allow the continued movement of capital and goods across international boundaries.

Increases in direct foreign investment and trade do not, however, have a positive impact for all actors. Globalization has costs as well as benefits. Some sectors and some economic interests that were previously isolated from international competition are now more threatened. Labor is much less mobile than capital and management. The high wages of workers in tradeable goods industries in industrialized countries are jeopardized by the increase in manufacturing activity in low wage countries. Increased trade and investment do not automatically produce political pressures that reinforce trends toward openness.

Aggregating societal attitudes toward economic openness is not straightforward. The impact of societal interests is always mediated by political structures. In general, higher levels of economic interdependence have diffuse benefits for the society as a whole. Departures from openness can have macroeconomic costs, such as higher levels of inflation. For small countries these general impacts will overwhelm any specific sectoral or class-based interests. The aggregate costs of closure impel especially small industrialized countries to pursue open policies.[4] Even small countries, however, might choose regional rather than global openness.

Larger countries have more options and may be more sensitive to specific pressures. If there are many cross cutting pressures with different actors and economic sectors engaged in both export-oriented and import-competing industries, then it is not likely that the government, even in a very large country, will experience much pressure for closure. In contrast, the more one country is characterized by import-competing industries that are not balanced by export-oriented industries or by managers of capital, the more pressure there will be to move away from multilateral liberal openness.

The most problematic configuration of societal interest groups is generated by Japan's interaction with its trading partners. Japan's overall trade surplus (a function of macroeconomic conditions and relative savings rates rather than trade policy) and Japan's low level of intrasectoral trade generate interest group pressures in other countries that are more supportive of protectionism, specific reciprocity, and regionalism than is the case for any other industrialized countries.

The changing international distribution of power and the configuration of interest group preferences suggest that management of a truly open multilateral economic system will be more difficult than has been the case in the past despite the trend toward globalization. Much of the success or failure of this management will depend on the relationship between the United States and Japan. Western Europe as a region is inherently stable because of economic interdependence, a multilateral balance of power, and strong institutional commitments reflected in the European Community. Likewise,

North America is a stable region because of the continued dominance of the United States; neither Canada nor Mexico have an attractive alternative to the American market.

Asia is not an inherently stable region. Heretofore, Japan has been the largest economic power in Asia, but it is not large enough to unilaterally dominate the region. Smaller Asian countries will always pursue options that allow them to balance against Japan. In terms of both security and economic considerations, the continued presence of the United States creates a more stable situation for Asia than would be the case if the United States withdrew.

The continued commitment of the United States, and other major states as well, to global multilateralism and open regionalism is, however, threatened by both the rising relative power of Japan and by the configuration of interests generated by Japan's pattern of international involvement. Japanese GNP, the best single indicator of underlying power capability, has continued to grow faster than that of both Europe and the United States. There is no indication that relative growth rates will change, even if absolute levels falter. We are already in the midst of a power transition centered on Japan, whose aggregate economic output has grown from about 10 percent that of the United States in 1950 to about 60 percent in 1992. Such power transitions are never easy to manage because they require the rising power to bear more responsibility and the declining power to bear less, a transition that can be psychologically and politically difficult. Japan is seriously rethinking its world role, as is the United States.

At the same time the configuration of interests generated by Japan's unique international trade pattern also threatens the viability of the contemporary multilateral global economy. High levels of trade and investment cannot be maintained without a secure political foundation. Such a foundation involves not only stable domestic order, but also at least roughly symmetrical international interests. Because of the low level of manufacturing imports and direct foreign investment in Japan, there are fewer interests with a stake in maintaining open relations with Japan than is the case for either Europe or North America. The most important contribution that Japan could make to the stability of the global political economy would be to give more actors a greater stake in Japan's economy. This would mean increasing the openness of the Japanese market for both goods and direct foreign investment.

DECLINING AMERICAN POWER

The United States emerged from World War II with extraordinary resources across a very wide range of issue areas. It had by far the largest GNP. It was the only state that possessed nuclear weapons. Although its army was partly demobilized after the war, it had a formidable blue water navy. It held far more international financial reserves than any other state and was the only significant source of international capital. Its industries possessed the lead in cutting edge technologies.

The relative position of the United States declined from the late 1940s until about 1970. There has not been much change in the last two decades as indicated by overall economic output, the single best indicator of underlying capabilities, albeit a very crude measure. The US share of aggregate production for all OECD countries fell from 58 percent in 1953 to 38 percent in 1975. Since that time it has remained relatively stable, accounting for 35 percent of output in 1988.[5]

Per capita output can be taken as a very rough proxy for technological capability and factor mobility, variables that are consequential for the ability of a state to redeploy its resource to either resist a foreign threat or to increase its leverage on another actor. The pattern here is similar to that in aggregate production with the position of the United States vis-à-vis other industrializing countries falling until the 1970s and remaining more or less stable since then. Only Japan has continued to close the gap with the United States.[6]

The American share of world trade has followed a similar pattern to that of aggregate output, declining in the immediate postwar period and stabilizing over the last two decades. The US share fell sharply in the late 1940s and 1950s, and then more or less stabilized between 24 and 28 percent. The composition of its share has, however, changed dramatically. In the 1950s, the US share of world exports was greater than its share of world imports; in the 1980s, the US share of world imports was greater than its share of world exports.[7]

One area where American capabilities have continued to decline is monetary reserves. The US share of world monetary reserves fell from 50 percent of world reserves in 1948 to 15 percent in 1970, remained at 13–17 percent during the mid-1980s and then fell to under 10 percent in 1988. Japan passed the United States as the country with the largest international reserves in 1987, the first time that the US had not ranked first in the postwar period.[8]

Most dramatically for global economic performance, the United States no longer has, as it had before 1970, surplus crude oil production capacity that could be used to offset cutbacks by Third World oil exporting states. Moreover, by the early 1970s the seven major oil companies (five of which were American) had lost effective control of crude oil production levels which they had enjoyed since the 1920s as a result of the higher levels of autonomy achieved by oil exporting states.

In the Gulf War the United States acted to prevent further price increases that would have resulted from the ability of Iraq to dictate production levels in the Arabian peninsula (Kuwait, Saudi Arabia, United Arab Emirates). This military action, which involved moving 450,000 troops halfway around the world, was an impressive demonstration of continued, indeed enhanced, American military power.[9] It would, however, have been easier to deal with the prospects of higher oil prices if the United States still had surplus production capacity of its own. In that case increasing production rates in Texas could have been a substitute for sending troops.

In sum, American power has declined since the peak immediately after the conclusion of World War II. This is hardly surprising. Western Europe and Japan were destined to recover from the devastation of the war, even if it was difficult to predict that they would recover so well.[10] This decline in relative American capability was most pronounced before 1970. Some major indicators of capabilities, especially share of world GNP, have remained fairly stable since then. The United States still remains by far the world's largest and most diverse economy.

Nevertheless, the recovery of Europe and Japan and other shifts in relative capabilities have eroded the relative position of the United States, even if it remains exceptionally formidable.[11] The United States has moved from being a net creditor to a major net debtor, making American financial markets sensitive to external developments and constraining the freedom of action of US policy makers. Japan has challenged the preeminence of the United States in many high technology industries. Most pointedly, the United States lost control of the world oil market shortly after 1970.

The changes in the relative international capabilities of the United States has resulted in a shift in American policies from the pursuit of very open handed milieu goals in the immediate postwar period to a much greater concern with specific American economic interests in more recent years. The United States has become increasingly focussed on pursuing its own specific economic interests and less concerned with preserving the stability of the system as a whole.

During the first part of the Cold War, American leaders presumed that all good things would go together; that they could accomplish all of their core objectives – the promotion of economic development in the non-communist world, economic growth for the United States, and increasing utility for American consumers – by pursuing a policy of liberal internationalism.[12] The possibility that promoting prosperity for the Western bloc as a whole could impede American growth, weaken the relative position of the United States, damage particular American industries, and even threaten the ability of the United States to effectively assume global leadership has not been seriously confronted by American policy makers.

In recent years American policy has begun to change in the face of increased external pressures, but there is, as yet, no articulated alternative to the guiding philosophy of liberal internationalism, even as the principles and norms of this approach are violated by an increasing number of specific American policies. While the general principles and commitments of American policy makers have not changed, however, both external and internal pressures have led to the adoption of new policies that are based more on specific than diffuse reciprocity.[13] American foreign economic policy has not been characterized by the replacement of one set of principles by another but rather by the accretion of new practices on top of earlier policies that were based on different principles and norms.[14]

Trade legislation since 1970 has been more concerned with specific American interests than the stability of the global economic system as a whole. The Trade Act of 1974 mandated that Congress, generally more protectionist than the executive, had to approve any trade agreement by a majority vote of both houses. The requirements for invoking provisions of the escape clause were relaxed, making it easier for American industries that were harmed by imports to get relief. Perhaps most importantly, the 1974 Act introduced a broad notion of unfair trading practices under section 301 of the Act. The 1979 Trade Act moved jurisdiction over the three elements of American law that dealt with what were considered unfair foreign practices – dumping, subsidies, and 301 violations – from the jurisdiction of the Treasury Department, which had been strongly committed to free trade, to the Commerce Department, which was more responsive to the interests of particular American industries.

The Trade and Tariff Act of 1984 gave the president the right to negotiate bilateral free trade agreements, a movement away from generalized most favored nation treatment. Agreements were concluded with Israel and, much more significantly, with Canada.

The Omnibus Trade and Competitiveness Act of 1988 created a number of mechanisms that could, if they were vigorously pursued by the executive branch, provide the United States with greater leverage to alter the behavior of foreign trading partners. The Super 301 provision of the Act provides for expedited action against countries that are judged to be engaged in unfair trading practices. Such practices can, under the provisions of the Act, be technically legal, but if they violate the spirit of international trade agreements the president is authorized to retaliate. Retaliation can be targeted against a specific country and can take a very wide range of forms. Super 301 is an instrument for coercive bargaining on the part of the United States. It has been used as leverage to get other countries to change their policies.[15]

The growing American concern with specific interests has not been limited to the area of trade. Since the early 1970s American international monetary policies are best explained in terms of the concrete and specific interests of the United States. American leaders have moved away from policies in the 1960s that were dominated by a concern for global stability. When the United States trade balance, as opposed to just the current account balance, fell into deficit in 1971, the Nixon administration brought down the value of the dollar by suspending gold convertibility and imposing an almost across the board 10 percent import surcharge, unilaterally ending the Bretton Woods system. In the early 1980s the Reagan administration conducted macroeconomic policy exclusively through monetary rather than fiscal policy, forcing up global interest rates, and greatly exacerbating the debt problems of Third World countries. American international monetary policy has been increasingly driven by specific interests rather than milieu goals.[16]

In the 1980s, American officials pressed other countries to open their telecommunications markets to both American products and services. A more market-oriented regime would undermine the system of national monopolies that has dominated domestic and international markets since the nineteenth century. In the fall of 1990, however, American policy makers backed away from their demand for national treatment fearing that foreign competitors would secure more advantages in the open American market than American companies could secure in more restricted European markets.[17]

In general, specific policies have increasingly diverged from the norms of diffuse reciprocity, openness, and non-discrimination. Various pressures, sometimes from domestic groups, sometimes from the international system, have compelled policy makers to adopt practices that are increasingly concerned with specific, well-defined American interests. Unlike the early Cold War years when power, rhetoric, and policy were internally consistent and reinforcing, the period since 1970 has been less coherent. Policies are inconsistent with espoused principles and norms because the relationship between underlying capabilities and commitments is more problematic.

CHANGING POWER CONFIGURATION AND SYSTEMIC OUTCOMES

There has been a relationship between declining American power, changing American policy, and the performance and stability of the international economic system. The critical link in that relationship has been oil. International economic flows have continued to grow, in most areas and for most countries, at higher rates than national economic activity. This is especially true for finance and direct foreign investment. Changes in American power and policy have not led to a collapse of the global economy or anything even resembling such a development. While the commitment of the United States to the stability of the global order may have flagged, that order itself appears to be robust.

While various measures of international economic transactions – trade, finance, investment – are either growing or only marginally declining, the performance of national economies has been more problematic. Overall economic performance has declined since 1970: growth rates are slower, and unemployment and inflation are higher as shown in the following Table 2.1.

Table 2.1 World economic performance 1960–87

	Average annual growth of GDP			*Average annual rate of inflation*		
	1960–70	1970–9	1980–7	1960–70	1970–9	1980–7
Low income countries excl. China and India	4.3	3.8	1.7	3.0	10.9	13.3
Middle income excl. oil exporters	6.1	5.5	2.8	3.0	13.3	62.3
Ind market economy	5.1	3.2	2.6	4.3	9.4	5.2

Sources: World Bank, *World Development Report* (1981 and 1989), Tables 1 and 2

Growth rates for poor, middle income, and developed market economy countries have all declined since the 1960s. With the exception of the industrialized countries, inflation rates have also grown steadily since the 1960s. Public debt service has increased dramatically from 7.1 percent of the export of goods and services for low income countries in 1970 to 21.9 percent in 1987, and from 11.7 percent for middle income countries to 23.9 percent.[18]

At least to some extent these negative aspects of international economic performance can be attributed to the declining power of the United States via changes in international energy markets. Higher and less stable oil prices are directly attributable to the declining power of the United States in this issue area. The United States lost control of the international energy market after 1970, primarily because it became a net oil importer, and secondarily because oil exporting states were able to nationalize their oil fields. Nationalization ended the full vertical integration that had previously been enjoyed by the major international oil companies, most of which were American. As a result oil prices rose precipitously in 1973–4, 1979–80 and 1990. Fuels accounted for 10 percent of world exports in 1963, 11 percent in 1973, 20 percent in 1979, and 21 percent in 1983. By 1987, however, fuels had fallen back to 11 percent of world exports.[19]

Higher and less stable oil prices worsened global economic performance. Many companies were forced to scrap some capacity and to alter their allocation of factors. This led to a fall in real wealth, a decline in aggregate demand because of government attempts to control rising inflation, and, for the United States, a worsening trade balance because of rising dollar exchange rates. These marcoeconomic changes reduced the rate of productivity growth.[20]

The Third World debt crisis, which began partly as a result of the exceptional incentives that international banks had to recycle petrodollars, also revealed an absence of American leadership, or any leadership for that matter. The funds flowing into these banks grew so precipitously as a result of the revenues generated by petroleum exporting states that the banks almost pushed oil importing Third World states into higher levels of borrowing despite the fact that high rates of inflation in the mid-1970s made real interest rates negative for some loans. When real global interest rates rose in the late 1970s, many Third World countries found themselves in a debt squeeze which contributed to economic downturns more severe than anything they had experienced in the 1930s. Debt service ratios (debt payments as a percentage of the export of goods and services) for non-oil developing countries increased from 11.5 percent in 1974 to 22.3 percent in 1982 and remained at about the same level through the late 1980s.[21] Mexico experienced a growth rate of only 0.5 percent for the period 1980–7 compared with 6.5 percent for the period 1965–80; Argentina had a negative growth rate of –0.3 percent for the period 1980–7 compared with a positive rate of 3.3 percent for the period 1965–80.[22]

There was an absence of any leadership, including American leadership, in dealing with the problem of petro-currency recycling. Little guidance was given to banks. Little effort was made to steer the activities of oil exporting states with surplus revenues. Most significantly, the decision by the Reagan administration to manage American macroeconomic policy virtually exclusively through monetary measures led to a large increase in interest rates around the world which severely disadvantaged highly indebted Third World countries. Only when Mexico threatened to default in the early 1980s did American public officials begin to take a more decisive role, and even then such leadership was initially limited to the Chair of the Federal Reserve, Paul Volcker.

In the past the United States could be depended on to step in and preserve the stability of various international economic regimes because it was very powerful and very politically ambitious. In the present, management of international regimes requires cooperation among a number of major powers. Such cooperation has increased in the last decade, especially in the area of macroeconomic policy coordination.[23] In other areas, however, such as international trade, conflict among major industrial countries has become more intense. The Uruguay Round was protracted and painful. Distrust between the United States and Japan has increased.

In sum, the most important explanation for growing anxiety about the future of the international economic system is the changing international distribution of power among states, especially the decline of the United States. As American power has fallen, US leaders have been less willing to accept diffuse reciprocity and less anxious to pursue general milieu goals. They have focussed more on specific American interests and have been less willing to provide support for the system as a whole. While economic interdependence has continued to grow, the political foundations of global regimes have become more frayed.

CONFIGURATIONS OF INTEREST

A second cause for concern about the stability of the global economic system arises from the configuration of specific interest in various countries rather than the distribution of power among states. Global interdependence results in higher levels of economic well being for societies as a whole. Politically, however, the general benefits of openness may be so diffuse that they do not lead to consequential political activity. Costs or benefits that are concentrated rather than diffuse are much more likely to be politically consequential; that is, to result in pressure group activity that can change government policy.[24] An open international system does create winners and losers. Internationally mobile factors of production and exportables are beneficiaries of an open system. Import competing sectors are losers.

The following taxonomy suggests the relationship between patterns of trade and interest group pressures.

1 The government of a country that has limited export sectors and many import-competing sectors (with trade deficits being financed in one way or another) will experience substantial society pressure to adopt more protectionist policies.
2 The government of a country that has both import-competing and export-oriented sectors will experience competing pressure with some groups pressing for greater protectionism and others supporting an open system.
3 The government of a country that has many sectors in which there are high levels of exports and imports, that is where there is considerable intra-sectoral trade, will experience little pressure for protectionist action. Those analysts who stress the development of globalization see this configuration of cross cutting interests as prototypical, at least for the advanced market economy countries. It is a world in which multinational corporations operate across many countries and compete against each other on a global basis. The usually implicit assumption of those who see a borderless world is that there will be high levels of symmetry with regard to investment, trade, and technology flows among advanced industrialized countries.

These configurations can only be a rough first cut. The translation of societal preferences into policy outcomes depends upon institutional structures, not just on societal interests. Nevertheless, the configur-

Table 2.2 Trade ratios (export to imports or imports to exports), 1988

	US–Japan	*Japan–EC*	*US–EC*
Food	21.1	–11.0	1.4
Raw materials	25.9	–2.4	3.9
Ores and other minerals	33.0	–9.3	3.5
Fuels	10.1	–7.5	–1.8
Non-ferrous metals	2.4	–8.0	–2.3
Iron and steel	–18.3	1.5	–13.1
Chemicals	1.8	–2.2	–1.1
Other semi manufactures	–2.7	–1.2	–2.7
Machinery and transp equip	–6.9	5.6	–1.0
Power generating machinery	1.1	2.1	1.2
Other non-electrical mach.	–5.4	2.5	- 2.0
Office and telecomm equip.	–5.8	32.3	3.7
Electrical machinery	–5.1	4.5	1.0
Automotive products	–46.6	3.5	–5.4
Other transport equipment	–1.1	4.1	1.7
Textiles	–3.1	–1.4	–1.8
Clothing	–1.9	–7.0	–8.7
Other consumer goods	–2.3	1.4	–1.4

Source: Derived from figures in GATT, *International Trade 1987/88* (Geneva, 1988) US and Japan country tables

ation of interests is a decent first approximation of the proclivity of different governments with respect to international economic policy.

Table 2.2 provides a very rough description of the pattern of interests generated by international trade. The table shows the ratio of imports to exports, or exports to imports by sector. In each case the larger figure is the numerator of the ratio. A positive figure indicates that exports are larger than imports; a negative figure indicates that imports are larger than exports for the first country in each named pair. (For instance, the figure of 21.1 for food in the US–Japan column indicates that the ratio of US food exports to Japan to food imports from Japan is 21.1.) If the figure is 1 it indicates trade balance; that is, exports and imports within the sector are equal.

The pattern of trade that is least likely to generate protectionist pressures occurs when the ratio of exports and imports is close to unity, because this indicates high intra-sectoral trade. Intra-sectoral trade will not generate pressures for protection among trading partners. In contrast, higher ratios indicate that trade within a sector is imbalanced generating a pattern of interests in which export-oriented industries will favor openness but import-competing ones will support closure.

With the exception of iron and steel and clothing, relatively small dollar value sectors, and automotive equipment, trade between the United States and the European Community is relatively balanced within sectors. Although the United States has run an overall deficit with the Community, it has been much smaller than the bilateral deficit with Japan.

The situation is much more problematic with regard to Japan. Not only is the total trade deficit between the United States and Japan very large (a figure that reflects macroeconomic policy and relative savings rates), but sectoral imbalances are also substantial with Japan importing raw materials from the United States, and exporting much more than it imports in most manufacturing sectors. Sectoral imbalances between the EC and Japan are also large in many areas although not as skewed as those between the United States and Japan. Regardless of the reasons for this pattern of exchange, it does lead to a situation in which there will be pressures for protectionism from import competing industries, even if they are somewhat offset by sectors that benefit from exports to Japan. In contrast the high level of intra-sectoral trade between the United States and Europe is less likely to lead to pressures for closure.

In addition to trade, direct foreign investment can also influence that pattern of interest group pressure. Higher levels of direct foreign investment will generally create more support for an open economic policy. Direct foreign investors will favor an open system because they want to repatriate or transfer their capital, to export as well as market domestically goods that are produced offshore, and to integrate production activities by sourcing components from several different countries. Labor employed by direct foreign investors, especially if plant activities depends on imported components or export markets, will also support international openness. In recent years, direct foreign investment has been growing much more rapidly than either trade or world GDP. From 1983 to 1989 direct foreign investment outflows grew at a compound annual rate of 28.9 percent, compared with 9.4 percent for exports and 7.8 percent for GDP.[25]

Table 2.3 Ratios of value of stock of direct foreign investment, 1988

Japan in EC to EC in Japan	7.35
Japan in US to US in Japan	2.98
EC in US to US in EC	1.47

Source: Derived from figures in UN, Centre on Transnational Corporations, *World Investment Report 1991: the triad of foreign direct investment* (New York: UN, 1991), p. 40, Figure II

Like trade, there is much more balance in direct foreign investment between the United States and the EC than there is between Japan and either the United States or the Community. In 1988 the stock of American direct foreign investment in the Community was $131.4 billion and the stock of Community investment in the US was $193.9 billion. In contrast, the stock of Japanese investment in the US was $53.4 billion compared with $17.9 billion worth of US investment in Japan, and the value of Japanese investment in the EC was $12.5 billion compared with $1.7 billion worth of EC investment in Japan. The ratios of the value of the stock of direct foreign investment are shown in the following table.

Japanese corporations have a much greater stake in the American and Community markets than American or Community investors have in the Japanese market.

Reliance on balance of trade statistics obscures the extent of imbalance in exchange between the United States and Japan. In 1989, majority owned US affiliates of Japanese corporations had total sales of $225.5 billion. In 1987, 94 percent of the sales of Japanese affiliates in manufacturing in the United States were made within the US. Assuming the same percentage continued to hold, Japanese corporations made about $212 billion in sales within the United States in 1989.[26] In 1989 majority owned US affiliates in Japan had total sales of $58 billion, about one-quarter the value of the sales of Japanese affiliates in the US.[27] Hence, the sales of foreign affiliates, like trade flows between the United States and Japan, are very imbalanced. Japanese firms have a much greater stake in the American market than American firms have in the Japanese market.

In contrast, in 1989 the affiliates of European corporations in the United States had total sales of $472 billion, and European affiliates of American corporations had total sales of $571 billion. Like trade, the sales of foreign affiliates of American corporations in Europe, and European corporations in the United States, are fairly balanced.[28]

Hence, a very simple interest group assessment of the societal pressures for protectionism suggests that these pressures will be much less in the US–European relationship than in the US–Japan relationship. Trade between the United States and Europe is relatively balanced overall and within sectors. Trade between the United States and Japan is much more imbalanced overall and within sectors. Likewise, both the stock of direct foreign investment and the sales of affiliates are much more equal in the case of the United States and Europe, than they are in the case of the United States and

Japan. Despite a number of highly visible policy conflicts, relations between the United States and Europe are much more interdependent than relations between the United States and Japan or Japan and Europe. If there is a rupture among the advanced industrialized countries in the economic realm, it is more likely to involve Japan than US–European relations.

REGIONAL INTEGRATION

Anxiety about the potential regionalization of the global economy, as opposed to a dramatic universal breakdown, has become more pronounced. The fear is that the current multilateral system will be replaced by more or less closed regional blocs.

The European Community and its move to a single integrated market in 1992, as well as its commitment to future monetary integration, is the most important regional initiative of the last decade. In the early 1980s the incentives for further regional integration increased. The European economies were suffering from stagflation. Euro-sclerosis, not Europe 1992, was the catch phrase of the day. Trade growth had stalled. Greater market integration, which could spur productivity and growth by taking advantage of economies of scale, was an attractive economic policy, especially given the fact that most European governments feared that expansionary monetary and fiscal policies would only increase inflation.

There were also a number of political and institutional factors that made greater market integration attractive. Ruling parties or coalitions in Britain, Belgium, the Netherlands, Germany, and Denmark all moved to the right in the early 1980s. The Mitterrand government abandoned its reflationary policies of the early 1980s and adopted more conservative positions. All of these governments were more interested in market-based solutions than their more liberal predecessors. A number of large European business interests supported a more integrated market since they were best situated to take advantage of new opportunities. The development of the European monetary system had brought the macroeconomic policies of the major European states more in line with each other, making the elimination of non-tariff barriers easier. Finally, rulings of the European Court, especially the Cassis de Dijon decision in 1979, which mandated mutual recognition of national standards, made it easier to move to an integrated market because it eliminated the need to develop a single European-wide standard.[29]

In December of 1991 the members of the Community concluded

an even more ambitious agreement, the Maastricht Treaty on European Union. The Treaty calls for monetary and political union. Maastricht was concluded at a moment when the basic conditions of the postwar order were changing as a result of the collapse of the Soviet empire and the Soviet Union itself, a development which has, at the same time, increased some of the incentives for greater integration and made such integration more difficult. Even if the Maastricht initiative were to badly flounder, however, the European Community would still be a far more integrated economic bloc than any other area of the world.

The second most prominent effort at regional economic integration is the North American Free Trade Agreement (NAFTA), which was preceded by the United States–Canada Free Trade Agreement. This is a much less ambitious arrangement than the single European market. It eliminates trade barriers but labor movement remains highly restricted and there is little effort to regulate other issue areas such as social policy and the environment except to the extent that they impinge on trade issues. There are no explicit provisions for macroeconomic policy coordination or exchange rate regulation.

The United States–Canada Agreement was primarily initiated by Canada. The United States is by far the largest market for Canadian products, accounting for almost 75 percent of Canada's trade. Trade barriers between the two countries were very low before the Agreement was signed. Canadian economic interests, however, feared that aggressive American trade practices could impede their access to their most important foreign market. The Free Trade Agreement was important for Canadian exporters because it provided them with higher levels of confidence about future transactions.[30] While the Agreement has received relatively less attention in the United States, it has generated major debates in Canada where its opponents have pointed to the danger of American cultural domination as well as to economic costs.

Mexico's motivations for joining a North American Free Trade Agreement are more complex. Traditionally Mexico has been leery of close ties with the United States because it has feared American domination. Mexico lost much of its territory in the nineteenth century. It nationalized foreign oil companies, many of which were American, in 1938. It has protested against the treatment of Mexican workers in the United States. Nevertheless, the prospects of a free trade agreement were attractive to the government of President Salinas. Part of the motivation is similar to Canada's; an agreement guarantees access to the American market which accounts for about

65 percent of Mexico's total trade, and a much higher percentage of trade in rapidly growing manufacturing sectors. The agreement is also an instrument that the Mexican government can use to spur market oriented reforms within Mexico.

For the United States, the NAFTA may be more of a bargaining lever and a reflection of faltering faith in the multilateral GATT regime. The NAFTA would create an economic bloc of 360 million people. It might enhance the bargaining leverage which the United States has vis-à-vis the European Community.

There are, however, political tensions which the NAFTA will have to confront that are not an issue for the European Community. The United States is by far the most powerful member of the NAFTA. The relative opportunity cost of changing the agreement would be far less for the United States than for either Mexico or Canada, giving the United States more leverage.[31] Mexico is at a lower level of development than either the United States or Canada. The disparity in per capita wealth between the poorest and richest members of the European Community is much less than between Mexico and the United States. The European Community, in contrast to North America, has four large countries – Germany, Italy, France, and Britain – which can balance among themselves. The largest European country, Germany, is anxious to be contained within the Community; it is not likely that the United States has any desire to be contained within NAFTA.

There has been much less progress toward formal regional economic integration in East Asia. Here the problem of power asymmetry is even more acute than is the case for the US and Mexico. Japan is by far the largest economic actor in the region. There is anxiety about Japanese economic dominance. There is a historical legacy of Japanese aggression. Unlike North America, where both Canada and Mexico are highly dependent on the United States market with or without an agreement, the major trading states of East Asia have, thus far, been able to maintain a more diverse trading profile. The United States, not Japan, is the largest export market for the East Asian NICs. Given current trading patterns it would be more important for Korea, Taiwan, Hong Kong, and Singapore to secure access to the American market than to the Japanese market.

It is very unlikely that a closed regional trading bloc will develop in East Asia. Trading patterns are too diverse. Institutional structures are too anaemic. The distribution of political power is too problematic. Empirically, there is no indication that trade has become more regionalized in East Asia if growth rates in the 1980s are taken into account.[32]

CONCLUSIONS

Anxiety about the erosion of the open multilateral international economic system of the postwar era has grown despite the fact that there are few indicators that the system is failing. Trade has continued to grow more rapidly than aggregate economic output. The integration of global capital markets has dramatically accelerated over the last decade. Direct foreign investment has grown much more quickly than trade, providing support for the argument that the world is becoming truly borderless with major multinational corporations as the primary instrument for global economic integration. The only area where regionalization is clearly manifest is Europe. There is no indication that trade is becoming more regionally concentrated in either North America or Asia, although Japanese investment in Asia increased substantially after the revaluation of the yen in the mid-1980s.

The concept of a borderless world suggests that trends toward greater global integration will continue. The optimistic vision of a borderless world is ultimately based on the assumption that changes in technology, especially reductions in the cost of transportation and communication, as well as more sophisticated labor forces, will create ever greater incentives for states to embrace open policies. Closure will inevitably lead to backwardness and failure.

This view ignores the fact that property rights and border controls are a function of political choices. The incentives influencing such choices will not automatically lead to liberal policies. In some cases, political leaders might simply be motivated by personal corruption; they might act to increase the opportunities for rent, seeking rather than pursue policies that would provide general societal benefits. Even in the absence of any rent seeking, if the costs and benefits of openness are asymmetrically distributed, interest group pressures will make it more difficult for political leaders to adopt liberal policies. In contrast, if there are many cross cutting cleavages, open trade and investment practices will encounter little societal resistance. Corruption and interest group politics aside, recent work in strategic trade theory suggests that openness is not necessarily a first best policy in a world that is characterized by increasing returns industries. Selective state action can made a country better off. Wise leaders might opt for intervention rather than diffuse liberalism.

Finally, at the general level of international regimes there are collective action problems. These problems are most easily settled if there is a hegemonic distribution of power, although several large states might also engage in effective cooperation. During the Cold War many collective action problems were resolved by the leadership of the United States, whose rulers enjoyed a preponderance of power in the West and were motivated by milieu objectives related to the containment of communism which discouraged them from making careful calculations about national economic gains.

In sum, technological changes will not inevitably lead to a borderless world. Stable property rights will remain a problem in many areas where political instability is increasing. The declining power of the United States and the collapse of communism will make the resolution of collective action problems more difficult. Finally, the unique pattern of Japan's involvement with the rest of the world weakens domestic political support for open trading and investment policies. It is startling that Kenichi Ohmae, the author most associated with the concept of a borderless world, is from the advanced market economy country that still has the most consequential borders.

The most significant contribution that Japan could make to the stability of the international economic system would be to give major societal actors in Europe and the United States a greater stake in the Japanese economy. This would require greater openness than has taken place in the past for both goods and direct foreign investment. If Japanese relations with Europe and the United States were characterized by the kind of interdependence that is reflected in European–American relations, there would be very little societal pressure to move toward a more closed system. Management of the global economy would be easier, even in an era of power transition.

Paradoxically, then, the most important arena for the exercise of Japanese leadership to preserve the stability of the global system involves domestic change rather than international initiatives. The provision of more foreign aid or the participation of Japanese troops in United Nations peace keeping operations, issues that have traditionally been seen as tests of a new international role for Japan, are much less important than the participation of foreign corporations in Japanese public works projects or the share of imported computer chips in the Japanese market. Globalization must be based on a political not just an economic foundation, and that foundation is not yet securely in place.

NOTES

1 For a discussion of the distinction between interdependence and globalism see Chapter 1 of this volume.

2 Simon Reich, "Roads to follow: regulating direct foreign investment," *International Organization* 43 (Autumn, 1989) pp. 543–84 for a discussion of Germany, France, Great Britain, and the United States.

3 Jeffry Frieden, "Invested interests: the politics of national economic policies in a world of global finance," *International Organization* 45, 4 (Autumn, 1991).

4 Peter Katzenstein, *Small States in the World Economy* (Cornell: Cornell University Press, 1985).

5 US–USSR comparisons 1960–84 from CIA, *Handbook of Economic Statistics* (1985); US–OECD comparisons 1960–86 based on OECD, *National Accounts 1960–1988. Volume I: Main Aggregates* (1990), Table 13, and *National Accounts 1960–1986*, p. 145. US–OECD comparisons 1953 calculated from UN, *Yearbook of National Account Statistics 1965.*

6 The situation in the advanced industrialized market economy countries can be contrasted with that in many LDCs which have limited capital markets and where labor is relatively immobile. Such countries are vulnerable to shocks from the external environment which they cannot control or easily adjust to. This argument is developed in Stephen D. Krasner, *Structural Conflict: the Third World against global liberalism* (Berkeley: University of California Press, 1985).

7 UN, *Yearbook of International Trade Statistics 1960* and *1970–71*; UN, *1984 International Trade Statistics Yearbook*; GATT, *International Trade*, various years.

8 Data on reserves can be found in IMF, *International Financial Statistics Yearbooks 1987 and 1989.* Susan Strange "The persistent myth of lost hegemony," *International Organization* 41 (1987), pp. 568–69, argues that the US is less constrained than other countries.

9 Had the Soviet Union opposed this action, as it almost certainly would have at any point before 1985, it is difficult to believe that American intervention would have taken place, although the Soviets might have kept their military client, Iraq, from invading Kuwait in the first place.

10 Kenneth Organski and Jacek Kugler have argued that states which are defeated in war ultimately return to the trend line of GNP growth established by their prewar experience. See A. F. K. Organski and Jacek Kugler, *The War Ledger* (Chicago: University of Chicago Press, 1980).

11 Bruce Russett, "The mysterious case of vanishing hegemony; or, is Mark Twain really dead?," *International Organization* 39 (1985). For other studies which emphasize the continued leadership position of the United States see Joseph Nye, *Bound to Lead* (New York: Basic, 1990), and Henry Nau, *The Myth of American Decline* (New York: Oxford University Press, 1990). Both of these studies place considerable strength on the potency of American ideology, its endorsement of democracy, the market, and, especially in contrast with Japan, its universalism.

12 The argument that American leaders were unable to make trade-offs, that they believed that all good things would go together is developed

in Robert Packenham, *Liberal America and the Third World* (Princeton: Princeton University Press, 1973).

13 The distinction between diffuse and specific reciprocity is developed in Robert Keohane, "Reciprocity in International Relations," *International Organization* 40 (1986).

14 Judith Goldstein, *Ideas, Interests, and American Trade Policy*, Unpub. manuscript (Stanford University, October, 1990).

15 Ibid., pp. 47–52.

16 Joanne Gowa, *Closing the Gold Window: domestic politics and the end of Bretton Woods* (Ithaca: Cornell University Press, 1983). John Odell, *International Monetary Policy* (Princeton: Princeton University Press, 1983) has pointed out that American policy was consistent with and could be rationalized by new economic ideas that extolled the virtues of flexible exchange rates. The specific decisions taken by American leaders in the summer of 1971, however, reflected specific interests not new intellectual ideas as evidenced by the fact that efforts to re-establish a fixed exchange rate system continued until the mid-1970s.

17 Stephen D. Krasner, "Global communications and national power," *World Politics* 43, 3 (April, 1991); Peter Cowhey, "The international telecommunications regime: the political roots of regimes for high technology," *International Organization* 44, 2 (Spring, 1990).

18 World Bank, *World Development Report 1989* (1989), Table 24.

19 Figures from GATT, *International Trade 87–88*, Vol. II, Tables AB 1, 2, and 3.

20 Zvi Griliches, "Productivity Puzzles and R&D: another nonexplanation," *Journal of Economic Perspectives* 2 (1988).

21 IMF, *World Economic Outlook* (1982), p. 173; (October, 1986), p. 110.

22 Figures from World Bank, *World Development Report 1989*, Table 2.

23 Michael Webb, "International Economic Structures, Government Interests, and International Coordination of Macroeconomic Adjustment Policies," *International Organization* 45, 3 (Summer, 1991).

24 Helen V. Milner, *Resisting Protectionism: global industies and the politics of international trade* (Princeton: Princeton University Press, 1988).

25 UN, Centre on Transnational Corporations, *World Investment Report 1991: the triad of foreign direct investment* (New York: UN, 1991), p. 4, Table 1.

26 Information from US, Department of Commerce, *Survey of Current Business* 71, 7 (July 1991), Table 10 and UN, Centre on Transnational Corporations, *World Investment Report 1991* (New York: UN, 1991), p. 45, Figure IV.

27 US, Department of Commerce, *Survey of Current Business* 71, 10 (October 1991), p. 42, Table 12.

28 Information from US, Department of Commerce, *Survey of Current Business* 71, 7 (July 1991), p. 81, Table 10; 71, 10 (October 1991), p. 42, Table 12.

29 David Cameron, "The 1992 initiative: causes and consequences," in Albert M. Sbragia (ed.), *Euro-politics: institutions and policymaking in the 'new' European Community* (Washington: Brookings Institution, 1992).

30 Rachel McCulloch, "The United States–Canada Free Trade Agreement,"

in F. Macchiarola (ed.), *International Trade: the changing role of the United States*, Proceedings of the Academy of Political Science 37, 4 (New York: 1990).

31 The relationship between bargaining power and the relative opportunity cost of change is developed by Albert Hirschman in *National Power and the Structure of Foreign Trade* (Berkeley: University of California Press, 1945/1971).

32 Jeffrey Frankel, "Is Japan creating a yen bloc in East Asia and the Pacific?," in Jeffrey Frankel and Miles Kahler (eds) *Regionalism and Rivalry* (Chicago: University of Chicago Press, 1993, pp. 53–88).

Part II

Global firms: confronting the imperatives of globalization and regionalization

3 The evolving nature of the transnational corporation

Cause and effect of globalization

David Gold and Azizul Islam[1]

INTRODUCTION

One of the major developments in the international economy during the 1980s was the rapid expansion of foreign direct investment (FDI) and the activities of transnational corporations (TNCs). Annual nominal flows of foreign direct investment grew from US$32 billion in 1983, the low point of the decade, to $225 billion in 1990. For the last half of the decade, 1985–90, FDI flows grew by 32 percent per year in comparison with a 13 percent annual growth rate for the value of merchandise exports and 12 percent for nominal world-wide gross domestic product (GDP).[2] Moreover, the growth of FDI, as impressive as it seems, understates the growing importance of TNCs since FDI does not include the many ways that TNCs are expanding their activities across borders without the commitment of substantial amounts of equity capital.

While a portion of the growth of FDI can be explained by the cyclical expansion of the world economy after 1983 – and the slow-down in FDI growth in 1991–2 in response to cyclical weaknesses in the world's largest economies suggests that this explanation remains important – there is widespread agreement that secular forces are also at work. Transnational corporations are widely seen as playing both a larger and qualitatively a more fundamental role in world-wide economic change. A series of policy changes liberalizing FDI in a wide spectrum of countries accompanied by the understanding that TNCs transmit a package of growth-inducing characteristics to host countries, often in concert with a variety of equity and non-equity links with local enterprises, is one example.[3] The possibility that FDI is partially replacing trade as the major force leading toward integration of cross-national economic relations is another.[4]

At the same time, there have been important paradigmatic

changes in the international economy. The increasing resort to market forces in economic decision making, the growing role of technology as a source of growth, the heightening of competition within industries and across countries, and the appearance of strong regional linkages involving trade, finance and investment, have led to rapid changes in many regions and sectors. These changes are creating a more integrated world economy, one that is increasingly being labeled as "global," and one which facilitates the cross-border activities of TNCs.

The issue examined in this chapter is how the two sets of changes are related. Is the expansion, and possible "globalization," of TNCs a cause of the larger changes observed in the world economy, or is this greater role of TNCs one of the effects of the larger changes? Part I of this chapter examines in closer detail the expansion of FDI in the 1980s and the accompanying concentration of the activities of TNCs within the largest economies. Part II looks at the factors behind the increasing integration of the world economy. Part III discusses how TNCs are becoming more integrated and the implications that has for how TNCs relate to the world economy. Part IV suggests that the globalization process is proceeding along different dimensions of economic activity at different rates. Part V draws some implications from the analysis.

I THE RECENT EXPANSION OF TNCS

The expansion of FDI flows described briefly above represents an extremely rapid period of expansion. At the end of 1990, the global stock of FDI stood at $1.7 trillion, up from $519 billion in 1980. Other measures also indicate the quantitative expansion of FDI, as well as providing a measure of the extended involvement of TNCs in the major determinants of global economic activity.

For example, the importance of FDI as a source of capital for host countries increased in the 1980s. Data on FDI as a share of domestic capital formation for host economies, both flows and stocks, show generally increasing ratios over the 1980s. For most countries, the ratio of FDI to domestic investment is fairly small, usually less than 10 percent of gross domestic capital formation (GDCF), and occasionally greater than 10 percent of GDCF.[5] However, even when FDI is small in relation to aggregate domestic investment flows, it is often much larger in key industries. For example, in the Republic of Korea, while FDI represented only 2 percent of GDCF in the mid- to late 1980s, it accounted for 19–31 percent of capital formation in manufacturing.[6] Such differences are partly accounted for by the inclusion of infrastructure and housing investment in GDCF, which are largely domestic activities and in many countries are fairly sizeable, but also because TNCs tend to be attracted to the faster growing and more outwardly oriented sectors of an economy.

There has been a marked shift toward services industries in the distribution of FDI across sectors. For seven major home countries (Canada, France, Germany, Japan, the Netherlands, the UK and the US), the share of the total outward stock of FDI attributed to the services sector grew between 1975 and 1990. Its share rose for all seven countries, and in some cases the rise was substantial (e.g. from 29 percent of the total stock to 47 percent for the US, and from 40 percent to 67 percent for Japan). For manufacturing industries, the percentage share of the total outward stock fell or stayed the same in six of the seven countries, the exception being the UK, where the share of its outward stock in manufacturing rose from 32 to 38 percent.[7]

Since services are generally less tradeable than goods and many services must be produced and delivered at the point of production, an increase in the relative importance of services in the world economy implies an increase in the relative importance of services FDI. At the same time, the deregulation of many services activities, as in communications, finance and transportation, and the privatization of many government-run enterprises in these sectors, contributed to the rapid growth of FDI in services.

A third important feature of the quantitative changes in TNC activities is the growing concentration of FDI within the developed economies, and especially within the three legs of the Triad, the European Community, Japan, and the United States. In the early to mid-1970s, approximately one-third of all flows of FDI were directed toward developing countries; by the end of the 1980s, this proportion had been cut almost in half, as 17 percent of FDI flows went to developing countries in 1986–90. Approximately 70 percent of annual flows go to the Triad economies, which, by 1990, accounted for more than half of the global accumulated stock of FDI, a share that will undoubtedly rise further given the size of annual flows.

This growing concentration within the Triad is partly due to a number of broad changes: the declining role of primary sector activity in worldwide economic growth has reduced the relative importance of FDI in many sectors important to developing countries; growth problems, especially during the debt crisis of the 1980s, reduced the attractiveness of developing country locations; restrictive host country policies, including nationalizations, made many host developing countries less attractive to TNCs in the 1970s, although widespread liberalizations in the 1980s have not, in general, stimulated larger FDI flows. The concentration of TNCs within the Triad can also be attributed to changes within the world of TNCs. Changes in the technology and organization of production, pioneered by Japanese TNCs, have reduced the importance of low labor costs and therefore reduced the importance of low labor-cost locations, while simultaneously increasing the role of coordination within the firm. These changes have emphasized the establishment of long-term relationships between producers and their suppliers, as well as increased the efficiencies from locating suppliers near assemblers. Thus, there appears to be an important incentive for locating production near the largest markets, and locating suppliers near final producers.

The growing concentration of FDI within the Triad is not the only important aspect of the concentration of FDI. An analysis of bilateral flows and stocks of FDI between the members of the Triad and those developing countries where such data is available reveals an important pattern of regional concentration. As shown in Figure 3.1, there is a distinct pattern whereby Triad members tend to dominate FDI positions within host developing countries located in the same region as the Triad member. With the rise of Japan as a major foreign investor, this pattern appears to be growing stronger over time.

A similar clustering of developing countries around a single Triad member is also observed when patterns of foreign trade are analyzed and, for the EC and Japan but not for the United States, the same holds for bilateral official development assistance.[8] The existence of trade and FDI clusters may be due to common historical linkages, including those established out of colonial ties, geographical proximity and cultural familiarity, as well as common causes in terms of policies and market incentives or disincentives. At the same time, the growing importance of TNCs in international trade, and the importance of trade, especially intra-firm trade, to the strategies of integrated TNCs suggests that the overlap of trade and FDI clusters may also be the result of the strategies adopted by TNCs. Similarly, there is evidence that home country governments from the Triad have utilized the distribution of ODA to support the trade, financial and FDI linkages with host developing countries established by TNCs.[9] Thus, the regional clustering of these important flows of resources may be a result of the regional strategies of TNCs.

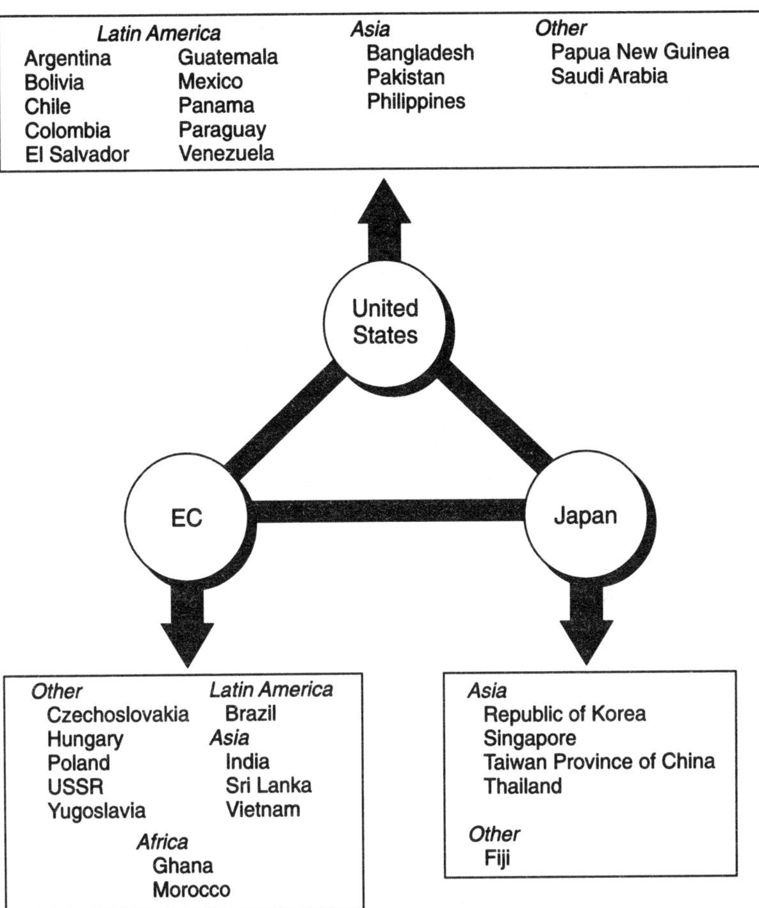

Figure 3.1 FDI clusters of Triad Members, 1968–9

Source: Transnational Corporations and Management Division, *World Investment Report 1992: Transnational Corporations as Engines of Growth* (New York, United Nations, 1992)

Regional clustering does not rule out important cross-regional flows of FDI and an important cross-regional presence of TNCs. Intra-Triad FDI flows are quite large, with the notable exception of flows from the EC and the US to Japan.[10] In the case of developing countries, the dominance of a single Triad member within a region has been accompanied by a substantial presence of TNCs from outside of the region. Thus, EC and US TNCs have substantial FDI in Asia, while EC TNCs are present in Latin America and the Caribbean and Japanese TNCs are expanding in that region.[11]

II IS THE WORLD ECONOMY GLOBALIZING?

Important changes in the nature of worldwide economic relations are continuing to occur and are re-shaping the world economy. National economies are becoming more open and economic activities, such as the movement of goods and services, financial flows, investment, and even the movement of people, are becoming more integrated across borders. Some have argued that this cross-national integration has proceeded to such an extent that the world economy is best characterized as a single, global economy, while others have emphasized that economic integration is assuming a distinctly regional character.

Globalization refers to two distinct phenomena. At the aggregate level, globalization implies that economic phenomena within a country are strongly influenced by developments of a worldwide nature. In that sense, both globalization and regionalization can be seen as examples of internationalization, which occurs as domestic economic variables, that is, prices and quantities, are increasingly determined by, or subject to influence by, factors outside of the national economy. Internationalization includes a number of phenomena, such as international trade, international financial flows, FDI and other cross-border activities of TNCs, the transfer of technology across national boundaries and the international movement of human capital. Internationalization, from the viewpoint of a single, national economy might be seen as regionalization if the external forces are largely within the same region, and might be seen as globalization if the forces are largely or pre-dominantly extra-regional. It is possible that some parts of an economy are global, others regional and still others largely national. For example, in a hypothetical economy, interest rates could be heavily influenced by global flows of financial capital, exchange rates primarily affected by regional trading patterns and wage rates largely determined nationally.

From the standpoint of the individual firm, globalization refers to the adoption of strategies and structures in which cross-border activities have a high degree of functional interrelationship. Under globalization, firms can potentially situate a growing range of corporate activities in a large number of international locations, with each activity and location evaluated in terms of its contribution to the firm's overall objectives. Thus, globalization strategies and structures involve an increase in cross-national integration. However, while the greater integration accompanying globalization strategies can occur across a large number of country locations, it can also exist in a small number of countries located in close proximity to one another. Thus, there may be no necessary link between the geographical and functional dimensions of globalization.

One of the key elements leading toward a changing and more integrated world economy is the increasing importance of market forces. The resurgence of market forces is perhaps most dramatically illustrated in the transformation of the economies of Central and Eastern Europe and the former Soviet Union from centrally planned to market based. Within both developed and developing economies, the withdrawal of the state from many key areas of economic life has also fostered the growth of market forces. The deregulation of domestic industries, many of which involve substantial participation by TNCs, the privatization of previously state-owned or state-run enterprises, in many cases allowing foreign ownership, and the liberalization of laws and regulations governing foreign transactions, including FDI, have been widespread. One important result is that TNCs have entered new industries and sectors in specific host economies, including telecommunications in Argentina, Mexico and Venezuela, the airline industry in the United States and even defense sector industries in many countries.[12] The growing importance of the market is one of the main factors behind the view that the world economy is becoming more integrated, and more global.

Accompanying the growing importance of the market is the shrinking of economic distance. Transport and communications costs as a portion of total product value have been declining, as a result of technological innovation and increased competition, which in turn have helped stimulate the expansion of more efficient transport and communications systems into more areas of the world.[13] For example, the privatization and modernization of telephone systems and computer networks in a growing number of developing countries is a factor spurring the integration of these countries into larger economic regions.

Transport and communications are examples of the growing role of services in the world economy. Other examples include finance, real estate, construction and business services. Services are also becoming more important within manufacturing processes. Research and development and management coordination have become important sources of value added within manufacturing, and they may appear at various and multiple points along a firm's value chain. Research and development outlays as a share of both aggregate GDP and of GDCF have been rising and the bulk of these outlays are undertaken by TNCs.[14] To give one example of the growing importance of services within manufacturing, it has been estimated that 80 percent of the cost of a computer is attributable to services activities.

One of the most remarked upon features of the world economy is the spreading uniformity of demand, which has stimulated a global proliferation of products such as automobiles, electronics goods, clothing and many foodstuffs, consumer services such as hotels and movies, producers services such as banking and advertising and even some capital goods such as computerized machine tools. Levi's, the Sony Walkman and the Marlboro Man are as well known in developing Asia as they are within the Triad.

Observers such as Kenichi Ohmae have emphasized the cross-national convergence of demand patterns as a major component of the globalization of the world economy and the globalization strategies of TNCs.[15] Yet Ohmae has also emphasized the importance of demand patterns that are distinctly local. For example, the booming market for four-wheel drive vehicles is largely a United States' phenomenon that has attracted transnational producers. In a related fashion, wider European integration is not likely to eliminate regional preferences in the demand for such basic household appliances as washers and dryers. Attempts to create pan-European production systems have to deal with such regional differences. Thus, while demand may be a force leading toward global markets, it simultaneously preserves or creates some that are national or regional.

Major changes in the technology and organization of production have also had an impact on global economic relations. Japanese firms have pioneered flexible, "best practice" manufacturing systems which are partly based upon innovations in microelectronics and partly upon innovations in the organization of work.[16] Japanese producers have succeeded in reducing unit costs while simultaneously expanding the quality and variety of their output. Their successes have helped foster the shift from a resource-based to a technology- and knowledge-based expansion of production on an aggregate level. In the process, Japanese TNCs have expanded rapidly on international markets, both as exporters and as direct investors, with the latter expansion being one of the sources of the rapid global growth of FDI. At the same time, the success of

Japanese TNCs has heightened competition, especially within the Triad, and led to many other companies adopting or seeking similar cost reducing production methods.

The heightened competition brought about by Japanese TNCs is part of a broader phenomenon, whereby competitive conditions have been intensified in many markets and across many countries. This is perhaps nowhere more evident than in the United States, where producers in many oligopolistic industries have found their market positions threatened by lower-cost and higher-quality producers from Japan, Western Europe and even a few developing countries. The strength of competition from outside the EC is one of the issues behind the formulation of trade and competition policies for the single market. Ohmae defines globalization as the need for TNCs to be present in all major markets, in part to gain market position and potential profits, but also to challenge the market position and profitability of competitors in order to weaken the ability of competitors to utilize their ownership advantages on a global scale.

The final phenomenon of note is a growing tendency for the establishment of regional arrangements among countries. The formation of a single market within the European Community and the possible extension of this market to the wider European Economic Area, the creation of a free trade area in North America, and the creation of formal and informal regional linkages in South America, the Caribbean, North Africa and Asia, are prime examples of this regionalization trend. The three largest and best known regions, the EC, North America and East Asia, have proceeded by different routes.

As articulated by Sylvia Ostry, political motives and external economic shocks – oil price rises amidst competitive pressures from Japan and the US – led the EC toward the single market. In North America, strong bilateral trade and investment relations between the US and Canada and between the US and Mexico, but not between Mexico and Canada, pushed the three countries into negotiations on a North American Free Trade Agreement (NAFTA); while in Asia, multilateral governmental arrangements are largely absent and the activities of firms, financial institutions and other actors are creating greater regional integration.[17] Whether TNCs are following, as Ostry feels is the case in Europe, leading, as in Asia, or moving parallel, as in NAFTA, there can be no doubt as to their importance. In addition, regionalization takes some of its cues from global developments. The impetus for NAFTA from the US side is both to protect the North American market from Japan and Europe and to improve competitiveness within the US. Similarly, Mexican interest in NAFTA increased when the president of Mexico realized that European companies and countries were more interested in exploring linkages with the newly-opened economies of Central and Eastern Europe and the former Soviet Union than they were in building extra-regional linkages in Latin America. While fostering greater cross-national economic integration, it remains an open question whether the creation of regional trade blocs will be a stimulant or barrier to greater global integration.

III INCREASING GLOBALIZATION AND THE CHANGING NATURE OF TNCs

Acting in concert with the various forces described above, TNCs have increasingly adopted globalization as a central element in their strategies. The evidence of increased globalization can be seen in different forms. First, the upsurge of FDI itself, noted earlier in the chapter, bears testimony to this phenomenon. Second, the growing share of FDI in developed market economies, particularly among the Triad members, spurred by the strategic decisions of TNCs to establish a presence in each other's markets, is a refleciton of globalization (Figure 3.2). It is also of interest to note in this context that a large part of FDI involves cross-border intercorporate equity investments. According to one estimate, such investments, which amounted to only $10 billion in 1985, rose to a peak of $115 billion in 1989 and amounted to $98 billion in 1990.[18] Third, there has been a considerable increase in the internationalization of R&D by TNCs. Finally, mention should be made of a variety of cross-border non-equity links among TNCs, particularly strategic technological alliances. These alliances are most common in the area of new technologies and are heavily concentrated among TNCs from the Triad (Table 3.1).

In addition to increasing globalization, the nature of TNCs as organizations is in the process of fundamental change. Available evidence indicates that TNCs have been evolving toward a more complex and integrated form of cross-border organization, both within TNCs and in their relations with other firms.[19]

In one simplified form of structure, affiliates in host countries have a linear link with the parent firm in the home country. Such affiliates tend to be largely resource based or oriented toward the domestic market within the host economy. An example would be

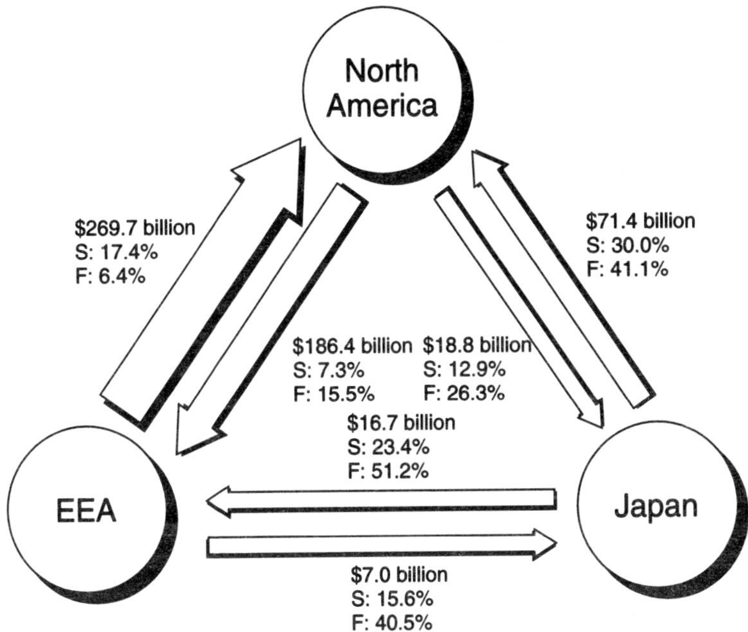

Figure 3.2 Intra-Triad foreign direct investment, 1989

Source: Transnational Corporations and Management Division *World Investment Directory* (New York: United Nations, 1992)

Note: Dollar figures show estimated value of stock of foreign direct investment based on data on inward and outward investment from North America and the European Economic Area (EEA), excluding Iceland and Liechtenstein. Intra-North American investment and intra-EEA investment has been netted out. Percentages show average annual growth rates for stocks (1980–9) and flows (1985–90). North America includes Canada and the United States. The European Economic Area included the European Community (EC) and the European Free Trade Association (EFTA), excluding Iceland and Liechtenstein.

FDI in an extractive industry within a host country, where the affiliate obtains a resource which it then transmits to its parent for further processing and sale in the home country or for export to third countries. Another example would be an affiliate within a desired market that assembles and sells a product using inputs supplied by the parent. In one simple case, a market-oriented affiliate may be largely a marketing or trading entity, and engage in little or no manufacturing value added. The linear form of parent–affiliate

Table 3.1 International distribution of technology cooperation agreements in biotechnology, information technologies and new materials, cumulative 1989 (number and percentage)

	Biotechnology		*Information technologies*		*New materials*	
Area	*Number*	*Percent*	*Number*	*Percent*	*Number*	*Percent*
Japan	58	5	95	4	88	13
United States	428	35	707	26	139	20
United States–Japan	155	13	406	15	94	14
United States–Western Europe	245	20	599	22	133	19
Western Europe	223	18	509	19	118	17
Western Europe–Japan	38	3	177	7	49	7
Other	66	5	225	8	67	10
Total	1,213	100	2,718	100	688	100

Source: John Hagedoorn and Luc Soete, "The internationalization of science and technology (policy): how do 'national' systems cope?" in H. Inose, M. Kawasaki and F. Kodarna (eds), *Science and Technology Policy Research: What Should be Done? What Could be Done*? (Tokyo: Mita Press, 1991), pp. 201–16

organization involves two-way resource flows, including finance and management skills as well as intermediate and final products, directly between the parent and the affiliate. The parent TNC can be seen as exploiting its ownership-specific advantages in the context of specific locational advantages within host countries, with the latter entering at a fairly well specified point in the production process.

The form of TNC organization that is now emerging is more complex and best described as integrated rather than linear. The parent still utilizes some affiliates in the linear manner as described above. However, the entire value chain is becoming more integrated, with affiliates not only interacting with parents but with each other, and both parents and affiliates are interacting more closely with firms that are not under the direct control of the parent firm. In the integrated form of international production, the flow of goods and services through the value chain will not proceed in a straight line from affiliate to parent to consumer, but will involve an extensive flow of resources and components among affiliates (see Figure 3.3 on Toyota's operations in four ASEAN countries), between affiliates and the parent, as well as between both parents and affiliates and companies linked via non-equity arrangements. Final assembly can occur within the home country for sale at home and/or for export, but it could also occur within an affiliate for sale within a host

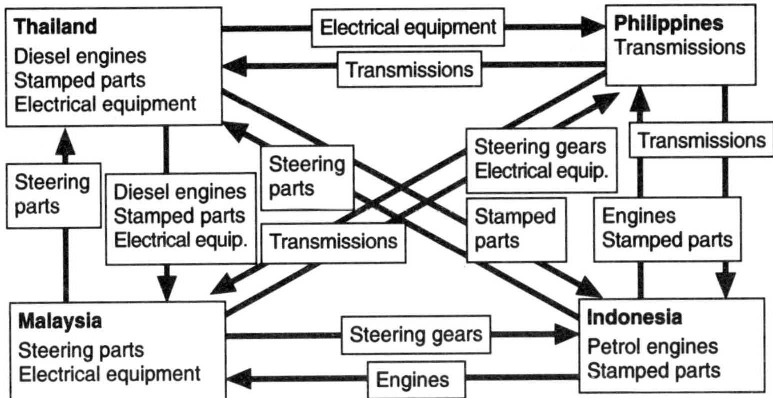

Figure 3.3 Automobile operations of Toyota in four ASEAN countries
Source: Far Eastern Economic Review, 21 September 1989

country and/or for export to the home country and to third countries.

Ghoshal and Bartlett describe a typical, integrated TNC, in this case N. V. Phillips of the Netherlands:

> The company has its own operating units in 60 countries as diverse as the United States, France, Japan, South Korea, Nigeria, Uruguay, and Bangladesh. Some of these units are large, fully integrated companies developing, manufacturing, and marketing a diverse range of products from light bulbs to defense systems. Such subsidiaries might have 5000 or more employees and might be among the largest companies in their host countries. Others are small, single function operations responsible for only R&D or manufacturing, or marketing for only one or a few of these different businesses. Some such units might employ 50 or fewer people. . . . Some of these units are tightly controlled from headquarters; others enjoy relationships with the headquarters more akin to those between equal partners than those between parent and subsidiary.[20]

Foreign direct investment can occur at almost any point on the firm's value chain as the TNC responds to both competition and cost differentials. In addition, TNCs adopt a variety of relationships outside of wholly-owned affiliates. They may secure inputs through long-term subcontracts, obtain a presence in host country markets via franchising and reduce the risks of transnational expansion through joint ventures. These non- or low-equity arrangements allow some degree of internalized decision making for the parent while also increasing their flexibility to produce internationally at different points on their value chains.

The integrated form of TNC organization represents, on the one hand, a more sophisticated mixing of ownership, locational and internationalization advantages and, on the other, a greater reliance upon coordinating mechanisms to achieve value added at all levels within the TNC. While the shift from a linear to an integrated form or organization does, in part, reflect recent historical evolution, it needs to be emphasized that the linear mode continues to exist within the world economy, and sometimes within a single TNC. Thus, some functions within an integrated TNC, or some product lines, may still be organized along the lines of a linear mode, even as the bulk of activities are more fully integrated.

One example of a combination of linear and integrated modes of organization is Ford's European operations. A single affiliate, Ford of Europe manages operations throughout Western Europe, mostly within the European Community. Ford of Europe coordinates assembly and component manufacturing facilities within Europe, as well as a network of suppliers and subcontractors, while maintaining a link with the parent company for the European network as a whole.[21] The Ford example, however, along with that of Toyota cited above, as well as numerous others, suggests that the integrated form of organization has a strong regional base.[22] TNCs are establishing regional core networks which combine intra-firm and inter-firm networks to produce for regional markets, and then establishing similar regional core networks when expanding into other regions. Thus, the global expansion of TNCs has a strong regional component.

Ford also provides a recent example of a move toward a cross-regional form of integration. Ford has introduced a new model, the Mondeo, in which the identical car is being assembled in both North America and Western Europe, with some sourcing occurring intra-regionally and some cross-regionally. The key innovation is that the research, design and development of the Mondeo was undertaken globally, with some 20,000 R&D workers linked electronically into a single network. Ford's previous attempt to construct a "world car," the Escort, did not succeed because the European and North American design teams worked separately. The result was two distinct products sharing a common name and little else. However, while the R&D for the Mondeo has been organized globally, production of components and finally assembly is confined to two regions; the Mondeo is being manufactured in North America and Western Europe, but not in Asia.[23]

Within the automobile industry, there are substantial cross-national differences in transnational corporation strategies. Ford, as mentioned above, along with General Motors, have networks covering two regions with additional countries served through stand-alone affiliates or via exports. Most of the large European producers have only European networks, with relatively small extra-regional production capabilities. The major Japanese producers, on the other hand, are rapidly establishing regional networks in all three legs of the Triad. These strategies reflect differences in the historical development of home country-based competitive advantages. The US companies developed skills in managing multi-plant operations and exploiting scale economies in a large internal market, which gave them advantages operating transnationally. European firms have been restricted by trade barriers and significant cross-national differences in demand patterns and regulations, and have been much slower in developing the type of ownership advantages that can yield dividends in foreign production locations. Japanese producers, on the other hand, developed innovations in management that gave them advantages in niche markets which they were then able to convert into advantages in all markets.

Over time, the strategies of the more successful automobile manufacturers may be merging, as competition has provided a powerful incentive for learning. US firms have moved toward utilizing many elements of Japanese production methods, while European firms have extended their regional networks to include Central and Eastern Europe. Most recently, firms such as BMW and Daimler-Benz have begun to utilize FDI as part of their strategies of international expansion. Substantial excess capacity and protectionist pressures remain important forces within the auto industry, however, and the evolution of strategies remains uncertain.

The development of more integrated strategies is also evident in the evolution of how various functions are performed within the firm. Finance was one of the first industries to be considered global and financial management within non-financial firms has taken on global characteristics, with the ability to transfer massive quantities of funds electronically and the existence of 24-hour trading days. Marketing and advertising functions have also taken advantage of new technologies to develop global strategies. Yet, while such strategies may work well for some products, strong regional, national and cultural patterns exist that new technologies have not been able to overcome.

Similarly, while research and development is far more dispersed and interconnected than previously, as the Ford Mondeo example, cited above, indicates, research for many products remains decentralized. Thus, in pharmaceuticals, while high research costs have pushed firms to seek wider international markets for their products and thereby foster globalization in one sense, the research itself is often best performed on a relatively small scale, which imparts a single-country orientation. Other functions, such as legal, accounting and personnel, may be limited in their globalization potential by the lack of widely accepted international standards, and by the continuing phenomenon that most labor is far less internationally mobile than capital.

IV CAUSE AND EFFECT OF GLOBALIZATION

Changes in the world economy and the evolution of TNCs are occurring simultaneously, and it is clear that there is substantial interaction, and mutual causation, between the two, rather than a one-way causal relationship. Some of the observed changes appear to fit a regionalization mode, while others are pushing toward globalization. The integrated form of TNC organization is becoming more important as TNCs seek advantages within the changing world economy. Increasing reliance on market forces gives TNCs more scope for extending networks both geographically and functionally, while at the same time the expansion of TNCs is a force pushing for greater openness. Globalization appears to be occurring at different rates along different dimensions of economic activity. It might be useful, therefore, to briefly describe the main dimensions of the interaction of broad economic changes and those observed among TNCs.

Demand-based globalization can be seen in the appearance of identical, or at least similar, products throughout the world's major markets, and in many smaller ones as well. TNCs are increasingly responding to the similarity of demand patterns across the Triad and within many developing countries. Demand is responding to growing per capita income, and the convergence of per capita income levels across countries, especially among the developed market economies. This process has been stimulated by the success of the new, flexible production technologies, which allow firms greater scope for offering variations of basic products to meet local variations in demand, and by the existence of high fixed costs, which increase the incentive for TNCs to seek global markets. Yet TNCs help foster these patterns through their transnational marketing and advertising operations, and through the exploitation of ownership advantages in marketing, brand names, etc. Thus, individual firms and products increasingly have a global presence.

Similarly, competition-based globalization leads to the presence of TNCs in multiple countries and regions as they attempt to undermine the ownership advantages possessed by their competitors as well as more fully exploit their own ownership advantages. Thus, TNCs may seek a presence, even a small one, in all of the world's major markets in order to protect their own home markets and establish footholds in the foreign markets they see as most important. In some cases, this may involve exploiting a niche advantage, while in others may include a larger presence in a host market.

The growing importance of R&D raises risks and fixed costs, providing pressure for expansion and greater competition, while simultaneously introducing motives for cross-firm cooperation. R&D is also a sign of increased specialization along the value chain, providing a further push toward integrated organizations and global production and marketing. One example is the aircraft market. At the industry's birth, an airliner could be produced in a single factory, with engines adapted from other uses.[24] Today, producing even a small passenger aircraft might involve thousands of separate units, including parents and affiliates of TNCs, subcontractors and vendors, who are often also TNCs, and firms allied through joint ventures, research agreements, etc.

Competition-based globalization is in part fostered by the convergence of technological excellence of TNCs from different countries. In the postwar period, as TNCs, first from the United States, then from Western Europe, later from Japan and more recently from some of the NIEs, have become world-class competitors, this process has intensified. Where it has proceeded the furthest, foreign TNCs have attained a substantial enough presence within host economies and taken on many of the characteristics of host country firms. Examples of this phenomenon include Ford, General Motors and IBM in Europe and Honda and Sony in the United States. Whatever the nature of foreign affiliates in host countries, quite clearly competition-based globalization could not thrive in the absence of supportive policy changes in a broad spectrum of areas, for example, ownership and operating conditions for FDI, including in services, and liberalization of access to domestic financial and capital markets.

It has been noted earlier that the reduction in transportation and communications costs has fostered globalization of the world economy. Such reduction in costs has been both spearheaded by TNCs and has assisted them in their pursuit of globalization strategies.

Thus, the relationship between the globalization of the world economy and that of TNCs is a mutually interacting process. In some cases, autonomous changes in the world economy have created conditions of which TNCs have taken advantage in implementing their globalization strategies; in others, the globalizing strategies of TNCs have helped globalize the world economy.

Whatever the direction of this causal relationship, there is no denying the fact that, overall, the 1980s have witnessed a significant increase in the globalization of TNCs. However, this observation should be modified by two caveats. First, globalization of TNCs is by no means a universal phenomenon. The extent of globalization differs widely among sectors and among firms. Second, even for so-called globalized TNCs, regional core networks are often the means of being present in multiple regions. This suggests either that the economics of production fosters greater firm-level integration yet limits globalization from the supply-side, or that national, bilateral and multilateral policies have placed limits on the global reach of TNC networks. What appear to be global strategies on the part of TNCs may, when looked at from the production side, be in reality a collection of regional strategies.

V POLICY IMPLICATIONS

The globalization of TNCs in an increasingly integrated world economy poses a number of policy challenges. Some of these are briefly discussed below.

It has been mentioned earlier that, to some extent, globalization of TNCs is competition-based. The competitive strength of a firm, partly determined by its own inherent strength, is also influenced by the interactions of its capabilities with the institutional and policy environment it faces in its home country. As TNCs tend to invest in each other's home countries in pursuit of globalization strategies, pressures for greater convergence of institutional and policy frameworks are likely to emerge with a view to the creation of level playing fields. In consequence, many policy issues traditionally considered to be in the domestic arena may become subject to international discussions and consensus. Some examples lie in the area of competition, support for R&D, the environment, etc.[25]

Transnational corporations are increasingly emerging as integrating agents of investment, trade, technology and human resources development. In consequence, they react to a diverse set of policy instruments, not only FDI policies per se. The increasing participation of TNCs in the global market as integrating agents, coupled with their perceived need for level playing fields, suggests that the existing multilateral frameworks are ill-suited to meet the growing challenge of policy coordination, both between nations and between regional groupings, in a broad range of subjects. Sooner or later, the international community will have to grapple with the question of a multilateral framework capable of dealing with issues of finance, investment, technology and trade in an integrated manner, including those that arise when a TNC fails, affecting many interest groups – consumers, suppliers, stockholders, employees, etc. – dispersed over several countries.

The integrated form of TNC organization has a number of important characteristics in terms of its impacts upon host economies. One is that it tends to generate substantial linkages with host country institutions in the form of supplier relationships, training of employees and local managers and the spillover of product and process technology. These linkages can benefit host country growth prospects, although the characteristics of the host economy are often a primary determinant of the effectiveness of the linkages. A second important impact is that an affiliate that is closely integrated into a TNCs organizational structure will tend to possess a range of the parent firm's ownership and internalization advantages. The affiliate brings a package of these advantages to its host country location which tends to increase the likelihood that the host economy will benefit from the affiliate's presence.

At the same time, as has been documented in this chapter, FDI remains heavily concentrated in the Triad and a few developing countries. Therefore, insofar as integration into the international economy and concomitant growth prospects are fostered by globalization or regionalization strategies of TNCs, the vast majority of developing countries run the risk of increasing marginalization. How to ensure a more even distribution of FDI flows among countries is likely to become a major policy challenge during the 1990s.

Access to and the capacity to make use of technologies, particularly new technologies, are of crucial importance to sustained growth and the competitiveness of nations. Transnational corporations are major actors in the generation of technologies as well as their transfer across nations. The concentration of FDI in a limited number of countries, high R&D costs of new technologies (largely developed and commercialized by or in association with large, global TNCs), strengthening demands for stricter enforcement of intellectual property rights and the growing tendency for the internalizing of technologies among TNCs of the Triad countries through a web of strategic alliances may limit access for many developing countries, except through FDI, to technologies required for sustaining their international competitiveness and growth. This again reinforces the policy challenge to effect a more equitable distribution of the global flow of FDI.

NOTES

1 We would like to thank our colleagues at the Transnational Corporations and Management Division for their assistance in preparing this chapter, and especially Persa Economou, Michelle Gittelman, Karl P. Sauvant and Telly Tolentino for allowing us to incorporate some of their ideas and research. The views expressed, and any remaining errors, are solely the responsibility of the authors and in no way should be taken to represent the views of the United Nations or any of its subsidiary bodies.

2 All data on FDI are taken from Transnational Corporations and Management Division (TCMD), *World Investment Report 1992: Transnational corporations as engines of growth* (New York: United Nations, 1992).

3 Ibid., especially Chapter X.

4 DeAnne Julius, *Global Companies and Public Policy: the growing challenge of foreign direct investment* (London: Pinter Publishers, 1990).

5 TCMD, op. cit., Table II.3.

6 Chung H. Lee and Eric Ramstetter, "Direct investment and structural change in Korean manufacturing," in Eric Ramstetter (ed.), *Direct Foreign Investment in Asia's Developing Economies and Structural Change in the Asia-Pacific Region* (Boulder, Colo.: Westview Press, 1991), p. 112.

7 TCMD, op. cit., Table I.3.

8 United Nations Centre on Transnational Corporations (UNCTC), *World Investment Report 1991: The Triad in foreign direct investment* (New York: United Nations, 1991), Chapter 3.

9 Shafiqul Islam (ed.), *Yen for Development: Japanese foreign aid and the politics of burden-sharing* (New York: Council on Foreign Relations, 1991); Bernard Wysocki Jr., "Japan plots development of other economies in Asia through aid, investment programs," *Asian Wall Street Journal* (August 27, 1990).

10 Robert Z. Lawrence, "Why is foreign direct investment in Japan so low?," paper prepared for National Bureau of Economic Research Conference on Foreign Direct Investment (May 15 and 16, 1992).

11 Terutomo Ozawa, "The dynamics of Pacific Rim industrialization: how Mexico can join the Asian flock of 'flying geese'," in M. Riordan Roett (ed.), *Mexico's External Relations in the 1990s* (Boulder and London: Lynne Reimer, 1991).

12 TCMD, op. cit., pp. 86–9; Brett Pulley, "USAir will get $750 million from British Air," *The Wall Street Journal* (July 22, 1992); Theodore Moran, "The globalization of America's defense industries: managing the threat of foreign dependence," *International Security*, 15, 1 (Summer 1990), pp. 57–99.

13 Helleiner states that "in terms of economic distance (transport and communications costs relative to total costs) the global market has by now shrunk to a size comparable to that of many national markets only a few decades ago." G. K. Helleiner, *The New Global Economy and the Developing Countries: essays in international economics and development* (Hants, England: Edward Elgar, 1990), p. 220.

14 OECD, *OECD Science and Technology Indicators Report No. 3: R&D, production and diffusion of technology* (Paris: OECD, 1989), Chapter 1.

15 See Kenichi Ohmae, *Triad Power: the coming shape of global competition* (New York: The Free Press, 1985) and *The Borderless World: power and strategy in the interlinked economy* (New York: HarperCollins, 1990).

16 For a description and analysis of the origins of the new methods in the Japanese automobile industry, see Michael A. Cusumano, *The Japanese Automobile Industry: technology and management at Nissan and Toyota* (Cambridge, Mass.: Harvard University Press, 1985). For analyses of the impact of these methods on the world automobile industry, see Kurt Hoffman and Raphael Kaplinsky, *Driving Force: the global restructuring of technology, labor, and investment in the automobile and components industry* (Boulder: UNCTC and Westview Press, 1988) and James P. Womack, Daniel T. Jones and Daniel Roos, *The Machine that Changed the World* (New York: Macmillan, 1990).

17 Sylvia Ostry, "The new international order: the regionalization trend," paper presented at an International Conference on the New Economic Order, Rio de Janerio (April 13–14, 1992).

18 Paul M. Healey and Kirhsna G. Palepu, "Crossborder equity investments among firms in industrialized countries," paper prepared for National Bureau of Economic Research Conference on Foreign Direct Investment (May 15 and 16, 1992).

19 See Transnational Corporations and Management Division, *World Investment Report 1993* (New York: United Nations, 1994).

20 Sumantra Ghoshal and Christopher A. Bartlett, "The multinational corporation as an interorganizational network," *Academy of Management Review*, 15, 4 (1990), p. 604.

21 See Peter Dicken, *Global Shift: the internationalization of economic activity*, 2nd edn. (London: Paul Chapman, 1992), pp. 298–302.

22 UNCTC, op. cit., pp. 44–53.

23 Kevin Done, "A model to Smash the mould," *Financial Times*, (January 6, 1993); Richard A. Melcher, "Meet Ford's brave new 'world car'," *Business Week* (January 18, 1993).

24 Wayne Biddle, *Barons of the Sky: from early flight to strategic warfare:*

the story of the American aerospace industry (New York: Simon & Schuster, 1991).

25 For further elaboration, see Sylvia Ostry, "The domestic domain: the new international policy arena," *Transnational corporations*, 1, 1 (February 1992), pp. 7–26.

4 New strategic challenges facing the global company[1]

George S. Yip

Turning a collection of country businesses into one worldwide business, that has an integrated, global strategy, presents one of the stiffest challenges for managers today. Many forces are driving companies around the world to globalize in the sense of expanding their participation in foreign markets. Companies also need to globalize in another sense – integrating their worldwide strategy. This global integration contrasts with the multinational approach in which companies set up country subsidiaries that design, produce and market products or services tailored to local needs. This multinational model is now in question, and may be considered a "multilocal strategy" in contrast to a truly global strategy.[2] This chapter discusses major challenges that multinational companies face in becoming global companies. The chapter also provides some evidence on these challenges from an interview-based study of the use of global strategy by eighteen worldwide businesses belonging to major US multinational companies.

Many managers are asking if they are in a global industry and whether their business should have a global strategy. The better question to ask is, how global is an industry and how global should a business strategy be? This is because virtually every industry has aspects that are global or potentially global and some industries have more aspects that are global and more intensely so. Similarly a strategy can be more global or less global in its different aspects. An industry is global to the extent that there are intercountry connections. A strategy is global to the extent that it is integrated across countries. Global strategy should not be equated with any one element such as standardized products, worldwide market coverage or a global manufacturing network. Global strategy should, instead, be a flexible combination of many elements.

Recent and coming changes make it more likely that in many

industries a global strategy will be more successful than a multilocal one. Indeed, having a sound global strategy may well be the requirement for survival as the changes accelerate. These changes include the growing similarity of countries in terms of what their citizens want to buy, a point argued forcefully and controversially by both Levitt (1983) and Ohmae (1990). Other changes are the reduction of tariff and non-tariff barriers, technology investments that are becoming too expensive to amortize in one market only, and competitors who are changing the nature of rivalry from country-by-country competition to global competition.

Trade barriers are also falling. The 1989 United States–Canada Free Trade Agreement and a possible similar arrangement between the United States and Mexico, and the increasing, albeit uneven, harmonization in the European Union provide some of the most dramatic examples. Under pressure from its Western trading partners, Japan is also gradually opening up its long barricaded markets. Maturity in domestic markets is also driving companies to seek international expansion. This is particularly true for American companies, who, nourished by a huge domestic market, have typically lagged behind their European and Japanese rivals in internationalization. The recent surge of foreign acquisitions in the United States has globalized the nature of competition in many industries. Between 1977 and 1986 the share of US manufacturing assets owned by foreign companies doubled from 6 percent to 12 percent.[3] Increased volatility in exchange rates has helped to spur cycles of acquisitions as companies in countries with temporarily high exchange rates buy assets in countries with temporarily low rates. The rise of the "NIEs" (newly industrializing economies like Hong Kong, Taiwan, South Korea, Singapore, Thailand, Malaysia, Mexico and Brazil) has also increased the number of viable sites for sophisticated manufacturing operations with low labor costs.

THE GLOBALIZATION TRIANGLE

The changes toward globalization pose severe challenges for multinational companies. These challenges can be best understood by examining each apex of what I term the "globalization triangle." The first apex constitutes "industry globalization drivers," which constitute underlying market, cost and other industry conditions and create the potential for a worldwide business to achieve the benefits of global strategy. This emphasis on industry conditions was initiated by Porter (1986) and further developed by Yip (1989). The second apex comprises the different aspects of global strategy itself or "global strategy levers," such as the use of globally standardized products. Authors have differed on the feasibility of global strategy. At one extreme Levitt (1983) advocated that all businesses should go global. At the other extreme Douglas and Wind (1987), Kashani (1989) and others stressed the pitfalls and near impossibility of global strategy or global marketing. The third apex is represented by global organization factors that affect a company's ability to implement global strategy. Organization factors have been particularly stressed by Prahalad and Doz (1987) and Bartlett and Ghoshal (1989). These three parts of the globalization triangle all affect each other. The new strategic challenges facing the global company relate to understanding, managing and changing not just each apex of the triangle but the relationships among them also.

This chapter discusses twenty different challenges in the globalization triangle for would-be global companies. These challenges have been conceived from a combination of previous literature, business periodicals, and the author's own consulting experience and research studies. The latter includes an interview-based study of the use of global strategy by major American multinational companies. This chapter uses some of the findings from this interview study to illustrate the challenges discussed. In addition, the chapter provides an extensive description of the findings in two of the individual businesses. In particular, these two case histories show how the companies responded to industry globalization drivers in their use of global strategy and in their organization design and management processes.

AN INTERVIEW-BASED STUDY OF THE USE OF GLOBAL STRATEGY

The interview study was conducted in 1989, with eighteen worldwide businesses belonging to eleven American companies. In each business I conducted lengthy (one and a half to two hours), semi-structured interviews with two senior executives (in separate meetings in most cases). The interviews covered each of the elements of industry globalization drivers, global strategy levers and global organization. So the interviews provided mini-case histories of how different businesses rated globalization forces in their industries, how they responded to these forces in terms of the use of global strategy, and how they were organized and managed in regards to being able to implement global strategy.

Participating businesses were recruited primarily from member companies of the Marketing Science Institute, the sponsor of this study. Qualifying businesses had to market in countries on more than one continent (in fact, all of the sample marketed in countries on three or more continents), and could sell products or services, although professional services were excluded.

The recruiting frame consisted entirely of major, Fortune 500 companies. Seven of the eleven participating companies ranked in the top twenty-five of the 1989 Fortune 500 list. Two of the eleven companies provided information on three businesses each, three of the companies on two businesses each, and the other six companies on one business each.

The sample comprised one consumer financial service business, three consumer packaged goods businesses (food and beverages, toiletries, and household products) four consumer durable goods businesses (personal apparel, passenger automobile, furnishings and housewares), five capital goods businesses (computer hardware and software, and control equipment) and five industrial components businesses (building supply, automotive parts, electrical supplies, plastics and chemicals). The businesses had on average 42 percent of their revenues outside the United States, which is much higher than the average for all Fortune 500 companies.

The respondents were mostly quite senior in position, with eight division or region heads, six deputy heads, seven heads of marketing and ten directors of marketing or planning. All of the respondents had close knowledge of the business. Also, twenty-four of the respondents currently had international (i.e. non-domestic) or global responsibilities.

CHALLENGES IN DIAGNOSING INDUSTRY GLOBALIZATION POTENTIAL

Getting a good understanding of industry globalization potential is the starting point for developing an effective global strategy. In diagnosing this potential managers face several challenges.

1 Most industries have some globalization potential

Unlike the assumptions in some of the earlier global strategy literature, industries are not either global or local. Instead, nearly every industry has globalization potential in some aspects and not others. When rated under different categories of globalization drivers, the eighteen industries in the study did not fall into extreme groups of high or low globalization. Instead, they ranged in total globalization strength from quite low to quite high. For example, when multiple measures of drivers were averaged, the detergent industry was rated fairly low in globalization drivers, the specialty chemical industry was rated moderate, and the microcomputer industry very high. While the measure is fairly crude it clearly demonstrates that the distribution globalization potential across industries constitutes a continuum rather than being bipolar. So managers in almost every company must face up to globalization challenges.

Industries also differ by category of globalization driver, the primary ones being market, cost, government and competitive drivers. A given industry might face strong market globalization drivers, but relatively weak cost ones, and so on. Figure 4.1 ranks the industries in the study (and a few additional industries) for each of the four categories of drivers. These comparative rankings are approximate only and will also change over time.

2 Globalization drivers have differing effects in the same industry

Different industry globalization drivers can operate in different directions, some favoring globalization and others making it difficult and inadvisable. The fifteen individual globalization drivers measured (such as "common customer needs" and "global scale economies") each showed great variation. Industries high on some individual drivers were often low on others. For example, the travelers check industry faces a very strong market globalization driver in terms of the commonality of customer needs around the world. Thus, globally standardized products are needed. On the other hand, the customers themselves, whether banks or consumers, are still entirely local, so that marketing needs to remain locally differentiated. In contrast, the automotive component industry has many regional, and increasingly global, customers which require a global approach to marketing. However, in many categories of automotive components, high capital intensity in production, and raw materials being a high proportion of the cost of goods, together push for locally dispersed rather than globally centralized manufacturing. These variations within any given industry renders management of global challenges and opportunities very difficult.

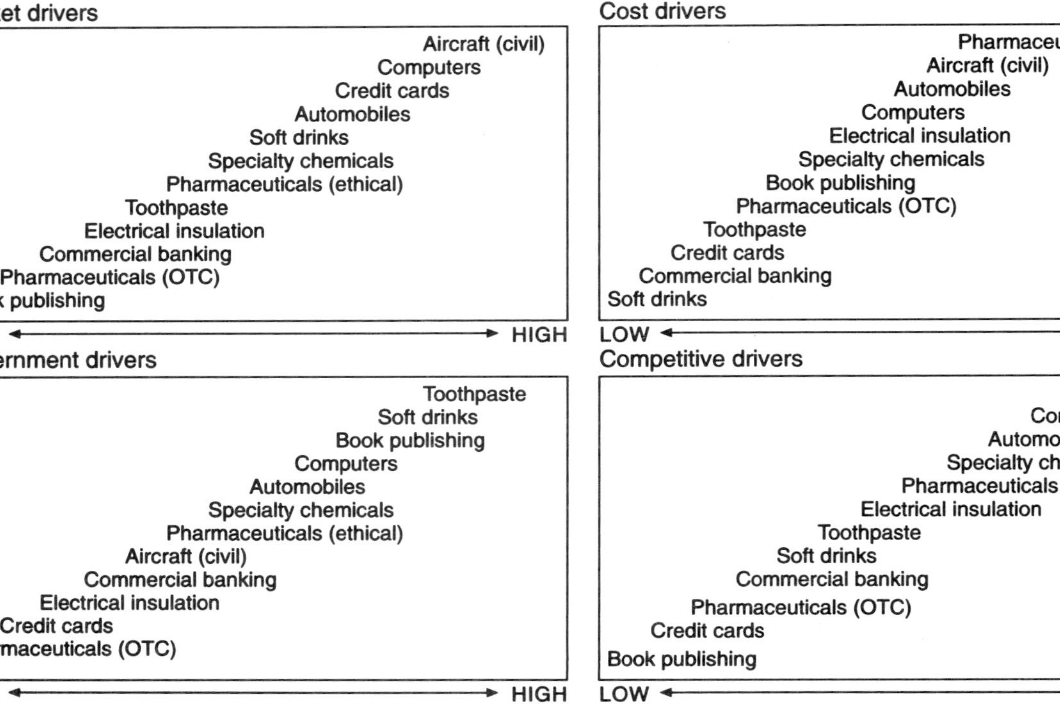

Figure 4.1 Strength of globalization drivers for selected industries

Source: George S. Yip, *Total Global Strategy: Managing for worldwide competitive advantage* (Englewood Cliffs, N.J., 1992)

3 The level of globalization potential changes over time

Changes over time in globalization potential add to the challenges of global management. Indeed, the current salience of global strategy springs from the rapid increase of globalization potential in many, if not most, industries. Most of the industries in the study faced globalization drivers – particularly market and competitive ones – that were increasing in strength. On the other hand, in some instances globalization can reverse itself. A study of the major appliance industry in Europe found that drivers shifted from favoring national strategies to pan-European strategies and back to national in the late 1970s and early 1980s (Baden Fuller, Nicolaides and Stopford, 1987).

4 Industry globalization drivers can work at a regional or continental scale as well as at a global scale

Managers also need to be alert to opportunities for integrated strategies at the continental rather than global level. The same types of drivers apply. For example, Europe 1992 provides an intriguing and highly important example of how industry globalization drivers can be analyzed for an entire region, the European Union, across all its industries. Europe 1992 increases the strength of all globalization (or Europeanization) drivers within the EU, and also affects overall globalization drivers for any industry for which Europe is part of the world market. Companies can also use integration at the continental level as preparation for later integration at the global level.

5 Industry competitors can themselves affect some globalization drivers

Some globalization drivers can be affected by the actions of competitors. For example, the introduction of globally standardized products can hasten the market's move toward more globally common customer needs and tastes. This strategy has had a powerful and advantageous effect, particularly for Japanese competitors in such industries as automobiles and consumer electronics. It seems that the competitors who stimulate these changes typically reap the major benefits. So managers face the additional challenge of whether and how to hasten globalization by using strategies that are ahead of their time. In some ways such a strategy is the globalization analogy ("globalizing ahead of the globalization wave") of the experience curve strategy ("pricing ahead of the experience curve") also exploited by Japanese companies.

CHALLENGES IN FORMULATING AND IMPLEMENTING GLOBAL STRATEGY

Just as there are multiple drivers of industry globalization potential there are multiple dimensions or elements of global strategy. Businesses can respond selectively to industry globalization drivers by globalizing only those elements of strategy affected by favorable drivers. Yip (1989) identifies five major global strategy dimensions:

- *market participation* (Ohmae, 1985) – the choice of country markets in which to conduct business, and the level of activity, particularly in terms of market share;
- *product standardization* (Levitt, 1983; Kogut, 1985; Walters, 1986) – the extent to which a worldwide business offers the same or different products in different countries;
- *activity concentration* (Hout, Porter and Rudden, 1982; Kogut, 1985; Bartlett and Ghoshal, 1989) – the choice of where to locate value-adding activities, particularly the extent to which the value chain is geographically concentrated rather than dispersed;
- *uniform marketing* (Takeuchi and Porter, 1986; Quelch and Hoff, 1986; Jain, 1989) – the extent to which a business uses the same brand names, advertising and other marketing elements in different countries;
- *integrated competitive moves* (Hamel and Prahalad, 1985; Porter, 1986) – the extent to which a business makes competitive moves in individual countries as part of a global sequence or pattern, as opposed to making moves in uncoordinated fashion.

Building global market participation

Participating in the right countries and at the right level provides the foundation on which a successful total global strategy needs to be built.

6 Participation in globally strategic markets is crucial

In a multilocal participation strategy, countries are selected on the basis of their stand-alone potential in terms of revenues and profits.

In a global market participation strategy, countries need to be selected in terms of their potential contribution to globalization benefits. There are several ways in which a country can be globally strategic as a market:

- large source of revenues or profits
- home market of global customers
- home market of global competitors
- significant market of global competitors
- major source of industry innovation

Global market participation may also mean concentrating resources on building share in a limited number of key markets than more widespread coverage. Ohmae (1985) advocates a pattern of major shares in major markets in his concept of the US–Europe–Japan "triad." In contrast, under a multilocal strategy no particular pattern of participation is required – the pattern accrues from the pursuit of local advantage. So the first challenge in global market participation is being able to identify globally strategic markets.

7 Globally strategic markets may be "unattractive" to enter

The second challenge in global market participation is that many globally strategic markets are unattractive in their own right. Indeed, many governments and competitors collaborate to make their national markets unattractive to outsiders. Reinforcing the findings of many other studies, most of the businesses in the interview study identified Japan as a globally strategic country but one where it was very difficult for American companies to succeed.

8 Different countries can play different strategic roles

A global strategy approach to market participation also means that different countries should have different roles within the total business. The collection of country businesses should be viewed as a strategic portfolio rather than as a passive one. The Boston Consulting Group popularized the use of cross-subsidization of businesses within a corporate portfolio. The same approach can be applied to countries in global strategy. Typically, the home country needs to subsidize markets that are newer to the business. That contrasts with what has been a common mindset in companies dominated by the home business. Such companies often treat international markets opportunistically as ways to balance capacity utilization.

9 Large global market share is not enough

Having a large global market share is important, but not sufficient for global market participation. A global business also needs to have its geographic distribution of revenues in reasonable balance with that of the worldwide market. That is, the business should usually not have most of its revenues concentrated in just a few countries, and its market share in each country should not be too different from its global market share. Global balance is important as a counterpoint to large market share, because the business usually needs to have significant presence in many countries in order to fully benefit from a global strategy. On a country-by-country basis, in some industries it may be better to have a large, significant share in some countries and a small share in others than to have a moderate share level everywhere.[4] But this effect may well be offset by the damaging effect of uneven market share on the ability to operate a global strategy.

10 Joint ventures can both help and hinder global strategy

Alliances and joint ventures can provide a quicker and easier way to build global market participation, but also weaken the potential for a fully integrated global strategy (Gomes-Casseres, 1989). Managers need to beware, however, of thinking that setting up a joint venture in a country means that market is covered and can be counted as part of a business's global presence. Whether joint ventures represent genuine market participation depends on how the venture is set up and on how the partners behave.

Designing global products and services

Successfully designing global products and services requires managers to make tough tradeoffs between global and local demands. Most of the businesses in the interview study sold products that were somewhat or highly standardized globally. All faced difficulties, however, in designing the right products.

11 The potential for global products is often greater than it appears

There are often more opportunities for globally standardizing products than many managers realize. Managers tend to focus on what is unique in their particular situation. The new challenge is to learn to look for commonalities also. For example, an electronics business, part of an American multinational company, had a product line that was potentially highly standardized – in fact, more so than its executives realized. They initially thought that their product was not standard across countries, because 40 percent of the product cost was in a decoder that was different in each country. But digging deeper, however, they discovered that within the decoder only the software was unique. Furthermore, the software was embodied in purchased parts (masked ROMs). Therefore, there was no difference in the manufacturing process, only in the inventory to be kept. Also, the cost of developing the unique software was amortized over a large sales base. As a result, what initially appeared to be 40 percent nonstandard turned out to be only 3 percent nonstandard.[5]

12 Global products are better designed from the start, while allowing for local tailoring

The best global products are usually those that are designed as such from the start rather than being adapted from national products later. This approach has the obvious advantage of taking into consideration the needs of major markets right at the start, rather than having to retrofit a product developed for one national market. Managers should start by identifying globally strategic markets, then understanding the needs of those markets. Perhaps most important, managers should search for commonalities rather than for differences. Such an approach should allow managers to design the largest possible standardized core, while allowing for necessary customization at the same time.[6] The challenge is to be able to maximize the size of the common global core while also providing for local tailoring around the core.

The second, less desirable but more common, approach is to adapt existing products or services. In adapting from an existing mix of national products, managers need to start by understanding the causes of the national variants. Have these variants arisen from a deliberate response to real differences in needs and tastes? Or are they accidents of independent development? Very often the answer is much more accident than deliberation. Many businesses wind up with product lines that are much less standardized than they could be, simply by not having a global perspective, so that countries make decisions independently of each other. The challenge here is to, first, recognize the problem, and, second, to find a feasible way of gradually moving to the optimal set of product offerings.

Locating global activities

In a multilocal activity strategy, all or most of the value chain is reproduced in every country. In another type of international strategy – exporting – most of the value chain is kept in one country. In a global activity strategy, the value chain is broken up and each activity may be conducted in a different country. The major benefits lie in cost reduction. One type of value chain strategy is partial concentration and partial duplication. The key feature of a global position on this strategy dimension is the systematic placement of the value chain around the globe (see Prahalad and Doz, 1987).

13 Different activities have differing needs for global centralization and local dispersion

One key challenge in the location of global activities is being able to identify which activities need to be centralized and which dispersed. In general, the activities that benefit most from economies of scale and tight quality control need to be centralized. In contrast, activities affected by high transportation costs, trade barriers and needing exposure to local customers are best localized, at least to some degree. The interview study found a very clear current pattern of activity location. There were three clear groups of activities. Those earliest in the value chain – research and development – were on average highly centralized. Those activities in the middle stages of the value chain – purchasing, production and marketing – showed a mixed pattern between being centralized and localized. The activities latest in the chain – selling, distribution and service – were mostly conducted locally.

14 The ideal pattern of location changes with circumstances and the evolution of the business

A further challenge for global managers is that the ideal pattern of location changes with circumstances and the evolution of the business. This was borne out in the interview study. In response to strengthening globalization drivers, most of the businesses wanted to make many of the activities more central.

Creating global marketing

In many ways marketing is the most difficult strategic element to globalize. Differences between countries are often greatest in the customer attitudes and behavior that marketers try to influence. Furthermore, many of the benefits of global marketing can be more subtle than for the other elements of global strategy. At the same time, using global marketing can integrate the worldwide efforts of an organization in a more visible and powerful way than any other.

15 Globally uniform marketing process is no longer enough

Conventional wisdom in international marketing has favored standardization across countries of the marketing process, but not of its content (e.g. Rau and Preble, 1987). But worldwide businesses can use globally standardized marketing content to great effect. Like the other global strategy levers, global marketing can achieve one or more of four major categories of potential globalization benefits: cost reduction, improved quality of products and programs, enhanced customer preference and increased competitive leverage. Much of the previous debate on global marketing has identified cost savings and increased recognition as the primary benefits, and reduced program effectiveness as a major drawback. However, a strong case can be made that *improved program effectiveness* is often the greatest benefit of global marketing. Good ideas in marketing are scarce. So a globalization program that overcomes local objections to allow the geographic spread of a good marketing idea can often raise the average effectiveness of programs around the world. Of course, objections are not couched as "not-invented-here" (often the real problem), but as "you-don't-understand-we-are-different" (the most common argument). In addition, globalization of some elements of the marketing mix, for example, the positioning strategy, would free up national managers' time to improve other elements, such as trade relations.

16 Each element of the marketing mix has its own unique opportunities and limitations in global uniformity

Every element of the marketing mix – product design, product and brand positioning, brand name, packaging, pricing, advertising strategy, advertising execution, promotion and distribution – is a candidate for globalization. As with other global strategy levers, the use of global marketing can be flexible. A business can make some elements of the marketing mix more global and others less so. Within each element, some parts can be globally uniform and others not. For example, a "global" pack design may have a common logo and illustration in all countries, but a different background color in some countries. So both marketing as a whole and each individual marketing element can be global to a greater or lesser extent in its *content*.

Businesses in the interview study showed a wide range in the extent to which they globalized individual elements of the marketing mix. Brand name was the most uniform element of the marketing mix. Capital goods businesses were particularly likely to use uniform brand names, while consumer packaged goods businesses were the least likely to. Packaging was also quite uniform. The least uniform element was promotion. There has recently been a great deal of attention paid to global advertising, particularly as advocated by advertising agencies (Peebles, 1989). These businesses were not great users of global advertising. The questions distinguished between absolute pricing and relative pricing, as it was expected that absolute pricing would be fairly variable because of currency and other market-specific factors. In contrast, pricing relative to competitors might be much more uniform, reflecting a consistent positioning strategy. Absolute pricing was, indeed, less uniform than relative pricing, but neither was very uniform.

The study results clearly demonstrate that global marketing is not all or nothing. None of these businesses applied the same extent of uniformity to all elements of the marketing mix. The challenge is to find the right mix of uniformity and variation. National marketing managers need to remember that they have been trained to look for local differences. Creating successful global marketing requires a reorientation to look for similarities.

Making global competitive moves

Perhaps the ultimate test of a total global strategy is whether a worldwide business can make globally integrated competitive moves. In many ways it is the most difficult of the five aspects of global strategy to use, because its consequences are less directly visible, unlike global standardized products or globally uniform advertising. At the same time, not making global integrated competitive moves can undermine the competitive advantages built up in individual countries and weaken a business's worldwide position.

17 Global competitive moves require coordination and agreement among national managers

A major reason for the difficulty in making global integrated competitive moves is that it often requires national sacrifices for the sake of the worldwide business. The businesses in the interview study generally found it difficult to make much use of globally integrated moves.

Regional versus global strategy

But there are barriers to MNCs implementing strategy on a worldwide basis. Obstacles arise from "bounded rationality" (the limited ability of managers to orchestrate worldwide activities) and from the potential resistance of subsidiary managers to their loss of autonomy (White and Poynter, 1990). In addition, the gradual creation of regional trading blocs (European Union, European Economic Area, the possible North American free trade zone, a South American free trade zone) may increase barriers to the inter-regional trade that is an essential element of global strategy. Some MNCs are beginning to seek a regional solution to globalization forces, either as a substitute for or as a complement to global strategy (Morrison and Roth, 1992).

The Pacific Rim region seems particularly difficult for regional strategy because of its huge distances and great disparities in income, culture and language. At the same time these same factors may make it more necessary to find the more localized solutions offered by regional as opposed to global strategy. The corporate population is also different from that of the other two major economic regions of North America and Europe. In the Asian Pacific Rim companies fall largely into two groups: many very large Japanese corporations that are already highly successful in international business, and smaller emergent corporations from the newly industrializing countries (NICs) such as Taiwan, Hong Kong and Singapore, with South Korean companies somewhere between the two types.[7]

Extending Porter's (1990) emphasis on the importance of the "home base," regional strategies are also important in that they can provide a distinctive platform of advantage for firms headquartered in the region. In this regard Japanese firms, which are the dominant force in the Pacific Rim region,[8] differ significantly from their American and European rivals. While the latter have engaged in extensive foreign direct investment (FDI) over the last fifty years, Japanese companies have relied much more to date on exports. Japanese MNCs also differ in their management approach. Because of their export orientation and for various cultural reasons, Japanese MNCs are typically managed much more tightly from the center than are American or European MNCs (Kono, 1984; Jaeger and Baliga, 1985). Together with the great geographic distances and differences in income, language and culture within the Pacific Rim any Japanese approach to regional strategy will be significantly different from regional strategy in North America and in Europe.

CHALLENGES IN BUILDING THE GLOBAL ORGANIZATION

Implementing strategy is always difficult. Implementing *global* strategy is particularly challenging because of the multiple countries and nationalities involved. Furthermore, in many cases a key part of the global strategy is not so much the content of the strategy (e.g. a globally standardized product) but the decision to operate with a globally integrated management process (e.g. a global product development process). Implementation can be so disruptive and difficult that there may not be enough benefit in pursuing a highly global strategy. In particular, strategy globalization often requires changes that involve one or more countries having to give up long established strategies, products and the like.

18 A global strategy cannot succeed in the face of organization barriers and resistance

In the interview study over two-thirds of the businesses reported that their overall strategy was less global than it should be. Respondents mostly cited implementation problems and slowness in changing as the key reasons for the gap between current and desired globalization of strategy. In particular, all the businesses made only limited use of the various organization and management devices advocated in the literature (e.g. Prahalad and Doz, 1987; Bartlett and Ghoshal, 1989). For example, in most of the businesses, control was split between domestic and international divisions, thus fragmenting global authority. Similarly, few of the businesses had global heads, whether line or staff for individual functions. These businesses also made only moderate use of global coordinating mechanisms such as global strategic planning, global budgeting, global performance review and compensation and global strategic information systems.

19 A global organization involves more than organization structure

A common mistake in reorganizing to support global strategy has been for companies to change the organization structure only. Instead, companies need to change several aspects of organization. These include

- *organization structure* – comprising the reporting relationships in a business;
- *management processes* – comprising the activities such as planning and budgeting that make the business run;
- *people* – comprising the human resources of the worldwide business and include both managers and all other employees;
- *culture* – comprising the values and rules that guide behavior in a corporation.

Each of these factors directly affects each other and the use of global strategy. Each operates powerfully in different ways. A common mistake in implementing *any* strategy is to ignore one or more of them, particularly the less tangible ones, such as culture. A blockage in even one dimension of organization can severely cramp the ability to think and behave globally.

One of the lessons from the interview study is that different aspects of organization – whether organization structure, management processes, people or culture – will be more difficult to globalize depending on the history and circumstances of the company. It seems best to work on the most easily changed aspects first, in order to prepare the way for the more difficult changes. As with the elements of global strategy, different aspects of organization can have different levels of being global. But globalization will not work fully unless all aspects of organization complement each other to support the desired global strategy. Lastly, changing the organization toward globalization takes a great deal of time. Top executives need to instill a sense of urgency to drive toward the desired changes. They need to recognize that global industries are not born, but are created by global companies. The rewards of globalization go to the first movers.[9]

TWO EXAMPLES OF THE USE OF GLOBAL STRATEGY

The challenges of globalization can be better understood by a comprehensive examination of how a couple of the businesses in the interview study responded to industry globalization drivers. The two businesses provide useful contrasts – one faced very strong industry globalization drivers while the other faced only moderate ones.

An industrial process control business – "Brown Controls"

An American industrial process control business, "Brown Controls," provided one of the more successful examples of globalization. This business was the global market leader. Its major competitors were other major multinational companies from the United States, Europe and Japan. I interviewed the company's vice president for international sales and distribution and its director of strategic planning.

Industry globalization drivers

This business faced some of the strongest industry globalization drivers of any in the interview study.

For *market globalization drivers* customer needs were highly common. A given customer would often demand a standardized control system for all its facilities around the world. For example, a customer like Royal Dutch/Shell might order sixteen identical units because it wants its plants around the world to be mirror images of each other. So it was very important to get in first with such global customers. Indeed, both global customers and regionwide customers accounted for about 20 percent each of worldwide market revenues, and their share was expected to increase. Global and regionwide channels of distribution were somewhat less important, accounting for about 10 percent of worldwide market revenues. Customers were somewhat favorably disposed toward foreign brand names, packaging, advertising and promotion, but somewhat unfavorable toward foreign sales personnel. In addition, because many customers were themselves multinational companies, overseas exposure to products, brand names and advertising had some positive effect on a customer's disposition to buy at home. Overall, market globalization drivers were very strong and expected to get stronger rapidly.

Cost globalization drivers were also quite strong and getting stronger. Economies of scale in production were very high – between

30 percent and 50 percent global market share was needed to maintain the minimum efficient scale. Transportation costs were moderate, at about 5 percent of product sales value for intercontinental shipping, which was great enough to deter the shipment of physically large items. Because labor was a small part of total costs, there was less than a 25 percent difference in production costs between the lowest and highest cost countries in which manufacturing occurred for this industry. Lastly, new product development costs were significant, at about 10 percent of expected global lifetime sales.

Government globalization drivers were overall quite favorable and slowly getting more so. Tariffs ranged from a minor barrier in a few countries to being major in a few Third World countries such as Brazil. Non-tariff barriers were perhaps more important, being a major problem in a few countries like Japan, Korea and, again, Brazil. Differences in technical standards were only a minor barrier, while differences in marketing regulations were scarcely a barrier anywhere.

Competitive globalization drivers were among the strongest in the study and were getting stronger quite quickly. The other major competitors all operated globally, were well spread around the globe, and used strategies that were moderately integrated globally. Particularly worrying for Brown Controls was that foreign competitors were able to achieve significant success in the US market. One of the respondents complained that American companies in this industry tended to react to competitive events rather than anticipate them.

Use of global strategy levers

Brown Controls made significant use of global strategy. To start with, the business had very strong *global market participation*, being present in countries that accounted for 90 percent or more of the global market, and having by far the largest global market share. Its sales were geographically generally well spread relative to the global market. As the market expanded from the developed countries to newly industrializing ones and Eastern Europe, Brown Controls was attempting to match that spread. Its product mix was about 70 percent in a standardized base line, while the rest was in customized products. Some adaptations were necessary because of differences in technical standards and to make local adaptations of the system. In contrast, Brown Controls' competitors sold more standardized products, partly because of their smaller market share and partly because as later entrants they had had less time to adapt their product lines.

Particularly given the strong industry globalization drivers that it faced, Brown Controls was one of the less centralized businesses in terms of *activity location*, being centralized "more as a concept than by location." Its research and development activities were somewhat spread out across different regions, unlike most other businesses studied. Its manufacturing activities were similarly spread on a regional basis, although Brown was trying to centralize these operations more. Its marketing activities were quite regional, too much so according to the executives interviewed, resulting in overstretch of resources and priorities. In addition, the respondents felt that selling, which was mostly local, did not have to be so de-centralized. On the other hand, the distribution operation, serving seventy different independent distributors had to be located locally.

Brown Controls used mostly *globally uniform marketing*. It used the same brand name everywhere and mostly the same packaging, with a strong logo concept. But its pricing varied somewhat geographically, causing problems with global customers who wanted the same price worldwide. These variations were driven by a combination of competitive actions and the company's own resource availability. Advertising, promotion, selling and distribution were all somewhat uniform across countries. Lastly, this business was one of the few in the study that made extensive use of *globally integrated competitive moves*. The executives interviewed believed that they "usually" or "almost always" integrated their competitive moves. This was particularly necessary for price changes and feature reconfigurations when up against other global competitors in this bid-based business.

Overall, the business's strategy was somewhat or mostly global and needed to be a bit more global than it was.

Use of global organization

Some aspects of Brown Controls' *organization structure* favored globalization. There was one worldwide head of the industrial process control business and the business controlled all of its own functions. On the other hand, there was no global head for individual functions, only coordinating individuals or teams for some of the functions. Also, the business was part of a matrix system in which the geographic dimension was very strong. Like most US companies, Brown Controls maintained an international division that was separate from the domestic one, making global integration more difficult.

The business had *management processes* that were moderate to strong in helping global integration. Cross-country coordination was viewed as very important. Because of global customers and integrity and safety concerns, any change in the control products had to be made consistently around the world. In consequence, each strategic business unit in the company had its own "Worldwide Business Team" made up of representatives from each region, including for this business a representative of a joint venture operation in Japan. In the words of one respondent, these teams had a "terrible responsibility" – for product rationalization, new products, marketing and manufacturing strategy. The teams would meet two or three times a year. Created ten years earlier, around 1980, these worldwide business teams constituted one of Brown Controls' greatest successes in its globalization efforts. Other global management processes were all moderately strong. The main problem was insufficient use of global performance review and compensation, although that was getting better, for the team members at any rate. A portion of their incentive plan was now based on worldwide achievement.

In terms of *people*, this business made very limited use of foreign nationals in the home country or in third countries, while the use of home country nationals (Americans) internationally was also quite limited.

Lastly, the *culture* of the company seemed balanced between being American and being international, although one respondent, a European, commented that "it is a hard life for a foreigner here in this very mid-Western company."

Comment

Facing strong industry globalization drivers, this business has been quite successful in developing and implementing an appropriate global strategy. Part of this success arises from its ability to put in place organizational mechanisms for global coordination.

An American personal apparel business – "Carter Wear"

A personal apparel business – "Carter Wear" – provided the only instance of a business for which the level of use of global strategy seemed to exceed what it should be (based on industry globalization potential). This business had the lowest globalization drivers of all those in the study. Carter Wear was the global market leader in this product category and was also the only global competitor. The other major industry participants were regional European and Japanese players. At least one of these competitors was attempting to go global. I interviewed the president of the international division for the entire company and the president of the personal apparel division.

Industry globalization drivers

This industry faced the weakest globalization drivers of any in the study. For *market globalization drivers* customer needs were not very common. The product category had a strong fashion element, so it was unsurprising that customer needs varied around the world, although there was some commonality with regions. Global customers and global channels did not exist. Regional channels of distribution were just starting to develop in Europe, but as yet accounted for only about 10 percent of global market volume. The strong fashion element also meant that in this business marketing programs would not travel well – marketing needed to be tailored to local ideas of what was fashionable in this category. On the other hand, being a product worn by consumers, and therefore prominently displayed, exposure to products, brand names and advertising while overseas was expected to have highly favorable effects on domestic purchases. These relatively weak market globalization drivers were not expected to strengthen. Indeed, one executive believed that trends were moving from global to regional as customer tastes became more differentiated across regions, and as local and regional competitors became more sophisticated in their product offerings.

Cost globalization drivers were not very strong either. Economics of scale were not very important in production – less than 10 percent share of the global market was needed to achieve the minimum economic scale. Transportation costs were also very low, at about 2 percent to 3 percent of product sales value for intercontinental shipping. Labor was also a sufficiently small part of total costs that there was little need to seek offshore manufacturing to reduce labor costs. On the other hand, the relatively simple manufacturing technology allowed many even less developed economies to produce the products successfully. As a result, currency fluctuations posed a special threat in this business, constantly changing the relative positions of competitors based in different countries. Lastly, developing a new product cost very little – probably less than 1 percent of its potential global lifetime sales.

Government globalization drivers were the only really favorable ones. There were few tariff or non-tariff barriers except in a small number of developing countries such as Brazil and Indonesia. Some governments, such as in Japan, almost encouraged parallel imports. Technical standards were either non-existent or very similar globally.

Competitive globalization drivers were the weakest out of all the industries in the study. The industry had only two global competitors, of which this business was one. Most other competitors were regional. Competitors made little use of global strategy. Furthermore, this industry enjoyed the absence of global Japanese competitors! So, overall, competitors provided little push for globalization.

Use of global strategy

Despite the relatively low industry globalization potential, this personal apparel business made quite extensive use of global strategy. To start with, the business had very strong *global market participation*, being present in countries that accounted for 90 percent or more of the global market, and having by far the largest global market share. Furthermore its sales were very evenly spread relative to the global market. The business also sold mostly *global products*, although the mix tended to differ from country to country. For example, the business sold more premium products outside the United States. In terms of *activity location* the business centralized its R&D in the United States, but used a global network for manufacturing. It maintained manufacturing facilities in the United States, Europe and Brazil, plus a couple of final assembly sites in the Far East. This partial dispersion of manufacturing was partly in order to reduce transportation costs and partly to provide quicker service to distributors. All of its marketing, selling, distribution and service activities were conducted locally. This business made some use of *global marketing*. It used the same brand name everywhere and mostly the same packaging, although in some cases the international packaging was "more flashy." Parallel imports were a major problem, so the business made significant efforts to maintain globally consistent pricing for many product segments. The business created advertising strategy centrally but left execution up to local managers. Promotion, selling and distribution were all mostly different from country to country. Lastly, this business was one of the few in the study that made much use of *globally integrated competitive moves.* The executives interviewed believed that they "usually" integrated their competitive moves.

But given the low level of industry globalization drivers, this use of global strategy was more than what seemed optimal. The head of the international division, one of the executives interviewed, believed that overall the strategy was more global than it should be. He felt that the business needed to become more regional in its strategy because of the differing nature of the regional markets. For example, the business had lost significant ground in Japan because of a global policy to not make products below a certain quality level. But a local competitor had introduced a specialty product, of relatively low quality, that proceeded to capture 20 percent of the Japanese market. Eventually this business changed its policy in order to be able to respond by offering a similar product.

Use of global organization

The business managed to maintain the moderately global strategy, just described, despite making the least use (along with one other business in the study) of global organization. The business's parent company operated with an international division that was responsible for all products sold outside the United States. Under this *organization structure* geographic management was exceptionally strong relative to business and functional management. Furthermore, there was no single head of this business, responsibility being split between US management and the various country managers. Similarly, none of the individual value-added activities had global heads with worldwide authority for their operation.

The business also had *management processes* that were not very global in nature. Only cross-country coordination was moderately strong, while global strategic planning was weak, global budgeting was very weak, and global performance review and compensation, and the global strategy information system were all quite weak. The business did make moderate use of global group meetings, with occasional participation from US managers. Lastly, the business did not use one single global advertising agency, maintaining a roster of five or more different agencies around the world.

In terms of *people*, this business made quite limited use of foreign nationals in the home country and very limited use of them in third countries, while the use of home country nationals internationally was also somewhat limited.

Lastly, the *culture* of the company seemed quite American,

although the head of the international division believed that it was becoming more international at a fast pace.

Comment

Carter Wear provides an unusual example of a business whose strategy was more globally integrated than it should be. Facing rather weak globalization drivers the business has over-standardized its products and some of its policies. At the same time its organization seems to have about the right level, quite low, of global integration. The biggest challenge for this business is probably that of developing responsive *regional* strategies.

CONCLUSION

Global companies and would-be global companies face severe challenges in formulating and implementing globally integrated strategies. Their task will be easier if they systematically analyze the many different globalization drivers that they face in their particular industries, and devise global strategies to match, exploit and anticipate current and expected industry conditions. Lastly, they need organization structures, management processes, people and culture that will support the desired global strategies.

NOTES

1 Presented at conference on *The Impact of Globalization and Regionalization on Corporate Strategy and Structure Among Pacific Rim Firms*, North Pacific Region advanced Research Center/East–West Center, Sapporo, Japan, August 1992. This chapter is based in part on George S. Yip, *Total Global Strategy: managing for worldwide competitive advantage* (Englewood Cliffs, N.J.: Prentice-Hall, 1992). The author thanks the Marketing Science Institute (Cambrige, Mass.) for supporting the research on which this chapter is based.

2 Hout et al. (1982) coined the term "multidomestic" to apply to industries rather than strategies. See Thomas Hout, Michael E. Porter and Eileen Rudden, "How global companies win out," *Harvard Business Review* (September–October 1982), pp. 98–108. The term "multilocal" seems better when applied to strategies, in that "domestic" implies a company competing in its home market, while a great deal of local competition occurs between companies, none of whom are in their home markets.

3 US Commerce Department, reported in "The takeover of American industry," *New York Times* (May 28, 1989), Section 3, pp. 1, 8, 9.

4 See, for example, Porter's ideas about the disadvantages of being "stuck

in the middle" in Michael E. Porter, *Competitive Strategy: techniques for analyzing industries and competitors* (New York: Free Press, 1980).

5 This example is drawn from George S. Yip, Pierre M. Loewe, and Michael Y. Yoshino, "How to take your company to the global market," *Columbia Journal of World Business* (Winter 1988), pp. 37–48.

6 See also Ilkka A. Ronkainen, "Product-development processes in the multinational firm," *International Marketing Review* (Winter 1983), pp. 57–65.

7 South Korean companies accounted for 60 percent of the 100 largest Asian companies outside Japan in 1990. See Hiroyuki Takeuchi, "Top 500: Asia's leading companies", *Tokyo Business Today* (September 1991), pp. 24–32.

8 Of the 150 largest industrial companies in the Pacific Rim in 1989, 126 were Japanese. See "The Pac Rim 150," *Fortune*, 122, 8 (Fall 1990), pp. 102–6.

9 Yip, Loewe and Yoshino, op. cit.

REFERENCES

Baden Fuller C., C. P. Nicolaides and J. Stopford, "National or global? The study of company strategies and the European market for major appliances," *London Business School Centre for Business Strategy Working Paper Series*, 28 (1987).

Bartlett, C. A. and S. Ghoshal, *Managing Across Borders: the transnational solution* (Boston: Harvard Business School Press, 1989).

Douglas, S. P. and Y. Wind, "The myth of globalization," *Columbia Journal of World Business*, 22, 4 (Winter 1987), pp. 19–29.

Gomes-Casseres, B., "Joint ventures in the face of global competition," *Sloan Management Review* (Spring 1989), pp. 17–26.

Hamel, G. and C. K. Prahalad, "Do you really have a global strategy?," *Harvard Business Review* (July–August 1985), pp. 139–48.

Hout, T., M. E. Porter and E. Rudden, "How global companies win out," *Harvard Business Review* (September–October 1982), pp. 98–108.

Jaeger, A. M. and B. R. Baliga, "Control systems and strategic adaptation: lessons from the Japanese experience," *Strategic Management Journal*, 6 (1985), pp. 115–34.

Jain, S. C., "Standardization of international marketing strategy: some research hypotheses," *Journal of Marketing*, 53 (January 1989), pp. 70–9.

Kashani, K., "Beware the pitfalls of global marketing," *Harvard Business Review* (September–October 1989), pp. 91–8.

Kogut, B., "Designing global strategies: profiting from operational flexibility," *Sloan Management Review* (Fall 1985), pp. 27–38.

Kono, T., *Strategy and Structure of the Japanese Enterprise* (New York: M. I. Sharpe Inc., 1984).

Levitt, T., "The globalization of markets," *Harvard Business Review* (May–June 1983), pp. 92–102.

Morrison, A. J., and K. Roth, "The regional solution: an alternative to globalization," *Transnational Corporations* (New York: UNCTC, February 1992).

Ohmae, K., *The Borderless World: Power and Strategy in the Interlinked Economy* (New York: Harper Business, 1990).

Ohmae, K., *Triad Power* (New York: Free Press, 1985).

Peebles, D. M., "Don't write off global advertising: a commentary," *International Marketing Review*, 6, 1 (1989), pp. 73–8.

Porter, M. E., *Competitive Strategy: techniques for analyzing industries and competitors*, (New York: Free Press, 1980).

Porter, M. E. , "Changing patterns of international competition," *California Management Review*, 28, 2, (Winter 1986), pp. 9–40.

Porter, M. E., *The Competitive Advantage of Nations* (New York: The Free Press, 1990).

Prahalad, C. K. and Y. L. Doz, *The Multinational Mission: balancing local demands and global vision* (New York: Free Press, 1987).

Quelch, J. A. and E. J. Hoff, "Customizing global marketing," *Harvard Business Review* (May–June 1986), pp. 59–68.

Rau, P. A. and J. F. Preble, "Standardization of marketing strategy by multinationals," *International Marketing Review* (Autumn 1987), pp. 18–28.

Takeuchi, H. and M. E. Porter, "Three roles of international marketing in global strategy," in M. E. Porter (ed.), *Competition in Global Industries* (Boston, MA: Harvard Business School Press, 1986).

Walters, P. G. P., "International marketing policy: a discussion of the standardization construct and its relevance for corporate policy," *Journal of International Business Studies* (Summer 1986), pp. 55–69.

White, R. E. and T. A. Poynter, "Organizing for worldwide advantage," in C. A. Bartlett, Y. L. Doz and G. Hedlund (eds), *Managing the Global Firm* (London: Routledge, 1990).

Yip, G. S., "Global strategy . . . In a world of nations?," *Sloan Management Review*, 31, 1 (Fall 1989), pp. 29–41.

Yip, G. S., *Total Global Strategy: managing for worldwide competitive advantage* (Englewood Cliffs, N.J.: Prentice Hall, 1992).

Yip, G. S., "Total global strategies," *Global Executive* (March/April 1993), pp. 16–20.

Yip, G. S., P. M. Loewe and M. Y. Yoshino, "How to take your company to the global market," *Columbia Journal of World Business* (Winter 1988), pp. 37–48.

5 Organizing technical activities within the globalizing firm

William A. Fischer

To live and work in the last decade of the twentieth century is to be blessed by being present at one of the most dramatic junctures in the history of international relations. To speak seriously of global markets is intoxicating: the quest for "new arenas," the construction of "transnational organizations," and winning of "final frontiers," is nothing short of dizzying. The simultaneous political opening of previously unattainable markets and the technical means of linking these markets has made the historic visions of a one-world marketplace, and truly transnational corporations, nearly a reality. With all of these changes, a spirited pursuit of the obvious attractions of the exploitation of natural economies of scale would appear to be irresistable, if not ineluctable. Ironically, however, the same two factors, dramatic political change and radical advancements in technological capabilities, are also creating strong and contradictory forces that are leading firms away from the pursuit of advantages of commonality, even away from the exploitation of economies of scale, and toward greater (micro-) market responsiveness and market individuality. In industry after industry, these contradictions, between economies of scale and market responsiveness, are being played out all along the series of value-adding activities and actors that constitute the modern business system. Nowhere is this more visible and more acute than in those technical activities associated with the concept and the fabrication of the product.

For those of us interested in the provision of goods and services in complex economies, the implications of such contradictions are profound. They threaten to overturn many, if not all, of our accepted concepts concerning effective manufacturing practice. As one observer put it a few years ago:

> the structure of the world economy may be in the first throes of

> a rearrangement as profound and as ramified as that of the industrial revolution. Here the crucial consideration is what might be called the logic of international production.[1]

Specifically, our whole logic of marshalling and arraying productive resources may be for substantial revision (or, what is popularly being referred to as a *paradigm shift*).

There are several movements that are currently unfolding, simultaneously, that appear, when taken in confluence, to be at the origins of this upheaval.

1 The first of these is the growing globalization of world markets, and the rapidly expanding new commercial arenas that are opening up as a result. It is not only the former centrally-planned economies, but virtually the whole developing world is today available for accommodation. Kenichi Ohmae has probably captured this dimension as vividly as anyone in the series of writings that originated in the concept of *Triad Power*.[2] Central to this theme are the notions that: i) the world market is growing increasingly more sophisticated and increasingly more cosmopolitan; creating important demand in many formerly peripheral markets; and ii) science and technology (S&T) have spread faster and further than anyone would have believed only a decade ago, resulting in a large number of new competitors and contributors to the S&T dimension of international commercial contribution. Today, Europe, the East Asian NIEs (newly industrializing economies), even China and parts of the former Soviet bloc, are all seen as potentially viable sources of new technologies, in addition to the more familiar North American, European, and Japanese industrial sources.

2 The second major event is the demise of the product life cycle as a useful guide to business operations strategy. It is increasingly obvious that product life cycles in many industries are becoming shorter as new innovations reduce the time during which any particular product-generation dominates a market. Consequently, with the length of time that a product can anticipate the successful economic exploitation of maturity reduced, the influence of scale economies is also reduced.

   The strategic notion of scale economies began with Adam Smith and *The Wealth of Nations*, in 1776, and was extended by writers such as Joel Dean, Joe Bain and Frederic Scherer. With the development of what we can only call neoclassical manufacturing strategy,[3] writers such as Wickham Skinner, Steven Wheelwright and

Robert Hayes, and Bill Abernathy fashioned a conceptualization of manufacturing strategy that institutionalized the prominence of economies of scale in both manufacturing process choice and technological innovation. Today, however, the rise of flexible manufacturing technologies and philosophies, and the influence of just-in-time manufacturing, the *lean manufacturer*, and concerns over *time to market*, have all worked to challenge the accepted paradigms of neoclassical manufacturing strategy and accelerate and exacerbate the strategic realities and implications of a diminished product life cycle.

3 The third major event is the regionalization of the world economy into several clearly defined sub-markets (e.g. the European Community) which may or may not be way-stations on the path to a truly global market. In the immediate term, however, what is important is that these regional markets represent distortions in the globalization phenomenon that have very real implications for the organization of production and production-related activities in the firm.

4 The fourth major event is that there are fundamental demographic changes occurring in the developed world. The rich markets of the north are no longer as young or as resilient as they were in the immediate postwar period. Consequently, they are no longer as hospitable to alternative competitors. Creeping protectionist fears, the hint of neo-mercantilism, and growing moves of zero-sum gaming, are all changing the philosophical nature of world trade. If, Lester Thurow is correct,[4] then increasingly we will see more pointed and more widespread *adversarial trade* (as Peter Drucker puts it) characterizing worldwide market competition,[5] with significant implications for patterns of trade and foreign direct investment, and the role of the multinational corporation.

It is the purpose of this chapter to explore the nature of the globalization/regionalization phenomenon on the organization of production and production-related activities in the market-sensitive firm. The discussion will be built around the concept of the business system and will concentrate on those activities that are *upstream* of marketing and distribution, namely R&D, design, sourcing, fabrication, and assembly. To a limited extent, warehousing and logistics will be alluded to, but not discussed fully. The chapter will draw heavily from interviews and case-writing that is presently going on at the International Institute for Management Development (IMD), including IMD's *Manufacturing 2000* project. The objects of the chapter are multifold. First, to represent the strategic technical interests of the firm in the debate over globalization and its effects. Second, to consider the strategic tradeoffs that exist amongst the *upstream* activities of a typical business system. And, third, to review both the literature and an opportunistic sample of corporate experiences and to draw hypotheses regarding the globalization phenomenon from these.

WHAT DOES GLOBAL MEAN?

One of the more important issues to understand at the beginning of this chapter is just what does it mean to be *global?* This is an issue that understandably plagues many of the writers who are currently thinking about this topic. One way to start might be to adopt the very simple taxonomy suggested by Alfred Zeien, Chairman of the Board and CEO of The Gillette Company, which distinguishes between three different types of corporate orientation.[6]

International An international company transports its business outside its own country. Normally, each of its operations is a replication of the company's domestic experience. Generally, an international business is structured geographically and involves subsidiary managers.

Multinational A multinational company, in contrast, grows and defines its business on a worldwide basis, but continues to allocate its resources among national or regional areas so as to maximize the total.

Global The so-called global corporation treats the entire world as though it were one big country. The global corporation may be the entire company or one or more of its major product lines.

More dramatic, but perhaps equally useful, is Kenichi Ohmae's concept of the *global* corporation:

> A global corporation today is fundamentally different from the colonial-style multinationals 1960s and 1970s. It serves its customers in all key markets with equal dedication. It does not shade things with one group to benefit another. It does not enter individual markets for the sole purpose of exploiting their profit potential. Its value system is universal, not dominated by home-country dogma, and it applies everywhere. In an information-linked world where consumers, no matter where they live, know which products are best and cheapest, the power to choose or

> refuse lies in their hands, not in the back pockets of sleepy, privileged monopolies like the earlier multinationals.[7]

According to Ohmae, globalization involves the

> denationaliz[ation of] their operations and creat[ion of] a system of values shared by company managers around the globe to replace the glue a national-based organization once provided. . . . In a genuinely global corporation, everyone is hired locally. No matter where individuals in an amoeba-like structure are, they can communicate fully and confidently with colleagues elsewhere.[8]

This concept of the global corporation appears to require what George Yip speaks about when he portrays globalization as a choice of strategies, rather than the creation of a global firm; in a sense, the process of choosing where and how to define the competitive arena is actually what defines the globalization imperative.

> Competitors are globalized to the extent that they use the global strategy levers of global market participation, global products and services, global location of activities, global marketing, and global competitive moves.[9]

Closely related to Yip's concept of globalization as a result of strategies are the thoughts of Hamel and Prahalad.

> In the past, several observers, including ourselves, drew a distinction between "multi-domestic" and "global" businesses or firms. We believe that *this distinction misses the central reality of the new international competition.*
>
> We believe that the process of globalisation begins with a particular sequence of competitive action and reaction, namely:
>
> (1) An aggressive competitor decides to use the cash flow generated in its home market(s) to *cross-subsidise* an attack on the home market(s) of foreign-based competitors.
>
> (2) A defensive-minded competitor then *retaliates* not in its home market(s) where the attack was staged, but in national markets where the aggressor firm is most vulnerable in a cash-flow sense. . . .
>
> We are now able to draw a distinction between a global corporation, global business and a global company:
>
> • *Global competition* is determined by the strategic intent of competitors, and their ability to cross-subsidise national market-share battles.

- *Global businesses* are those where the minimum volume necessary exploit scale economies and experience effects is unavailable within a single national market.
- *Global companies* have the distribution and brand positions in key foreign markets which enable cross-subsidisation and world-scale volume.[10]

Synthesizing from these observations, one gains the impression that the global firm is characterized by transnationalism in terms of strategy, and resource acquisition and deployment. The global firm is agile and informed. The global firm views the world as a playing field, and picks and chooses its moves in any one particular country market with reference to its positions, experiences, and implications in other country markets.

One of the interesting implications of Hamel and Prahalad's thoughts on globalization is that they serve to remind, in the midst of what is frequently euphoria over the potential of unified markets, that boundaryless markets also work for what were formerly foreign, or "irrelevant," competitors, as well. As Cantwell has observed:

> the rate of growth and the size of the market actually served by firms in the Member States [of the European Community] may be reduced by the greater force of competition incurred by firms based in other European countries.[11]

THE DILEMMA OF NEOCLASSICAL CONCEPTS OF OPERATIONS IN AN INCREASINGLY GLOBAL MARKET

For over 200 years, operational logic has been based upon concepts of economies of scale. This began with Adam Smith, in *The Wealth of Nations*, and his example of the economies available within a pin factory through the exploitation of an increased division of labor, but awareness of the concept existed well prior to this book, for example, in the Venice Arsenal.[12] It formed the basis for the fundamental choice of operational formats (between job-shops and flow-shops) which many believe was (and still is?) the essential pure issue at the heart of manufacturing strategy.

In Smith's example, the economies of scale were largely static, depending primarily upon the rated capacity of the operation. More modern descriptions of scale economies recognize the often more powerful *dynamic* economies associated with the mass production of standardized items, and obtainable through the "learning curve" or "experience curve" phenomena.[13] Both models of scale economies, however, are typically associated with high volume, mass production, of mature products in an effort to compete on the basis of low-price. Except for labor-intensive assembly operations in developing countries, the pursuit of economies of scale typically involves relatively large commitments of capital investment. As Jack Welch, CEO of General Electric in the US, has aptly observed:

> The winners in these global games will be those who can put together the world's best in design, manufacturing, research, execution, and marketing on the largest scale. Rarely are all of these elements located in one country, or even on the same continent, scale will be the dominant factor.[14]

Consequently, for this and the foregoing reasons, the profitable realization of the benefits of economies of scale have traditionally been associated with long duration, mature phases in a product's life cycle. Yet, as we have seen in the introductory comments, while regionalization and globalization are making such scale achievable, shortened product life cycles, and increasing preferences for customization, may be working against the achievement of these scale economies.

THE OPERATIONAL IMPLICATIONS OF GLOBALIZATION: THE BASIS FOR HYPOTHESES

The business system

In the emerging global market, characterized as it is by increasing and uncertain institutional, political, social, economic, and technological complexity,[15] it is useful to rely on a device that both reduces and still appreciates the richness of the real world, when portraying, in conceptual fashion, the actors and events that are pertinent to any analysis of the unfolding pageant of the times. The concept of *the business system*, which emphasizes the institutional dimension of the value chain, is used at IMD almost as a leitmotif for engraving a corporate signature on programs designed for international executives.[16]

The idea of the business system, according to Werner Ketelhöhn of IMD,[17] grew out of the pioneering work by Ray Goldberg on agribusiness systems, and is useful to "identify the chain of existing *businesses* between the supplier of raw materials and the final consumer of the product. . . . This way we could talk about what the different participants in the system were actually doing, how they were competing, and what could be done to outpace them" (emphasis added).

According to Xavier Gilbert and Paul Strebel, also of IMD:

> Rather than considering the company as competing *in an industry*, it should thus be seen as competing *within a business system*, in the same way as a chess player uses the resources of a chessboard. A chess player does not try to win by asking simply, "How do I win at chess?" Instead, the player asks, "How should I use my pawns, my rooks, my knights, my bishops, my queen, and even my king?" Similarly, each ... company should see itself as competing with other companies on design, on component manufacturing, on assembly of specific configurations, on software development, on marketing, on selling, on distribution, and on service support to the customer, and not simply as competing "in the personal computer industry."[18]

It is the upstream "technical" activities of a firm's business system that will be looked at here, and how these activities are adjusting to the new world of globalization and regionalization. Excluded from this chapter's examination of the business system operations are such downstream issues as logistics, distribution, warehousing and related inventory and marketing requirements. Although these are often of critical importance to the working of the business system, and the rivalistic outcomes of global commercial competitiveness, they were viewed as being outside of the charter given to this chapter.[19]

The R&D function

The international dispersion of R&D activities is not a new phenomenon. Fourteen years ago, I had the privilege of co-authoring a book with Jack Behrman, entitled *Overseas R&D Activities of Transnational Corporations,*[20] in which we found a relatively healthy amount of "R&D" being performed in a variety of foreign locales by the roughly fifty-five North American and European multinational corporations that we interviewed. Much of this R&D was a natural extension of the work that was already going on within the firm, and virtually none of it (with the exception of a few truly "world market" firms) represented a serious diversion from the paths being followed by the firms' traditional S&T assets. Most of this R&D, however, was lower level than that performed "at home." R&D of any substance tended to be brought back into the corporate R&D

center. R&D not brought back tended to either have evolved from local technical activities, or be reasonably closely controlled by the center. The globalization of R&D, however, is a totally different, and quite brand new, phenomenon.

In the past, then, to speak of international R&D was almost to implicitly acknowledge a single corporate center-of-gravity of science and technology, with subordinate and satellite R&D activities possibly being allowed to evolve out of a variety of foreign commercial activities, such as manufacturing, maintenance and repair, and/or local marketing. "Offshore, overseas, or foreign" R&D was something that happened as a natural consequence of siting technical activities in, or being responsive to, foreign markets, and was frequently a very complex *minuet*, danced out with the host country government.[21] The R&D *agenda* of these firms were composed of classical issues of project selection relating to scheduling and size. Locational or partnering decisions had absolutely no place in the repertoire of the R&D manager's concerns or alternatives. R&D was unilateral, unicultural, and unidirectional. The legacy of such a conceptualization can still be seen in those discussions of R&D that implicitly suggest hub and spoke R&D organization (with corporate and/or domestic R&D at the center and all subsidiary S&T activities on spokes of a wheel, emanating from the hub, with the great majority of interlaboratory communications passing through the hub), and the deliberate, yet unilateral *siting* of foreign R&D activities.[22] Economies of scale among corporate S&T resources remain an important dimension of managerial consideration in such firms. Intra-group S&T communications, in the tradition of Tom Allen's classic work, remains the best vehicle for understanding the ecology of such activities.[23]

With increasing globalization, however, it would appear that an alternative view of corporate S&T might be emerging. This new conceptualization would recognize the differences within the R&D agendas of a set of firms who acknowledge the futility of attempting to "go it alone, technologically,"[24] and, consequently, address not only the classical project selection issues, but also issues of who and where new technologies shall arise or be accessed. Partners, alliances, and arrangements now all appear to be a part of R&D decision making. The sharing and protecting of S&T assets are critical issues in the R&D manager's portfolio of responsibilities, and the idea of the *network*, growing almost naturally out of "the simultaneous presence of conflicting and common inerests," are increasingly useful in capturing the realities of S&T activities.[25]

Issues such as the mechanisms for collaboration, the ultimate ownership of the resulting intellectual property, and the nature of inter-organizational articulation become the primary operational decisions in such a model.

The design function

> There are 600 million in Western Europe, the United States and Japan. And the young people in their 20s, 30s and even 40s are more similar than different. They wear the same clothes and listen to the same music. . . . You can't be a regional or national designer anymore.[26]

The key issue associated with growing globalization/regionalization to be faced in the design function of the business system is the appropriate degree of product homogenization to encourage across national/regional boundaries. Hartmut Esslinger, the founder of Frogdesign, a well-known design house with offices in each of the major Triad markets, that counts among its clients Next (the Next computer system), Apple Computer, AEG (the AEG Telefunken car telephone), Villeroy & Boch, Zeiss, Louis Vuitton (Challenge luggage), and Logitech (the Scanman and Logitech mouse), is quoted above to vividly reflect those views which strongly support the advantages of becoming a *global* designer. But, in fact, it would appear worthwhile to ask: "Just how important is design to globalization strategies?" And, "How useful/desirable is the notion of a *global* design?"

It would appear that the real "substance" of design has to do with the dimensions of both output and input that we associate with so-called "knowledge resources" of the firm. We have all heard, for some time, that the future belongs to knowledge organizations. But exactly what that means and how such knowledge organizations would operate is never precisely spelled out. Yet answers appear to form in the wake of competitive implications which stem from observations such as those of Robert Reich:

> [There are] twelve thousand people [who] are entering the world market every hour, most of whom are willing to labor for a fraction of the wages of unskilled workers in the [industrialized nations].[27]

or Lester Thurow:

> In the twenty-first century being born rich becomes less of a

> competitive advantage. Advances in telecommunications, computers, and air transportation have led to a logistics revolution where global sourcing is possible. Multinational companies bring First World capital availability with them when they build production facilities in Third World countries.[28]

The implications of such forces are obvious. There is very little reason to hope that one can continue to compete on the basis of cost performance alone in a world where competitors can source cheap labor and capital relatively easily. However, without cost advantages, and in the face of almost inevitable and rapid reverse-engineering/copying of technical advantages, where should the firm look for sustainable differentiation? Clearly, the answer may well be in the mobilization of knowledge, of which design cleverness, style, and fashion are all partial, but essential, elements. In fact, in a recent survey of European executives, design is seen as being a significant competitive advantage for European firms, almost across the board!

> There should be no surprises here. Simply mention the word *Ferrari* and the message is clear. However, it is important for American managers to understand just how pervasive and significant the design dimension really is for European manufacturers. Alessi, for example, has transformed the everyday . . . juice squeezer into both an art object and a best seller. The power of Dieter Rams design concept, that makes any Braun product instantly recognizable, can even be seen as an influence in the *Sensor*, parent-company Gillette's flagship razor. The recent opening of several A/X Armani Exchange departments in three top American retailers: Bloomingdale's, Saks Fifth Avenue, and Neiman Marcus, again underlines how serious, and how successful, European manufacturers have been in using product design as a competitive advantage.[29]

Most of these examples are concerned with styling. Design, however, is more than simply the shaping of the envelope. It is also, very much, the orchestration of the situation.[30] Here, innovations such as McDonald's fast food, Apple's Graphic User Interface, Federal Express' service concept, and *USA Today's* user-friendly format are also representative of design improvements and distinctive competitive advantages, and are also all relatively successful across a range of global markets.[31]

In fact, the use of a common global design for products and

services is one of George Yip's *global strategy levers*. Yet, as obvious as such a path toward globalization might be, its attainment is not an easy, or even necessarily desirable, achievement.

> Globally standardized products or "global products" are, perhaps, the one feature most commonly identified with global strategy. But *the idea of a fully standardized global product that is identical all over the world is a near myth that has caused great confusion.* Such products are very rare and hard to attain, like an "edible Walkman" – the dream of multinational food companies.[32]

Returning to matters of style, Hugh Aldersey-Williams, the editor of *International Design*, suggests the need to both define "global design," which he characterizes as tending to be:

> work that is solidly rooted in the tradition of the Bauhaus and Ulm schools. Platonic geometry dominates the form. The function is generally transparent. Decoration is kept to a minimum, although colors are bright. The use of simple shapes rounded off with large radii is well suited to the process by which molded plastic parts are produced in large numbers. It would seem that in stylistic terms global design is nothing more than good old-fashioned functionalism decked out in softer shapes and brighter colors.[33]

And the need to be able to differentiate between truly global design and "global distribution of a national product." Here, he argues that

> Most global products reflect nothing more profound than the power of their manufacturers. Global food and drink is American food and drink. Global movies are Hollywood movies, despite the fact that the environment and behavior they portray is patently alien to much of their audience. Global electronics goods are Japanese electronics goods. The world's luxury items are French luxury items, and so on.[34]

In some cases, in fact, *globalization* takes on both the appearance and reality of *homogenization*. The rise and demise of many so-called pan-European products are a case in point of increased standardization failing in the face of persistent national differences.

The alternative to globalization is greater differentiation to reflect local tastes and differences. Loek van der Sande, of Global Design in the Netherlands, has observed:

> Culture is the world commodity of the twenty-first century. In

> the seventeenth and eighteenth centuries, he argues, wealth was determined by access to natural resources, and in the nineteenth and twentieth centuries it came through the ability to manufacture goods and control the money and credit supply. In the future, he believes, national character will become a tradeable resource.[35]

But, if this is truly the case, then what are the implications for *global* design? And what are the implications for corporate decision making, responsiveness, and manufacturing, in either case?

The manufacturing function

Despite the prevalence and persistence of the idea of (static) economies of scale to understanding strategic manufacturing decisions, especially with respect to the preference for larger and more centralized capital-intensive operations, there are, and have been, good reasons to challenge the rigidity of such doctrine. Among the most important reasons for such belief was empirical work done by the American economist Joe Bain in the 1950s. Although Bain's work is now quite old, it is nonetheless still quite relevant as it deals with operationally *inflexible* capital investment, and as such represents an extreme caricature of the traditional flow-shop strategic choice.

Bain's work is liberating in that it showed, empirically, that the familiar long-run average cost curve associated with static economies of scale was more severe in reaching the threshold of economies of scale (i.e. these economies were achieved at smaller production volumes than was generally assumed), and was more shallow upon reaching these thresholds. In brief, static economies of scale were easier to achieve and had relatively less impact once achieved than traditional strategic thinking held. Big was not necessarily that much more beautiful, relatively speaking.

Nonetheless, despite such realizations, and despite the emergence in the late 1970s of increased flexibility in manufacturing processes and procedures (e.g. flexible manufacturing systems, group technology, and just-in-time manufacturing), the prevailing notions in Western manufacturing circles, both academic and practicing,[36] continue to, at least implicitly, reflect traditional, classical, economies of scale logic. This also appears to be true at the level of the firm, where plant-chartering decisions also continue to be, implicitly, based on choices centering on economies of scale.[37]

Recently, much attention has been lavished, by academics and practitioners alike, on the virtues of subcontracting and outsourcing.

By relying on someone else to play a major fabricating or assembling role, frequently in developing countries so as to purportedly be able to take advantage of cheap labor, the global manufacturer is seen as being able to increase its own operational flexibility (mostly, through a reduced need to incur the fixed costs associated with specific process choices, thus allowing them to be in a position to "walk away" from past choices if radical new approaches are called for), while at the same time reducing per unit manufacturing costs by capturing both economies of scale and the advantages of low wage/focussed labor. In fact, it has been argued that the spread of "smart" technologies, and electronic data interfacing, has significantly enhanced the ability of smaller and independent partners to participate in the integrated business systems of global market players.

> This . . . network system allows each component participant to pursue its particular competence. Because of the complementary nature of network participants, a dynamic network can accommodate a vast amount of complexity while maximizing specialized competence, and provides much more effective use of resources in various locations than would otherwise have to be accumulated, allocated, and maintained by a single organization at a single location.[38]

Although fashionable, outsourcing is not without costs, not the least of which is the emigration offshore, and hence the loss of, a nation's design and manufacturing skills. John Harvey-Jones, former chairman of Britain's ICI, has eloquently captured the fears of many, when he deplores the erosion of his nation's manufacturing skills.

> I have always believed that the future well-being of every person in the United Kingdom depends on improvements in manufacturing performance, for I see no other means by which we can pay our way in the world.[39]

The primary risk to the firm associated with such outsourcing strategies lies in what Sony's Akio Morita has referred to as the *hollowing* phenomenon, in which the firm gives up the intellectual property or knowledge assets that form its future, and assumes a form of dependency upon the supplier in order to equip the subcontractor for the present.[40] This is a risk, incidentally, in both low-tech firms, where design skills might well be lost, as well as in high-tech firms, where intellectual property associated with technologies are at risk. From the (developing) country's perspective, a concern of such arrangements is frequently that of increased domination of the local economy by foreign economic interests. On the other hand, the author has argued that such arrangements might well be the most effective means of economic growth in such countries, *even if it means partial economic domination!*[41]

PRELIMINARY CONCLUSIONS: BASED ON FRAGMENTARY OBSERVATIONS

It is still too early in the globalization phenomenon to fully understand what is happening and why. Perhaps, at this point in time, the most that should be asked for are indications of directions and impressions of how seriously the old paradigms are being challenged. That is what this section of the chapter will attempt to do. Relying on a diverse and opportunistic set of observations, anecdotes, and reports, an effort will be made to form some very preliminary observations regarding the organization and structure of the technical activities of the firm in the face of increasing globalization.

Furthermore, the observations to be considered will largely come from the European experience in handling the full-fledged development of a common market. While this clearly will introduce a certain geocentric bias to the discussion, the European Community experience is unique and should serve as not only a good test of the emergence of challenges to the existing paradigms concerning technical activities within a business system, but also as an indicator of likely behavior in similar regional economic blocs in the future, including an eventual globalization of the world market. William F. Miller, past president of SRI International, has referred to Europe 1992 as a "Schumpeterian event", to capture the sense of economic stimuli associated with "sea changes" emanating from technical, social and/or political changes.[42] Europe 1992 includes all three.

To begin with, it is useful to note that the little evidence that is available strongly indicates the profound impact that the emergence of the European Community is having on the alignment and arrangement of most technical activities within the business system. Incipient regionalization, in this case, is causing firms to explicitly reconsider the configuration and coordination of their technical activities, and consequently implicitly alter their corporate culture as well.[43]

At the same time, there is also the impression that we are at the *beginning* of globalization, rather than being in the position to carefully examine a large set of experienced global veterans. It is instructive in this regard that Jarillo and Martinez's study of fifty Spanish subsidiaries of multinational corporations, in 1988, found

> no clear "active" subsidiaries (i.e. subsidiaries that have *both* a high degree of integration and a high degree of localizaiton).... This may be due to the fact that the "transnational" strategy is still little implemented, or that Spain is, for whatever reason, not a good country to place one of the more active nodes within a transnational firm, at least in the industries included in the sample.[44]

However, they also found a notable degree of increased integration and decreased localization between historical data from 1983 and forecasts for 1991, which portends movement toward activeness, and which they ascribe to Spain's entry into the European Economic Community.

The R&D function

Based on discussions within the Manufacturing 2000 set of firms, it appears quite clear that in the last decade a whole new level of complexity has been added to the agenda of R&D issues and concerns that are traditionally addressed by corporate R&D managers. There should be no mistaking that the contradiction between economies of scale and market responsiveness, that is common to all *upstream* activities, is clearly still very much an issue for R&D, as well, and that no one generalizable textbook solution exists to deal with it. Nestlés going about "de-centralizing" R&D in order to correct a situation where its formerly centralized (and heavily academic) R&D, removed from much of the day-to-day activities of the operating units, had become, in the opinion of one observer

> a sterile backwater, cut off from Nestlé's global network of development centres and largely ignored by its operating divisions. As a consequence, much research never found commercial applications.[45]

The company has arrived at a "solution" where "Each SBU now includes a research co-ordinator, responsible for two-way communications with the labs, which are encouraged to view the SBUs as clients."[46] The automobile industry, on the other hand, is moving in much the reverse direction.

> Ford [of Europe] has embarked on a controversial programme

> to concentrate – by the end of 1994 – all its R&D activities at two sites at Dunton, Essex, in the UK, and at Merkenich, near Cologne in Germany, in place of the present six locations, four in the UK and two in Germany. . . .
>
> Ford has been converted to the gospel of simultaneous engineering, but has faced a big hurdle in matching its rivals: not only is its R&D split between the UK and Germany, but the design and manufacturing engineering has been scattered between several plants.
>
> "Product engineers and manufacturing engineers must be in the same country, and ideally in the same office," says Mr. [John] Oldfield [Ford of Europe's vice-president for product programmes, vehicle engineering and design], "You cannot achieve simultaneous engineering by telephone or video-conferencing. . . ."
>
> The movement of engineers between the UK and Germany is Ford's attempt to make the best out of a less than ideal situation. If it were starting afresh, Ford would undoubtedly locate all its R&D effort at one site in one country to gain the full advantages of simultaneous engineering.
>
> "If two sites are better than six why not one instead of two?" says Mr. Oldfield.[47]

But none of this is new. There has been an ongoing struggle, and historic cycle, between more and less centralized R&D, probably since R&D was first institutionalized. And, in fact, the old paradigms, based on the resolution and accommodation of contradictions between economies of scale and responsiveness, would predict the moves actually made by Nestlé and Ford respectively.[48] What is really new, and what is almost very definitely also the direct consequence of the globalization phenomenon, is that institutionalized R&D, in transnational or global companies, no longer works the way it used to. In essence, worrying about centralized versus decentralized structuring of knowledge resources may be futile, if not irrelevant. Increasingly, for the most part, the newer general theme that appears to be running through this additional set of issues is: the creation of knowledge-intensive (and often virtual)[49] organizations where the management of R&D involves (depends upon) activities in geographically diverse locations, often involving significantly different organizational partners, and sources of technology.

One way that a new paradigm of corporate R&D appears to be manifesting itself is through fundamental differences in intra-firm

R&D operating behavior from that suggested by the hub and spoke model of a decade ago. Increasingly, significant alternative R&D activities are appearing within firms, either because S&T at a new site has something to bring to the firm on its own, or because alternative sources of technology are being sought-out to remedy voids in the corporate portfolio.[50]

Recent research on the globalizing of research and development[51] by transnational corporations has shown that so-called overseas R&D facilities are now often being counted on to play a much greater and more creative role than was formerly the case. At the new $500,000 R&D facility that Campbell Soup Asia is building in Hong Kong, for example, the goal is to place product-related R&D closer to the customer to "spearhead the company's thrust into Asia" and develop a family of pan-Asian products:

> Every market has particular tastes. We need to give what the consumer wants, that's the principle of the R&D center here. [In Hong Kong] we're close to the market and can respond to that market easily.[52]

In the case of the European pharmaceutical industry, on the other hand, despite the significant world market positions held by a number of its members, there has been significant aggressive expansion of R&D recently into foreign locales in order to access local S&T.

> The research facilities of MNEs [European Multinational Enterprises] in the industry have been increasingly decentralized, and many drugs are now developed through the combined efforts of co-ordinated research in establishments located in different countries [including non-European locations]. . . . The main reason for carrying out R&D outside of the home country is to gain access to foreign science and technology, and to potential new avenues of innovation complementary to those already established by the firm. Interviews with pharmaceutical companies for various studies confirm the overwhelming importance of this consideration. Taking the four highest capacity countries, MNEs from each have set up R&D facilities in each of the others, with just one exception. The only case in which cross-research activity is at a low level is that of the MNEs of West Germany and Switzerland, presumably because of the already close links that exist between research in these two countries.[53]

Britain, in particular, has appeared to gain significant amounts of foreign pharmaceutical research commitments in the wake of the drive toward community, largely as a result of the "quality of British science."[54] In the motor vehicle industry, on the other hand,

> the local research base of UK production has been disastrously weakened as foreign MNCs have moved research away from the United Kingdom, and British Leyland has lost market share so rapidly that it has been unable to sustain substantial and diversified technological activity. At a time when the intensity of technological competition has been rising, Britain has not only seen its share of R&D fall, but even the absolute level of R&D expenditure in real terms has been falling.[55]

A second, equally important, recent change in the calculus of corporate R&D in the global corporation is the deliberate addition of corporate R&D resources through acquisition. This is not to suggest that R&D resources weren't being augmented in the past through acquisition; they were. But, rather, in the study of a decade ago, R&D resources acquired as the result of mergers and/or acquisitions were after-thoughts or bonuses; never the central assets which originally motivated the M&A activity. Today, that has changed. Increasingly, firms appear to be acquiring and merging explicitly to obtain specific R&D assets and capabilities. Or such assets and capabilities form an important reason for the M&A. The result, post-merger, is that the new R&D resources are regarded with a considerably greater degree of respect than was formerly the case, and the role and coordination of the new resources are handled in a considerably different fashion. The lengths to which Hoechst and Celanese, for example, have gone in an effort to create a synergistic melding of their existing portfolios of S&T assets and activities, following their 1987 merger, has been discussed in considerable detail and provides an illustration of the magnitude of managerial attention that is involved.[56]

Perhaps more typical, however, is the conflict and contradictions that grow out of attempting to orchestrate and learn from multiple coequal R&D activities. While Pearce and Singh assert that "skill in handling multinationality [in R&D] may itself become an ownership-advantage of the MNE",[57] the experience of a European biotechnology company, with a global market presence and R&D activities on two continents, is illustrative of the problems that are found here. In this firm efforts to blend R&D agendas have been frustrated by a variety of not very esoteric concerns, and, ultimately, two separate R&D programs have evolved:

> There were good reasons for doing it this way [i.e. two separate corporate R&D activities working semi-independently]. The alternative of doing it in joint teams wasn't really feasible. People were not ready to move to ... [Europe] or the US for 3–4 years for a specific project. Furthermore, there would have been questions of communication on a day-to-day basis, and ultimately this would have delayed the project for another six months. Having different approaches in different locations was only possible because the company was doing so well overall. The idea was to minimize the risks and to get the products into the marketplace as soon as possible. There were also arguments that customers in Europe and the US were different, that they had different needs, preferences for delivery, and so on.
>
> [The result is that] We now have two areas, each with a high local sales volume and a full R&D structure developing a different ... system, and each with a different view on how the business should develop. In effect, we have two opposite portfolios running – one for the US and one for the rest of the world. The reality of doing it this way was more brutal than we thought.... The people in these organizations don't like each other, which is easy to understand historically, and they are fiercely competitive. At best, only a handful of people on either side can talk to each other. The biggest challenges are getting people to talk to each other, getting complementary parallel development, and dealing with internal competition.[58]

In general, the external acquisition and sharing of technologies has become a much bigger phenomenon than was ever thought about ten years ago. A growing reliance on alliances and partnering as an essential source of new technologies has changed the way in which R&D managers think about their positions and their corporate R&D portfolios. The recent partnership between IBM, Siemens, and Toshiba to develop a 256-megabyte DRAM (dynamic random access memory) chip is symptomatic of the sort of multipartner technology arrangements that are evolving in the face of increasingly burdensome costs of state-of-the-art technology development.[59]

The movement toward partnering suggests, at first glance, the existence of a *global market for technology*, and, indeed, this concept has made numerous appearances in both professional and academic discussions. Yet, increasing evidence suggests that the external technology relationships of many firms are more of a familial than a market phenomenon. Håkansson, in a study of small and medium-sized Swedish companies, for example, found that customers and suppliers made up almost 75 percent of the partners in cooperative technology ventures.[60] Similarly, a study of a small sample of French firms involved in the external acquisition and sharing of technology found that a neighborhood search among firms with whom they had had prior relationships was much more characteristic of technology acquisition and sharing than it was a true market characterization.[61]

The design function

Of all of the upstream activities within the business system, the design function probably has less invested in issues of economies of scale than any of the others. Design groups are typically small, in and of themselves, and while economies of scale are certainly influenced by such design considerations as modularity and parts-commonality, these are more typically considered to be manufacturing issues than design issues. Instead, when we speak of the interrelationships between design and globalization/regionalization, we are typically concerned with the ability of the firm to establish a common product design across a wide geographic/cultural area. In *Triad Power*,[62] Kenichi Ohmae argued that there is a growing cosmopolitaness within all societies and that, to continue as a global player, a firm must arrange to be in all major markets, with state-of-the-art technology and design, simultaneously. Well-known, *world market*[63] firms, such as Sony, IBM, Coca-Cola, apparently all do this. Accordingly, we should expect that increasing globalization should, in fact, lead to greater design commonality across regions.

The very fragmentary data that has been collected to date in support of this chapter suggests, however, that "global design" is still very much a concept rather than a reality. Sony, Toshiba, and many of the other world market consumer electronics firms, for example, actually vary their designs considerably in response to major market differences. Similarly, the automobile industry appears to have moved well away from the idea of a world car or common vehicle. Instead, it would appear that even more, rather than less, attention, and more professional attention at that, will be paid to designing-in regional diversity in the future.

Mark Lee, formerly one of three partners in Priestman Associates, successful British design firm, and now a partner in the well-known British design firm called "The Partners," suggests that basic functions, for example paper clips, zippers, and disposable pens, will always share a universal design, but "where there is room for embellishment, you still, and will, see national tastes and styles expressed, such as the British fondness for quirkiness as found in the Morgan [automobile]."[64] To the extent that such national idiosyncrasies actually enhance the exportability of the product into foreign markets (such as the Morgan in the US, or Harley-Davidson into Japan), we see the impact of van der Sande's observation, cited earlier, that national character will become a tradeable resource. The increasing formation of international design teams, and the hiring of design consultants for specific regions, are ways of ensuring that such national and regional preferences are designed-in around globally-common core design platforms.[65]

The manufacturing function

For too long, manufacturing was considered a non-strategic element within the modern Western firm's overall planning scheme. Manufacturing interests were not well-represented in corporate strategy sessions, and manufacturing frequently participated in the influencing and implementation of strategy only by denial; by being unable and/or unwilling to carry out plans and strategies that they had no hand in developing. At some point in the late 1970s/early 1980s, all this changed. A series of articles and arguments involving the strategic aspects of manufacturing not only appeared in the professional media, but catalyzed the profession. Over the past decade and a half, manufacturing has become increasingly more sophisticated, increasingly more vocal, and increasingly more strategic. Nonetheless, the age-old struggle between the advantages of scale economies versus the benefits of greater manufacturing responsiveness still remains as the heart of most decision making related to manufacturing strategy. In Europe, NAFTA, and elsewhere where regionalization and globalization are forcing firms to reconsider the arrangement of their manufacturing resources, manufacturing strategy and restructuring continue to be discussed and operationalized within the context of this essential trade-off between scale and responsiveness.

There is also, however, a demassification of the manufacturing resources of many firms taking place as a result of the current penchant for restructuring. The downsizing of manufacturing workforces and facilities is leading to if not leaner (in the currently popular use of the word),[66] then certainly thinner factories. Production performance, however, has largely been maintained by greater productivity achieved as a result of increased application of automation. In addition, instead of flexibility being built into the manufacturing process at an elemental level, the roles, responsibilities, and linkages among business system actors is changing, so that greater flexibility is achievable throughout the business system. Benetton, for example, is an excellent illustration of how this can be accomplished through a clever combination of product and process design, information, and organization. At the same time, in many firms, outsourcing is also increasing, which provides greater organizational agility. But, as opposed to the simple subcontracting of the past, today's outsourcing relationships often require greater intimacy, capability, and reliability: greater linkages! Benetton, which styles itself as being vertically de-integrated, subcontracts 95 percent of its value-adding activities; without extremely intimate relationships, such a situation would be unthinkable.

We are also seeing factories becoming more product-oriented. Two relatively recent case studies, written at IMD concerning manufacturing restructuring in anticipation of a single market Europe (post-1992), provide clear illustrations of this phenomenon.[67] One implication of all this is that the movement offshore of value-adding elements will no longer mean the necessary loss of complete value-adding chains or broad product capabilities. A second implication is that such focussing, to some extent in contradiction to efforts to co-locate the actors involved with product design and manufacture in order to reduce time-to-market and improve concurrent engineering, creates a real need to think about how to build better linkages and still restructure/redeploy. Global supply-chain management appears to be a key to future market-supply success and, consequently, to some extent, it appears that telecommunications and electronic orchestration appear to be the key, and that the creation of new organizations based on electronic experiences may be the wave of the future. this, in turn, means a greater emphasis on local infrastructure in offshore locations.

CONCLUSIONS

In summary, while there is an undeniable effort on the part of many, if not most, firms to take action within their technical resources in order to adjust to an emerging global (or regional) business environment, it does appear that frequently the present efforts toward greater operational globalization are fairly inelegant, incoherent, opportunistic, and non-strategic. This may very well be because they often appear to be person-specific (e.g. layering of

Euro-wide responsibilities on an existing person or site and often a person with unusual language, lifestyle, or other accomplishments that make him or her appear to be pan-European or globally-adept) rather than truly organizationally *strategic* (i.e. based on well-thought-out and developed organizational competencies). Or, that long-term strategic objectives are temporarily under attack from more pressing short-term economic pressures in recessionary times.

When strategic organizational changes do take place, they often tend to devolve into a "lead-division" approach, rather than a real attempt at worldwide orchestration of corporate (and extra-corporate) assets. In other words, firms go with that portion of the organization that appears, at present, to be best positioned to function within the new environment, rather than reorganize, or reculturize, the entire organization so as to really move into the future together. The danger here is that such moves could ultimately result in organizations that are distorted in terms of shape, abilities and cultures; the regional-scale extrapolation of business-as-usual, rather than a dramatic rearrangement of resources/activities. Such change is often project- rather than process-based, and is often the result of matrix structures becoming critically unbalanced in one direction or another (i.e. ad hoc, incremental, spasmodic approaches, rather than carefully thought-out procedures). On the other hand, there are certainly more than a few companies which are exceptional in their movement toward developing a coherent and strategic global focus. These would include ABB, Nestlé, Volkswagen, Bally, General Electric (US), Sony, Matsushita, and Acer (Taiwan). In fact, Volkswagen's success in winning Skoda (Czech Republic) over other strong suitors was due to its ability to capitalize on its experiences and successes with Seat in Spain.

It is clearly possible, then, to conclude that significant changes are taking place in the restructuring of business activities in response to global or regional market changes, particularly technical resources, but that they are not necessarily symmetrical across regions or markets, nor are they even necessarily internally consistent within firms. Alliances and partnerships are flourishing, and they give an unprecedented degree of freedom to corporate planners in creating global strategies.

As for whether the phenomenon we are seeing around the world amount to globalization in the making, or, instead, are acts of regionalization, the answer remains unclear. The restructuring of operational activities within the European Community appears to be much more regionalization than globalization, as do the initial penetrations of Central Europe and the former Soviet Union. While there are relatively few signs of global optimization in the experiences that we have explored, it is still too early to rule out European restructuring as a way-station on the road to global operations, although at present, I am not persuaded that this is really the case. As a case in point, in their study of Spanish subsidiaries of multinationals, Jarillo and Martinez have found

> A trend can be observed where firms rationalize manufacturing by specializing in the production of a few items for both national consumption and export to the rest of Europe. This trend is now going beyond traditional industries . . . to sectors that have traditionally operated as multidomestic. These "autonomous" subsidiaries in food processing or health care are rapidly drifting towards "active" strategies: an increased interchange of products with other subsidiaries across Europe is to be expected. At the same time some firms that had manufacturing units in Spain for political or trade-barrier-related reasons plan to close them altogether.[68]

For the developing countries, especially the Third and Fourth Worlds, the future appears to actually be dimmer rather than brighter. In the face of the fragmentation of much of the Second World (the former Soviet bloc), there is now an abundance of cheap manufacturing platforms available to potential Western investors. For those countries that remain mired in the depths of poverty and inadequate infrastructures, what are the compelling advantages that they offer multinational firms? Relative to the proliferating competition that they face as sites for foreign investment, their advantages, whatever few there might be, appear less and less compelling.

NOTES

1 Robert Heilbroner, "Hard times", *The New Yorker* (September 14, 1987) pp. 96–109.
2 Kenichi Ohmae, *Triad Power* (New York: The Free Press, 1985).
3 *Neoclassical* because at the heart of these conceptualizations was the very stark process choice between high-volume mass production of relatively standardized items (the pursuit of economies of scale) or low-volume production of customized items (the "job shop").
4 Lester Thurow, *Head To Head* (New York: William Morrow & Co., 1992).
5 Peter F. Drucker, *The New Realities* (London: Mandarin, 1989).
6 Alfred Zeien, "International, multinational, and/or global?," *Prism* (Fourth Quarter, 1991), pp. 85–8.

7 Kenichi Ohmae, *The Borderless World* (New York: HarperPerennial, 1990), p. 90.
8 Ibid., p. 91.
9 George S. Yip, *Total Global Strategy* (Englewood Cliffs, N.J.: Prentice-Hall, 1992), p. 60.
10 G. Hamel and C. K. Prahalad, "Creating Global Strategic Capability," in Neil Hood and Jan-Erik Vahlne, *Strategies In Global Competition* (London: Croom Helm, 1988), pp. 9 and 11. Emphasis added by present author.
11 John Cantwell, "The reorganization of European industries after integration: selected evidence on the role of multinational enterprise activities," in John Dunning and Peter Robson (eds), *Multinationals and the European Community* (London: Basic Blackwell, 1988).
12 Claude George, *The History of Management Thought* (Englewood Cliffs, N.J.: Prentice–Hall, 1968).
13 James C. Abegglen and George Stalk, Jr., *Kaisha* (Tokyo: Charles E. Tuttle, 1985).
14 Jack Welch, as quoted in William F. Miller, "Europe 1992: regionalism and globalism," *The International Executive* (September/October 1991), pp. 28–35.
15 David Warsh, *The Idea of Economic Complexity* (New York: Penguin Books, 1984).
16 Xavier Gilbert and Paul Strebel, "Developing competitive advantage," in William D. Guth, *Handbook of Business Strategy: 1986–1987 Yearbook* (Boston, Mass.: Warren, Gorham and Lamont, 1986).
17 Werner Ketelhöhn, "Competitive analysis for MCR," Internal IMD Memorandum (November 14, 1990). Ketelhöhn's thoughts on the business system have subsequently been collected and published in Werner Ketelhöhn, *International Business Strategy* (Oxford, UK: Butterworth Heinemann, 1993).
18 Gilbert and Strebel, op. cit. Emphasis added by present author.
19 "Logistics activities contribute some 20–30% of the GDP of industrialized countries and provide employment to 20–30% of the working population." Pavel Dimitrov, "Logistics in national economies: structures, strategies and international trends," in Pavel Dimitrov (ed.), *National Logistics Systems*, Collaborative Paper CP-91-06, International Institute for Applied Systems Analysis (IIASA), Laxenburg, Austria (June 1991), p. 29. More vivid, however, is the observation that "In less than two decades, Japanese companies have built a significant and identifiable worldwide market presence. Today, Sony, Casio, Seiko, Canon, Toyota and Honda enjoy the same recognition that was once reserved for names like Coca-Cola, Kodak, Nestlé and Philips. This reflects the enormous investments in distribution made by Japanese firms in the most recent stage of their global competitive onslaught." G. Hamel and C. K. Prahalad, "Creating global strategic capability," in Neil Hood and Jan-Erik Vahlne (eds), *Strategies in Global Competition* (London: Croom Helm, 1988), p. 7.
20 Jack N. Behrman and William A. Fischer, *Overseas R&D Activities of Transnational Corporations* (New York: Ogelschalger, Gunn & Hain, 1979).

21 William A. Fischer, "Trade, technology and other contradictions in economic development," *Business in the Contemporary World* (Summer 1989), pp. 99–105.
22 Scott D. Julian and Robert T. Keller, "Multinational R&D siting," *The Columbia Journal of World Business* (Fall 1991), pp. 46–57.
23 Tom Allen, *Managing the Flow of Technology* (Cambridge, Mass.: MIT Press, 1977).
24 The Dutch commercial vehicle producer, Daf, which failed in February 1993, cited its inability to compete with "its much bigger competitors, such as Mercedes-Benz and Iveco (Fiat), in continuing to develop and renew its entire truck range without strategic partner" as part of the reasons for its demise. Kevin Done, "Desperate days in Daf's demise," *Financial Times* (April 17–18, 1993), p. 10.
25 Håkan Håkansson, "Technological collaboration in industrial networks," *The European Management Journal* (September 1990), pp. 371–9.
26 Hartmut Esslinger, *Newsweek*, as quoted by Hugh Aldersey-Williams, *World Design: Nationalism and Globalism in Design* (New York: Rizzoli, 1992), p. 184.
27 Robert Reich, as quoted in Lloyd Dobyns and Clare Crawford-Mason, *Quality Or Else* (Boston: Houghton Mifflin, 1991), p. 107.
28 Thurow, op. cit., p. 42.
29 Robert S. Collins and William A. Fischer, "American manufacturing competitiveness: the view from Europe," *Business Horizons* (August 1992), pp. 15–22.
30 Ralph Caplan, *By Design* (New York: McGraw-Hill, 1982).
31 Except for Federal Express, which has largely failed to successfully export its design to Europe.
32 Yip, op. cit., p. 85. (Emphasis in original).
33 Hugh Aldersey-Williams, *World Design, Nationalism and Globalism in Design* (New York: Rizzoli International, 1992), p. 9.
34 Aldersey-Williams, ibid., p. 8. Could the NBA (National Basketball Association), in the face of being touted as "the game for the Nineties," and in the midst of an astonishing "global" marketing bonanza, ever be anything but *Made in the U.S.A.*? Even despite the growing numbers of foreign players? Wouldn't even the entry of China's Ma Jian into Pro Basketball be an Asian sharing of the American schoolyard dream, rather than the globalization of the sport? See Associated Press, "In Asia, NBA gears up with a full-court press," *International Herald Tribune* (July 4–5, 1992), p. 13. In 1992, the NBA expects sales of $22 million in branded merchandise in Asia. In Asia there are more than 1,000 NBA concept shops.
35 Loek van der Sande, "Design and cultural identity," Internationales Forum für Gestaltung, Hochschule für Gestaltung, Ulm, Germany (September 1989), as quoted in Aldersey-Williams, ibid., p. 15.
36 See Ramachandran Jaikumar, "Postindustrial manufacturing," *Harvard Business Review* (November–December 1986, pp. 69–76), for evidence of the persistence of traditional thinking in industry, despite the availability of flexible manufacturing capabilities.
37 Robert S. Collins, Roger W. Schmenner, and D. Clay Whybark, "Pan-

European manufacturing: the road to 1992," *European Business Journal*, 1, 4 (1989), pp. 43–51.

38 Masaaki Kotabe, "The relationship between offshore sourcing and innovativeness of U.S. multinational firms: an empirical investigation," *Journal of International Business Studies* (Fourth Quarter, 1990), pp. 623–38. This argument was also strongly made by George Gilder in *Microcosm* (London: S&S Trade, 1990).

39 John Harvey-Jones and Anthea Masey, *Troubleshooter* (London: BBC Books, 1990), p. 8.

40 Akio Morita, *Made in Japan* (London: Fontana, 1990).

41 William A. Fischer, "China as a player in the global economy," *China Economic Review*, (Spring 1989), pp. 9–21; "China's potential for exported growth," in The Joint Economic Committee's *Chinese Economic Dilemmas In The 1990s: The Problems of Reforms, Modernization, and Interdependence* (Washington, D.C.: U.S. Government Printing Office, 1991); and "China and the opportunities for economic development through technology transfer," in Tamir Agmon and Mary Ann Von Glinow (eds), *Technology Transfer in International Business* (New York: Oxford University Press, 1991), pp. 159–75.

42 Miller, op. cit.

43 The idea of restructuring in the face of such regionalization being understandable through some combination of coordination, configuration, and culture is a central theme in Manufacturing 2000's Industrial Restructuring project. See Robert S. Collins, Michael D. Oliff and Thomas E. Vollmann, "Manufacturing restructuring: lessons for management," *Manufacturing 2000 Executive Reports Series*, 2 (August 1991, IMD).

44 J. Carlos Jarillo and Jon I. Martinez, "Different roles for subsidiaries: the case of multinational corporations in Spain," *Strategic Management Journal*, 11, November–December (1990), pp. 501–12.

45 Guy de Jonquiéres, "Research comes back to the nest," *The Financial Times* (July 14, 1992), p. 13.

46 Ibid.

47 Kevin Done,"From design studio to new car showroom," *The Financial Times* (May 11, 1992), p. 17.

48 William A. Fischer and Jack N. Behrman, "The coordination of foreign R&D activities by transnational corporations," *Journal of International Business Studies* (Winter 1979), 28–35.

49 John A. Byrne, Richard Brandt, and Otis Port, "The virtual corporation," *Business Week* (February 8, 1993), pp. 98–103.

50 This conclusion is also shared in "The management of international research and development," in Peter J. Buckley and Michael Z. Brooke, *International Business Studies: An Overview* (Oxford, U.K.: Blackwell Business Press, 1992), pp. 495–509.

51 Robert D. Pearce and Satwinder Singh, *Globalizing Research and Development* (London: Macmillan, 1992).

52 Allen Ho, director of technical development at Campbell Soup Asia, as quoted in "Campbell Soup targets Asia with new R&D center", *Business Asia*, Business International (January 27, 1992), pp. 29–30.

53 Cantwell, op. cit., pp. 35–6.

54 Ibid., p. 38.

55 Ibid., p.43.
56 Leon Starr, "R&D in an international company," *Research Technology Management* (January–February 1992), pp. 29–32.
57 Pearce and Singh, op. cit., p. 2.
58 These observations were related by a senior corporate executive with international market and R&D responsibilities, quoted in an IMD case study, *Reflotron (A)*, written by Joyce Miller and Mary Rose Greville (June 1992).
59 Steven Butler and Louise Kehoe, "Partners thank each other for the memory," *The Financial Times* (July 14, 1992), p. 17.
60 Håkansson, op. cit., p. 376.
61 Francis Bidault and William A. Fischer, *The Technology Market*, IMD working paper (Summer 1992).
62 Ohmae, op. cit.
63 Jack N. Behrman and William A. Fischer, "Transnational corporations: market orientations and R&D abroad," *Colombia Journal of World Business*, 15, 3 (Fall 1980), 55–60.
64 Personal communication, July 1992. Harvey Jones, op. cit., devotes a chapter to the Morgan motor car, and captures some of the fondness of which Lee speaks.
65 Michael E. McGrath and Richard W. Hoole, "Manufacturing's new economies of scale," *Harvard Business Review* (May–June 1992), pp. 94–102.
66 J. Womack, D. Jones and I. Roos, *The Machine that Changed the World* (London: Macmillan, 1990).
67 Roger W. Schemner, *International Plow*, IMD Case POM 129 (April 4, 1987), and Mark E. Brazas, Robert S. Collins, and Michael D. Oliff, *Prentice Products Europe (A)*, IMD Case POM 138, (Rev. June 17, 1991).
68 Jarillo and Martinez, ibid., p. 508.

Part III

Pacrim firms: structure and strategy

6 Strategic responses of Canadian firms to globalization

Alan M. Rugman and Joseph R. D'Cruz

INTRODUCTION

The business sector must play a leading role in Canada's drive toward competitiveness. Indeed business leaders must provide the leadership that governments cannot in meeting the new challenges of competitiveness. Alterations to government regulations, policies and fiscal measures are all necessary preconditions for improving Canada's ability to compete, but by themselves these adjustments will be far from sufficient.

This chapter shows how business leaders can actively nurture competitiveness. It covers an area neglected by most Canadian business – the development and employment of business networks. After describing business networks, we will show why they are crucial to the development of competitive advantage in global industries. Next, we will specify the important elements of an effective network, including the role of government as part of the "non-business infrastructure." Finally, we will outline strategies for advancing the effectiveness of Canadian business networks.

This chapter is a summary of the new conceptual framework for business networks developed in more detail in our recent study, *New Concepts for Canadian Competitiveness.*[1] That study contains an updated scorecard on Canada's international competitiveness, extensive discussion of the role of government and other parts of the non-business infrastructure, an action agenda for the leaders of the clusters, and a set of specific recommendations. Here we explain the core framework of the larger study and focus on the role that managers can play in improving Canada's international competitiveness in this era of emerging globalization.

WHAT IS A "BUSINESS NETWORK"?

The term "business network" has entered the vocabulary of competitive strategy, along with terms such as "strategic alliance" and "joint venture." Yet there is considerable confusion about the meaning of these terms. Let us define business networks within the context of strategic clusters.[2]

To put it simply, a strategic cluster is defined as a group of firms within a small geographic region, all of which participate in the same industry or a closely related group of industries. Each cluster includes a "flagship" firm (or a small number of firms), which plays a dominant role in exports from the cluster, as well as a number of other firms that participate in business dealings with the flagship firms. The flagship firms compete globally, so their strategies and internal organizations need to reach the benchmark of international standards. In *Fast Forward: Improving Canada's International Competitiveness*,[3] we described, in depth, the ten major strategic clusters in Canada.

A business network is the web of strategic relationships that tie the members of a cluster together. It is important to distinguish network linkages from two other relationships: transactions between firms in a market and internal transactions within individual firms. Market transactions cover the buying and selling of goods and services; they are governed by the terms of contracts or by commercial practice and legal requirements. Intra-firm transactions are conducted by means of organizational structures and policies.

Network linkages are achieved through the harmonization of the strategies of the firms within a cluster. In other words, firms within a network agree to align and harmonize their competitive strategies for mutual advantage. Thus, network linkages involve some of the characteristics of both market transactions and intra-firm structures and processes. If this appears perplexing, it is. Business networks are difficult, troublesome relationships that require a high level of sophistication on the part of management. Yet, for many types of global competition, business networks are essential for survival.

By networking, firms can make use of resources owned by others. While some of these external resources are tangible and can be bought when needed, others are based on the skills and relationships of the people in the firms concerned, and are therefore hard to acquire through market transactions. The global competition for Canada's key industries has become so demanding and so complex that few Canadian firms possess the resources essential for long-term success. Even the world's largest multinationals are finding that they cannot rely solely on internal resources. For this reason Asea, Sweden's largest electrical products manufacturer, merged with Brown Boveri, one of the largest firms in Switzerland. Similarly, IBM is forging network links with other multinationals. The leading firms in Canada's major strategic clusters need to forge comparable networks to develop their strategic advantage.

BUILDING AN EFFECTIVE NETWORK

Canada's flagship firms are now locked in competition with European, Asian, and American multinational enterprises, many of whom already use networks to gain competitive advantage. How should a Canadian firm develop similar networks? Responsibility for forging the basic structure of the networks within a strategic cluster must lie with the flagship firm. Only they have the necessary influence to effect change. Choices must be made concerning what activities should take place inside the flagship firm and what should be left to network partners. These are key decisions for forging a modern global strategy. Suppliers, customers, competitors, and the non-business infrastructure must all be included in an effective network. We shall discuss each in full.

1 Suppliers

In Figure 6.1 the structure of an effective network for suppliers as displayed in normal arm's length commercial relationships are shown as solid arrows that do not cross organizational boundaries.

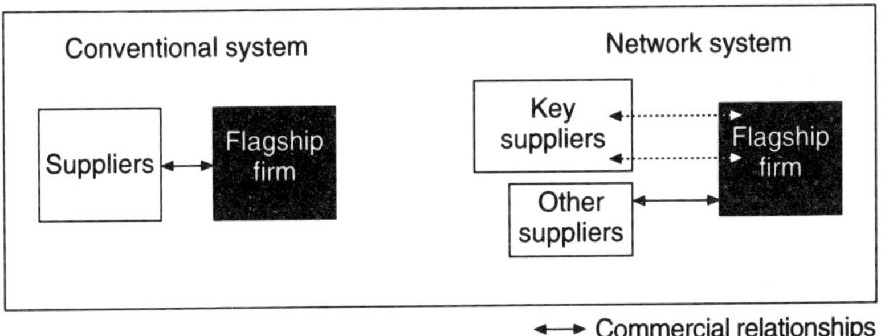

Figure 6.1 Major multinationals are making fundamental changes to their supplier systems

Network linkages, which involve the development of close relations, are shown as shaded arrows that go beyond organizational boundaries.

Two apparently contradictory trends have changed supplier relations dramatically. First, many businesses have adopted programs to decrease the number of suppliers with whom they deal. Following the example of the Japanese, Ford has dramatically reduced the number of its component suppliers; for a few components, it has adopted a single source policy. Previously, Ford management had feared that single source suppliers would develop substantial market power and use it to Ford's disadvantage. To overcome its fears, Ford has developed sophisticated means for managing its suppliers. It has recognized that special efforts must be made in order to align the strategies of Ford and its suppliers in a manner that minimizes conflicts of long-term interests.

The second trend has been a general increase in the supplier's share of value-added when it becomes a network partner. Whereas suppliers were previously held responsible for only manufacturing and assembly tasks, now network partners are also being asked to develop new materials and components to perform industrial engineering functions for their customers, and, in some cases, to assume liability for warranties. However, an increase in the share of value-added in the business system does not necessarily result in increased profits. On the contrary, profitability (measured by returns on sales) can actually decline because many of the newer activities are more risky, in large part because they are more fixed-cost intensive. It is therefore equally in the supplier's interest to participate actively in the processes of strategic alignment with the flagship firm.

2 Customers

Forging network linkages with customers involves changing the focus of the relationship from one in which the emphasis is on trying to get the best from individual transactions, to one in which the goal is to optimize the long-term prosperity of both parties. Canadian firms need to shift from arm's length relationships toward the shaded arrows, i.e. a commitment to closer relations.

The new network linkages between business leaders and customers are depicted in Figure 6.2. Such linkages are changing the shape of distribution systems, particularly across international borders.

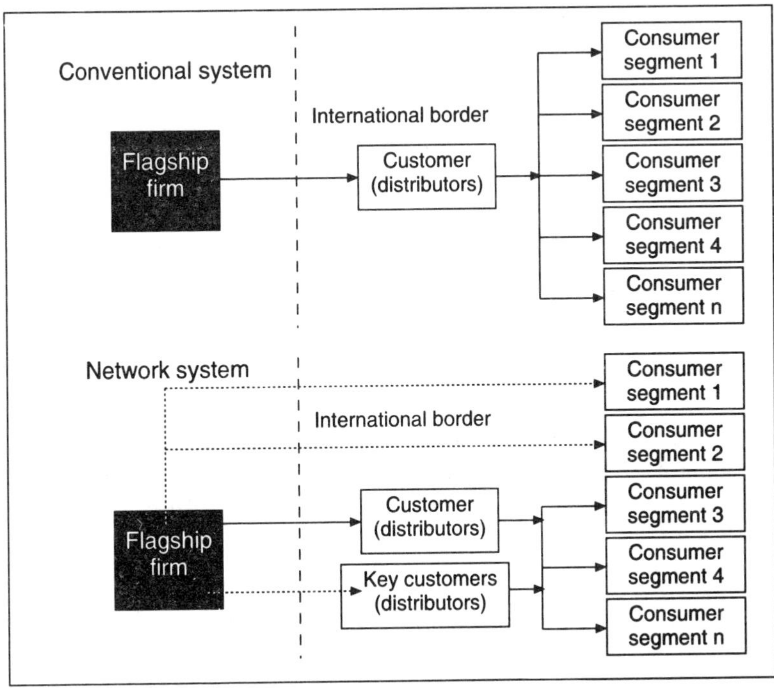

Figure 6.2 Network linkages are changing the shape of international distributional systems

In the conventional model, the flagship firm and its customers maintain an arm's length relationship, as shown in the top half of the diagram. With this approach, there is little direct contact between the firm and the actual consumers of its products. Instead, the firm deals from a distance with distributors who it regards as its immediate customers. Our view is that these arm's length linkages should be maintained for many customers, but that new relationships are required for key customers. In Figure 6.2, a direct link has been developed between the flagship firm and its most important customers in segments 1 and 2, while traditional relations were kept up with some distributors to serve the firm's less important customers. As a third alternative, network linkages could be developed with key distributors to better serve other customers in segments 2, 3, and n.

Achieving the full benefit of networking with customers requires much more than the improvement of communication channels and procedures; it necessitates alignment of strategies. This requires the divulgence of sensitive information, which makes many companies nervous. They fear that the disclosure of their strategies might allow the customer to develop powerful market advantages. Certainly, discussing details of the firm's strategies with every customer would not be sensible. Indeed, the selection of customers to include within the primary network of the firm is itself a major strategic decision.

3 Competitors

Network linkages with customers, as described above, are substantially different from those with competitors. Anything older than arm's length relationships with competitors is usually avoided in the United States because of combines/antitrust legislation, and, even in Canada, close relations are looked on with suspicion. Recently, Canada's competition policy has been reinterpreted to consider Canada's global competitors, but the law and its administration is still in an evolutionary stage, lagging behind global reality.

When it comes to international trade, network linkages between competitors are fairly common. They can take the form of joint ventures in third countries, agreements to market one another's products, technology-sharing arrangements, and combination efforts to develop the capabilities of a supplier base. Figure 6.3 illustrates the variety in the network linkages that major multinationals have been developing with their competitors.

Traditionally, network arrangements between international competitors have taken the form of joint ventures or technology-sharing arrangements. For example, Caterpillar and Mitsubishi Heavy Industries formed a joint venture, Shin Caterpillar–Mitsubishi. Today, the latter is a substantial company in its own right, which has a whole new set of network linkages with its "parents." Joint ventures of this nature have become the preferred entry strategy of Western companies going into Japan.

Another common form of traditional network linkage between competitors has been to share technology. For instance, Hymount, a major chemical producer, has licensed its polyproplyne technology to competitors in many parts of the world, to the extent that these systems for manufacturing now hold the dominant market share in that field. Similarly, technology-licensing has been a successful strategy for Union Carbide in its polyethylene manufacturing process.

The newer forms of network linkages between competitors are more varied and more subtle than the traditional forms. Instead of

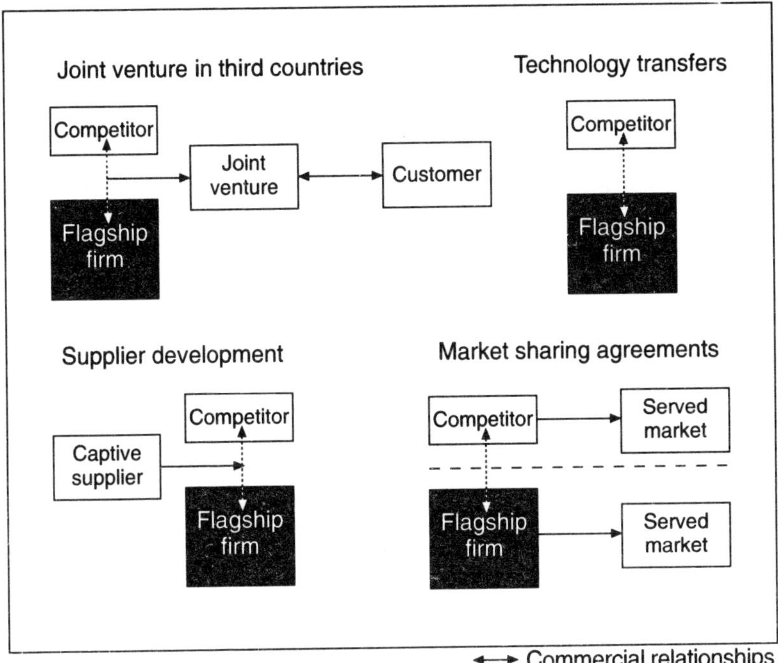

Figure 6.3 Network linkages with competitors take a variety of forms in international business

relying on the establishment of jointly-owned but separate business entities or on elaborate structures based on painfully negotiated contractual arrangements, the new ventures achieve integration through the day-to-day interaction of managers from both parties who are working together toward the achievement of mutual goals.

Sometimes these ventures take the form of back-to-back market-sharing arrangements. A Japanese company might agree to sell the products of a European firm in Japan in return the European firm agreeing to sell Japanese products in Europe. Successfully implementing such arrangements has proved much more difficult than their originators imagined. The deals make sense at the strategic level to those involved in striking the partnerships. However, the sales forces may have little interest in implementing the deal, and can usually find many plausible reasons for dragging their feet, thus scuttling any chance of success.

An interesting variation is Ford's network arrangement with Mazda. In addition to owning a significant minority interest in

Mazda (25 percent), Ford has an umbrella structure for specific joint venture deals with Mazda. Although each deal is treated as an entity that is separately negotiated and managed, the umbrella arrangement provides an indication of the good faith of both parties and sets out a framework for their negotiations. The initial deal was negotiated at a time when Mazda was in serious financial difficulty, and has survived the changed circumstance of the two firms.

The history of network linkages between multinationals holds an important lesson for Canadian-based multinationals. Frequently, the first attempt at such a relationship fails to meet the expectations of the firms involved. The popular business press contains many stories about failures of initial network linkages, all of which seem to feature how disappointed each is with the other. However, firms that persist in developing second and third network linkages usually find that they can avoid the mistakes they made the first time around; subsequent linkages are more robust. Curiously, linkages that do work are those that tend to rely less on formal mechanisms, such as contracts and joint management structures, and more on informal arrangements based on mutual trust. The truly adept firms apparently come to prefer network linkages to all other forms of international expansion – they certainly use this arrangement more often.

4 The "Non-business Infrastructure"

The role of the non-business sector is also important in improving Canada's international competitiveness. By non-business sector we mean, in particular, the non-traded service sectors which employ well over half of the 70 percent of Canadians working in services. These include education, health, social services and cultural industries – which, along with transportation, were the five sectors exempted from the Free Trade Agreement – and government at all levels.

There is a widespread misconception in Canada that because these service sectors do not engage in international trade, they are not pertinent to competitiveness issues. Nothing could be further from the truth. They have a vital role to play because the quality and costs of the services they provide directly influence the ability of the exporting sector to remain internationally competitive.[4] Their performance affects the quality and costs of business firms that compete globally. These non-traded sectors are, in fact, indirect participants in world trade. Effective linkages between business firms

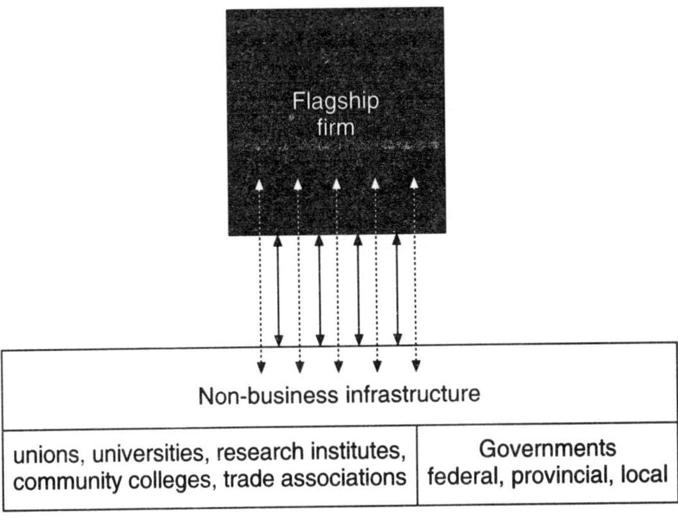

Figure 6.4 Flagship firms must be leaders in developing network linkages with institutions in the non-business infrastructure

and the non-business infrastructure are a critical component of competitiveness. As illustrated in Figure 6.4, similar types of network linkages should be developed between flagship firms and the institutions in the mainly service-based non-business sector. A few links already exist between flagship firms and non-business organizations such as universities, community colleges, research institutes, and government departments. However, these links must be reformed to surpass the traditional arm's length connections that are common today.

It should be noted that Figure 6.4 differentiates governments from the other institutions in the infrastructure. This separation was done deliberately to emphasize the differences between the two types of institutions. Building links with governments should follow, not precede, the creation of a network structure with the rest of the infrastructure. If governments are brought into the process too early, their agendas will tend to deflect attention from competitiveness issues. Governments do have a role to play, but they are not likely to be in the vanguard of a drive toward competitiveness.

Most network arrangements with non-business organizations will be of a project nature. For example, a flagship firm may develop a scheme with a community college to provide specialized courses tailored to the particular needs of the firm and the industry. Employees of the flagship firm are encouraged to take these courses as part of the upgrading of their personal skills. Tuition fees may be partly or fully subsidized, and classes may be conducted during work hours and even on company premises. The firm benefits because professional educators tailor the content of their courses to the particular needs of the industry. The community college does not have to advertise or promote the courses, so it benefits. In return for a guaranteed class size, it can lower the fee per student. Most important, the long-term character of the link encourages both parties to work in the interests of the other.

Network linkages change the frequency, intensity, and honesty of the dialogue between the firm and the non-business institution. As the alliance assumes true strategic dimensions, the institution can begin making adjustments to its program structure, including capital commitments, with greater confidence. The firm can then consider implementing technological changes that require order-of-magnitude improvements in the skills base of the workforce. Obviously, these plans must include workers outside the firm. People who work for the suppliers of the network must also participate in skills upgrading.

THE ROLE OF SMALL BUSINESS

A final point to note is the role of small firms in the business network strategy. Some small firms will be an integral part of the business networks described above; that is, they are suppliers, customers, or competitors of the flagships firms. Their relationships with the flagship firm is critical to both their own success and that of the entire cluster. The more managers and workers in these small businesses develop a global perspective, the better. Other small businesses will be in the service sector component of the non-business infrastructure. These are local firms such as doughnut shops, barbershops, and dry-cleaning establishments that, on the surface, appear to have absolutely no international component to their businesses. However, their costs have an impact on the competitiveness of the clusters, since they are suppliers to these firms.

Another group of small firms to consider consists of those that operate internationally by exporting their products. These businesses are most certainly selling into niches in a foreign market. In the case of such small-business exports, network linkages with the cluster will be just as important but quite different from the linkages described above. The small business that exports on its own is responsible for gathering all its own export market intelligence, foreign exchange information, customer profiles, and so on. These small businesses can be helped by government officials in federal and provincial trade offices, as well as by experts familiar with foreign markets. They are beneficiaries of the expertise developed by the suppliers of the cluster, and may also benefit from the development of the non-business infrastructure as described next.

In terms of the relative importance of small-business exports, while there are thousands of such exporters their share of Canada's exports is quite small. In contrast, the fifty largest Canadian exporting firms account for over 70 percent of Canada's exports. This is why our focus on competitiveness has been devoted to the nature of the global competition facing larger firms.

THE FINAL FRAMEWORK

The final framework for the structure of effective networks across Canada appears in Figure 6.5. At first glance the figure may appear to be rather complex and forbidding. In fact, it is just the aggregate of the four components of the network relationships developed sequentially. While not a simple diagram it does provide a powerful

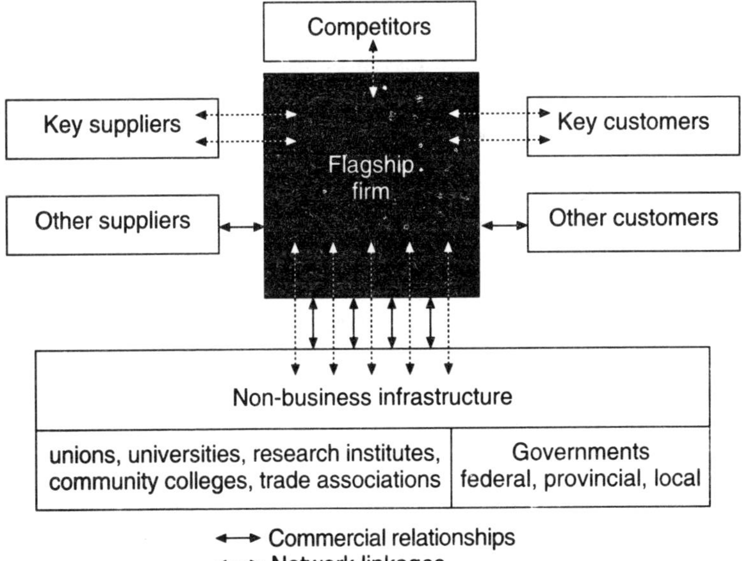

Figure 6.5 Basic structure of an effective network

statement about the need for a network to be developed with the flagship firm in four areas as follows:

1 suppliers;
2 customers;
3 competitors; and
4 the non-business infrastructure

Within Figure 6.5 we demonstrate the traditional arm's length relationships by solid arrows and the more desirable network linkages by shaded arrows. As explained in earlier discussion of the four components, moving toward network linkages will not be easy, but it is feasible. Canada can and must develop more network linkages in order to compete globally. In the next section we consider how, in practice, Canada's leading clusters can achieve the new relationships demonstrated in Figure 6.5.

RESHAPING THE FLAGSHIP FIRM

The network strategies described above require a radical new vision for the flagship firm itself. It needs to formulate and implement new global strategies in concert with other members of the cluster. To succeed, its own strategy must be first rate, with a constant ability to manage change internally as the external environment becomes ever more challenging. The lesson of history dictates that changes in strategy must be accompanied by appropriate adjustments to organizational structure and process. What has been discussed so far are changes in the external relationships of the flagship firm. Major internal changes will also have to be made in order for the new strategies to work. The flagship firm will be sharing strategy with its partners in the cluster; new thinking is required.

First, adopting network strategies will lead to major changes in the scope of activities conducted within the flagship firm itself. Functions that can be performed more effectively or efficiently by others should be transferred to network partners. Just a few examples will illustrate the types of changes that should take place in this realignment of strategies:

- shifting labor-intensive tasks to suppliers by integrating them into production components rather than final-assembly operations;
- eliminating incoming inspection and quality-control procedures

by helping suppliers adopt total-quality systems of their own that meet the needs of the flagship firm's quality system;

- outsourcing all activities peripheral to the core business of the firm. Examples include everything from snow plowing to medical services for employees;
- mobilizing the non-business infrastructure to provide services such as training, research and development, and certification of standards; and
- encouraging key customers to develop strategic alignment with the flagship firm by taking responsibility for some aspects of distribution and sales.

Figure 6.6 graphically portrays the overall impact of adopting a network approach. The scope of activities of the flagship firm will shrink over time as the cluster network develops. The shaded area in this diagram shows the range of activities that can be transferred to network partners. The scope of activities conducted within the network firms shrinks as a consequence of the success of the cluster in sharing strategies. What remains will represent the core competencies of the flagship firm: strategic management, nurturing of the major technologies on which distinctive competencies are based,

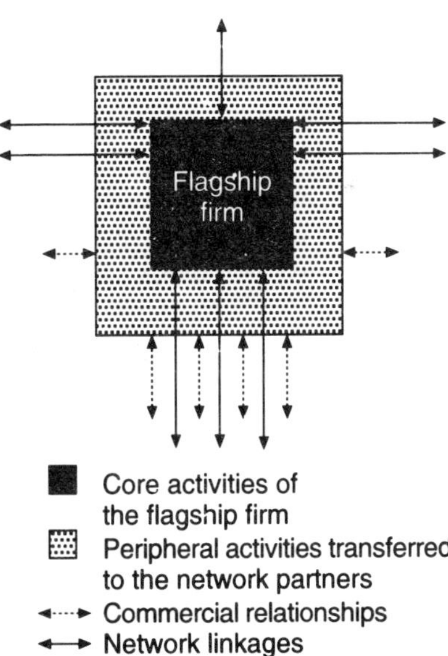

Figure 6.6 Adopting network strategies will lead to major changes in the scope of activities conducted within the flagship firm

capital-and-knowledge-intensive operations, and maintenance of the network itself.

Second, adopting network strategies will have profound implications for the internal structure and management processes of the flagship firm. The model of the new organization is shown in Figure 6.6. The major changes to implement this model are:

1 to replace the traditional "command and control" organizational structures that are in place in the majority of Canadian businesses with new structures that are supportive of upgrading and continuous enhancement of all aspects of competitiveness;
2 to empower front-line workers to take initiatives in the day-to-day aspects of upgrading the competitive capabilities of the firm;
3 to redesign the role of middle managers in the firm, whose antiquated concepts and privileges will be the most difficult hurdle to overcome before implementing the new organizational forms; and,
4 to foster the new mindset and attitude toward workers that management must adopt for the new compacts to work.

THE ROLE OF CEOS IN CREATING EFFECTIVE NETWORKS

Like most complex business strategies, building a network is best accomplished one step at a time rather than in a few sweeping moves. Thus, rather than investing much effort in an elaborate strategic plan complete with details of the many steps needed to implement an effective network strategy, flagship firms should instead undertake many small initiatives on a variety of fronts, building network linkages with suppliers, customers, and competitors wherever appropriate.

The overall vision of the complete network has to come from the chief executive officer (CEO) of the flagship firm, as does the initial impetus toward networking as the central element of the firm's strategy. The detailed strategies and specific projects should be developed largely through bottom-up initiatives by members of the senior management team.

Creating an organizational climate within the firm that is supportive of experimentation is crucial for developing networks. This requires a tolerance of the failures of many of the initial efforts and a determination to proceed with networking as a basic objective of the business strategy for the flagship firm despite occasional set-backs. Successful network linkages, no matter how minor, need to be celebrated to provide others with the incentive to experiment.

As the number of small successes increases, a stage will come when the pace of development of the network can be increased substantially. At this point, a number of role models of successful linkages will be available, and the management team will have learned how to build linkages that suit the nature of their firm and the international competitive environment of the industry. But to start the process of change leadership is required. The CEOs of Canada's ten clusters leaders – the flagship firms – must provide this leadership. Today, Canada has no cluster with these fully developed network linkages. It is time to start building them.

DATA ON CANADA'S CLUSTER LEADERS

In this section we will report on a preliminary study of the potential leading companies within each of Canada's ten clusters. As noted earlier, we have identified ten clusters across Canada. In *Fast Forward: Improving Canada's International Competitiveness* we explained the rationale for the choice of these ten clusters, especially their regionally-based nature, and the focus on the development of a competitive global strategy for the clusters.

In Table 6.1 we list the major companies active in each cluster. Our methodology for doing this needs to be carefully described. We have only used publicly available information on the sales and foreign sales of the largest companies in Canada. A company needs to have sales of over $1 billion to be in the cluster. To be more specific, a company must meet the following criteria to be included in Table 6.1 as a flagship firm:

1 the company must be listed as one of the largest companies in Canada in the *Financial Post 500*, using data from their latest publicly available annual reports, that is, for the 1990 reporting year;
2 the company must have sales of at least Canadian $1 billion for 1990, and it should be one of the ten largest companies in the cluster. (Only in the Alberta energy cluster do we include more than ten firms and only in the Atlantic seafood cluster do we include firms with sales under $1 billion; many other companies could be added to the clusters if we go under $1 billion, but we are interested in the cluster leaders, so ranking by size is the key factor governing inclusion);

3 the company must have a core business located in the geographical area of the cluster, or it must have a recognizable independent corporate strategy that can be identified with that of the cluster. Some foreign-owned firms can be included in the cluster on these grounds;
4 the company is excluded if it is a conglomerate, such as Brascan, Canadian Pacific, or BCE, although large self-standing companies within the conglomerate may be included, such as Trilon, CP Rail, and Northern Telecom;
5 the company is not a flagship firm if it is a retailer or food-based company, such as George Weston, Sears, or Canadian Tire, as these are multi-domestic firms with a focus on sales in Canada rather than abroad;
6 the company cannot be a flagship firm if it is a "supplier" in the sense of this report. This excludes large and influential companies such as Hydro Québec, Ontario Hydro, Air Canada, and Mitsui. These type of firms can, of course, be essential members of a cluster, but not its leader.

Table 6.1 The largest companies in Canada's ten key strategic clusters

1. The Western Canadian forest products cluster

Firm (Ranking in 500)	*Sales*				*Ownership*
	Total ($m)	*US (%)*	*Offshore (%)*	*Foreign (%)*	
1 Macmillan Bloedel (–)*	3,003	48	33	81	Canada
2 Fletcher Challenge (101)	1,160	n/a	n/a	n/a	New Zealand
3 Crown Forest (113)	1,061	n/a	n/a	n/a	New Zealand
Average	1,741			81	
Total	5,224				

2. The Alberta energy cluster

Firm (Ranking in 500)	*Sales*				*Ownership*
	Total ($m)	*US (%)*	*Offshore (%)*	*Foreign (%)*	
1 Imperial Oil (6)	10,223	5	n/a	5	US
2 Shell Canada (16)	5,508	20	n/a	20	Netherlands
3 Petro-Canada (17)	5,317	n/a	n/a	n/a	Canada
4 Nova (19)	4,736	12	7	19	Canada
5 Amoco Canada (24)	4,444	n/a	n/a	n/a	US
6 Total Petroleum (37)	3,180	n/a	n/a	n/a	France

Table 6.1 Continued

Firm (Ranking in 500)	Sales				Ownership
	Total ($m)	US (%)	Offshore (%)	Foreign (%)	
7 TransCanada Pipelines (41)	3,033	28	0	28	Canada
8 Mobil Oil Canada (84)	1,870	n/a	9	n/a	US
9 ATCO (82)	1,442	n/a	n/a	n/a	Canada
10 Suncor (89)	1,374	8	2	10	Canada
11 Alberta & Southern Gas (110)	1,076	n/a	n/a	n/a	US
12 TransAlta Utilities (112)	1,064	n/a	n/a	n/a	Canada
13 Chevron Canada Resources (114)	1,058	n/a	n/a	n/a	US
14 Norcen Energy Resources (115)	1,052	7	7	14	Canada
Average	3,241			16	
Total	45,377				

3 The prairie farming cluster

Firm (Ranking in 500)	Sales				Ownership
	Total ($m)	US (%)	Offshore (%)	Foreign (%)	
1 Canadian Wheat Board (27)	4,111	n/a	87	87	Canada
2 Saskatchewan Wheat Pool (61)	1,943	n/a	n/a	n/a	Canada
3 Cargill (74)	1,612	n/a	n/a	n/a	US
4 Alberta Wheat Pool (98)	1,223	n/a	n/a	n/a	Canada
5 United Grain Growers (104)	1,125	n/a	n/a	n/a	Canada
Average	2,003			87	
Total	10,014				

4 The Eastern Canadian forest products cluster

Firm (Ranking in 500)	Sales				Ownership
	Total ($m)	US (%)	Offshore (%)	Foreign (%)	
1 Noranda Forest (–)*	4,555	n/a	n/a	n/a	Canada
2 Moore (36)	3,231	60	31	91	Canada
3 Abitibi-Price (39)	3,088	27	0	27	Canada
4 Domtar (51)	2,314	11	0	11	Canada
5 CP Forest Products (–)*	2,313	n/a	n/a	n/a	Canada

Table 6.1 Continued

Firm (Ranking in 500)	*Sales*				*Ownership*
	Total ($m)	*US (%)*	*Offshore (%)*	*Foreign (%)*	
6 Repap Enterprises (97)	1,227	41	0	41	Canada
Average	2,788				
Total	16,728				

5 The base metal mining cluster

Firm (Ranking in 500)	*Sales*				*Ownership*
	Total ($m)	*US (%)*	*Offshore (%)*	*Foreign (%)*	
1 Alcan Aluminium (7)	10,217	33	54	87	Canada
2 Inco (31)	3,627	31	58	89	Canada
3 Horsham (34)	3,253	100	0	100	Canada
4 Noranda Minerals (–)*	2,671	n/a	n/a	n/a	Canada
5 Falconbridge (60)	2,032	39	48	87	Canada
6 Cominco (86)	1,403	39	43	82	Canada
7 Rio Algom (91)	1,343	31	13	44	Britain
8 Placer Dome (107)	1,093	9	58	67	Canada
Average	3,205			79	
Total	25,639				

6 The Southwest Ontario automotive cluster

Firm (Ranking in 500)	*Sales*				*Ownership*
	Total ($m)	*US (%)*	*Offshore (%)*	*Foreign (%)*	
1 General Motors of Canada (1)	18,458	64	n/a	64	US
2 Ford Motor of Canada (3)	13,706	n/a	n/a	n/a	US
3 Chrysler Canada (10)	7,067	71	n/a	71	US
4 Varity (26)	4,155	38	57	95	Canada
5 Honda Canada (46)	2,454	n/a	n/a	n/a	Japan
6 Magna International (62)	1,927	86	2	88	Canada
7 Toyota Canada (81)	1,505	n/a	n/a	n/a	Japan
Average	7,039	65	30	80	
Total	49,272				

Table 6.1 Continued

7 The Ontario advanced manufacturing cluster

Firm (Ranking in 500)	*Sales*				*Ownership*
	Total ($m)	*US (%)*	*Offshore (%)*	*Foreign (%)*	
1 Northern Telecom (–)*	7,899	58	6	64	Canada
2 Bell Canada (–)*	7,655	n/a	n/a	n/a	Canada
3 IBM Canada (22)	4,578	0	n/a	n/a	US
4 Dofasco (35)	3,250	16	10	26	Canada
5 Stelco (57)	2,101	n/a	n/a	n/a	Canada
6 Dow Chemical of Canada (73)	1,630	15	12	27	US
7 General Electric Canada (77)	1,581	17	5	22	US
8 Du Pont Canada (85)	1,411	n/a	n/a	n/a	US
Average	3,763			35	
Total	30,105				

8 The Toronto financal services cluster

Firm	*1990 Assets ($m)*	*Ownership*
1 Royal Bank of Canada (1)	125,938	Canada
2 CIBC (2)	114,196	Canada
3 Bank of Montreal (3)	87,369	Canada
4 Bank of Nova Scotia (4)	87,230	Canada
5 Toronto Dominion Bank (5)	66,900	Canada
6 Trilon Financial Corp. (6)	45,192	Canada
7 Royal Trusco (-)	40,946	Canada
8 CT Financial Services (10)	35,087	Canada
9 Sun Life Assurance (-)	31,920	Canada
10 National Trustco (12)	15,653	Canada
Average	65,043	
Total	650,431	

Table 6.1 Continued

9 The Montreal aerospace and manufacturing cluster

Firm (Ranking in 500)	*Sales*				*Ownership*
	Total ($m)	*US (%)*	*Offshore (%)*	*Foreign (%)*	
1 Bombardier (58)*	2,093	11	79	90	Canada
2 Pratt & Whitney Canada (76)	1,584	45	39	84	US
3 CAE Industries (105)	1,120	51	28	79	Canada
4 Asea Brown Boveri (111)	1,065	n/a	n/a	n/a	Switzerland
Average	1,466			84	
Total	5,862				

10 The Atlantic seafood cluster

Firm (Ranking in 500)	*Sales*				*Ownership*
	Total ($m)	*US (%)*	*Offshore (%)*	*Foreign (%)*	
1 McCain Foods (49)	2,396	n/a	n/a	n/a	Canada
2 National Sea Products (162)	608	45	31	76	Canada
3 FPI (183)	535	n/a	n/a	n/a	Canada
Average	1,180			76	
Total	3,539				

Sources: Except where noted all data are adapted from *The Financial Post 500* (Summer 1991), except for data on ratios of foreign to total sales, which are from *Canadian Business* (June 1991)

Notes: * Data are from the 1991 corporate annual report.
For cluster No. 8, rankings are from "The Top 100 Financial Institutions"

Using these criteria, Table 6.1 reports the names of the leading companies in Canada's ten clusters. It is from these companies that the flagship firm (or firms) must emerge to lead each cluster.

Within the ten sections of Table 6.1 readers should be aware of several definitions that affect the interpretation of the data. All tables report the following:

1 the company's ranking (as measured by sales) in the *Financial Post 500* (if the company is a consolidated subsidiary its ranking is not reported, e.g. Macmillan Bloedel is owned by Noranda Products);
2 total sales for 1990 (except for the financial services cluster, where assets are used);

3 percentage of sales to the United States (i.e. exports from Canada plus sales of any US subsidiaries);
4 percentages of sales to offshore (i.e. excluding the United States);
5 ratio of foreign to total sales (where foreign sales equals exports and subsidiary sales to the United States, plus all other offshore sales);
6 the country of ownership, which identifies foreign-owned firms, by nationality of the major shareholder (including Canadian firms).

In addition, for each of the ten groupings, Table 6. 1 lists the average sales and foreign sales. These averages need to be interpreted carefully because intra-group comparisons may be inappropriate. For one cluster, Alberta energy, we include fourteen firms with sales over $1 billion. For all other clusters, there are ten or fewer firms.

Readers should scan these lists for their own purposes. Our agenda in using them is to demonstrate that there are several potential companies which can become the flagship firms for these clusters. Every one of the ten clusters has the potential to develop a cluster leader. Some clusters are already better able to identify a flagship firm or develop business linkages and a network of activities with the non-business infrastructure. In some clusters the process has not begun.

We should emphasize that this is only a preliminary assessment of the potential cluster leaders. We hope that the flagship firm – the leaders of the clusters – will emerge soon. At this time we cannot identify the other players in the clusters. Some of the key suppliers and key customers will have a major influence on the development of a successful cluster strategy. However, the flagship firm must set the pace and nurture all the components of the cluster. In a similar vein, some government agencies and crown corporations can be useful participants, but their role as part of the non-business infrastructure must be as supporters, not leaders.

We have not listed any small firms, though they may be of great help to a cluster. There are, for example, many small business firms that do extremely well in export markets. They are often exporting into global niches, but their vitality and awareness of global conditions can help raise the level of understanding in Canada about international competition. So if the name of your company is not mentioned here it does not mean that you are unimportant in the drive to competitiveness; only that the flagship firms must be the key players in the process of change.

CONCLUSION

In conclusion, as there are ten clusters in Canada, we envisage that ten CEOs will take up the challenge to organize a system to revamp the international competitiveness of Canada's leading clusters. In all our research, we have not observed any cluster operating in the manner described in this chapter. There is no cluster with the fully developed business networks and successful linkages to the non-business sector that we believe are critical for success in the twenty-first century. We do not call on government to promote industrial policies, or to identify provincial clusters (as has been attempted in Québec). Instead, we recommend that the leadership comes from Canada's flagship firms. They are the crown jewels of Canadian business, and without their leadership successful networks for business and government will never be developed.

NOTES

1 Joseph R. D'Cruz and Alan M. Rugman, *New Concepts for Canadian Competitiveness* (Toronto: Kodak Canada, March 25, 1992).
2 The focus on strategic clusters has been re-introduced into the literature by Michael Porter, *The Competitive Advantage of Nations* (New York: Free Press, 1990).
3 Alan M. Rugman and Joseph R. D'Cruz, *Fast Forward: Improving Canada's International Competitiveness* (Toronto: Kodak Canada, 1991). The clusters are:

i The Western Canadian Forest Products Cluster
ii The Alberta Energy Cluster
iii The Prairie Farming Cluster
iv The Eastern Canadian Forest Products Cluster
v The Base Metal Mining Cluster
vi The Southwest Ontario Automotive Cluster
vii The Southern Ontario Advanced Manufacturing Cluster
viii The Toronto Financial Services Cluster
ix The Montreal Aerospace/Advanced Transportation Cluster
x The Atlantic Fisheries Cluster.

4 This point is developed in more detail in Alan M. Rugman and Joseph R. D'Cruz, *New Visions for Canadian Business* (Toronto: Kodak Canada, 1990).

APPENDIX: THE EARLIER LITERATURE ON NETWORKS AND MULTINATIONALS

In the past the predominant organizational form for US and Canadian multinationals has been internalization, i.e. centralized strategic control over integrated functional divisions of the firm. In contrast, many Japanese multinationals are not internalized; instead they participate in an extensive networking system. The essential characteristics of the network system include the existence of ownership – independent component suppliers and a more flexible approach to inventory planning and production management than has normally been practiced by North American multinationals.

Networks and internal markets

It is apparent that the network system and clusters are an alternative form of organizational structure to the hierarchical markets of North American multinationals. As Williamson (1975) noted, a hierarchical structure will replace a market when transaction costs impede the efficient operation of the latter. Internalization occurs when the benefits of control through internal markets exceeds the governance costs, and when environmental factors preclude exporting, licensing or joint ventures as viable methods of servicing foreign markets (Rugman, 1981). Both the strength and weakness of internalization is the nature of centralized control and strategic planning over key production and marketing decisions. Its strength lies in the exploitation of scale and, today, scope economies on a global basis through a system of wholly-owned subsidiaries where dissipation of the firm-specific advantage is minimized. Its weakness lies in the costs of running such a large integrated, hierarchical internal market, in which managerial and administrative complexity eventually limit the successful growth of the firm (Rugman, 1986).

North American multinationals have used internalization in order to monitor, meter and regulate the use of firm-specific advantages in either technology, managerial "know-how", marketing or financial strength. Internal markets substitute for regular external markets in the face of natural transaction costs and government-imposed regulations which disturb the international environment (Dunning and Rugman, 1985). Fully-owned subsidiaries are required, even though many North American multinationals have moved from ethnocentric to more geocentric management structures.

Japanese multinationals also secure control over similar types of firm-specific advantages, yet they do so without internalizing within formal organizational structures. Instead, the nature of Japanese cultural systems ties the outside suppliers and contractors to the multinationals in just as solid a manner as internalization.

Japanese multinationals can also achieve the production benefits of scale and scope economies but they avoid the costs of internalization by use of their network system. The great advantage of a network is that formal control need not be exercised, so management time and administrative costs are avoided. Instead, control in Japan is exercised through an informal system. Instead of an internally organized hierarchical structure Japanese multinationals achieve all of the same benefits of control over affiliates by the network system. Members of the network are tied to the "parent" multinational by culture-specific factors. The Japanese affiliates are bound by traditional relationships based upon trust, respect and personal integrity. Similarly, the "parent" multinational is tied to its suppliers by similar cultural constraints and objectives. The cultural bonds are so strong that independent affiliates are known to supply rival Japanese multinationals without any possibility of opportunistic behavior occurring.

The hypothesis which needs to be evaluated is the extent to which the Japanese network system is culture-specific. Can the advantages of networks, in their saving of administrative organization and governance, be secured in North America? Would production by Japanese firms in a Western culture dependent upon market forces and competition lead to the breakdown of the altruistic behavior exhibited in networks? Or would Japanese firms be forced to become more self-serving and controlled rather than autonomous and informally linked?

It is possible that the answer is already known. Observation of the entry of Japanese auto firms into North America reveals a preference for Japanese suppliers over American suppliers (Fortune, 1986). While it is stated that this is due to the lower quality and poorer plant conditions in American firms, it is just as likely that it is because of the Japanese preference to deal with compatriot firms versed in the nuances of the informal network system. Thus, Japanese networks are being transferred to North America (and other areas), demonstrating that they are culture-specific and that American firms cannot operate in the same manner. Instead, North American-based multinationals should probably continue to rely on the strengths of the Western tradition of organization by either markets or hierarchies; networks are the third option and are Japanese-specific.

Incrementalism and networks

One of the key attributes explaining the competitive advantages in production of Japanese multinationals is incrementalism. Japanese manufacturing firms excel in incremental innovations. They have demonstrated a remarkable capacity to rapidly develop new product lines based on information about changing techniques and market environments. Japanese firms frequently adapt and commercialize Western technology and knowledge in ways which were not apparent to the original producers (Westney, 1986).

Yet incrementalism in research, production and technological development is only part of the reason for efficient Japanese multinationals. The other is the existence of an organizational structure which builds upon the strength of Japanese culture. This is the network system. The combination of incrementalism and networks yields important firm-specific advantages to Japanese multinationals which are not readily available to rival multinationals from North America and elsewhere.

Evidence of the importance of incrementalism is presented in the study by Imai, Nonaka and Takeuchi (1985). They discuss the success of major product launches by five companies: Fuji-Xerox, Honda, Canon, NEC and Epson. They argue that all five product lines were based on incremental improvements. However, they also state that all were "hero projects," i.e. that the successful development of the products were managed within the organization context of each firm.

In general, there were several key aspects of organizational development: i) top management acted as a catalyst for the product launch; ii) there were self-organized project teams; iii) there were overlapping development phases; iv) there was multi-learning; v) subtle controls existed and vi) there was an organized transfer of learning within the firm. It should be noted that such managerial factors required for successful product development would be much the same for a North American company. Therefore, the success of Japanese multinationals must be due to incrementalism being coupled with something else. This is the Japanese ability to use networks as an external supplement to the regular internal management and organizational skills utilized by any well run corporation.

The theory of networks was developed earlier by Japanese scholars at Hitotsubashi University in Tokyo. Their models explained networks as alternatives to both markets and hierarchies (Kagano, Nonaka, Sakakibara and Okumura, 1985). A summary account is in the journal article by Imai and Itami (1984). The theoretical advantages of networks (as we understand them) are that they provide the benefits of control without the governance costs associated with internalization. The Japanese multinationals pass off the governance costs onto their suppliers and associates, economizing on internal control and management systems. Thereby they delegate the risks, information costs and other organizational expenses of an internal market to a set of separate but closely-related firms which are ultimately dependent on the multinationals and therewith informally controlled by them.

Critical to the global success of Japanese manufacturing multinationals is the ability to couple incremental improvements with the benefits of an interorganizational network. The speed and flexibility of new product development is enhanced by the existence of a close network of affiliated, but not owned, outside suppliers. These companies often participate in the product development of the multinational. Thereby these subcontractors, components suppliers and vendors, service and other affiliates, are all involved in the success or failure of the Japanese multinational. Yet they remain small autonomous companies with their own management. Therefore, the large Japanese multinationals do not bear the same burden of internal administrative and organizational costs as would a rival North American multinational operating under the precepts of internalization. Thus, the key advantage of "externalization" is the savings on internal costs of governance, i.e. an ability to assign these administrative costs to smaller independents within the company's network.

The affiliated companies in the network are independent in name only. They rely on the large multinational(s) for the bulk of their business, so they are extremely responsive and adaptive to the multinational. In essence, the multinational is like a "parent" firm to the smaller companies, which are almost as dependent on it as are "subsidiaries" in a North American internalized multinational. The ownership-independence of Japanese networks should not blind us to the underlying economic reality of dependence and power, which is little different in Japan than in North America.

Networks and the Japanese management system

The strengths and weaknesses of Japanese management have been widely discussed in recent years, and increasing attention has been given to the network approach. The older books (Franko, 1983 and Thurow, 1985), did not pay sufficient attention to networks.

The organizational consequences of emerging Japanese FDI have been studied in a collaborative cross-cultural research project reported in Takamiya and Thurley (1985). Takamiya examined the management production of four electronics firms (making televisions) operating in Britain; two Japanese, one American and one British-owned. He found that the comparative success of the Japanese multinationals was due to the smooth cooperation between individuals, sections and departments. While there was no explicit test of networks, the focus of Takamiya's work on the importance of good personnel management was confirmed by other researchers on the project. Good linkages between functional areas and their employees are also the objective of North American multinationals, but formalized control by internalization may not always be as effective as the informal control exercised by Japanese multinationals.

Moritani (1982) explains the linkages between Japanese culture and its success in incremental industrial technology. He argues that receptivity to technology differs between North America, Europe, Japan and other nations. Cultural and social conditions in these nations determine the quality of industrial products and the success or failure of technology transfer, a process which he terms "comparative technology." Moritani defines comparative technology as the study of technology through cultural and historical traditions. This is a strong position which implies that successful networks will foster the commercialization and production of incremental technology only in a Japanese context. It implies, for example, that North American multinationals cannot penetrate the Japanese market on the same terms as their home country rivals. But it would also imply that Japanese multinationals operating in North America or Europe may not be successful in new product development unless they transport a network system with them, or can build one up in a niche-type segment of the foreign nation (which is perhaps an unlikely prospect).

Perhaps one neglected aspect of the literature on Japanese management is discussion of the actual diversity of approach in Japanese management. Observations that employees are with the same company for thirty or forty years, that executives move up slowly and are carefully groomed for senior management positions, that there are excellent employee–management relations, etc. are all correct and help to explain a country-specific advantage. Yet there is diversity within this picture. For example, Nonaka and Johansson (1985) extend the conventional view of the nature of organizational learning in Japan by discussing the contrasts between "bottom up" participatory decision making (in Hitachi, Mazda and Nissan) with the "top down" management styles at Honda, Sony and Matsushita. The latter style seems to be more similar to North American management than the current simplistic view of a Japan characterized by quality circles and the singing of company songs.

Johansson (1986) has also argued that most Western commentators have been blinded by the dazzling success of Japanese management, to the extent that several notable Japanese failures have been ignored. Johansson traces these failures to marketing, not to incrementalism in production and technology. He argues that many Japanese multinationals are handicapped by organizational structures wich are culture-specific and cannot readily adapt to the different circumstances in foreign markets. He believes that many Japanese marketing practices are essentially ethnocentric. These work well for sales of products using scale economies where price competition is the key to global competitive success. However, they are less successful for niche strategies. They will also be unsuccessful as trade in services becomes more important and marketing skills become even more essential.

Globalization versus niche strategies

A key constraint in the development of good marketing intelligence is the country-specific and hierarchical nature of Japanese management. While there is effective participation by employees and junior managers in production-based work, the organizational structure of the typical Japanese multinational is often not sufficiently responsive to absorb marketing information gleaned by foreign subsidiaries. Networks are good systems for incremental production-based systems but they are not effective in providing intelligence about foreign markets to the multinational. Even the *sogo shosha* are better geared toward finite production than intangible service information due to the risk of recovering expenses incurred in new product systems. Also their experience is based on the marketing of goods rather than services. Yoshino and Lifson (1986) report that the *sogo shosha* have been most successful in steel, machinery, chemicals and other basic goods sectors. They have been less successful in computers, telecommunications and electronics where large Japanese multinationals do their own trading.

It is necessary for a service-based multinational to have a very decentralized, even polycentric, organizational structure in order to have host country marketing information drive the firm. The successful Canadian multinational, Moore Paper Forms, is a good example of such a polycentric organization (see Rugman and McIlveen, 1985). However, Japanese multinationals find it difficult to delegate such autonomy to managers in foreign subsidiaries, perhaps because the production-based globalization strategies have not required such actions. In general, Japanese multinationals lack experience in the use of subsidiaries since they rely on networks. Bartlett and Ghoshal (1989) also found that the Japanese firms were the least successful in the Triad at being "nationally responsive," i.e. adapting their products to host country markets. Instead, the Japanese were best at pure globalization strategies (i.e. cost and price-driven scale economies plus differentiation).

The problem of successful management of network systems outside of Japan will become particularly acute as the proportion of foreigners (host country nationals) increases in the subsidiaries of Japanese multinationals. For example, the American managers of a Japanese multinational (production or service-based) in the United States often find it difficult to convince headquarters of the importance of the marketing intelligence gathered by their subsidiary. In Canada, Japanese subsidiaries lack autonomy. If the strategic decisions in Japanese multinationals are generated in head office, either by a "consensus" method or a Honda "top down" method, it is apparent that the Japanese multinationals will be transmitting but not receiving. Previous production-based network strategies successful in the cultural milieu of the Japanese market may be difficult to transfer abroad (Simon, forthcoming).

The perceived advantages of technological and production incrementalism, networks and Japanese culture may become disadvantages in the future. The network system requires informal control mechanisms. There are few costs borne by the Japanese multinational in using a network system in Japan, or in translating a mini-network system to America or Europe (as is being done in autos and electronics). However, when marketing intelligence and service customization call the tune then decentralization and autonomy, within the organizational structure of the firm, are required. There is little evidence to indicate that Japanese multinationals can separate the benefits of networks from the cultural-specificity of this form of organization.

In contrast, North American multinationals are aware that firm-specific advantages can be obtained in both production and marketing areas, and that both sources need to be controlled by internalization. The experience gained in organizing internal markets is now an asset in moving toward North American cluster networks. The rival Japanese multinationals do not yet possess these skills outside of Japan.

References for appendix

Bartlett, C. and S. Ghoshal, *Managing Across Borders* (Boston: Harvard Business School Press, 1989).

Dunning, J. H. and A. M. Rugman, "The influence of Hymer's Dissertation on the theory of foreign direct investment", *American Economic Review* (May, 1985), pp. 228–32.

Fortune. "Are Japanese managers biased against Americans?," *Fortune Magazine* (September 1, 1986).

Franko, L. G., *The Threat of Japanese Multinationals: how the West can respond* (New York: Wiley, 1983).

Imai, K. and H. Itami, "Interpenetration of organization and market: Japan's firm and market in comparison with the US", *International Journal of Industrial Organization* 2 (1984), pp. 284–310.

Imai, K., I. Nonaka and H. Takeuchi, "Managing the new product development process: how Japanese companies learn and unlearn", in Kim B. Clark, Robert H. Hayes and Christopher Lorenz (eds), *The Uneasy Alliance: managing the productivity-technology dilemma* (Boston, Mass.: Harvard Business School Press, 1985), pp. 337–76.

Johansson, J. K., "Japanese marketing failures", *International Marketing Review* 3, 3 (Autumn 1986), pp. 33–46.

Kagano, T., I. Nonaka, K. Sakakibara and A. Okumura, *Strategic vs. Evolutionary Management: a US–Japan comparison of strategy and organization* (New York: North-Holland, 1985).

Moritani, M., *Japanese Technology: getting the best for the least* (Tokyo: The Simul Press, 1982).

Nonaka, I. and J. K. Johansson, "Organizational learning in Japanese companies", in Robert Lamb and Paul Shrivastava (eds), *Advances in Strategic Management*, 3 (Greenwich, Conn.: JAI Press, 1985).

Rugman, A. M., *Inside the Multinationals: the economics of internal markets* (New York: Columbia University Press, 1981).

Rugman, A. M., "New theories of the multinational enterprise: an assessment of internalization theory," *Bulletin of Economic Research* 39, 2 (May 1986), pp. 101–18.

Rugman, A. M. and J. McIlveen, *Megafirms: strategies for Canada's multinationals* (Toronto: Methuen, 1985).

Simon, Denis Fred, *The Technology of Japanese Firms Towards the Pacific Rim* (Cambridge: Cambridge University Press, forthcoming).

Takamiya, S. and K. Thurley, *Japan's Emerging Multinationals* (Tokyo: University of Tokyo Press, 1985).

Thurow, L., *The Zero-Sum Solution: Building a World Class American Economy* (New York: Simon & Schuster, 1985).
Westney, E. D., *Imitation and Innovation: the transfer of Western organizational patterns to Meiji Japan* (Cambridge, Mass.: Harvard University Press, 1986).
Williamson, O. E., *Markets and Hierarchies* (New York: Free Press, 1975).
Yoshino, M. Y. and T. B. Lifson, *The Invisible Hand: Japan's sogo shosha and the organization of trade* (Cambridge, Mass.: MIT Press, 1986).

7 Strategic responses of Korean firms to globalization and regionalization forces

The case of the Korean electronics industry

Yongwook Jun

INTRODUCTION

There are increasing studies on the impact of globalization and regionalization on the strategy development of multinational corporations from developed countries. However, studies on the strategic behavior of small multinational corporations or companies from the outside of Triad Power are rare. In a sense, it is these small players which are most heavily influenced by the globalization and regionalization forces because of their weak technological and managerial bases. In this context, this chapter tries to provide a perspective from the small country firm's viewpoint on the globalization and regionalization trends. The chapter has two particular objectives to achieve in pursuing the theme. One is to assess which forces are more demanding and relevant for Korean firms in their strategy development, the globalization forces or the regionalization forces? The other objective is to look into the response profile by the major value activity. How do the globalization and regionalization forces influence the production, technology and marketing strategies of Korean firms? By looking into the major value activities, we can have a better understanding of the impact of globalization and regionalization forces at the micro-level. At the same time, we can also identify the unique challenges and responses of small country firms which are distinct from those of established multinational companies.

In order to achieve these research objectives, I have chosen the Korean electronics industry for the case study. Due to the exploratory nature of this research, a one-industry study is adopted rather than a multiple-industry study in order to increase the internal validity of this research. The electronics industry is chosen, not only because of its importance to the Korean economy, but also because of its simultaneous exposure to both globalization and regionalization forces. In pursuing this research, we not only utilized published literature on global strategies and the Korean electronics industry, but also conducted personal interviews with twenty executives of four major Korean electronics firms (Samsung, Goldstar, Daewoo and Hyundai).

The first section of this chapter will suggest a conceptual framework which provides a strategic response profile by value activity of firms in the face of globalization and regionalization trends. An attempt was made to integrate existing literature on this issue by the major value activity. The second section will look into the specific strategic responses Korean electronics firms have taken by value activity in response to the oncoming globalization and regionalization forces. In the process, we have tried to identify how each strategic response is related to the conflicting forces of globalization and regionalization. The final section will suggest a few concluding remarks on the strategic behavior of Korean electronic firms in responding to globalization and regionalization forces and the implication of such behavior for the future strategic direction of Korean firms.

I A CONCEPTUAL FRAMEWORK: THE STRATEGIC RESPONSE PROFILE BY VALUE ACTIVITY

In essence, a firm is actually nothing more than the aggregation of discrete business activities performed within the same organization (Porter, 1986). When we view a firm from this perspective, environmental changes – whether they are related to global or regional forces – will likely have different types of impact on the various separate and distinct activities being carried out.

It is only at this level of discrete activities, rather than the level of the firm as a whole, that the impact of globalization and regionalization on corporate strategy can be better understood. Porter accommodates this disaggregated view of the firm in his "value chain concept" (Porter, 1985). According to him, the value chain provides a systematic means of displaying and categorizing activities which are grouped into two broad types: primary activities and supporting activities. The former are those involved in the physical creation of the product or service, its delivery and marketing to the buyer, and its support after sale. The latter are those which provide inputs of infrastructure that allow the primary activities to take place on an ongoing basis such as procurement, technology development, human resource management and firm infrastructure.

This value chain concept cannot only be applied to the domestic setting, but also extended to the global setting. Kogut (1985) summarizes the core of international business strategy as answering the following two principal questions: 1) where should the value-added chain be broken across borders?; 2) in what value activities should a firm concentrate its resources? In a similar context, Porter (1986) looked at the corporate strategy issue in the global setting within the configuration and coordination framework. According to him, the distinctive issue in international, as contrasted to domestic, strategy lies in two key dimensions of how a firm competes internationally. The first dimension is the configuration of value activities, which refers to where in the world each activity is performed, and the second dimension is coordination, which refers to how like activities performed in different countries are coordinated with each other.

What all these studies point to is that activity-level micro analysis is relevant and useful in analyzing the impact of global environmental changes on corporate strategy. In the following, we will create a catalogue of the strategic responses a firm could make in each value activity in the face of globalization and regionalization forces respectively (Table 7.1). This catalogue has been generated from the existing literature. We focussed only on three major value activities: production and marketing from the primary activity group and technology development from the supporting activity group. The first

Table 7.1 Strategic response profile by major value activity

Environment value activity	*Globalization forces*	*Regionalization forces*
Production	Global production network Rivalistic production relocation (exchange of threats; follow-the-leader)	Self-sufficient integrated manufacturing FDI in market countries FDI in quota-hopping countries
Marketing	Global launch Standardization of marketing programs	Regional adaptation of marketing programs
Technology development	Strategic coalition Global mobilization of R&D resources	Participation in regional R&D consortium Localization of R&D

two activities roughly represent downstream activities and the latter represents an upstream activity of the value chain.

Production activity

Typical strategic responses in production activities in the face of globalization forces are global production rationalization or networking and rivalistic production location decisions such as "exchange of threat" and "follow-the-leader" type behavior.

With the reduction of tariff and other trade barriers, firms in the globalizing industries have freer access to worldwide production factors and markets and this helps firms take advantage of the different comparative advantages of each nation. This, what Kogut calls a "real option", is one of the major sources of competitive advantage an international firm must exploit along with economies of scale, learning curves and economies of scope (Kogut, 1984). A typical strategic response to this trend is global manufacturing rationalization or global networking. Global rationalization means shifting from a set of local-for-local plants, each serving its own national markets with a broad product range, to an integrated network of large-scale production-specialized plants serving the world market (Doz, 1987). This kind of global networking can be made, not only horizontally across different product lines, but also vertically along the production process (Daniels, 1992).

Another group of major strategic responses to globalization forces can be manifested in rivalistic behaviors in production location. As globalization increases, the battleground of competition extends beyond each national market. A firm's competitive position in one country is increasingly influenced by its position in other countries (Hout, Port and Rudden, 1982). Each company becomes very sensitive to its counterpart's move to other countries. Especially in the oligopolistic industries such as automobiles and electronics, this risk-reducing mimicking behavior in foreign direct investment is very apparent.

The rivalry in foreign production can occur among foreign as well as domestic rivals. The former is what we call a follow-the-leader pattern and the latter, exchange-of-threat. Knickerbocker (1973) found that there is a strong tendency for US firms to follow each other in foreign production investments in oligopolistic industries. On the other hand, there were also strong cross-investments across borders in the same set of industries, especially between the US and Europe (Hymer and Rowthorn, 1970). Threatened by the establishment of a foreign-owned subsidiary in their home market, the response of the leading firms in that market is to set up subsidiaries in the invader's home market as an exchange of threat (Graham, 1985).

Meanwhile, in production the strategic response to regionalization forces is mostly to move sites inside market countries in order to bypass trade barriers imposed on exports. Vernon (1966) has emphasized the role of trade barriers as "triggering events" for foreign production in market countries. Most market seeking investments belong to this category. Another major response may be quota-hopping investment in less developed countries. In many cases, when firms face trade barriers in their major markets, they move their production sites to third countries so bypassing the trade barriers of their final market. A case in point is the textile investments by NIE firms in the Caribbean countries where the final product is for the US market. A third strategic response to regionalization can be to establish an integrated manufacturing operation which relies heavily on local resources. The stringent domestic content regulation of host countries often forces firms to abandon a screw-driver type assembly operation in favor of an integrated manufacturing one.

Technology development activity

The two major strategic responses to globalization forces in technology development activities are increasing utilization of technology-development coalitions and global search for R&D resources. As new product development costs have risen considerably in a range of industries, and timely introduction of new products becomes a key success factor in global competition, there is a strong incentive to share the financial cost as well as development risk with other firms. Furthermore, in today's high-tech industries, no single company can control all the critical technologies. In order to avoid the risk of losing out totally in a new game, a firm may well cross-fertilize with a complementary company, domestic or foreign, across a wide spectrum of the business system (Ohmae, 1985). In particular, coalitions in technology development are often preferred to arm's-length transactions because technology is kept out of the open market, preserving entry and mobility barriers (Porter and Fuller, 1986).

Another strategic response to globalization forces in technology development is the global mobilization of R&D resources. In many industries, multinational corporations no longer compete primarily with numerous national companies, but with a handful of giants who tend to be comparable in terms of size, international resource access and world market position. Under these circumstances, the ability to innovate and to exploit those innovations globally in a rapid and efficient manner has become essential for survival and perhaps the most important source of a multinational's competitive advantage (Ghoshal and Bartlett, 1987). In fact, key scientists are potentially more dispersed geographically than they have ever been. Some European pharmaceutical or electronics firms find it easier to locate laboratories for new technologies such as genetic engineering or microchips in the United States than in Europe. Exploiting a large pool of talent and avoiding the cost of expatriation are strong motives for locating R&D in various countries (Doz, 1987).

Meanwhile, the forces of regionalization suggest different directions for technology development. The emergence of regional blocs and the increasing involvement of local or regional governments in the global technology race have tended to force international firms to be more sensitive to local or regional demands. As competition between nations and regions is increasingly based on technology rather than on traditional production factors, such as capital and labor, more and more governments at local or regional level are involving themselves in the high-tech development issues. This, what Prahalad and Doz (1987) have called "political imperative," requires firms to set up more locally or regionally integrated R&D capacities. According to a survey conducted by Behrman and Fischer (1980), "host market" firms, with their national market focus, were particularly sensitive to the relationship with host country governments. This sensitivity resulted in the establishment of foreign R&D activities, thereby helping placate local governments' desire for the creation of skilled jobs. Furthermore, in order to be eligible for national or regional R&D subsidies or access to local or regional technological resources, firms may opt to participate in national or regional collaborative R&D projects.

Marketing activities

In marketing activities typical strategic responses of firms to globalization forces are the global launching of new products and the standardization of marketing programs. On the other hand, the response with respect to regionalization forces is regional adaptation of marketing programs.

The increase in development costs of new products, along with the homogenization of worldwide consumers, offers a mandate to introduce new products to the entire world simultaneously rather than introducing sequentially in order to amortize the heavy front-end investment. Companies that choose to develop the domestic market first may find themselves totally blocked out by well-entrenched competitors set to invade their own home markets (Ohmae, 1985).

Besides global launching in terms of timing, another major strategic implication of globalization of markets is the standardization of international marketing programs. This means using common product, pricing, promotion and distribution programs on a worldwide basis. Levitt (1983) argues strongly for the need to develop "global" products and brands. In a world of growing internationalization, the key to success is a focus on the marketing of standardized products and brands which will allow firms to achieve substantial economies of scale in production and marketing. According to Levitt, the world is being driven toward a converging commonality by the force of technology, and the resulting commercial reality is the emergence of global markets of standardized products on a previously unimagined scale. Ohmae (1985, 1989) also noted this phenomenon, especially among the Triad Power zone of the US, Europe and Japan.

The strategic response in marketing to the regionalization forces may be regional adaptation of marketing programs, which is basically developing different product, pricing, distribution and promotional programs for different regional markets. Douglas and Wind (1987) criticize the pitfalls of standardization arguments by pointing to the limitations of its underlying assumptions. These include the homogenization of customer needs, people's preference for lower prices at high quality by sacrificing product features, functions and the like, and the achievement of substantial economies of scale. They suggest that, in reality, there are many operational constraints to the effective implementation of a standardization strategy. Along with a few internal constraints, such as problems of fit with the existing international organization and concerns about the motivation and attitudes of local management, there are four major external constraints, one of which is the governmental and trade restrictions that is a manifestation of regionalization trends. According to them, government and trade restrictions, such as tariff and other trade barriers, and product, pricing or promotional regulation, frequently hamper standardization of product, pricing or promotion strategy. Tariffs or quotas on the import of key materials or components may affect production costs and thus hamper uniform pricing or alternatively result in the substitution of other components and modifications in product design. Local content requirements or compensatory export requirements, which specify that products contain a certain proportion of components manufactured locally or that a certain volume of production is exported to offset imports of components or other services, may have a similar impact. In this situation, adaptation to local or regional differences may yield better results. Baden-Fuller and Stopford (1988) show a good example of the above result with the case of the European washing machine market. According to them, due to non-tariff barriers to trade among European countries, nationally focussed strategies have been more successful than global strategies in this industry.

II STRATEGIC RESPONSES OF KOREAN ELECTRONICS FIRMS TO THE GLOBALIZATION AND REGIONALIZATION FORCES

In this section, we will discuss the response of Korean electronics firms to the conflicting forces of globalization and regionalization in terms of changes in R&D, production and marketing strategies. We will be particularly interested to see which forces are more demanding on Korean firms for each value activity.

Production strategy

It seems that Korean firms are sensitive to both globalization and regionalization forces in changing their production strategy. In the past years, Korean firms' production strategies have undergone four conspicuous changes: fast increase in foreign investments in developed countries such as the US and the EC; accelerated production relocation to developing countries such as South East Asia and China; increased efforts in domestic production rationalization; and shared production with rival firms.

Foreign direct investment in developed countries

Korean firms' direct investments in developed countries seem to be mostly in response to the regionalization forces. Korean firms' foreign investment in developed countries started with Goldstar's investment in color TV production in the US in 1981 in the face of

Table 7.2 Foreign direct investment of major Korean electronics firms in developed countries, as of December 1991

Name of firm	*Country*	*Year of establishment*	*Ownership (%)*	*Product*
Goldstar	US	1981	100	C-TV
		1986	100	MWO
	W. Germany	1986	100	C-TV, VCR
	UK	1989	100	MWO
	Italy	1990	30	Refrigerator
Samsung Electronics	Portugal	1982	55	C-TV
	US	1984	55	C-TV
	UK	1987	100	MWO, VCR
	Spain	1989	100	VCR
Daewoo Electronics	UK	1988	100	VCR
	France	1988	70	MWO
Inkel	UK	1991	100	Audio
Haitai	France	1990	51	CDP, Car Audio

Source: Company data

trade barriers on color TV exports from Korea. Since then, more than ten plants have been built up in the US and Europe for the production of consumer electronics goods (Table 7.2). Without exception, all these investments were made to overcome the trade barriers which were already imposed on them or in the expectation of future barriers.

Facing the increasing entry barriers by developed countries, it was inevitable that Korean firms would invest in these countries in order to maintain their export market share. Even if production economics in these countries was much worse than in Korea in terms of high labor cost, material cost and overheads (Table 7.3), Korean firms did not have any option but to invest there due to their high dependence on these markets for their business volume. It was not the luxurious decision of "export or foreign investment," but the decision of "foreign investment or die." Given the high proportion of major export items of Korean electronics firms going to these markets, they simply could not give up these markets in the face of market protectionism. Due to the "structural irreversibility" in the short run of their current cost leadership strategy and the difficulty of achieving export market diversification in a short time, they had to make "premature" and "defensive" investment there in order to maintain their current export share.

Table 7.3 The comparison of production cost of a 19 inch color TV in the Republic of Korea and the United States

		Production in Republic of Korea	*Production in United States*	*Difference*
Firm "A" (1983)	Material cost	82.1	98.0	15.9
	Wage cost	1.4	4.0	2.6
	Factory overhead	2.2	5.0	2.8
	Total production cost	85.7	107.0	21.3
	Transportation cost	7.0	–	–7.0
	Tariff	7.3	–	–7.3
	Total	100.0	107.0	7.0
Firm "B" (1983)	Material cost	82.2	98.8	16.6
	Wage cost	1.1	4.5	3.4
	Factory overhead	3.5	4.0	0.5
	Total production cost	86.8	107.3	20.5
	Transportation cost	6.7	–	–6.7
	Tariff	6.5	–	–6.4
	Total cost	100.0	107.3	7.3

Sources: Cho Dongsung, "Case studies in international business," Seoul, undated; Y. W. Jun, "The reverse direct investment: the case of Korean consumer electronics industry," *International Economic Journal*, Vol. 1, No. 3 (Autumn, 1987), p. 18

The way they tried to overcome the location disadvantages initially was to build screwdriver-type plants which were mostly fed by Korean parts from the parent plant in Korea, thereby "internalizing" Korean low labor cost as much as possible in the parts trans-shipped. However, the effectiveness of this strategy did not last long. The imposition of antidumping on parts in addition to finished goods (e.g. color picture tubes in the case of color TVs) and the increasingly stringent local content regulation on so-called "screw-driver plants" have nullified this production strategy. As a result, the US operations of two major Korean consumer electronics firms were withdrawn and merged into their Mexican operations.

Another outcome of these difficulties is a recent change in production strategy by Korean firms. Most Korean firms try to bring their affiliated parts makers overseas. This follow-the-customer investment by parts makers will help Korean assemblers to achieve a higher local content ratio. A case in point is the recent investment by Samsung

Electric in Portugal to supply TV tuners and FBT's for Samsung Electronics' three plants located in England, Spain and Hungary. However, one problem with this is that the production volume of the parts maker may not achieve sufficient economies of scale due to the limited captive use by the assemblers (Simon et al., forthcoming).

Foreign direct investment in less developed countries

Another important change in the Korean firms' production strategy has been the increasing investment in less developed countries (LDCs) (Table 7.4), in particular in the regions of Mexico and South East Asia. The investments in Mexico especially are in response to regionalization forces. With the formation of North American Free

Table 7.4 Foreign direct investment of major Korean electronics firms in less developed countries, as of December 1991 (unit: %)

Name of firm	*Country*	*Year of establishment*	*Ownership*	*Product*
Goldstar	Turkey	88	25	MWO, washing machine
	Mexico	88	100	C-TV
	Thailand	88	49	C-TV, B/W-TV, cassette tape recorder, washing machine
	Indonesia	90	70	C-TV
	Philippines	88	60	Washing machine
Samsung	Mexico	88	100	C-TV
	Thailand	88	51	C-TV, VCR
	Indonesia	89	49	Refrigerator,
		91	80	VCR, C-TV
	Turkey	89	20	C-TV
	Hungary	89	50	C-TV
	Malaysia	89	100	MWO, audio
Daewoo Electronics	China	89	48	Refrigerator
	Miyanmar	90	55	Refrigerator, C-TV, B/W-TV, audio
	Mexico	91	100	C-TV, MWO, refrigerator

Source: Company data.

Trade Area covering the US, Canada and Mexico, Korean firms felt the need to respond to this new regionalization mood in North America by planting a foot in Mexico. The Mexican operation is basically replacing the role of former US operations in penetrating the US market. The easy access to the US market and the advantages in production cost have made the investment in Mexico a natural choice for Korean firms.

In contrast to the investment in Mexico, the Korean investments in South East Asian countries seem to be a response to both globalization and regionalization forces. Korean firms set up operations in South East Asia partially to maintain global export competitiveness by relocating production sites in the face of worsening domestic factor cost conditions. At the same time, they wanted to check the dominance of Japanese firms in South East Asia by competing with them for the local market share. These aspects of strategy are in response to globalization forces. However, there is also a strategic purpose in the Asian investment which is to bypass the import restrictions imposed on Korean exports. By producing those products under restrictions in South East Asia, such as color TVs and CPTs, Korean firms can have free access to the European and US markets. This aspect of the strategy reflects the response to regionalization.

One interesting aspect of these dual purpose operations of Korean investments in the South East Asian countries is that they maintain joint ventures for local business, but 100 percent subsidiaries for export business. The latter is to have a faster decision mechanism which is free from intervention by local partners. The timeliness in production and delivery is a key factor for success in the export business.

Domestic production rationalization

Another major change in the production strategies of Korean electronics firms has been the increased division of labor between large integrated electronics houses and small and medium-size subcontractors which is largely in response to globalization forces. The large electronics houses rationalize their production systems by transferring a series of product lines in which the larger houses no longer have any competitive advantage and, instead, concentrate their resources on new products or new businesses. Typical product lines transferred are small screen TVs, vacuum cleaners, humidifiers, electric fans and printed circuit boards. They rent or sell their production facilities to those small and medium-size companies along with the assistance of technical training. This move, along with upgraded efforts in factory automation, is an attempt to remain globally competitive. Firms are adjusting their production strategies on the basis of changes in comparative advantages which are being forced by the globalization trend.

Production facility sharing

Being pinched by the many dimensions of globalization forces, Korean firms have been making some progress in cooperation among themselves. The threat from Japanese operations in South East Asia and the opening of domestic markets to foreign firms have pushed Korean firms to attempt successful cooperation in areas where economies of scale cannot be achieved by individual companies. A case in point is the specialization in production of large size refrigerators which used to be imported by two rival firms. Samsung develops and makes 720 liter class refrigerators and Goldstar do the same with the 650 liter class and then they swap them with each other and sell them under their own brand names. As there is not sufficient domestic demand for these refrigerators, no one company can achieve economies of scale in production by going alone. This kind of domestic cooperation in production helps save product development costs significantly by avoiding overlap.

From the discussion above, we may see that Korean firms have changed thier production strategies not only in response to regionalization forces, but also in response to globalization forces. They responded to regionalization mostly by trying to localize their production activities within developed countries. At the same time, they have also responded very actively to the globalization forces by going into LDCs and rationalizing their production systems in accordance with the changing comparative advantages of their home country.

One possible response which is not too apparent in the case of Korean firms, unlike in that of advanced multinational firms, is networking efforts. Though most of major Korean electronics firms have multiple production sites overseas, there do not seem to be any significant flows of information, parts, semi-finished products, human resources or capital between their operations. This seems to be mostly due to their early stage of internationalization. However, there is a limited attempt at integration. By establishing international procurement offices in Singapore, firms try to economize on sourcing of some materials, parts and goods for the scattered plants in the region.

R&D strategy

The strategic responses in R&D activities are mostly in reaction to globalization forces, in particular technology protectionism which takes the form of patent infringement suits and increased royalty charges. Korean electronics firms have been trying to overcome these threats by forming strategic alliances, diversifying technology acquisition channels and joining domestic research consortiums coordinated by the Korean government. The Korean electronics firms do not feel the regionalization pressures strongly yet. Because of the relatively early stage of multinationalization, they do not face the pressure for localizaiton of R&D functions in host countries or in the host region. Even in the case of established local R&D centers in major industrialized countries, this strategic response is not in reaction to regionalization forces, but rather to globalization forces. They set them up there as a way to acquire foreign technologies in face of global competition (Simon, 1995a).

Diversification of technology sources

Korean electronics firms have tried to diversify their technology sources. Not only do they acquire foreign technologies through licensing, Korean firms have resorted to more diverse methods such as the establishment of foreign R&D labs in major centers of world technology, utilization of retired foreign engineers, partnering with foreign venture capitals, cross licensing and joint development. By maintaining diversified channels for the acquisition of technologies, the Korean firms wanted to achieve a higher level of independence in their technology strategy.

A unique mode, utilized by Korean firms in recent years for the acquisition of foreign technologies from developed countries, is merger and acquisition (M&A) activities. When the timing of entry into the business is critical and the product life cycle gets shorter, M&A is a very effective strategy. By purchasing high-tech firms in developed countries, Korean electronics firms can not only quicken the access to the new technologies, but also catch up the forerunners in terms of technological capabilities.

However, this method is not without its pitfalls. First, Korean firms have found it hard to manage the acquired foreign high-

Table 7.5 Foreign R&D centers of Korean electronics firms

Name of firm	*Country*	*Local name*	*Activity*
Samsung	US	Samsung Information System	200 MB Hard Disk Drive, Notebook, Notepad Computer Development/Technology Transfer
		Samsung Semiconductor	Semiconductor Technology Development/Transfer
		Samsung Software	Workstation related Technology Development/Transfer
	Japan	Samsung Electronics	LCD Drive IC Development/ Technology Transfer
Hyundai	US	Hyundai Electronics	DRAM Development/ Technology Transfer
		Telecom R&D Center	Software Development
Goldstar	US	GS Tech Chicago R&D Center	Consumer Electronics, HDTV
	Germany	GS Germany R&D Center	Study of European Standards
	Ireland	Design Center	Design
	Japan	Goldstar Japan	
Daewoo	US	ID Focus Santa Clara R&D Center	Design
	Japan	Tokyo Lab	

Source: Various Korean economic newspapers 1987–92

tech firms, not only because of cultural reasons, but also because of gaps in technological understanding. Second, it was hard for Korean firms to assess correctly the value of the firms to be acquired. Not only the technology may be unproven due to its newness, but also there may be some hidden debts which are difficult to check in advance. If they could not check the tehnological and financial soundness in advance, Korean firms might be stuck with the wrong firm in the longer term. Some firms fell into an awkward situation where they had to decide whether to commit more resources to bail out the firm or to give up the venture altogether.

Another mode of diversifying the technology source was the direct establishment of research labs in advanced countries such as the US and Japan (Table 7.5). These research labs hire local scientists and pick up technologies from their experience and knowledge. These organizations are also utilized as training centers for Korean technicians dispatched to these labs for on-site education.

Along with the diversification of acquisition mode, the Korean electronics firms have also tried to find a way to diversify their technology sourcing countries. The Korean electronics industry relied on Japan and the US for 88 percent of its technology acquisition during the period 1962–88. In this respect, a series of attempts to explore alternative sourcing countries is warranted. Though the heavy dependence on Japan and the US has been significantly reduced, Korean firms are trying to establish new technology channels with previously unfamiliar countries. Some of the possible candidates for this arrangement are European firms and Russian institutes. However, unfamiliarity in doing business with these parties has been a psychological burden for Korean firms. The outcome of such efforts has yet to be seen.

Formation of strategic alliances

It is a boom for Korean firms to establish strategic alliances with foreign firms to face off global competitive forces. The prevalence of strategic alliances among Triad Power firms in almost all dimensions of electronics areas renders a great threat to the follower group, such as Korean firms, as the technology gap seems to expand rather than contract as the globalization of the electronics industry unfolds.

The major purpose of these alliances is to establish access channels to technology. Korean firms can obtain advance foreign technologies if they can utilize effectively their complementary assets such as financial resources, production capacities and business links in other product lines, and exploit the competition among major global firms in the industry to their advantage.

A case in point is the technical tie-up in March 1990 between the Goldstar Electron Co. and Hitachi of Japan for the production of 1MB DRAM and later 4MB DRAM chips. It was the first major Korean–Japan technical tie-up for the production of an advanced semiconductor device. The Goldstar Electron Co. is a newly-established company of the Lucky-Goldstar Group which is supposed to integrate under one roof the previously scattered operations of the memory chip business of several firms within the group. The technical tie-up has been the result of the convergence of mutual interests of both parties. The partnership was basically spurred by Hitachi's need for additional production facilities for 1MB DRAMs and Goldstar's need to advance its DRAM technology and make up the ground lost to Samsung in the DRAM race. Hitachi's monthly production capacity of 5.5 million 1MB DRAM was overshadowed by its arch rival Toshiba's 9 million at that time. By establishing a technical tie-up with Goldstar, Hitachi could assure itself of secured supply of 1MB DRAM while it concentrated its resources on the development of 4MB DRAMs. It was agreed that most of Goldstar's production be exported to Hitachi on the OEM basis. On the part of Goldstar, it wanted to catch up its arch rival Samsung in their DRAM race. Goldstar was not only behind Samsung in terms of production capacities, but also in terms of technology.

However, these strategic allliances are not without problems. One of the major problems Korean firms are facing is that the complementary assets they possess are not those of an enduring quality. Unlike the technological power of foreign partners, the assets of Korean firms, such as production capacity, local market access and some pool of financed resources, are not of a long-standing nature. These asymmetric relations, either real or perceived, provide constant sources of conflict and anxiety and make the relationship a temporary one. Furthermore, due to the lack of experience in corporate-level cooperation in Korean business culture in general, and in international strategic alliances in particular, there are many management conflicts. Thus it is especially so because there are three layers of management involved in a typical strategic alliance. One is that of top management, who share the spirit of cooperation. The second is that of senior management who are heavily involved in most decision-making on production, marketing and finance. The last group is engineering staff who are the actual catalysts for technology exchange. However, there is a significant lack of coordination among these three levels of managers and it often leads to delay in decision making and conflicts with foreign partners.

Besides, Korean firms mostly view strategic alliance as an engineering rather than a management task. This too narrow perspective hinders the smooth operation of strategic alliances whose real focus should lie in the delicate handling of the decision process of both parties. As a result, many strategic alliances are at a crossroad and some have already broken down. A case in point is the Samsung–Micron technology alliance in the semiconductor sector.

Table 7.6 Domestic alliances in the Korean electronics industry

Participator	*Product*	*Activity*
Samsung, Goldstar, Daewoo, Alps, Hankuk, KIST, KIET, Others	HDTV	Joint R&D
Samsung, Daewoo, Goldstar	Large size refrigerator	Shared manufacturing/swap
Samsung, Daewoo and 20 Others	CATV and CATV Parts	Joint R&D
Samsung Corning, Goldstar	All products	Cross licensing
Goldstar, Hyundai, Daewoo, KAITECH	G4 fax machine	Joint R&D
Goldstar, Daewoo	Word processor	Joint R&D
Goldstar, Anam	TV teletext technology	Technology transfer
Samsung, Goldstar	TDX	Joint R&D
Samsung, Goldstar	LDP Mechanism	Technology transfer

Source: Annual Statistics, Ministry of Trade and Industry, 1992, Seoul, Korea

Cooperation among domestic firms

Facing an increasing competitive check from foreign firms, the time has come for Korean firms to resort to cooperation in the acquisition of parts (e.g. joint purchase), localization of parts, and the development of technology (Table 7.6). One recent event in the direction of this cooperation is the mutual exchange of patents among two arch rivals in the Korean electronics industry. Samsung Corning and Goldstar agreed to share their patents, with total more than 4,000 cases altogether. They expect that this kind of cooperation will be made beyond the individual company level and will reach the whole group, which comprises more than forty companies each. The joint R&D effort and the swap of technologies between rival firms are the result of the recognition that no one company has enough resources to cover major technology investment, and that technology protectionism by foreign technology leaders is hard to be borne by one single company. The companies found that the solution to global competitive forces is mutual cooperation. In the past, Korean firms looked for global firms as their partners, neglecting their domestic rivals. However, the fast rising costs of development and the need to defend against foreign competition have pushed Korean firms toward alliances with each other.

The Korean government often plays a very important role in these joint efforts in technology development. In the 4MB DRAM project, the Korean government adopted two new approaches in order to successfully finish the project on time. One was the utilization of competition among firms. Some of the fund was allocated to member firms on a merit basis. Only those firms which achieved required performance on time had the right to obtain the fund. The failed firms were not reimbursed for their expenditures on R&D. Another approach was that the government provided only a part of total financial requirements, making member firms share the rest of the burden. This sharing of cost made firms more cost- and time-sensitive throughout the process. One interesting thing to note in this development process is that the very oligopolistic structure of the Korean electronics industry has made competition a very effective tool for speeding up the development process. Besides the differential financial benefit, each member firm places a great emphasis on its pride. A similar approach has been adopted in other government–industry joint projects, such as development of 16M DRAM. The role of the government will become more important, but the mode of the government intervention will be less explicit, especially in the case of Korean government which is subject to trade disputes with industrialized countries.

Marketing strategy

It seems that most of the recent changes in marketing strategies in Korean firms have been in response to globalization forces rather than regionalization ones. The threats from the low cost suppliers of South East Asia and China and the domestic market opening have been forcing Korean firms to change their marketing strategies. Two major responses to these forces are the shift from the original equipment manufacturer (OEM) brand to the own brand strategy and beefed-up efforts in domestic marketing.

Changes in brand strategy

The most prominent marketing strategy of Korean electronics firms has been OEM brand strategy which is the marketing end of the two poles of the salient industrial strategies: cost leadership and dependent development. This OEM strategy has enabled Korean firms to realize economies of scale in production by taking volume orders and, at the same time, to supplement their marketing weakness by relying on foreign buyers for delicate local marketing activities. The strategy has also partially contributed to enhancing the production and quality control capabilities of Korean firms in the process of meeting the stringent price and quality requirements of OEM buyers.

However, it seems that the effectiveness of the OEM strategy has been rapidly decreasing, especially in the consumer electronics and personal computer sectors, which are sensitive to changes in factor costs and vulnerable to threats from low cost producers in the Third World. The unfavorably changing competitive condition of the Korean electronics industry, arising from escalating domestic labor cost and the threat of Third World countries, rapidly deteriorates the utility of the OEM strategy. Furthermore, Korean firms have recognized that the most inherent disadvantage of the OEM strategy is the lack of brand name recognition by end users which is indispensable to product differentiation. Korean firms have realized that they will not become true global firms without establishing their own brand names in the global market. Currently, the lack of global recognition of own brand names is one of the weakest links of the industry's value chain, along with the weakness in technological capabilities. These internal needs, as well as the unfavorably changing economic environment, have pushed Korean firms to shift their brand strategy toward that of the own brand. Accordingly, there is an explicit recognition among Korean firms that marketing expenditures should be regarded as "investment" rather than periodic "expenses." As a result, Korean electronics firms have been increasing their budget for enhancing their global brand identity and using more diverse ways of advertising, including media advertising and sponsoring of major sports events in order to appeal to the mass public. However, establishing an own brand in the global market is not easy. It demands a big commitment to marketing investment on the part of the Korean firms. They have not only to develop an appropriate brand image, but also to set up their own marketing channels in major local markets which will supplement the diffusion of their brand names. To firms which were accustomed to dependent marketing, this transition is destined to be a slow process.

Reinforcing domestic marketing efforts

The globalization forces which have opened the Korean domestic market to foreign firms have significantly changed the way Korean firms in consumer electronics and computer sectors perform their marketing activities. First of all, Korean firms have become much more customer-oriented than before and more attentive to customers' needs. Many firms take "value creation for customers" as their marketing motto. Major consumer electronics firms have recently established lifestyle research institutes which are monitoring customers' changing needs and providing new product ideas to product development departments. Many new products specifically designed for Korean customers are being developed.

Another change in domestic marketing activity has been the reinforcement of logistics systems to shorten the delivery time to customers and the expansion of service networks to improve the quality of customer services. As Korean firms now have to compete with better quality and better designed foreign products, they have found it necessary to create their own competitive advantages in other parts of value chain such as outbound logistics and after-sale services. In other words, they are trying to offset disadvantages in product differentiation with strength in service differentiation.

A third major marketing activity undertaken to compete with foreign rivals has been the strengthening of their marketing channels. They are not only enlarging the size of their retail outlets in order to carry wider product lines and sufficient inventories, but also increasing the number of retail shops and specializing them according to product lines carried (i.e. audio/video, white goods, etc.). All these changes in marketing strategies reflect Korean firms' changed attitude toward consumer needs. Korean firms are learning the importance of customer value through the threat of foreign imports.

Although I listed above strategic responses in marketing mostly to globalization forces, it has to be noted that, unlike global class firms, Korean firms have not gone far enough to initiate global launching of world class products or global standardization programs in marketing due to their limited experience in international marketing and lack of technological capabilities. They are at the stage of beginning to recognize the importance of world class brand identity.

Meanwhile, there have been also some efforts in responding to the regionalization trend. Especially in the integrated European market, some companies are setting up local design centers to develop products which conform to local tastes instead of simply modifying domestic or American export models. However, this kind of effort has been pursued only on an ad hoc basis so far. More localization attempts are to be expected in the future in international marketing activities as part of companies' attempts to be "insiders" in target countries.

Table 7.7 Strategic responses of Korean firms

Major value activity	*Salient responses*	*Major environmental forces*
Production	1 FDI in DCs	R
	2 FDI in LDCs	R/G
	3 Oligopolistic reaction in FDI	G
	4 Rationalization in production	G
	5 Collaboration among domestic firms	G
R&D	1 Diversification of technology sourcing	G
	2 Formation of strategic alliances with foreign firms	G
	3 Cooperation among domestic firms in technlogy	G
Marketing	1 Emphasis on brand image	G
	2 Reinforcement of domestic marketing	G
	3 Local design	R

Note: G = globalization forces; R = regionalization forces

III CONCLUSION

From the overall observations on the strategic responses of Korean electronics firms to the conflicting forces of globalization and regionalization, we can recognize that Korean firms tend to feel more pressure from globalization forces, which are mostly driven by the competitive behaviors of global firms. Specifically, the global technology war and ensuing technology protectionism, strategic alliances among major global players, and domestic market opening pressures render great threats to Korean firms.

As a result, Korean firms' recent strategic responses in major value activities such as production, marketing and R&D are mostly formulated to accommodate globalization forces (Table 7.7). Only in the limited dimensions of production (FDIs in developed countries) and marketing (local design adaptation) strategies are Korean firms responding to the regionalization forces. It seems to be very natural behavior if we consider the high globalization potential of this industry in accordance with the Yip's industry drivers model (Yip, 1992). It is also interesting to note that Korean firms are relatively more sensitive to globalization forces in upstream activities such as R&D and more sensitive to regionalization forces. In downstream activities such as production and marketing, which

confirms the past research on global competition (Takeuchi and Porter, 1986; Doz, 1987).

Another major observation on the strategic responses of Korean firms is that strategic alliances with foreign or domestic firms are no more the monopoly of global giants. It seems that strategic alliances have become an indispensable weapon, even for small firms from the minor league. We have seen that Korean firms have resorted to cooperation schemes widely in R&D, production and marketing in response to the globalization forces. In fact, it seems that strategic alliances have become a way of life for any firm that has to compete in a globalizing industry. The only difference is that the strategic alliance is utilized as a defensive strategic weapon rather than an offensive one in the case of Korean firms. As such, strategic alliances seem to be established as a legitimate area of business research.

A third major observation is that Korean firms are not yet so advanced as to utilize the global networking game which becomes the core strategy in the globalizing industry. Due to their early stage of internationalization, Korean firms have not yet built up the internal capability to run such a network, even if they currently possess multiple production, R&D and marketing operations overseas. In future competition in a globalizing industry, not only the locations of separate plants, but also the linkage between them will be important in order to achieve the economies of scope advantage. The major competitive advantage in the global industry does not lie in economies of scale but in economies of scope. Korean firms may have to develop a global production and sourcing network among their multiple plants scattered around the globe.

A few policy implications for the future strategic direction can be derived from the above analysis. One is that Korean firms may have to develop some solid complementary assets in technology, production or marketing as fast as possible in order not to be excluded from the global strategic alliance game between major players, which will become more prevalent in the future in the technologically intensive global electronics industry.

Another implication is that Korean firms may need to foster "soft" know-how to manage the global or regional networks of their operations scattered around the globe (Simon, 1995b). As the internationalization process accelerates, Korean firms will develop a wider network of foreign operations. Then, the strategic task facing them will be to coordinate efficiently the multiple flows of tangible and intangible goods in the network. This coordinating capability will be a determining factor in the future global business game.

Though this chapter has suggested an insight into the strategic behavior of Korean firms in an industry which is heavily exposed to both globalization and regionalization forces, it leaves many areas to be researched further in the future. One possible area of future research is to analyze the process of harmonizing the two conflicting forces of globalization and regionalization within Korean firms. Given the reality of having to face the two forces, it would be interesting to see how firms adjust the configuration of their major value activities and what kind of coordination mechanisms they invent to handle management issues deriving from such a configuration. Another area of research would be to compare firms' behavior in different industries. It may be expected that the behavior of firms in the very competitive industries, such as apparels or athletic shoes, will be quite different from those of firms in the oligopolistic industries such as electronics or automobiles.

REFERENCES

Baden-Fuller, C. and J. M. Stopford, "Why global manufacturing?," *Multinational Business*, No. 1 (1988), pp. 15–25.

Bartlett, Christopher A., "Global competition and MNC managers," Harvard Business School Case Study no. 02163, 1985.

Behrman, J. N. and W. A. Fischer, "Transnational corporations: market orientations and R&D abroad," *Colombia Journal of World Business* (Fall, 1980), pp. 55–60.

Daniels, J. D. and Lee H. Radebaugh, *International Business*, 6th edn (Reading, Mass.: Addison Wesley, 1992).

De Meyer, A. and A. Mizuhima, "Global R&D management," *R&D Management*, Vol. 19, No. 2 (April, 1989), pp. 135–46.

Douglas, S. P. and Y. Wind, "The myth of globalization," *Colombia Journal of World Business* (Winter, 1987), pp. 19–29.

Doz, Y. L., "International industries: fragmentation vs globalization," in Bruce K. Guile and Harvey Brooks (eds), *Technology and Global Industry* (Washington, DC: National Academy Press, 1987), pp. 96–118.

Ghoshal, S. and C. A. Bartlett, "Innovation process in multinational corporations," Proceedings of the Symposium on Managing Innovation in Large Complex Firms, INSEAD, Fontainebleau (September, 1987).

Graham, E. M., "Intra-industry direct investment, market structure, firm rivalry and technological performance," in A. Erdilek (ed.), *Multinationals as Mutual Invaders* (London: Croom Helm, 1985).

Hymer, S. and R. Rowthorn, "Multinational corporations and international oligopoly: the non-America challenge," in C. P. Kindleberger (ed.), *The International Corporation: A Symposium* (Cambridge, Mass.: MIT Press, 1970).

Hout, T., M. E. Porter and E. Rudder, "How global companies win out," *Harvard Business Review* (September–October, 1982), pp. 98–108.

Jain, S. C., "Standardization of international marketing strategy: some research hypotheses," *Journal of Marketing*, Vol. 53 (1989), pp. 70–9.

Jun, Y., "The structural analysis of the global consumer electronics industry and the oligopolistic behavior of Korean firms in their internationalization," KIET Occasional Paper, No. 88–07 (May, 1988).

Jun, Y., "Korean overseas investment: patterns, characteristics and strategic behavior," *TNC Review* (New York: United Nations, 1990).

Knickerbocker, F. T., *Oligopolistic Reaction and Multinational Enterprise* (Cambridge, Mass.: Division of Reserach, Graduate School of Business Administration, Harvard University, 1973).

Kogut, B., "Normative observations on the international value-added chain and strategic groups," *Journal of International Business Studies* (Fall, 1984), pp. 151–67.

Kogut, B., "Designing global strategies: comparative and competitive value-added chains," *Sloan Management Review* (Summer, 1985), pp. 15–28.

Levitt, T., "The globalization of markets," *Harvard Business Review* (May–June, 1983), pp. 92–102.

Ohmae, K., "Becoming a Triad Power: the new global corporation," *Mckinsey Quarterly* (Spring, 1985), pp. 7–20.

Ohmae, K., "Managing in a borderless world," *Harvard Business Review* (May–June, 1989), pp. 152–61.

Porter, M. E., *Competitive Advantage* (New York: The Free Press, 1985).

Porter, M. E., "Changing patterns of international competition," *California Management Review*, Vol. 28, No. 2 (Winter, 1986), pp. 9–40.

Porter, M. E. and Mark B. Fuller, "Coalition and global strategy," in M. E. Porter (ed.), *Competition in Global Industries* (Cambridge, Mass.: Harvard Business School, 1986), pp. 315–44.

Prahalad, C. K. and Y. L. Doz, *The Multinational Mission* (New York: The Press Press, 1987).

Simon, Denis Fred (ed.), *The Emerging Technological Trajectory of the Pacific Rim* (Armonk, New York: M. E. Sharpe, 1995a).

Simon, Denis Fred et al., *Globalization, Korean-style: the emergence of Samsung as a world class corporation* (Boston, Mass.: Harvard Business School Press, 1995b).

Takeuchi, H. and M. E. Porter, "Three roles of international marketing in global strategy," in M. E. Porter (ed.), *Competition in Global Industries* (Cambridge, Mass.: Harvard Business School, 1986), pp. 111–46.

Vernon, R., "International investment and international trade in the product life cycle," *Quarterly Journal of Economics* (May, 1966), pp. 190–207.

Yip, G, S., *Total Global Strategy* (Englewood Cliffs, NJ: Prentice-Hall, 1992).

8 Strategic responses of Taiwanese firms to globalization

Chi Schive

INTRODUCTION

Judging from its development record following World War II, Taiwan had one of the most dynamic economies in the developing world, if not the most dynamic one. The evidence can be found in a wide variety of sources, such as GNP growth rates, health and welfare indicators, income distribution, economic stability, and various measures of structural change.[1] It may be argued further that the speed of change, or progress, of Taiwan's economy has not slowed down in the last decade. On the contrary, Taiwan's economy has gone through an unprecedented restructuring process on all fronts. Its economy has become more liberalized and internationalized through a series of reform and adjustment; even its political reform has achieved a high degree of success during this time. As far as the trade issue is concerned, although Taiwan did not increase its dependence on trade as measured by the trade to GNP ratio in the 1980s, it had accumulated the world's largest foreign exchange reserves by the end of 1991, even larger than Japan. The persistent trade surplus during that period created a significant degree of pressure on the NT (New Taiwan) dollar, and it did push the NT dollar to appreciate against the US dollar by more than 50 percent over a short period of four years, beginning in 1986. A severe impact on Taiwan's economy was therefore expected.

All local companies in Taiwan, regardless of their size, faced different challenges in this new economic environment, although opportunities did exist simultaneously. The first impact hit traditional, labor intensive, export-oriented manufacturers, who were damaged by the strong NT dollar plus rising wages. The situation for local market-oriented producers was relatively better because of the expanding local market. Nevertheless, gradually introduced trade liberalization reforms, beginning in 1985, have reduced protection in the domestic market, and an intensified competition from imports at a lower price than before can be felt everywhere. On the opportunity side, local companies with or without foreign links, helped by strong local currency, have become interested in taking actions to form foreign ventures. The first group of countries targeted for Taiwanese investors were ASEAN countries. There were a variety of reasons, abundant low wage labor being a particular one although, the United States still attracted a large amount of Taiwan's capital for its lucrative market and as a major supplier of new technology. Then, after the melting down of the political tension between the two sides of the Taiwan Strait, mainland China quickly became a new frontier for Taiwan's entrepreneurs. The size of the private long-term capital outflow, estimated at 4 percent of GNP in 1990, or 6.16 percent if the short-term capital is included, was outstanding compared to any Western economy. Last but not least, the undervalued NT dollar was corrected in the foreign exchange market and the bilateral trade negotiations between the United States and Taiwan have forced Taiwan to diversify its trade. The emerging single market in Europe, the reunion of West and East Germany, and the collapse of the non-market economy in East Europe all represent new market opportunities for Taiwan's traders.

No matter how regionalism and globalism are defined, Taiwan has experienced significant changes in economic relations with other countries over a short period of time. Foreign operations are no longer the privilege of large companies. Small and medium-sized businesses (SMEs) also play an active role in this new game. This chapter is aimed at exploring how Taiwan's firms have managed to accommodate all these challenges and changes.

The following section will examine Taiwan's new economic environment as it emerged in the 1980s. Some unique features during this period will be pointed out, such as the unbalanced economy, the quickly adjusted exchange rate, and trade liberalization reforms. The next section will describe the process of Taiwanese firms becoming "multinational", namely, the gradually emerging large international companies and the new wave of SMEs. In order to have a better view of how a large company reacts to the emerging new world, and to the globalization trend in particular, a company case study of Tatung will be presented. As Taiwan attempts to build up its financial strength in this region, some interesting developments are under way. Several foreign companies have tried to list themselves in the local stock market. By doing so, a foreign company is localized not by national authority, but by market force. A profound result is expected. Moreover, some international giants are considering Taiwan for their regional centers to take advantage both of Taiwan's financial strength and its ideal geographic location in order to improve competitiveness in this region.

THE EMERGING NEW ECONOMIC ENVIRONMENT

An unbalanced domestic economy in the 1980s

Taiwan's rapid economic growth in the 1980s, averaging approximately 7.9 percent per annum, was characterized by large trade and savings surpluses. Statistical data shows that the exports over GNP ratio remained about 52 percent between 1980 and 1983, then increased to 56 percent in 1986 and 1987 (see Table 8.1). But the imports over GNP ratio declined steadily until 1987. The net effect is clear: Taiwan started to deviate from balanced trade in 1980 and began accumulating a rapidly growing trade surplus. By 1986, the trade surplus accounted for 19.3 percent of GNP, which was not only a record level for Taiwan, but was also unparalleled among other trade surplus non-oil producing countries, West Germany and Japan for example. Although this figure dropped sharply to 5.8 percent in 1990, and further down to 4.8 percent in 1991, bringing

Table 8.1 External imbalance in Taiwan's economy 1980–91

Year	*(1) Exports/GNP*	*(2) Imports/GNP*	*(3) External imbalance (1)–(2)*
1980	52.6	53.8	–1.2
1981	52.2	50.2	2.0
1982	50.2	45.0	5.2
1983	53.0	44.4	8.6
1984	55.6	44.5	11.1
1985	53.3	39.8	13.5
1986	56.7	37.4	19.3
1987	56.4	39.3	17.1
1988	53.4	42.6	10.8
1989	49.2	41.6	7.6
1990	46.5	40.7	5.8
1991	47.0	42.2	4.8

Source: Quarterly National Economic Trends, Taiwan Area, the Republic of China (Directorate-General of Budget, Accounting and Statistics, Executive Yuan, Republic of China, various issues).

more balance to the import and export figures, the trade imbalance still raises serious problems.

The adjustment of exchange rate

When exploring the cause of the imbalance, a market disequilibrium is most likely attributable to a malfunctioning of the price system. In the external trade sector, the price is exchange rate. Figure 8.1 presents Taiwan's balance of payments as well as two measures of Taiwan's "real effective exchange rate" (REER) given in reciprocal terms and weighted by exports as well as total trade respectively. By taking into account both the changes in nominal exchange rates and price variations in Taiwan's major trade partners, the reciprocal of the REER of the NT dollar reflects the competitiveness of Taiwan's exports (imports) in the international (domestic) market. That is to say that a weak NT dollar encourages Taiwan's exports, other things being equal, and creates a trade surplus, and vice versa.

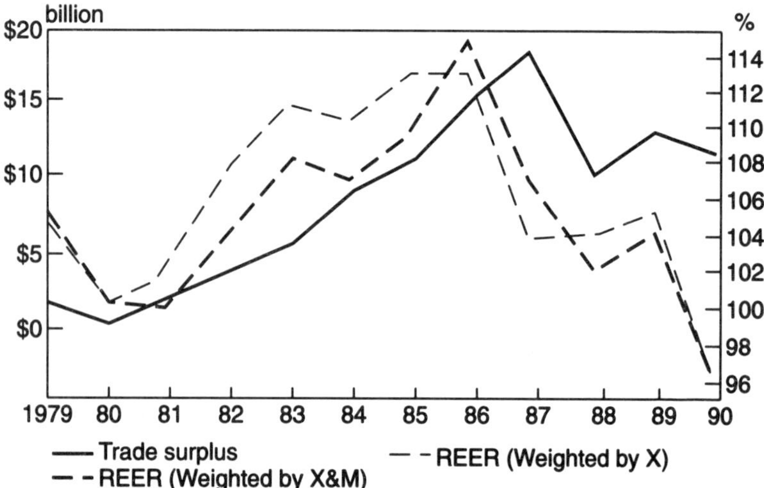

Figure 8.1 Trade surplus and the REER, 1979–90

Sources: Tainwan Statistical Data Book (Council for Economic Planning and Development, ROC, 1991); Hon Li-chun, "A study of the real effective exchange index of the NT dollar," paper presented at the 1988 annual meeting of the Chinese Economic Association, Taipei, and updated from the same author

Notes: X = exports; M = imports

The three curves shown in Figure 8.1 all move in a similar fashion.[2] It is evident that Taiwan's booming exports in the early 1980s have benefited from the weak NT dollar. As a result of this, the sharp appreciation of the NT dollar solely against the US dollar since the middle of 1986 was basically a means to correct the undervalued NT dollar by taking into account all the currency movements of Taiwan's major trading partners. A recent study in both Japan and Taiwan also suggests that "the balance of trade is more important than the balance of payments or the purchasing power parity (ppp) rate in determining the movements of the real exchange rate" (Sato and Lii, 1991).

The Taiwanese economy has been adjusting to the imbalances of the 1980s quite well (see Schive, 1991). It is no doubt that the major source for adjustment came from the sharp appreciation of the NT dollar. Table 8.2 indicates that the unit labor cost measured by the US dollar in Taiwan remained relatively stable between 1981 and 1985. However, since 1986 the unit labor cost index for Taiwan has increased so quickly that the country indeed has faced the highest surge of labor cost compared to all major industrial countries. For instance, when the index of unit labor cost stayed at 167 in 1988, the same figure for Korea was 101, and 136 for Japan. Because the comparison of labor cost among different countries is made on the dollar base after taking into account the variations of exchange rates, wage rate, and labor productivity, the index reflects the effect on the international competitiveness of each country from the variation of exchange rates, other things being equal. As a matter of fact, this argument is more applicable to the labor intensive export-oriented industries. Thus, it will not be too difficult to see how these industries or firms were affected by such a sharp change in their daily operational conditions.

Trade liberalization

When Taiwan began experiencing a persistent trade surplus in 1980 and thereafter, the surplus was mainly attributable to the US market. By 1987 Taiwan was the fourth largest supplier of goods and services for the United States, or the sixth largest market for US products. For several years Taiwan was the second largest creditor, second only to Japan, in financing the US trade deficit. On the Taiwan side, the United States absorbed nearly 50 percent of Taiwan's total exports, although this percentage figure has been going down stably and quickly and was below 30 percent in 1991. Given the trade

Table 8.2 Unit labor cost in US dollars, 1980–91

Unit%

Year	*Taiwan*	*Japan*	*Korea*	*US*	*UK*	*France*	*W. Germany*	*Netherlands*	*Canada*	*Denmark*	*Belgium*	*Norway*	*Sweden*	*Italy*
1980	87	107	104	87	118	125	124	127	83	126	155	110	130	117
1981	97	114	100	94	112	109	104	103	89	108	126	105	120	103
1982	100	100	100	100	100	100	100	100	100	100	100	100	100	100
1983	97	103	94	98	86	93	95	92	99	93	86	93	84	99
1984	108	99	90	96	77	87	86	77	91	87	79	85	81	89
1985	112	97	88	97	77	88	85	76	88	90	81	86	85	88
1986	127	142	83	97	91	117	120	104	91	128	110	110	109	116
1987	160	157	91	94	103	138	156	130	99	167	129	132	130	138
1988	170	173	112	92	112	138	160	130	111	170	126	141	141	140
1989	192	161	153	93	106	128	150	119	123	160	122	130	146	143
1990	199	–	160	–	–	–	–	–	–	–	–	–	–	–
1991	200	–	163	–	–	–	–	–	–	–	–	–	–	–

Source: Monthly Labor Review, Department of Labor, Bureau of Labor Statistics, US; *Monthly Bulletin of Earnings and Productivity Statistics*, Directorate-General of Budget, Accounting and Statistics, Executive Yuan, ROC.

Table 8.3 Trade liberalization in Taiwan

Unit: %

Year	*Average nominal tariff rate*	*Average real tariff rate*
1980	31.17	9.00
1984	30.81	7.72
1986	22.83	7.67
1988	12.79	6.13
1990	8.15	4.96
1991	7.54	4.00[a]
1992	6.60[a]	3.50[a]

Source: Import Tariff Analysis Tables, Ministry of Finance, Taipei, Japan, 1992.

Note: [a] Estimated figures.

imbalance situation, meetings on trade issues were constantly held between the two governments in the 1980s. One significant result of the meetings was that the Chinese government on Taiwan committed itself to lowering the tariff burden, i.e. the actually collected tariff over the total value of imports, to 3.5 percent by 1992, which is equivalent to the existing protection level of the OECD countries.

Table 8.3 indicates that Taiwan did try very hard to bring down the tariff protection level in the 1980s, especially in the second half of that period. The average nominal tariff rate stayed above 30 percent before 1984. In the two years between 1985 and 1986, the average nominal tariff rate was reduced from 30.81 percent to 22.83 percent. It was further cut to 12.78 percent in 1988. As far as the average real tariff rate is concerned, it did not start going down until 1986.[3] It can now be claimed that Taiwan has finally got rid of tariff protection as a major means for promoting its industrial development. Moreover, Taiwan also moved into abolishing several non-tariff protections, such as a discriminatory treatment of harbor dues against import and an upward-biased price imputation for dutiable goods. Restrictions and regulations on foreign investment were either removed or made more liberal. In short, Taiwan has been opening up its domestic market at an unprecedented speed.

The direct impact from a series of trade liberalization reforms can be read from the continuous decline of import prices. During the six-year period between 1986 and 1991, the import price index went down 27.18 percent totally, or 4.5 percent per annum. The sharply reduced price of imported goods had to intensify the competition in those import-competing industries to a degree never experienced before, which helped stabilize the domestic general price level.

THE PROCESS OF BECOMING "MULTINATIONALS"

A multinational company does not grow up over night. Taiwanese companies follow general patterns when they change their role and become more active players in international business. The first type are those gradually emerging, large, local companies that went abroad but gained little public attention. The second are the thousands of companies, most of them SMEs, that have invested in the ASEAN countries and mainland China.

The birth of large Taiwanese multinational corporations

Officially, the first Taiwanese outward investment was made in 1959 when a local firm invested $100,000 worth of machinery in a Malaysian cement plant. After a lull of two years, a jute-bag manufacturer restarted Taiwan's capital outflow in 1962 by setting up a plant in Thailand. Throughout the 1960s, Taiwan's direct foreign investment hovered around $800,000 annually, and then $5.17 million in the 1970s. However, the average annual capital outflow of direct investment amounted to $306 million in the 1980s; the average annual growth rate excluding abnormal years was 83.7 percent between 1981 and 1991. Thus, we may divide Taiwan's outward investment into two subperiods, before and after 1980.

By the end of 1981, the government had approved a total of 163 investment applications; of these firms, forty-eight (29 percent) were by then no longer in existence (Schive, 1990a: Ch. 7). This can be taken as evidence that the foreign operation of Taiwanese companies is highly risky.

Taiwan's investors went abroad before 1980 for four primary reasons: (1) to secure supplies of raw materials; (2) to pursue profits by supplying host-country markets; (3) to facilitate exports; and (4) to have access to technology in its country of origin. The first reason probably plays the least important role except for some plywood producers, fishing companies and canned foods producers. The second motivation can best describe the behavior of those investors in the food and beverage, textiles, plastics and plastic-products, and non-metallic materials (basically cement) industries. Their interest is to supply the domestic markets of the host countries. The third motivation refers to those companies which set up foreign trading offices or factories assembling semi-finished products for the local market. The existing trade barriers between Taiwan and its trading partners encouraged such a move. Another way to penetrate the fenced markets of major trading partners, particularly those with quota systems, is "quote hopping." Taiwanese export companies may set up offshore production in other countries to bypass quota restrictions. This has been the case for Taiwan's light industry investment in Latin America, the Caribbean, Singapore, and even in some French colonies aiming at the European market. The fourth motivation is limited to those ventures in developed countries, especially in the high-technology area. More on this point will be discussed later.

To say that Taiwan's outward investments were relatively small in size before 1980 in general, probably with the exception of Formosa Plastics[4] and Tatung's ventures, does not imply that Taiwanese multinational corporations (TMNCs) themselves were also small. Theories formulated by Hymer (1966), Kindleberger (1968) and Caves (1971) suggest that when a firm owns intangible assets such as knowledge, which is difficult to patent effectively but relatively easy to move from one national market to another, it will prefer to exploit them through direct foreign investment rather than through licensing or direct exports. When the firm is operating in an oligopolistic environment, with a limited market and keen competition, its desire to go multinational will be further intensified. The relatively large fixed information cost required before a large firm is ready to develop such assets internationally provides still more incentive to expand abroad.

Data on the relative size of Taiwanese MNCs before 1980, shown in Table 8.4, confirms this theory on the size of MNCs. With the exception of firms in timber and bamboo products, metals and construction industies, the largest companies in all the industries listed became multinational sooner or later. In the metals industry, a nut maker and a welding rod manufacturer were the largest companies in their specific areas. Moreover, all but five Taiwanese MNCs were among the top 500 companies in Taiwan when they went multinational. Many large companies not engaged in foreign ventures were either subsidiaries of foreign companies themselves, or they were public enterprises.

New wave in the 1980s – small and medium businesses going abroad

Although large Taiwanese firms have gone multinational since the late 1960s, outward investment did not become an overwhelming movement until recently. According to the outward investment data on the approval base, in 1986 the amount was US$56.9 million, and

Table 8.4 Relative size of Taiwanese multinational corporation, by industry
Unit: %

Industry	*Rank of firm in industry (by sales)*	*Rank of firm among Taiwan's top 500 firms (by sales)*
Food and beverages	1, 2, 8, X, X[a]	11, 19, 63, 101, 125
Fiber	1	5
Textiles	1, 3, 7, X, X, X, X	6, 54, 170, 366, 453, 483, Y[b]
Textile printing and dyeing	1	50
Lumber and bamboo products	2, 7	75, 161
Plastic products	1, 4, 6	1, 87, 129
Chemicals	1, 2, 5,10	2, 18, 65, 142
Cement	1, 2, 8	7, 16, 179
Glass	1	66
Metals	6, 9, 10, X, X	196, 244, 261, 308, Y
Machinery and equipment[c]	1, X	97, 130
Cable and wire	1, 2	23, 24
Electrical and electronics	1, 3, 5, X, X	4, 9, 17, 143, Y
Construction	1, 2, X	430, Y
Trade	1, 69	57, 731
Retail and service	1, X	50, Y

Sources: China Credit Investigation Co., Top 500 Firms in Taiwan, 1980; primary data.

Notes: [a] X = not among top ten firms in the industry.
[b] Y = not among Taiwan's top 500 firms.
[c] Excluding transportation equipment.

since then investment has doubled every year, reaching US$1,552 million in 1990, and US$1,656 million in 1991. Even so, the figures of investment from Taiwan capital outflow has been far more significant than just shown.

Table 8.5 reveals Taiwan's investment in ASEAN countries (apart from Singapore) over the last five years in both the amount approved by the Taiwan government and by the respective local governments. The dispairty is more than 100 times in some cases. For instance, the official approved data of investment in Indonesia was US$1.9 million in 1988, but according to Indonesia government sources investment from Taiwan reached US$910 million. The same figures in 1989 were US$0.3 million and US$158 million respectively. Taiwain's investment in these four ASEAN countries amounted to US$2.17 and US$1.99 billion in 1988 and 1989 respectively on the

Table 8.5 Taiwan's investment in ASEAN countries: amount approved by Taiwan and local authorities

Unit: US$ million; ( ) number

Year	*Thailand*		*Malaysia*		*Philippines*		*Indonesia*	
	Taiwan approved	*Local approved*	*Taiwan approved*	*Local approved*	*Taiwan approved*	*Local approved*	*Taiwan approved*	*Local approved*
1987	5.4	300.0	5.8	47.4	2.6	9.0	1.0	7.9
	(5)	(102)	(5)	(37)	(3)	(18)	(1)	(3)
1988	11.9	842.0	2.7	307.3	36.2	109.9	1.9	913.0
	(15)	(308)	(5)	(111)	(7)	(86)	(3)	(17)
1989	51.6	871.0	158.6	815.0	66.3	148.7	0.3	158.0
	(23)	(214)	(25)	(191)	(13)	(190)	(1)	(50)
1990	149.4	761.0	184.9	2383.0	123.6	140.7	61.9	618.0
	(39)	(144)	(36)	(270)	(16)	(158)	(18)	(94)
1991	86.4	567.6	442.0	1314.2	1.3	11.6	160.3	1056.5
	(33)	(69)	(35)	(182)	(2)	(109)	(25)	(57)

Source: Investment Commission, Ministry of Economic Affairs, *Outward Investment Analysis Report* (Taipei, 1991)

basis of host country data. That investment in 1990 was $3.90 billion. Although the approval figures from the host countries may be an overestimation of the actual capital outflow to a certain degree, Taiwan's outward investment is by no means negligible. As far as the number of investors is concerned, there have been a total of 160, 522, 645, 666 and 417 investment applications approved by these five ASEAN countries in the four consecutive years since 1987. Certainly many of these investments were not taken by large corporations.

Another new territory for Taiwanese investment capital is mainland China. In the 1980s Taiwan began a completely new relation with the mainland. Given the very low labor cost in the mainland, the coastal provinces such as Kwangtung and Fukien are ideal places for Taiwan's capital and technology in locating labor intensive industries. Table 8.6 confirms this point strongly. There are several unique features in Taiwan's investment in mainland China. First, although initially a small number, the number of investments in mainland China outpaced those in ASEAN countries in 1989. However, as far as the total amount of capital committed is concerned, ASEAN countries were still ahead of mainland China in attracting Taiwanese capital. One implication is that the scale of Chinese ventures was smaller than that of ASEAN countries. As a matter of fact, the average size of investment in the mainland is about US$1 million, compared to US$6 million in the ASEAN countries. The concern over risk and the lack of language and cultural obstacles in the neighboring "host country" can explain the cautious yet active behavior of Taiwanese investors in the mainland.

The analysis of these new waves of going abroad can be carried out further with respect to industrial distribution,[5] market orientation, organizational structure, and relations with the parent companies. It is clear that SMEs, instead of large companies, dominated the latest wave of outward investment. Their impact is quite discernible in Taiwan's industrial and trade structure (see Schive, 1991). Taiwan is moving very quickly from being a major supplier of many consumer nondurables to a major source for materials, semi-finished products, machinery and equipment. In addition to serving as a funding center for capital, Taiwan has also become a "regional" center for technology and information. The two-way flows of trade between Taiwan and the ASEAN countries and mainland China, both visible and invisible, have increased very fast ever since the capital flow started.

Table 8.6 Taiwan's cumulative investment in the mainland, 1987–92

	1987		*1988*		*1989*		*1990*		*1991*		*1992*	
Region	*Item*	*Negotiated amount*	*Item*	*Negotiated amount*	*Item*	*Negotiated amount*	*Item*	*Negotiated amount*	*Item*	*Negotiated amount*	*Item*	*Negotiated amount*
Total	80	1.0	435	5.2	982	10.37	2,099	20.21	3,800	34.1	10,200	89.7
Fukien	58	0.39	230	2.6	497	7.5–8.0	900	11.5	–	–	–	–
Shiah Men	20	0.2	120	1.65	231	6.44	357	9.9	–	–	–	–
Kwangtung	–	–	100	–	–	–	–	–	–	–	–	–
Shen Jiunn	11	–	38	0.86	–	–	–	–	–	–	–	–
Peking	–	–	22	0.84	–	–	27	2.42	–	–	–	–

Source: Chung-hwa Institution for Economic Research

A GROWING MULTINATIONAL AND EUROPE 1992: THE TATUNG COMPANY

Tatung's growth and its global strategies

Founded in 1918, Tatung Company is one of the oldest and largest companies in Taiwan. By 1990, the company registered a total capital of NT$8.5 billion, or roughly US$315 million, and sales of NT$51.0 billion, or roughly US$1.9 billion. The company has slightly more than 21,000 employees. At present the company stands as the seventh largest conglomerate in Taiwan, and the largest manufacturer in the electrical and electronics industry. It has eight subsidiaries and twelve overseas ventures, including liaison offices (see Table 8.7). The company's production lines were highly diversified in 1990: 60.5 percent of the total sales consisted of electronics, computers and communication; 13.5 percent belonged to industrial equipment; 17.6 percent to home appliances; and 4.1 percent was attributable

Table 8.7 Tatung's overseas investment, 1990

Company name	*Year of foundation*	*Location*	*Functions*
Tatung Co. of America	1972	Los Angeles	Marketing with an annual turnover of US$91 million
Tatung Science and Technology, Inc.	1983	San Jose	R&D
Tatung Co. of Japan, Inc.	1975	Tokyo	Marketing and procurement
Tatung Electronics (S) PTE Ltd.	1972	Singapore	Marketing
Chunghwa Picture Tubes Co. of Malaysia	1989	Malaysia	TV tubes
Tatung Company of Thailand, Inc.	1989	Thailand	TV manufacturing
Tatung Liaison Office ROK	1979	Seoul	Marketing
Tatung Liaison Office Australia	NA	Sydney	Marketing
Tatung (UK) Ltd.	1981	UK	Home appliances mfg
Tatung International Corp., SA	1981	Luxemburg	European headquarters
Tatung International (Deutschland) GmbH	1985	Düsseldorf	Marketing

Source: An Introduction to Tatung Co. (Taipei: Tatung Co., 1991)

to trade. Clearly the company has switched the production lines away from the traditional home appliances into high-tech products quickly over the years.

As shown in Table 8.7, the company became a native multinational corporation in 1972 and took the first move in Europe in 1981. In the early 1970s, Tatung began to establish a network of manufacturing subsidiaries in Japan, Singapore, Hong Kong, the United States, and Northern Ireland, in addition to a global network of sales and purchasing offices in Europe, the Middle East and Africa. By 1977, its overseas investments totaled about US$5 million. Tatung's entry into international business followed the classic pattern of development. Its success with exports led to outward technical cooperation and licensing of technical know-how and, subsequently, to direct investment. Its subsidiaries in Japan, Singapore, the US and Ireland primarily manufacture and assemble the same products, such as household appliances and electronic goods, with which it first attained domestic success.

Besides its manufacturing subsidiaries and its network of sales offices to service export markets, Tatung has also entered into technical cooperation agreements and joint ventures with local manufacturers in several less developed countries (LDCs). These cases include technical assistance agreements and joint-equity ventures in electrical household appliances in Indonesia and Malaysia.

A combination of factors seem to have spurred Tatung's multinationalization. The company's success in its domestic market appears to have provided the initial thrust, both by conferring upon it the ability to invest abroad and by engendering a need for it to internationalize in order to maintain an image of leadership and prestige among its competitors. A closely parallel reason was the reinforcement of its brand name in the international markets to which it had already been exporting. The immediate motive of circumventing the tariffs and quota restrictions of the EEC and high-tariff LDC markets may also have contributed to Tatung internationalizing its production. As European protectionism against Asian electronics exports went up, many Asian firms moved their plants to excess-quota countries in order to maintain their European sales from those locations. For instance, Tatung's television plant in Singapore was established both to circumvent the EEC quota and to supply completely knocked-down units to high-tariff countries in the region. Tatung's recent move into Iceland was motivated solely by the same goal.

Tatung's view on Europe 1992

The company unmistakenly has a global view which is followed through in its management strategies. The formation of a single market in Europe has had a broad and strong impact upon the company's policies. A recent interview of high ranking managers of the company indicated, first, that the company will concentrate its production more in Europe, rather than rely on import from the production elsewhere, including less developed countries.[6] Since 1992, the European market looks bright though the price competition will also be intensified. Second, as far as the subcontracting system is concerned, the size of firm in Europe will increase with more local subcontracts. As a result, more intra-market, instead of inter-market, trade will take place due to more investment taken by foreigners within the market. Third, it is felt that a certain degree of preferential treatment for EU firms will exist well beyond 1992, although fair trade will still be promoted and enforced.

The company itself will adopt strategies of low cost, product diversification, and more forward integration as a response to the new situation in Europe. More precisely, the company will push its product lines into a higher degree of automation, higher value-added products, larger scale, more sourcing from non-EU developed countries, and some relocations within the EU. On specific products, policies such as Euro-brand name and price competition will be adopted. The company will put more effort into R&D in relation to its EU operations to promote two-way technology flows between the host countries and homeland. This move is expected to have a long-term impact on the company's global operation. For the time being, no decision has been made on any investment plan in East Europe.

The impact of Europe 1992 on Taiwan

The formation of a unified single market in Europe in 1992, as believed and also illustrated by the Tatung case, has led to closer economic relations between Taiwan and European countries. As a matter of fact, the impact came sooner than expected. Aside from those favorable factors commonly discussed, such as the enlarged domestic market and purchasing power, the uniformity of the monetary system, and more cultural exchange programs, there are two promising developments on the Taiwan side which are in line with this trend.

First, as pointed out already, Taiwan has been under pressure to reduce its trade surplus with the US ever since the middle 1980s. As a result, Taiwan had to diversify its trade to other markets, of which Europe is an ideal target. Two-way flows of commodities and services between EU countries and Taiwan increased at 15 percent annually over the four years between 1988 and 1991. More interestingly, Taiwan's exports to West Germany grew at more than 20 percent during the same period, an indication that Taiwan's traders responded quickly to the new opportunities created by the unification of the two markets.

Second, as far as direct investment is concerned, European investors started making investments in Taiwan only in the 1960s and accounted for merely 7 percent of the total direct foreign investment in Taiwan, based on the approval data. Nevertheless, the percentage figure of investment share from Europe increased to 10 percent in the 1970s and to 17 percent in the 1980s. On the other hand, Taiwan's investment in Europe reached US$10.2 million in 1987 and jumped to US$265.9 million in 1990.[7] These promising developments paint a bright future for the prospects of Europe–Taiwan economic relations.

TAIPEI: A REGIONAL CENTER FOR FUNDING

Over the past thirty years or so the government has maintained an open and welcoming attitude to direct foreign investment, and the resulting inflow of DFI has made significant contributions to Taiwan's economy. In recent years the government has also begun to welcome other forms of foreign investment as part of its liberalization and internationalization policies. In order to promote internationalization of the securities market, to improve Taiwan's credit position in international financial markets, and to create channels for foreign portfolio investment in Taiwan, in 1983 the government permitted the establishment of four securities companies allowed to raise funds abroad for investing in the domestic stock market. In January of 1991 the government also opened the domestic securities market to foreign specialized investment firms. The next stage will be to permit foreigners to invest directly in the securities market.

In consideration of the steady trend toward a more open securities market, and also the need to utilize fully the abundant domestic capital, quite a few local subsidiaries of foreign firms have been seeking to go public in the local stock market. What sort of effect on the domestic economy would such a step have? What are the problems and implications? The next section will give brief analysis of these and related questions.[8]

Motivations for stock listing

Most companies have the following motivations to list on the stock-market: raising operating capital, increasing name recognition, taking advantage of preferential tax treatment, and giving management incentives. Foreign firms have additional motivations for stock market listing: changing the nature of the parent–subsidiary relationship to allow the subsidiary to become more independent, withdrawing capital for other uses, and earning capital gains in order to raise the stock price of the parent company. In recent years the richness of Taiwan's capital market, the enlargement of the local consumer market, the increased strength of R&D, the growing high-technology industries helped by the establishment of the science-based industrial park located in Hsinchu, and the progress of the East Asian regional economy have all combined to make stock market listing more attractive for foreign firms. High stock prices in Taiwan mean large capital gains for listing firms, while the increasing maturity of the local economy suggests that foreign subsidiaries need no longer be so closely tied to their parent companies.

Effect on domestic industry

Research on foreign subsidiaries has found that they are heavily dependent on foreign technology from their parent companies, that they rely on their parent companies for marketing information and marketing channels, and that they have a low propensity to buy domestically (Schive, 1990b). Therefore, if listing on the stock market leads to a substantial reduction in the equity share of the parent company, the likely effect is increased engagement in R&D, development of independent marketing information and channels, and greater domestic purchasing by the subsidiary. The increased proportion of domestic purchasing is likely to have backward linkage effects that can help promote the development of local materials and parts industries. Increased decision-making independence for foreign subsidiaries after stock market listing is also likely to increase flexibility and decrease the likelihood of a gradual loss in competitiveness.

The likely results pointed out above are not hypothetical, but are based on actual observations of foreign firms operating in Taiwan.

For example, foreign firms with majority ownership tended to buy less than those minority owned ones in the domestic materials markets (Schive, 1990b). Therefore, to lower the degree of foreign control will increase the incentive to buy more locally. Singer's famous investment in the 1960s was a good example of how the lack of decision independence could lead to a gradual loss of its competitiveness in the market. A foreign TV producer began its own R&D investment and even considered setting up its own foreign subsidiary right after the company was sold and the original tie to its giant international parent company was cut off. Thus, a far-reaching impact on the domestic economy is expected when a foreign firm becomes localized by shifting the ownership and management responsibility from foreigners to local investors.

There are several interesting change-of-hand cases taking place in the high-tech industry. For example, after the successful acquisition of American Wyse Technology by a group of local investors at the cost of US$270 million in 1989, the new company owners showed a great intereset in letting the company go public in the local market. If this becomes realized, it represents a new model of outward investment, i.e. the capital from the local stock market was mobilized to finance the acquisition of a foreign company. Another example is that Mosel, an American company producing IC at Silicon Valley, holds 51 percent of Taiwan Mosel's stock. In 1990 Taiwan Mosel raised a significant amount of capital in the local market and reduced the parent company's stock holding to 27 percent. Not waiting too long, Taiwan Mosel went a step further to buy up its founder in 1991. In this case a subsidiary grew up to become a parent company, and the original parent company became a subsidiary. There have also been cases where a foreign subsidiary has become completely independent from any foreign control.

Impact and implications

Foreign subsidiaires listing on the stock market can provide stock investment opportunities, expanding the scale of the stock market and increasing the choices available to average investors. But because of the close relations between the foreign parent and subsidiary, the effect on investors can be both advantageous and disadvantageous. Potential disadvantages include profit transfer from the subsidiary to the parent, the subsidiary being affected by problems of the parent company, and the parent company transferring its investments and cutting off its original assistance to the subsidiary.

As for the potential advantages, there is no shortage of large, structurally sound and reputable parent companies of foreign subsidiaries, meaning that investors often need not worry about the parent company encountering difficulties or acting opportunistically to the disadvantage of the subsidiary. In fact, investors can attain greater security in their investment since the parent company is well-positioned to offer assistance to the subsidiary if it encounters problems and certain connections can be maintained.

The general feeling on policy recommendation is that liberalizing rules for foreign subsidiaries listing on the stock market not only can promote the further internationalization of the securities market, increase the scale of the stock market, and effectively use foreign exchange, but it can also spur the development of local industry through linkage effects due to increased domestic purchasing by foreign subsidiaries as they become more localized. In addition, since foreign firms can list their Taiwanese subsidiary on the stock market, but maintain a controlling interest or a large stake, allowing foreign subsidiaries to be listed on the stock market can encourage foreign companies to make Taiwan play a more active role in their regional operations in the Asian Pacific.

The last implication is more significant given that the world is on the verge of forming several economic blocs. The government should attract European and American companies to make Taiwan their Asian Pacific regional operations center, one from which they can invest in other regional areas such as mainland China and South East Asia. This would help the government achieve its recognized need for internationalization and liberalization of foreign trade and assist its policy of developing Taiwan into the trade, finance, transportation, maintenance and even R&D center of the Asian Pacific. This may be the new role for Taiwan in the wake of the rapid fermentation of regionalization and globalization.

CONCLUSIONS

As Taiwan has integrated into the world economy during its rapid development process, there has been no difficulty for decision-makers both in the government and in the business community to understand the meaning of globalization or internationalization. In the 1980s, when Taiwan's economy went off balance, it solved the problem to a certain degree by investing heavily in neighboring countries. If this capital flow is part of the ingredient of the regionalization, then Taiwan's economy is also moving in this direction.

Therefore, both globalization and regionalization are essential characteristics of Taiwan's modern development. Taiwan's experience in this regard may offer some policy lessons for others. For example:

1 Internationalization does not imply the penetration of foreign markets only. It also means the constant effort to liberalize or deregulate existing government policies governing capital flows both inward and outward. The latter may be more effective and far more difficult to implement than the former, as shown in Taiwan's case.
2 Taiwan's outward investment began in the late 1960s. By 1980 Taiwanese MNCs, although they did not commit a large amount of capital in their foreign ventures, were large, old, and leading companies in their fields of specialty. A significant percentage of outward investment failed. It does take a long time to nurture a native multinational corporation.
3 If there are both push and pull factors driving a company to become a multinational, then the Taiwanese experience suggests that the "push" effect is more effective than the "pull". It may be argued that the "push" effect is a matter of survival while the "pull" effect is more on the incentive of growth or profit seeking.
4 To encourage native firms becoming "multinationals" does not mean the abandonment of those companies with difficulties at home. Many things can be done in order to smooth the capital outflow benefiting both home and host countries. For example, letting local banks expand their foreign operations, strengthening the local R&D capability and the supportive industries, even improving the local infrastructure may all benefit native "multinationals."
5 The new European Union presents both a challenge and an opportunity to Taiwan's enterpreneurs. Companies like Tatung are preparing fully for the significant changes ahead. Judging by the booming trade and investment between Europe and Taiwan over the past years, Taiwan may enjoy some lead in taking advantage of the rapidly growing single market in Europe.
6 Taiwan's abundant reserves of foreign exchange give it an excellent position to build up Taipei as a regional financial center. Many foreign companies have already taken advantage of this opportunity by listing their subsidiaries in the local stock market. World-famous giant companies are also considering making Taiwan their Pacific operation center for production, funding, mar-

keting, transportation, training and even R&D. The first inflow of capital and technology will lead to a series of outflows of capital and technology later by utilizing local resources. Whether this will be the new role for Taiwan in the coming decade depends on the government's further liberalizing policy, continuing effort to advance the domestic industrial base, infrastructures and, of course, on companies' strategy in response to the rapidly changing world economy.

NOTES

1 It would be a waste of space to cite the figure for all these measures, but readers who are interested in details may consult two data sources: *Taiwan Statistical Data Book, Republic of China* (Taipei: Council for Economic Planning and Development, Executive Yuan, 1991), and *World Development Report 1992* (Oxford: Oxford University Press, 1992). Taiwan's performance is consistently outstanding in comparison with others.

2 More precisely, a one-year time lag may be detected between the movement of the REERs and the trade imbalance. For instance, the first drop in the reciprocal of the REER in 1980 and then a six-year increasing trend of the reciprocal of the REER preceded the accumulation of the trade surplus, while a sharp reverse in the REER in 1989 did not dampen the trade surplus until a year later.

3 There are two reasons for the real tariff burden on imports being lower than the nominal tariff rate on the average base. First, tariff rates of many agricultural products and luxury goods were so high that no import actually took place, and hence no tariff revenue was collected. Second, Taiwan still maintained the tariff rebate system for a handful of products. No matter how tariff rates were cut, no tariff revenue was received and no impact would show on the tariff burden.

4 Formosa Plastics initiated a $24 million series of investments in the United States in 1980 with its acquisition of a vinylchloride monomer (VCM) plant. Part of the VCM produce was shipped back home. This investment, therefore, can be considered as taking advantage of low materials costs, i.e. the low prices of ethylene and energy.

5 In spite of the serious underward bias of Taiwan's approved outward investment data, those traditionally export-oriented, labor intensive industries have attracted most of Taiwan's direct investment capital in ASEAN countries and mainland China. For detail, see appendix.

6 The company interview is part of the project "Europe 1992 and Transnational Corporation" carried out by the United Nations Center on Transnational Corporations in cooperation with the Commission of the European Communities and the Japan External Trade Organization in 1990.

7 This figure to a significant extent is an overestimation of Taiwan's investment in Europe because a significant amount of the investment was concentrated on the territories governed by the UK, the Netherlands and Belgium to form a holding company, which, then, made a reinvestment

Appendix Taiwan's outward investment in ASEAN countries and mainland China by 1991, by industry

Unit: %

	ASEAN		*Mainland China*	
Industry	*Case*	*Amount*	*Case*	*Amount*
Total number of cases and amount	371	1,614,569	2,503	753,955
Primary	2.43	0.94	3.68	4.87
Manufacturing	81.92	96.30	92.36	86.79
foods and beverage	4.30	1.75	1.56	1.83
textile	8.89	6.29	3.16	4.51
garment and footwear	1.62	0.12	20.50	12.84
lumber, bamboo and rattan products	4.58	1.17	4.35	3.82
pulp, paper and products	2.43	6.00	3.32	3.06
leather and fur products	0.80	0.22	2.31	0.89
plastic and rubber products	5.93	3.87	8.19	9.19
chemicals	5.66	12.85	2.64	1.83
non-metallic products	4.58	11.42	12.62	14.16
basic metals and metal products	11.32	24.15	13.70	18.70
machinery equipment and instrument	2.43	0.85	1.88	2.77
electronic and electric appliances	27.22	26.79	1.48	1.77
others	2.16	0.82	16.65	11.42
Service	15.65	2.76	3.96	8.34
construction	2.16	1.14	0	0
trade	7.55	0.86	1.48	0.85
banking and insurance	2.43	0.23	0	0
transportation	1.08	0.15	0	0
service	2.43	0.38	2.48	7.49

Sources: Statistics on Overseas Chinese & Foreign Investment, Technical Cooperation, Outward Investment, Outward Technical Cooperation, the Republic of China (Investment Commission, Ministry of Economic Affairs, 1991); Investment Commission

Note: ASEAN countries include Philippines, Indonesia, Thailand and Malaysia

back home. This type of investment should be better considered as outward portfolio investment, instead of direct investment. More precisely, it represents domestic investment although with an international connection.

8 For details, see Hon and Schive (1993).

REFERENCES

Baker, H. Kent and M. Johnson, "A survey of management views on exchange listing," *Quarterly Journal of Business and Economics* 29, 4 (1990), pp. 3–20.

Caves, R. E., "International corporations: the industrial economics of foreign investment," *Economica*, 149 (Febuary, 1971), pp. 1–27.

Hon, C.-L. and C. Schive, "Listing of foreign companies in Taiwan," *Bank of Taiwan Quarterly*, 1 (1993) (in Chinese).

Hymer, S., *The International Operations of National Firms: A Study of Direct Foreign Investment* (Cambridge, Mass.: MIT Press, 1966).

Kindleberger, C. P., *American Business Abroad* (New Haven, Conn.: Yale University Press, 1968).

Sato, K. and S.-Y. Lii, "Exchange-rate deviation and trade flows in Japan and Taiwan," paper presented at the conference on US–Asia Economic Relations, Tokai University, Tokyo, June, 1991.

Schive, C., *The Foreign Factor: the multinational corporation's contribution to the economic modernization of the Republic of China* (Stanford: Hoover Press, 1990a).

Schive, C., "Linkages: do foreign firms buy locally in Taiwan?" *Asian Economic Journal*, 3 (1990b), pp. 1–15.

Schive, C., "How did Taiwan solve its Dutch disease problem?" paper presented at the conference on US–Asia Economic Relations, Tokai University, Tokyo, in *Journal of Asian Economics*, June, 1991.

9 Structural upgrading and concatenated integration

The vicissitudes of the Pax Americana in tandem industrialization of the Pacific Rim

Terutomo Ozawa

INTRODUCTION

The Asian economies, especially in the East and South East regions, are undergoing rapid structural changes both in production and consumption activities. These changes are not a mere summation of structural metamorphoses that are occurring separately in each individual economy, but are rather an interactively agglomerating phenomenon, a regional economic growth feeding on the synergistic interactions among the constituent economies through transborder business operations (trade and investment). There are clearly some motive forces at work in generating this type of *regionally clustered* industrial expansion or *regionalization* of economic activities. To paraphrase Michael Porter, who has studied the competitive advantages of both firms and nations (Porter, 1980, 1990), the competitive advantage of the Asian Pacific as a *region* seems to exist as a rather distinct phenomenon.

Elsewhere I have captured the elixir of Asian regional dynamism in terms of the concept of what may be called "economies of concatenation (or hierarcy)" by drawing upon the insights of Adam Smith (Ozawa, 1992a, 1992b). Smith observed:

> Private people who want to make a fortune, never think of retiring to the remote and poor provinces of the country, but resort either to the capital, or to some of the great commercial towns. They know that where little wealth circulates, there is little to be got; but that *where a great deal is in motion, some share of it may fall to them*. The same maxims which would in this manner direct the common sense of [individuals] ... should make a whole nation regard the riches of its neighbours as a probable cause and occasion for itself to acquire riches. A nation that would enrich itself by foreign trade, is certainly most likely to do so

> when its neighbours are *all rich and industrious* (Smith, 378; emphasis added).

Thus Smith explicitly recognized the economies of concatenation that exist in a hierarchically structured world of industrialization from the point of view of the less developed countries which, if properly motivated, can capitalize on gaps in incomes and productivity vis-à–vis the more advanced. In Smith's day, trade was the main form of international business operations, and foreign direct investment (international production as we know it today) obviously did not exist except in the nascent colonial type. He advocated free trade as a means of making the best use of the existing hierarchy of nations.

Moreover, relevant also is a similar observation made by Karl Marx: "The country that is more developed industrially only shows, to the less developed, the image of its own future."[1] For him, the cross-border spread of capitalism from the advanced to the less advanced was inexorable and unavoidable; it eventually would create the advanced countries' own competitors through the transmission of the capitalist mode of production to the less advanced.

Although these classic observations are intuitively very powerful and perspicacious, we need more detailed explanations of under what circumstances and how the less developed can catch up with – and in some cases, even surge ahead of – the more advanced "teacher" nations by exploiting the economies of concatenation. In other words, we need to specify *an operational causal mechanism through which the benefits of hierarchical relationships are generated and captured by the constituent members of a particular region or an economic bloc*. More specifically, we need to explain the process through which an advanced nation's superiority in industrial structure and technological progress is transmitted to lower-echelon nations within their hierarchy characterized by different stages of economic development. The staggered stages of industrial advancement within such a group of economies, when made the best use of by international commercial activities, can serve as a powerful environment in which a tandem industrialization of the entire group can ensue.

I posit that the dual phenomena, regionalization and globalization, with which we are concerned are the manifestations of the above-described fundamental integrative forces generated within the global hierarchy of economies, which are divided, at the top, into tripolar regions with their separate political economic systems: North

America, Europe, and Pacific Asia. Regionalization is proceeding in each of these regions, globalization basically *across* them. "Pure globalization" in the sense that economic activities spread *evenly* throughout the world has not, and will not, occur for the very reason that nations are at different stages of economic development in terms of factor endowments, technological sophistication, and demand conditions. They are pulled and pushed toward the tripolar centers (i.e. globalization) and into one particular center (regionalization) more deeply than into another. What may be called "triadized globalization" is, therefore, the reality.

The agenda for my analysis is as follows. The next section explores my basic theme that Asian Pacific regionalization of economic activities manifested in its industrial vibrance is the vicissitudinary outcome of the evolving Pax Americana, (the post-World-War-II global hierarchy) under which the dynamics of tandem industrialization have been set in motion throughout the region. The postwar period created the extremely favorable circumstances under which the economies of concatenation were purposefully disseminated by the United States as the leader of the liberal regime through trade, investment and technology transfers. These opportunities have been actively exploited by the constituent nations, first in Europe and then in the Asian Pacific – initially by Japan but soon by other Asian nations as well.

The third section elaborates on the industrial transfer mechanism of tandem industrialization in terms of the principle of increasing factor incongruity. Two channels – the "product-cycle" and the "structural upgrading" channels – are discussed.

The fourth section examines the common underlying motivational forces for the similar inter-temporal sequence of overseas investment waves by capitalist nations with the classical growth models as conceptual frameworks; the firms strive to prevent the profit squeeze (that causes growth stagnation) by escaping from the Ricardian bottlenecks via labor – and resource-seeking overseas investments and by searching for the Smithian growth *élan* via market expansion and technological progress, both at home and across national borders. It will be seen that Japanese corporations have so far largely found a way of escaping from the Ricardian bottlenecks in terms of their local business operations in the developing host countries, especially in Asia (as part of their *regionalization* efforts); and that they are also endeavoring to seek the Smithian growth *élan* mostly in the context of the tripolar growth centers (that is, through *triadized globalization* efforts).

THE VICISSITUDINARY UNFOLDING OF THE PAX AMERICANA

Why has so much industrial vibrancy and commercial outburst occurred in the Asian Pacific over the past three decades – early on in Japan, then in the Asian NIEs, and currently in some ASEAN countries in a sequence of strong chain reactions? Where has its *élan* of industrial expansion come from? I would maintain that it has emanated from the self-transformative – mostly self-consuming – internal mechanism of the Pax Americana, a hegemonic regime that came into existence at the end of World War II.

As a by-product of economic mobilization for the war effort and of the outcome of the war, the United States came to dominate the world in practically every industry as the victorious power whose economic infrastructure and industrial base had been not only left unscathed by war but rather vastly strengthened by its war-time quest for technological progress and manufacturing efficiency. In contrast, war-devastated Europe and Japan, America's closest rivals, were on their knees with their industries in a shambles. America's hegemony constituted the most powerful dynamo capable of transmitting growth impulses to its constituents, especially in the context of the Cold War and the postwar liberalization of international commerce – more powerful than the world had previously experienced, say, during the late eighteenth century and during the late nineteenth century. But the US dominance then was structurally an anomalous situation and was not expected to last long once normalcy was restored to the world economy.

The allies and the former enemies alike soon began to reconstruct their economies and engage in international commercial exchanges. Indeed, the United States, as the leader of the free world, "foresightedly" took the initiative to establish a liberal commercial world in which free trade, investment, and technological transfers were encouraged. The Marshall Plan and other magnanimous aid programs exemplified the concrete positive measures taken by the US to facilitate economic reconstruction.[2] America's industrial hegemony and leadership served as a nursery, as it were, for the quick recovery and miraculous economic growth, first of Europe and then of Japan.

And that is not the end of the story. The saga of American hegemony continues. More recently, the Asian NIEs (Hong Kong, Singapore, Taiwan, and South Korea), the new NIEs (Thailand, Malaysia, Indonesia, and the Philippines) and the "new" new NIEs

(China, Pakistan, India, Bangladesh, and Sri Lanka) have been benefiting from the still-reveberating dynamics of tandem industrialization set in train during the course of the vicissitudinary evolution of the Pax Americana, as detailed below. Indeed, the postwar world witnessed the golden age of capitalism, which some say lasted till the mid-1970s,[3] but which still lingers on throughout the Asian Pacific in a localized though often rejuvenated form. The "liberal regime" introduced by the United States at the conclusion of World War II (Krasner, 1983) has been increasingly embedded in the soil of the Asian Pacific and is strongly spreading.

This self-transformative motion of the Pax Americana as it relates to Japan and other Asian countries is illustrated in Figure 9.1. At the war's end, the US economy held competitive advantages in every industry; the world's industrial energy seemed stored only in America. It had a full set of *all* manufacturing industries, a complete set ranging from the technologically most sophisticated down to the labor-intensive standardized industries. The whole range of industries created since the Industrial Revolution was congregated and displayed in the United States. It was an unprecedented situation, indeed, in which one nation was so totally self-sufficient, so enviably affluent, and so dominantly powerful in every respect.

For analytical purposes, America's industrial colossus in the immediate postwar years can be vertically broken down into the four basic tiers distinguishable in declining order of capital–labor intensity and technological sophistication (Figure 9.1):

Tier 1 Innovation-intensive industries which may be identified as the "Schumpeterian" industries in which R&D and close customer orientation are the key inputs (e.g. aircarft, computers and other sophisticated electronic goods, and pharmaceuticals).

Tier 2 Assembly-based industries or the "differentiated Smithian" industries where product differentiation and scale/scope economies dominate (e.g. automobiles, TVs, and other consumer durables).

Tier 3 Heavy and chemical industries or the "undifferentiated Smithian" industries characterized by high resource-intensity and scale economies (e.g. steel, nonferrous metals, fertilizers, synthetic resins and fibers, and basic chemicals).

Tier 4 Labor-intensive light industries or the "Heckscher-Ohlin" industries in which unskilled/semi-skilled workers are

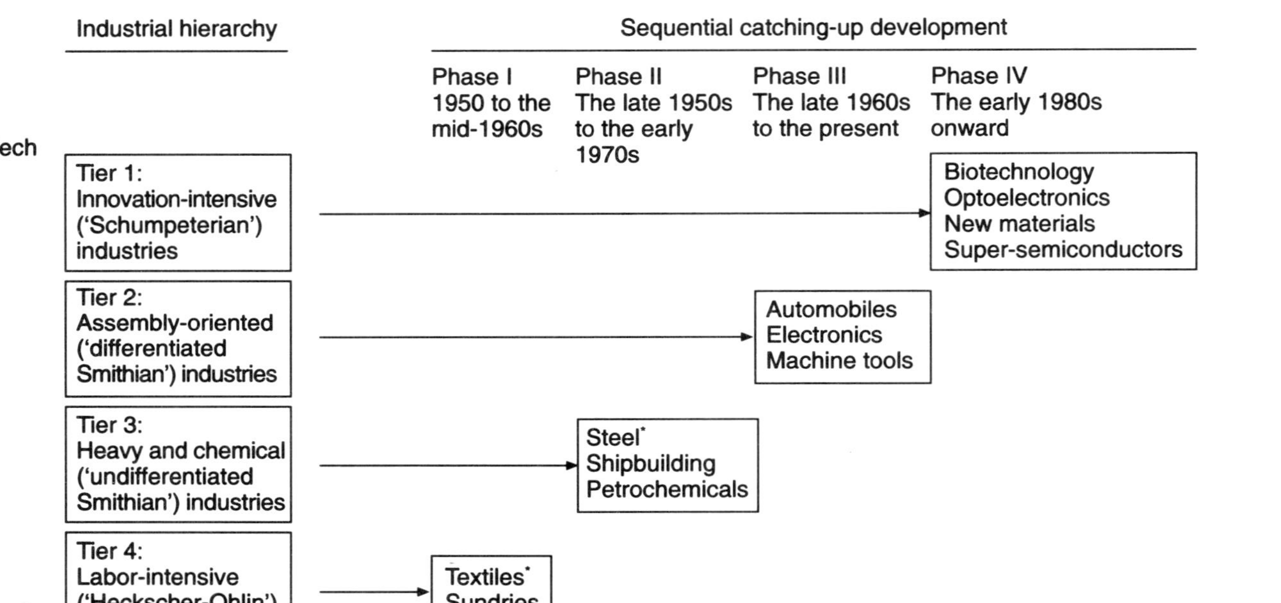

Figure 9.1 Sequence of Japan's postwar structural upgrading under the aegis of the Pax Americana

Note: In the pre-Second World War period Japan had already succeeded in building Tier 4 and Tier 3 industries. But these early phases of industrialization were reworked for export competitiveness in the postwar period, providng the new momentum to build upper-echelon industries intensively employed mostly by small and medium-sized firms (e.g. apparel, footwares, sporting goods, and sundries).

At the end of the war, the United States thus enjoyed an *absolute* advantage in every single manufacturing industry because Europe and Japan were severely destroyed by the war and their technological capacities were way behind. However, being abundantly endowed with capital and natural and technological resources, plus affluent mass markets, the United States obviously had a very strong *comparative* advantage in the upper-ranking types of industry (tiers 1 and 2), but only a passing comparative advantage in the mid-ranking type (tier 3) and a comparative disadvantage in the low-ranking type (tier 4).[4] What mattered most as a basis for international trade at that time was essentially the working of comparative advantage, and this principle was fully activated by the United States as an effective tool of assisting Europe and Japan in economic reconstruction. The United States, in fact, allowed – and even encouraged – Japan to export to the US market whatever Japan was able to manufacture immediately after the war; it was mostly labor-intensive light industry goods (textiles, toys, and sundries).

Yet Japan did not remain long as a happy toy-maker. It soon began to catch up with the US by proceeding from the bottom tier (tier 4) and moving up toward the upper tiers (tier 3, tier 2, and finally – and most recently – tier 1). This is indeed the very sequence of how modern industry has evolved under capitalism, the sequential path of industrial development explored previously not only by the United States but also by other advanced Western countries *albeit* over a much longer span of time, a century or even longer.[5] Moreover, this is the sequential path of catching-up development which Japan, as a latecomer capitalist economy, has been following ever since the start of its modernization effort by the Meiji government in 1868, although temporarily disrupted by World War II. In the prewar years, Japan first took up textiles (first cotton and then rayon), iron and steel, industrial machinery, and heavy industries and chemicals – step by step, through the state-guided process of import-substitution turned export-promotion. (Akamatsu, 1960; Smith, 1955; Arisawa, 1967; Yamazawa, 1990).

It is, however, in the post-World-War-II period that the sequential catching-up process – all the way from tier 4 to tier 1 in one sweep – has been accomplished at such an astonishing pace. Japan was able to achieve such an economic miracle because it had an excellent industrial road map to follow; the dominant US industry only showed Japan "the image of its own future." Japan also used the industrial foundations (mostly tier 4 and tier 3) built in the pre-World-War-II era, and during the war itself, as a launchpad for postwar industrial modernization. Most of all, however, the United States as the system leader had generated an extremely favorable wave of "systemic openness" and global expansion characterized by the "diffusion of technlogy, [the] catch-up of system followers, and freer trade" (Thompson and Vescera, 1992: 513).

Given the above pattern of Pax Americana-sponsored catch-up development, the postwar sequencing of Japan's industrial reconstruction and expansion can also be chronologically divided into four phases, although they naturally overlap and are not clear-cut in intertemporal demarcations; yet the dominance of a certain type of industry as the growth *cluster* of industrial activities is observable for each phase (Figure 9.1):

Phase I Expansion of labor-intensive manufacturing in textiles, toys, sundries, and other low-wage goods (the "Heckscher-Ohlin" goods), particularly as foreign-exchange earners (1950 to the mid-1960s).

Phase II Scale economies-based modernization of heavy and chemical industries, such as steel, shipbuilding, petrochemicals, and synthetic fibers (the "non-differentiated Smithian" goods) (the late 1950s to the early 1970s).

Phase III Assembly-based mass production of consumer durables, notably automobiles and electric/electronic goods (the "differentiated Smithian" goods) (the late 1960s to the present).

Phase IV Innovation-driven, service-focussed industries; mechatronics-based flexible manufacturing, small-lot, multi-variety production, along with innovations in HDTV, new materials, fine chemicals, high-performance microchips, and opto-electronics (the "Schumpeterian" goods) (the early 1980s onwards).

Japan's industrial structure has metamorphosed in three continuous phases ever since the end of the war, building on – and extending – the prewar efforts for industrialization, and is currently in the midst of the fourth stage (Ozawa 1991a). What we have witnessed here is the *gradual erosion* ("chipping-away") of America's once full-set industrial hierarchy at the hands of Japanese industry, working from the bottom tier and then upward toward the top, one by one, over the past four decades. Europe, too, contributed to this

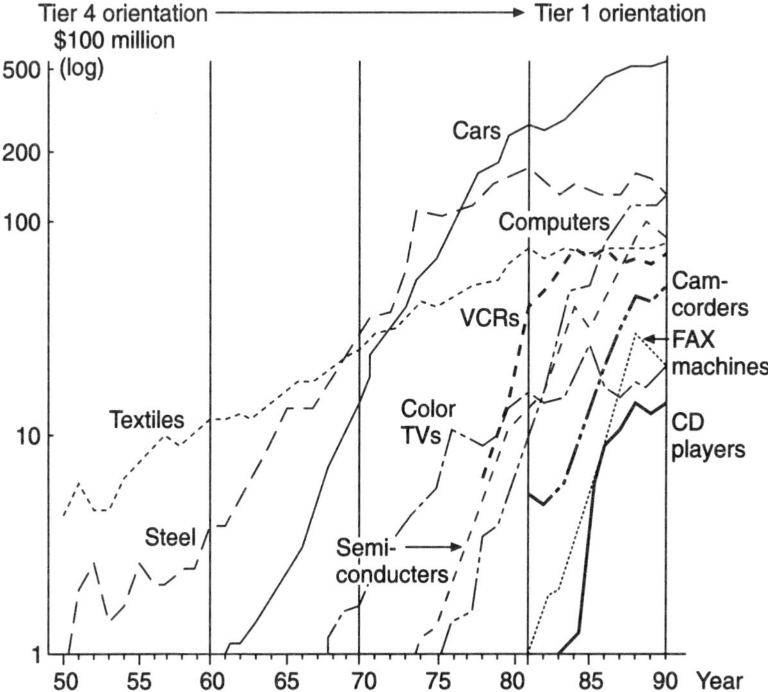

Figure 9.2 Trends of Japan's major exports of manufactures

Source: Ministry of International Trade and Industry, *Tsusho Hakusho* (White Paper on International Trade) (Tokyo, Government Printing Office, 1991, p. 145)

industrial dispersion process by absorbing American technology and reviving the former's traditionally strong industries such as basic chemicals and pharmaceuticals.

It should be emphasized that although Japan has acquired industries "off the shelf," as it were, its catching-up efforts were not mere borrowings. Japanese firms simultaneously added numerous competitively significant improvements (i.e. an emulator's advantages) along the way. In fact, some even see Japan as the leader of "lean production" (or flexible manufacturing), after America's leadership in "mass production," which had in turn replaced Europe's leadership in "craft production" (Womack, Jones and Roos, 1990).

This fact is well reflected in the export competitiveness of Japanese manufactures not only in prices but also in quality, delivery, and services. In fact, as shown in Figure 9.2, *pari passu* with Japan's structural upgrading, its pattern of manufactured exports has changed both qualitatively and quantitatively from low-tech to higher-tech categories in a wave-like sequence – from textiles (labor intensive goods) and steel (resource intensive, scale-based goods), to cars (assembly-oriented goods), to color TVs, VCRs, camcorders and CD players (consumer electronics), and computers and fax machines (R&D-based office equipment). *A particular pattern of export competitiveness mirrors a particular stage of structural upgrading.*

Let's call the upscaling from the first stage of labor-driven development to the second stage of heavy and chemical industrialization "Mark I restructuring," that from the second to the third stage of assembly-based manufacturing "Mark II restructuring," and that from the third to the fourth stage of innovation-driven flexible manufacturing "Mark III restructuring."

For all the stages of restructuring, the absorption (adoption, adaptation, and assimilation) of advanced Western technologies has been a crucial driving force for Mark I and Mark II. Japan initially absorbed modern industrial knowledge through the hiring of Western engineers and technicians in the early stages of Japan's industrialization during the Meiji period (Smith, 1955; Hayashi, 1990) and the joint ventures with Western firms (such as General Motors, Ford, General Electric and Siemens) in the pre-World-War-II period. However, since the end of the war, the learning channel has been mostly through licensing agreements, adaptive domestic R&D and shopfloor process improvements (Ozawa, 1974; Moritani, 1982). But for Mark III, the absorption channel is increasingly that of foreign direct investment, both inward and outward, and stepped-up domestic R&D and overseas strategic alliances in research and product development.

Moreover, as the Japanese economy climbed up the industrial ladder provided by the Pax Americana and graduated from one state to another of competitive development, those stages have been passed on to the less developed countries, especially to the NIEs, in the Asian Pacific via foreign direct investment and other forms of industrial transplantation.[6] It thus has been Japan's turn to show to the rest of Asia "the image of its own future." Indeed, ever since the mid-1960s, Japanese corporations, small and large alike, have suddenly and rapidly grown into multinational operators. They are actively recycling Japan's superannuated industries to other countries and increasingly straddling its multi-layered industrial activities (especially, of the vertically divisible structure of assembly industries such as automobiles and electronic goods), with the Schumpeterian-innovation-rent-seeking (marketing) end of its value-added chain mainly in the advanced countries' markets and the Ricardian-resource-rent-seeking (production) end largely in the Asian Pacific economies (Ozawa 1992b).

We can summarize the postwar configurations of Japan's foreign investment activities, both inward and outward, as the stage-specific concomitants of its structural upgrading;

Phase-I-linked-foreign-investment: selective imports of capital goods (embodied technology) and purchase of licensing agreements (disembodied technology) (i.e. inward investment); and the "low-cost-labor-seeking" type of outward investment in standardized, labor-intensive light industries, mostly in the neighboring Asian countries (originating in the late 1950s, but notably after the mid-1960s and growing strongly, especially after the revaluations of the yen in the early 1970s).

Phase-II-linked–foreign-investment: the incessant adoption and adaptation of advanced Western technology, mostly through licensing but also via joint ventures (inward investment) in petro-chemicals, machinery, and chemicals; and the "resource-coupled" (initially "resource-seeking", but later simultaneously "house-cleaning") type of overseas investment in resource-extractive and resource-processing industries (most actively throughout the 1960s and 1970s).

Phase-III-linked-foreign-investment: continuous adaptation of, and improvement on, imported technology and stepped-up domestic R&D; and the "assembly-transplanting, market-securing" type of overseas investment in automobiles, electronics and related parts and components, as well as the "trade-surplus-recycling" type in banking and finance, notably in the United States and Europe (especially after the Plaza Accord of 1985).

Phase-IV-linked-foreign-investment: hosting inward investment in chemicals, pharmaceuticals and machinery; and the "innovation-enhancing, strategic alliances" type of overseas investment in R&D-intensive, client-interactive and flexible-manufacturing-based industries (the mid-1980s onward).

In short, *a particular pattern of foreign investment, inward and outward alike, thus also mirrors a particular stage of structural upgrading.*

As shown in Figure 9.3 (in a highly stylized fashion), Japan's phenomenal sequential metamorphosis and its accompanying outward investment activities have been creating the *opportunities for industrial and market recycling* throughout the Asian Pacific. The NIEs – and even the new NIEs – themselves are joining Japan in this regional game of transplanting their now obsolete phase of industrial development onto the lower-ranking followers. While Japan is currently shifting away from tier 2 and consolidating tier 1 (that is, Mark III restructuring), South Korea and Taiwan are bent on building up tier 3 and 2 industries (that is, Mark I and Mark II restructuring simultaneously). Because of geographical constraints, Hong Kong and Singapore have largely skipped tier 3 industries (heavy and chemical industrializaiton), but are eagerly laying the foundation for tier 1 (in their leapfrogging attempt). On the other hand, the new NIEs (especially Thailand and Malaysia) are about to graduate from tier 4 and are actively developing tier 3 and tier 2, though clearly still behind South Korea and Taiwan. Indonesia reportedly will lose its competitiveness in low-wage-based tier 4 industries in five years. The "new" new NIEs (notably China and Pakistan) are eagerly inviting foreign direct investment to expand tier 4 industries.

The net result is intra-Asian tandem investment; the NIEs have grown as important investors in the new NIEs (ASEAN nations), as shown in Table 9.1. Regionalization of tier 4 and tier 3 industries is in progress through intra-Pacific investments by the multinationals, not only from the advanced countries (the US and Japan) but increasingly also from the Asian NIEs themselves.

It is worth stressing that all these outward-looking, export-promoting Asian economies are still heavily dependent on the United States as their most important export market. In the recent past, however, Japan has emerged as another key market, and the NIEs and the new NIEs themselves have become non-negligible markets – together creating an ever-growing pan-Asian market. Yet, all in all, the Asian Pacific has not yet quite weaned itself from the nurturing system of the Pax Americana.

In sum, the dynamics of tandem industrialization unleashed during the course of the self-transformative evolution of the Pax Americana still continues to activate and vitalize the whole Asian Pacific region. At the heart of this intra-bloc concatenated integration is the phenomenon of *industrial recycling* through foreign direct investment and other forms of industrial transplantation; especially as labor-intensive tier 4 industries – and the labor-intensive segments

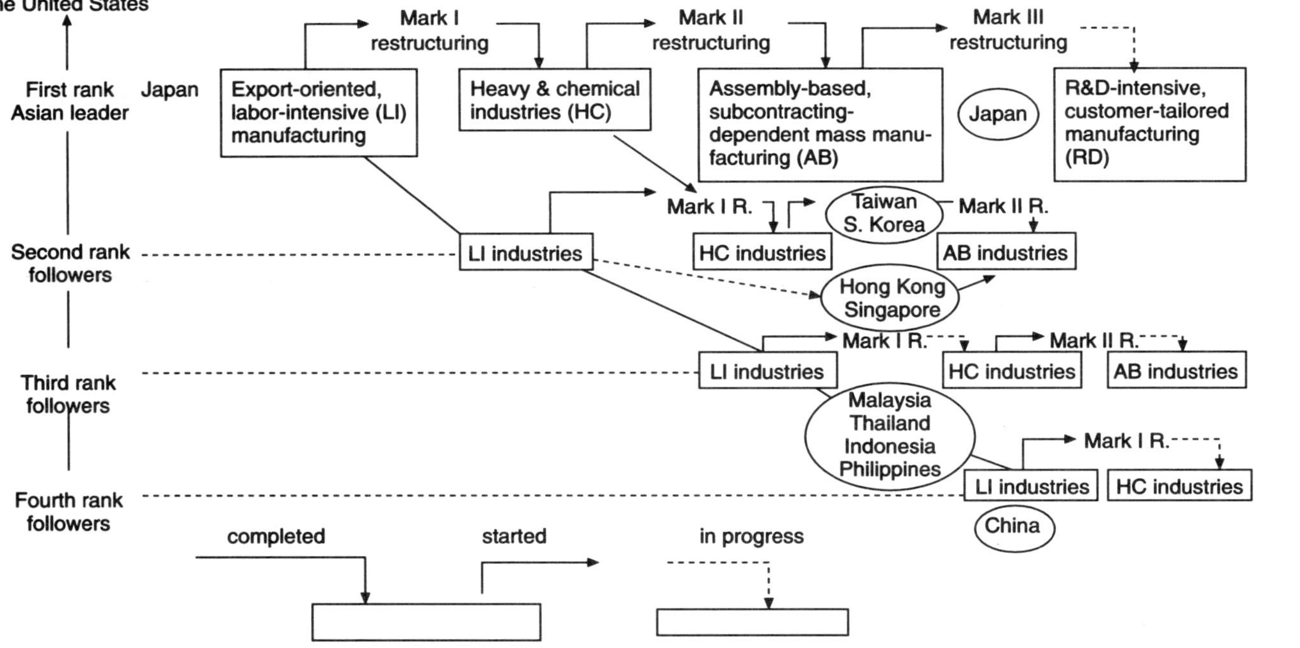

Figure 9.3 Cross-border industrial recycling and intra-Asian spread of tandem economic development

Source: Terutomo Ozawa, "The dynamics of Pacific Rim industrialization: how Mexico can join the Asian flock of flying geese," in Riordan Roett (ed.) *Mexico's External Relations in the 1990s* (Boulder, Colo. and London, Lynne Rienner, 1991)

Table 9.1 Foreign direct investments in major "new" NIEs

		Investors						
		US	*Japan*	*S. Korea*	*Taiwan*	*Hong Kong*	*Singa-pore*	*Total*
Hosts								
Indonesia (million US$)	1988	671	255	206	912	258	250	4,409
		(8)[a]	(44)	(31)	(20)	(25)	(24)	(215)
	1989	58[b]	499	385	156	244	156	3,750
		(8)	(63)	(64)	(501)	(16)	(19)	(294)
Malaysia (million ringgits)	1988	253	561	23	384	129	172	2,010
		(55)	(82)	(11)	(111)	(50)	(134)	(470)
	1989	127	1,065	79	1,013	113	270	3,401
		(30)	(127)	(29)	(191)	(40)	(150)	(608)
Thailand (million bahts)	1988	92,767	148,221	3,679	54,287	20,108	n.a.	394,212
		(136)	(389)	(40)	(400)	(126)		(888)
	1989	31,500	135,800	9,500	30,300	36,300	18,520	205,500
		(76)	(233)	(39)	(207)	(106)	(45)	(752)
Philippines (million pesos)	1988	3,216	1,996	n.a.	2,306	564	n.a.	9,523
	1989	1,718	448	n.a.	n.a.	206	n.a.	3,105

Source: compiled from MITI (1990, 1991b)

Notes: [a] Figures in parenthesis are the numbers of ventures; [b] January–June

of tier 2 – were passed around from one developing country to another, what may be called a "tandem development multiplier" has been at work in expanding the demand for local labor and putting upward pressures on wages – hence, rising incomes – throughout the Asian Pacific (Ozawa, 1991b).

In addition to Japan's industrial shedding which is centered on Asia (hence, leading to *regionalization*), its upgrading efforts need to be equally emphasized as they are made more on a global basis, namely as part of the *globalization* of its business activities. The fact that Japan is now in the Phase-IV-linked phase of overseas business means that many Japanese corporations are clearly on an equal footing with Western firms in technological, financial and marketing sophistication. So-called strategic alliances across borders involve an exchange of some *core competencies* (firm-specific assets) between the partners involved, although some partners may be more senior than others. Strategic alliances are a form of business carried out by firms mostly from advanced countries; they are basically a high-income phenomenon.

Three different types of technology-related alliances may be conceptualized: asset-seeking; asset-sharing; and asset-creating.[7] Each of these types becomes dominant in the order listed as a country moves up the ladder of industrialization and technological advance. Many Japanese firms are now sought as asset-creating partners by advanced Western firms. The prime example is a recent three-way mega-alliance between IBM, Toshiba and Siemens intended to design 256-megabit dynamic random access memory chips for computers of the twenty-first century. Only about a decade ago, however, Japanese tie-ups with Western firms were mostly either asset-seeking (technology-acquiring via original equipment manufacturing or OEM, for example) or at best asset-sharing (cross-licensing agreements). Most recently Japanese firms are participating in the asset-creating type of alliances (joint R&D and joint product development). All the three types of technology-related alliances are used to enhance the technological capacity of Japanese industry, thereby facilitating industrial upgrading. (As will be elaborated below, they represent a search for the Smithian growth *élan.*)

It is worth stressing that the Asian NIEs, especially South Korea and Taiwan, are largely still in the asset-seeking stage of alliance, the stage in which Japan was, say, in the mid-1970s (Jun, 1992; Schive, 1992). Taiwan's dream of becoming "an Asian Pacific regional center" for European and American multinationals who invest in other Asian regional areas such as mainland China and South East Asia (Schive, 1992) is an interesting idea as Taiwan tries to sell its location-specific advantages in exchange for Western multinationals' corporate assets (such as R&D facilities in Taiwan).

THE PRINCIPLE OF INCREASING FACTOR INCONGRUITY: TWO VITAL MECHANISMS

Given the fact that America's postwar hegemony has led the way for the dramatic recovery and expansion of other nations, what is the causal mechanism that facilitates industrial transfers, thereby transmitting growth impulses down the hierarchy? In other words, what are the economic laws or principles that can explain the transmigration (recycling of industries from advanced countries to the less advanced via overseas investment that results in tamden development within a stages-differentiated hierarchy of nations? One such principle is identified as the principle of increasing factor incongruity (Ozawa, 1992a). Factor incongruity means a phenomenon of incompatibility that appears over time between the factor intensity of a good and the factor endowments of an economy in which the good is produced, an incompatibility that necessarily occurs under two different circumstances.

First, it occurs for a good whose technological nature changes rapidly along the path of its product life cycle as it is transformed from a newfangled good to a standardized one even though the factor endowments of the economy remain the same. Second, such a factor incongruity emerges in any fast-growing economy whose factor endowments become quickly labor-scarce and more capital-abundant, as well as more skill (human-capital) abundant, thereby making the production of a good of a fixed-input proportion (say, a relatively labor-intensive good) ever more costly. As a result, the economy has to be restructured (upscaled) so as to produce much higher value-added (more capital-intensive) goods which are compatible with the ever-rising availability of human capital.

There are thus two essential mechanisms through which factor incongruity emerges and intensifies: one type is the product-related ("product-cycle") phenomenon; the other is the economy-related ("structural upgrading") phenomenon. In either case, an emerging – and intensifying – factor incongruity enervates the nation's *trade* competitiveness and drives its business firms to seek a more appropriate production environment abroad – hence cross-border industrial migration.

Put differently, a nation has a chain of comparative advantages, which, however, is constantly altered by dynamic economic factors (technological advances and factor growth), and the "weak links of the chain of comparative advantages" inevitably appear (Kogut, 1985: 22), calling for remedial strategic measures on the part of individual firms and activist governments.

Channel 1: the "product-cycle" mechanism

The technical nature of a new product changes very quickly from a very high to a less human-capital intensity, that is, to high labor-intensity as the new product matures and becomes standardized, although the factor endowments of the economy where it is originally innnovated scarcely change. The firm that has innovated the new product can no longer retain a competitive advantage in manufacturing at home and will have to transplant production abroad (to restore an appropriate factor congruity). This is essentially the scenario of the product-cycle theory of trade and investment (Vernon, 1966; Hirsh, 1967). In short, the emergence of factor incongruity is inevitable in a dynamic world of innovation and the spread of production occurs mostly from the advanced to the less advanced countries.

Channel 2: the "structural upgrading" mechanism

When the factor endowments of a country become increasingly more capital-abundant and labor-scarce, a product whose factor intensity used to be compatible with the initial state of labor abundance will no longer be produced cost-effectively at home, although the product itself may remain unchanged in its factor requirements, which is usually the case with already standardized, labor-intensive products.

This type of factor incongruity occurred – and is occurring – in the rapidly catching-up Asian economies after World War II, first in Japan, and then in Hong Kong, Singapore, Taiwan, and South Korea and most recently in Thailand and Malaysia. All these economies started out at the bottom of an industrial ladder, that is, at the labor-superfluous stage of development, and had to emphasize labor-absorbing light industries (tier 4) such as apparel, toys, and sundries. As detailed below, their reliance on initially low wages, however, paradoxically led to a rapid rise in wages and shortages of unskilled workers. The concentrated build-up of labor intensive industries made possible through successful export expansion to the advanced countries' markets inexorably causes rapid wage increases in a once-labor-superflous developing country over even a short span of time.

The result is a rapidly emerged incongruity in productive conditions between labor-intensive, low-wage-based manufactures and the ever-rising local wages. Those firms that are successful in capturing export markets now have to seek still lower-wage labor in developing countries by transplanting production. This phenomenon has been the driving force for the intra-Asian transmigration of labor-intensive, foot-loose manufacturing activities, generating the resultant pattern of tandem industrialization.[8]

On a more theoretical level of analysis, both the "product-cycle" and the "structural upgrading" channels of industrial recycling can be illustrated in terms of Figures 9.4 and 9.5 respectively.

In Figure 9.4, HH is the prevailing factor-price line in an advanced country, and QQ the initial isoquant of a new product introduced in that country. FF is the factor-price line in a less develop
In the beginning, the new product is produced at point A,
a relatively high capital–labor input ratio. As the tech

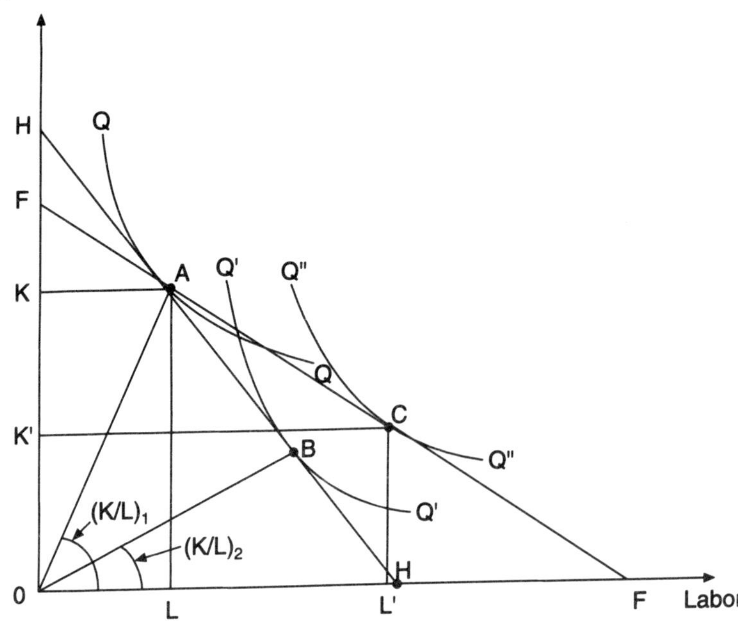

Figure 9.4 The "product-cycle" channel of industrial migration

new product is perfected in terms of both product and process characteristics aimed at large-scale manufacturing, its isoquant shifts from QQ to Q′Q′, with capital–labor input ratio dropping from (k/L)1 to (k/L)2. Production now can occur at point B. As this change in the factor intensity of the new product occurs, however, it becomes increasingly desirable (cost-effective) to transplant production onto the less advanced country where labor cost is lower. When this industrial migration takes place, production takes place at point C in a low-wage country. The result is a rise in output from Q′Q′ to Q″Q″ without any increase in total production costs (OK + OL = OK′ + OL′, since KK′ equals LL′). This explains the economic rationale for transplanting those innovations (products) that have been quickly standardized from the advanced country to the less advanced, lower-labor-cost country.

The only way for the advanced, high-wage country to maintain manufacturing activity is to keep introducing innovations one after another so as to retain its competitive advantage in the R&D (human-capital) intensive, upstream segments of manufacturing. Then, the cycle can continue: innovation, dissemination, again inno-

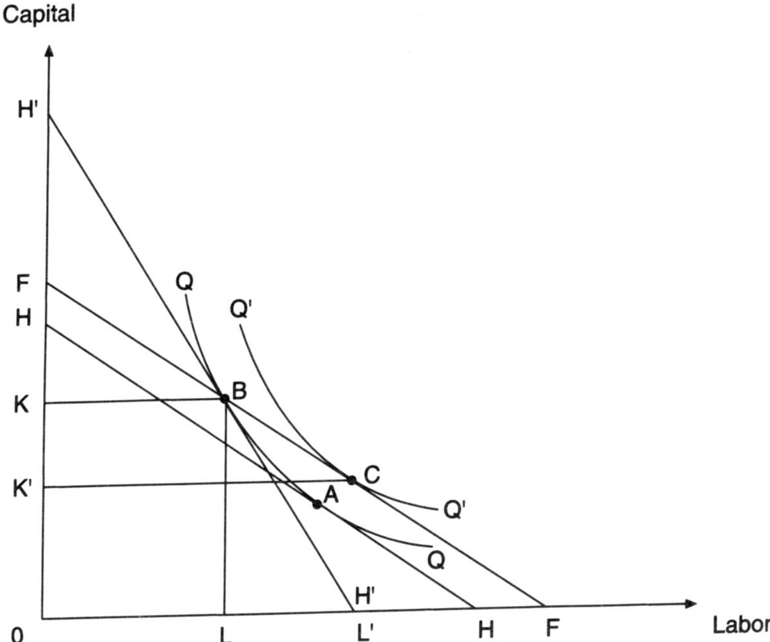

Figure 9.5 The "structural upgrading" channel of industrial migration

vation, dissemination, *ad infinitum*. But because of advances in communications and transportation technology and because of the global tend for market-oriented approaches, the rate of technological diffusion is faster than the rate of technological infusion; hence, the leader economy is often frustrated over the "premature" loss of innovations to its upstart competitors.

In contrast to the "product-cycle" channel, which focusses on the standardization process of a new product without any change in the country's overall factor endowments, the "structural upgrading" channel (Figure 9.5) illustrates the process of capital intensification, a change in the country's factor endowments but without any technological change in the nature of an already standardized product. HH is the initial factor-price line in a relatively labor-abundant country. The production of a technologically standardized manufacture occurs at point A. But such production, particularly when concentrated economy-wide (all-out-labor-driven development), leads to a quick rise in wages due to the fac magnification effect (Stolper and Samuelson, 1941). When price ratio changes from HH to H′H′, production occurs at point B. But if production is transplanted onto a lower-wage location (where the initial wage–rental ratio still prevails), output can expand from QQ to Q′Q′, with the same total production cost.

ESCAPE FROM THE RICARDIAN BOTTLENECKS AND SEARCH FOR THE SMITHIAN GROWTH *ÉLAN*

As we have seen earlier, Japan has so far experienced the four modes of overseas industrial recycling, in a wave-like sequence, each of which corresponds in a causal relationship to one of the four sequential stages of catching-up development: (1) the "low-cost-labor-seeking" type represented by overseas investments in light industry goods; (2) the "resources-coupled" type best exemplified by investments in the extraction of minerals and energy resources such as iron ore, coking coal, oil and natural gas, and, increasingly, resource-processing ventures; (3) the "assembly-transplanting, market-securing" type characterized by investments in auto-assembly operations; and (4) the "innovation-enhancing, strategic alliances" type related to investments in R&D/design/engineering centers and joint product-development ventures abroad.

As hinted earlier, these sequential waves of overseas investment which Japan has generated over the past four decades, notably the first three waves, were exactly those undergone by advanced Western nations over a span of a century or even longer subsequent to the Industrial Revolution that ushered the world into the age of capitalism. The latest mode of overseas investment, the "innovation-enhancing, strategic alliances" type, is currently pursued most actively by the high-tech firms in the advanced market economies. For Japan, the lengths of the first three waves have simply been compressed, reflecting its rapid catch-up along the path of capitalist development trajectory pioneered by the West (Ozawa, 1992a).

But why this commonality in the intertemporal configurations of capitalist countries' overseas investment activities? Does the particular system and nature of production and consumption inherent in the regime of capitalism produce such an identical pattern of overseas investment waves?

Here, David Ricardo's theory of economic growth (Ricardo 1817) (which is actually the first macroeconomic theory of secular stagnation or profit squeeze rather than of long-term growth) provides an ideal conceptual framework to explain why these waves of outward reach have been generated during the course of capitalist, market-oriented economic development.

As is well known in classical economics, Ricardo's model consists of five basic relations:

$$Q = w + r + p \tag{1}$$

where total output (real income) is divided into money wages (w), rents (r), and profits (p);

$$K = f(p),\ f' > 0 \tag{2}$$

which specifies that K, the rate of capital accumulation, is a positive function of profits;

$$PO = g(w > w^*),\ g' > 0 \tag{3}$$

where PO, the rate of population growth, is positively associated with money wages, w, as long as w is greater than a subsistence wage, w^*;

$$p = h(w, r) = Q - (w + r),\ h' < 0 \tag{4}$$

which means that profits are determined as the *residual* of total output after wages and rents are paid; and finally

$$r = j\ (K, PO),\ j' > 0 \tag{5}$$

which says that rent is a direct function of capital accumulation and population growth, since a rise in industrial activities brought about by capital accumulation increases the demand for labor, hence money wages; and rising wages (under the conditions of $w > w^*$) lead to population growth, which in turn raises the demand for food, hence rents.

Ricardo's scenario begins with an initially "happy" state of affairs. In an early stage of development, the classical economy has only a small population relative to natural resources; consequently, profits, the rate of accumulation, and wages are all relatively high (except rents). The high level of accumulation expands production of industrial goods, but simultaneously drives up the demand for labor, hence wages. This inevitably leads to population growth, as predicted by the Malthusian population principle. Since agricultural land is assumed to be subject to the law of diminishing marginal returns (as less and less futile tracts of land need to be cultivated), food prices, and therefore rents, go up, putting further upward pressures on money wages. The combined result is a profit squeeze as rents and wages eat up more of the total output (as seen in equation 4), leaving less for profits. But as long as profits are positive, capital accumulation continues, yet creating more and more unfavorable conditions for profits and, finally, an end to the process of capital accumulation. The economy reaches and remains trapped in a stationary state. Thus, Ricardo pessimistically saw the inevitability of this type of profit squeeze at the firm's level and stagnation at the marcoeconomic level.[9]

Can the economy escape from this fate? Ricardo pointed out that under two possible circumstances the economy would be able to postpone the day of reckoning: first, if free trade is pursued, thereby allowing imports of cheap food from overseas so that rents would not rise so much and so fast; and second, if technological progress increases productivity in both agriculture and industry. But on the whole, he believed that the profit squeeze would not be eliminated by cheap food imports and technological progress since they are considered exogenous variables.

In this regard, Ricardo apparently failed to see – or rather did not stress – another important solution, that is, overseas investment as a means of transplanting industrial activities onto new locations in foreign countries where arable land is still plentiful and money wages still low. (More on this point will be explored below.)

The basic features (elements) of Ricardo's secular stagnation model had actually been conceptualized much earlier by Adam Smith (1776/1908), though not in as well structured and operational a form as a theory.[10] Smith equally knew that economic growth depends on capital accumulation, which in turn depends on profits. He too was concerned with wage hikes that might cause a profit squeeze and hence an industrial slowdown. Yet Smith was very optimistic – certainly far more so than Ricardo – and believed that an expansion of markets via free trade would lead to the gains from increasing returns to scale (hence declining production costs) and learning-by-doing through the division of labor (hence cost-reducing technological progress), which would fully offset the profit squeeze caused by wage increases. In Smith's conceptualization, the dynamic *élan* of growth, namely the scale economies achieved through trade-led market expansion and the gains from learning-by-doing, are treated as *endogenous* variables within the economic system.

So, what are the relevance and implications of these classical growth models for the interface between the present-day process of economic development and operations of multinational corporations? In our modern economy, rents represent not only the return to land (and directly food prices) but also the prices of natural resources that are used as industrial raw materials and fuels, as well as the environmental costs associated with economic growth. The economy is considered capable of continuing to grow so long as profits are positive and capital accumulation continues. This is the *fundamental* law of growth in any capitalist economy. Hence, any rise in real wages needs to be kept within the bounds of productivity growth, and industrial inputs need to be secured at as low prices as possible. That is to say, these potential Ricardian bottlenecks (rising wages and rents) that cause a profit squeeze need to be avoided. The "low-cost-labor-seeking" type of overseas investments and the "resource-seeking" type, as well as the "housecleaning" type, are all the instruments to escape from the Ricardian bottlenecks.

Yet, modern nations are also actively involved in the creation of the Smithian growth *élan* (market expansion and organizational and technological advances) in terms of trade promotion, the promotion of R&D, education, skill formation through training, and entrepreneurial activities. And the more advanced the economy is, the more intensive the search for these dynamic Smithian factors becomes in order to overcome the negative forces of the Ricardian bottlenecks that cause a profit squeeze. In other words, the advanced nations are more strongly oriented to the Smithian-*élan*-seeking efforts than the less developed nations.

This difference in motivational orientation comes from their structural characteristics determined by stages of economic development. As pointed out earlier, capitalism has gone through the four basic forms of industrial metamorphoses; the very sequence of industrial catch-up Japan has traced in a time-compressed fashion. A nation's competitiveness in the first and second phases is largely determined either by the domestic "natural" factor endowments or by its ability to secure and import the necessary natural resources from abroad, hence the Ricardian bottlenecks are the primary concern. On the other hand, the third phase (which exploits scale economies and a vertical division of labor in components procurement under mass production) and the fourth phase (which is nearly totally liberated from the natural factor endowments and derives from "man-made" economic resources, that is, knowledge and information) more directly represent the Smithian growth *élan*. The advanced nations are thus ever more dependent on "man-made" competitive advantages, while the developing countries are still on "natural" comparative advantages.

The twin concepts of the Ricardian bottlenecks and the Smithian growth *élan* thus serve as additional key variables, along with the principle of increasing factor incongruity, in the stages theory of industrial upgrading and overseas investment. Labor-intensive industrialization, phase I of development, lasts only as long as wages are kept low. But wages inevitably rise because of the very active use of the relatively abundant labor. Once shortages of unskilled labor are experienced and a profit squeeze occurs, firms in labor-intensive light industries are induced to transplant labor-intensive production to low-wage countries, thus the phenomenon of the elementary "labor-seeking" type of overseas investment. Resource-intensive heavy and chemical industrialization, phase II of development, makes the economy dependent on overseas resources, all the more if it is a resource-scarce country. Any rise in prices of imported resources (rents), both actual and potential, causes a profit squeeze (or heightens such a prospect) and induces the "resource-seeking" type of overseas investment in order to secure the stable sources of overseas supply. The rising environmental costs (rents) of heavy and chemical industrialization, at home, especially if the economy is geographically confined and small, similarly encourage the "house-cleaning" type of overseas investment in those host countries where the marginal social benefits of resource-processing activities still outweigh the marginal social costs.

Assembly-based industrialization derives competitiveness from the exploitation of scale/scope economies and learning-by-doing technological progress (augmented by R&D activities and intensive on-the-job training, especially for quality control). These advantages are the Smithian growth *élan*. For this phase of industrialization, then, the maintenance and expansion of market share are critical in order to secure a large volume of production. Hence any possibility of protectionism in export markets induces the "market-seeking" or "market-retaining" type of overseas investment in search for, or in efforts to retain, the Smithian growth *élan*, as seen in the transplantation of auto-assembly operations onto the export markets. At the same time, those labor-intensive components, parts, and accessories of the assembly-based industries will be increasingly produced either in low-cost-labor countries abroad or through labor-saving automation, especially robotics, at home in order to escape from the Ricardian bottlenecks of labor shortages and high wages. Profit-squeezing pressure occurs not only internally as a result of increases in labor costs and prices of natural resources (including the environment), but also externally as the result of international competition and changes in exchange rates (appreciation of home currency).

The latest phase of R&D intensive industrialization further adds to the importance of firms' search for the Smithian growth *élan* (market expansion and organizational and technological efficiency). The term "strategic alliances" has become a catchword among the international business community. Instead of colluding to divide up the existing markets (which will certainly hinder the attainment of organizational and technological progress, hence a negative welfare effect on the consumers), multinationals are now actively cooperating to set up joint research, development, engineering ventures and marketing arrangements (which will create further dynamic rivalry to the advantage of the consumers, hence a welfare improvement in the long run).

In short, the elimination of the Ricardian bottlenecks is the primary concern of tier 4 and tier 3 industries (the phases of labor-intensive light industries and resource-intensive heavy and chemical industries), while the pursuit of the Smithian growth *élan* is the central strategy of business both at the levels of individual firms and nations for promoting tier 2 and tier 1 industries (scale-based, assembly industries and innovation-driven industries). It is worth noting that Japan's efforts to solve the Ricardian bottlenecks (particularly labor shortages) have so far been made largely within the Asian Pacific, but its search for the Smithian growth *élan* (market expansion and technologicl progress) is being carried out globally, especially in other advanced countries.[11] In other words, Japan's production is increasingly *regionalized* in the Asian Pacific (in terms of securing low-cost-labor and industrial raw materials), while its marketing and technological efforts are more and more *globalized*. This observation exactly jibes with an observation made by Hasegawa and Urata (1992) to the effect that in the advanced host countries, Japanese firms are actively engaged in business tie-ups in R&D and marketing, while in the Asian host countries, mostly production cooperation. The above analytical framework also sheds light on the generally known fact that Japanese ventures in the advanced countries are more often than not majority-owned, whereas in the developing countries mostly minority-owned. Management of the Smithian growth *élan* requires much stronger controls – hence majority ownership becomes more prevalent.

The firms in the Asian NIEs, though they began to be involved in overseas investment at the elementary stages, are essentially striving to avoid the profit squeeze by focussing on the solution of the

Ricardian bottlenecks, since their industrial structures are largely of the tier 4 and tier 3 types, with tier 2 industries only in the formative stage of development (with the exception of South Korea and Taiwan which have made significant inroads into some segments of tier 2, notably automobiles, auto-parts, semi-conductors, and personal computers). But as they strive to upgrade their industries, more and more efforts will be made to secure the Smithian growth *élan* through R&D at home and strategic alliances in product and market development across national borders (Smith, 1995).

CONCLUSIONS

The phenomenal economic growth in the Asian Pacific is nothing but the outcome of the dynamics of tandem development set in train under the aegis of the Pax Americana. The region's economic growth has been implemented in the stages-delineated sequence of structural upgrading beginning with tier 4 (labor-intensive light industries), moving up to tier 3 (heavy and chemical industries) and then to tier 2 (components-based assembly industries). So far, Japan is the only Asian economy that has successfully reached tier 1 (innovation-driven, high-tech industries). In the past, once Japan had graduated from the earlier phases of economic development, those industrial activities that were no longer factor-congruous were actively transplanted by Japan's emergent multinationals onto the Asian NIEs through overseas investment. But as the NIEs' own productive conditions similarly altered and became relatively labor-scarce *pari passu* with their structural upgrading, their firms – as well as Japanese ventures there – in turn began to transmigrate factor-incompatible industrial activities to the new NIEs (mostly the ASEAN nations) and to the "new" new NIEs (especially south China). New multinationals have thus begun to appear most noticeably on the Asian scene.[12] Those industrial activities actively recycled to lower-echelon nations are mostly tier 4 and the labor-intensive, low-tech intermediate goods (parts, components, and accessories) of tier 2 industries, the types of production that expand the demand for local labor – hence an upward-spiral of wages.

Sequential structural upgrading, economic growth, overseas investment (both inward and outward), and trade expansion are thus all the mutually reinforcing elements of industrial dynamism that are turning the Asian Pacific into the dynamo of concatenated economic integration and development. The faster the growth of the region, the greater the need for firms' efforts to escape from the Ricardian bottlenecks (rising labor and resource costs) and simultaneously secure the Smithian growth *élan* (expanded markets and technological progress) to ease the perennial pressure of the profit squeeze. In this process, the role of the individual firm's multinational operations, particularly those regionally motivated and anchored, becomes ever more strategically critical in facilitating the continuation of economic growth in the Asian Pacific. They strive to remove the Ricardian bottlenecks through concatenated integration in production and securing the Smithian growth *élan* globally. The result is the intensifying regionalization in production and the ever-widening globalization in marketing and search for technological opportunities through strategic alliances.

The governments of Japan and other Asian nations have been, on the whole, very active in promoting a market-based economy and, at the same time, facilitating by appropriate structural adjustment policies the upgrading of their industrial structures.[13] They are heavily involved in policies for economic development, trade and cross-border investment. In fact, the Japanese government is busily engaged in what may be called "cross-border industrial policy." It promotes a program of "comprehensive economic assistance" by blending its official development aid (ODA) with Japanese industry's overseas investments, as best demonstrated by the "New AID (Asian Industries Development) Plan."[14] The function of government as a facilitator of structural upgrading changes in nature and operational modality depending on what stage of competitive development the economy happens to be in. In other words, a stages theory of government involvement may be developed in close correspondence with the stages theory of structural upgrading and overseas investment. Important as the topic may be, nevertheless, it is beyond the scope of this chapter as it requires a great deal of analysis. It certainly remains as an area for future research.

Another important question that remains unanswered is the future prospect of tandem industrialization. What comes after tier 1 industries? Can the advanced nations continue to create new growth industries (to extend "technological trajectories")[15] so as to stay ahead of the pack of the challenging latecomers who are now closely on their heels? In particular, will Japan as an active recycler of industries be able to keep upgrading its industry? It has been relatively easy for Japan to climb up the ladder of industrialization since the West has provided the needed rungs for each climb. The competitive behavior and strategies of Japanese corporations, along with government policies, have no doubt altered with the changing phases of catching-up development. What will be the direction of change in the policies and strategies of Japanese industry and government, and how will the present process of regionalization and globalization be affected? Japan has accomplished its century-old goal of catch-up, and is now confronted with many emerging issues associated with its status as a superpower in the global economy.

To sum up, this chapter has explored the phenomenon of regionally concatenated industrialization (the supply-side phenomenon) and the ever-deepening globalized links of trade in goods and services (the market-cum-technology-seeking-side phenomenon) in terms of new conceptual frameworks, namely, the reinterpretation (an open-economy version) of the classical Smith/Ricardian growth models and the principle of increasing factor incongruity with the focus on the market mechanisms of cross-border investment activities.

NOTES

1 As quoted by Pitelis (1991: 142).

2 Stephen Krasner (1987: 2–3) describes the US policy as follows: "through the 1960s the United States presided over a global economic system that was theoretically based upon liberal principles and diffuse reciprocity, but which operated in fact to promote the economic prosperity and political stability of its major allies even if this meant accepting practices that discriminated against America itself. This strange world was one the United States could accept because of its unique global position. The extraordinary political, military, and economic dominance it was bequeathed by the consequences of World War II made it possible for the United States to adopt a very long time-horizon and pursue generous policies. Japan and Western Europe could act as free riders on the liberal economic regime without incurring the wrath of the United States, which was more concerned with political and economic stability than with strict adherence to liberal rules."

3 For this view, see Marglin and Schor (1990).

4 This classification of industries matches the stages theory of competitive development introduced by Michael Porter (1991: 546). He maintains that "despite the diversity of most economies, we can identify a predominant or emergent pattern in the nature of competitive advantage in a nation's firms at a particular time" by way of four distinct stages: (1) factor-driven; (2) investment-driven; (3) innovation-driven; and (4) wealth-driven. But "the first three stages involve successive upgrading of a nation's competitive advantages and will normally be associated with progressively rising economic prosperity," while "the fourth stage is one of drift and ultimately decline." At the end of World War II, however, the United States also possessed competitive advantages even

in the labor-driven industries (light manufacturing) because the war disrupted trade (international division of labor) and forced the United States – for that matter, practically all the major countries – to be self-sufficient.

5 Thompson and Vescera (1992: 510–11) date the heyday of the representative growth industries in the West as follows: textiles and iron working led by Britain, 1780s–1820s; railways, steam engines, and machine tools led by Britain, 1830s–1890s; steel, heavy engineering, electrical engineering, and heavy chemicals led by the United States, and petrochemicals, 1940s–1990s; and computer software, electronic equipment, robotics, fiber optics, and ceramics led by Japan or the United States, 1900– ?.

Similarly, Kitschelt (1991) describes the evolutionary path of capitalism in terms of technological trajectory: "Mark I technology" (textiles and machine tools); "Mark II technology" (iron and steel and basic chemicals); "Mark III technology" (cars, appliances, and electronic devices); "Mark IV technology" (aircraft, nuclear technology, and space technology); and "Mark V technology" (software, biotechnology, and high chemistry).

6 In particular, the so-called "new forms of investment" have become prevalent throughout the Asian Pacific, partly because of the high propensity of Japanese multinationals to use such forms. See Oman (1984).

7 For this classification I am grateful to Michel Delapierre and our exchange of ideas at the Symposium on New Technology Policy, Technical Alliances and Social Innovations within the Enterprise held at Université du Québec at Montreal, Canada, October 28–30, 1992.

8 This aspect of the intra-Asian spread of multinationalism has been the focus of my study since the early 1970s (Ozawa 1979) and Kojima's (1978). For a more recent examination of these issues, see Denis Fred Simon, *The Technology Strategy of Japanese Firms Towards the Pacific Rim* (Cambridge: Cambridge University Press, forthcoming).

9 Marglin and Schor (1990) also use the theme of the profit squeeze in their analysis of how the golden age of capitalism ended in the postwar period as the full employment policy commitment pursued by the West caused slow productivity growth and raised the efficiency rate of wage and as the OPEC's oil price hikes in the 1970s raised production costs. But their analysis is couched in the best tradition of Marxism.

10 Letiche (1960: 65) observes that "Adam Smith made an important contribution to the analysis of economc growth by discussing it in terms of general economic principles, rather than in terms of a theory of economic growth."

11 Here, what Cantwell (1989: 94) calls the "technological accumulation" theory of international production is relevant. "One reason for this [overseas R&D] is that carrying out research and production in a variety of international centres of innovative activity increases the capacity for and the complexity of technological accumulation within MNCs." Interactions between firms of different countries in a particular industry through cross-border operations in R&D and production contribute to the growth of international (multinationalized) industries characterized by the global networks of MNC rivals.

12 The region is witnessing the emergence of what Gilpin (1987: 252–60)

calls the "new multinationalism." It is characterized by (a) the pragmatic relationships between multinationals and governments, (b) the greater willingness of the developing countries to open their doors to the multinationals, (c) the increasing importance of "vertical" as opposed to "horizontal" foreign direct investment, notably in the area of off-shore production and sourcing of components and intermediate goods, and (d) the expansion of intercorporate alliances across national boundaries.

13 For industrial and structural adjustment policies in the Asian Pacific, see, for example, Rhee, Larson, and Pursell (1984); Komiya, Okuno, and Suzumura (1988); Okimoto (1989); Noland (1990); Wade (1990); and Balassa (1991), and Shimada (1991).

14 Under this program, Japan provides a comprehensive set of cooperative measures designed to assist the development of a number of carefully chosen manufacturing sectors as export industries. See Ozawa (1993).

15 Kitschelt (1991: 474) examines the "sectoral governance structures" for technological progress by conceptualizing an interesting multiple-level analytical framework for "the linkage between historical phases of industrialization, properties of technological systems, and institutional forms of governance." But prognosis is certainly more difficult than the diagnosis of past technological trajectories.

REFERENCES

Akamatsu, K., "A theory of unbalanced growth in the world economy," *'Weltwirschaftliches Archive*, Band 86, Heft 2 (1960), pp. 196–215.

Arisawa, H. (ed.), *Nihon Sangyo Hyakunenshi* [A 100-year History of Japanese Industry], 1 and 2. (Tokyo: Nihon Keizai, 1967).

Balassa, B., *Economic Policies in the Pacific Area Developing Countries* (New York: New York University Press, 1991).

Cantwell, J., *Technological Innovation and Multinational Corporations* (Oxford: Basil Blackwell, 1989).

Gilpin, R., *The Political Economy of International Relations* (Princeton, NJ: Princeton University Press, 1987).

Hasegawa, S. and S. Urrata, "Global strategies of Japanese firms," paper presented at the Gobal Business Seminar on "The Impact of Globalization and Regionalization on Corporate Strategy and Structure Among Pacific Rim Firms," Sapporo, Japan (August 3–7, 1992).

Hayashi, T., *The Japanese Experience in Technology: from transfer to self-reliance* (Tokyo: United Nations University Press, 1990).

Hirsh, S., *Location of Industry and International Competitiveness* (Oxford: Oxford University Press, 1967).

Jun, Y., "Strategic responses of Korean firms to globalization and regionalization forces: the case of the Korean electronics industry," paper presented at the Global Business Seminar on "The Impact of Globalization and Regionalization on Corporate Strategy and Structure Among Pacific Rim Firms," Sapporo, Japan (August 3–7, 1992).

Kitschelt, H., "Industrial governance structures, innovation strategies, and the case of Japan: sectoral or cross-national comparative analysis?" *International Organization*, 45 (Autumn, 1991), pp. 453–93.

Kogut, B., "Designing global strategies: comparative and competitive value-added chains," *Sloan Management Review*, 26 (Summer, 1985), pp. 15–28.

Kojima, K., *Direct Foreign Investment: A Japanese Model of Multinational Business Operations* (London: Croom Helm, 1978).

Kojima, K., *Japanese Direct Investment Abroad* (Tokyo: Social Science Research Institute, International Christian University, 1990).

Komiya, R., M. Okuno and K. Suzumura (eds), *Industrial Policy of Japan* (Tokyo: Academic Press Japan, 1988).

Krasner, S. D., *International Regimes* (Ithaca, NY and London: Cornell University Press, 1983).

Krasner, S. D., *Asymmetries in Japanese–American Trade: the case for specific reciprocity* (Berkeley, Cal.: Institute of International Studies, University of California, 1987).

Letiche, J. M., "Adam Smith and David Ricardo on economic growth," in Bert F. Hoselitz (ed.), *Theories of Economic Growth* (New York: Free Press, 1960).

Marglin, S. A. and J. B. Schor (eds), *The Golden Age of Capitalism: reinterpreting the postwar experience* (Oxford: Clarendon Press, 1990).

Ministry of International Trade and Industry (MITI), *Tsusho Hakusho* (White Paper on International Trade) (Tokyo: Government Printing Office, 1991a).

Ministry of International Trade and Industry (MITI), *Sekai to Nihon no Kaigai Chokusetsu Toshi* (White Paper on Foreign Direct Investment) (Tokyo: JETRO, 1990 and 1991b).

Moritani, M., *Japanese Technology: Getting the Best for the Least* (Tokyo: Simul International, 1982).

Noland, M., *Pacific Basin Developing Countries: prospects for the future* (Washington, DC: Institute for International Economics, 1990).

Okimoto, D. I., *Between MITI and the Market: Japanese industrial policy for high technology* (Stanford: Stanford University Press, 1989).

Oman, C., *New Forms of International Investment in Developing Countries* (Paris: OECD, 1984).

Ozawa, T., *Japan's Technological Challenge to the West, 1950–1974: motivation and accomplishment* (Cambridge, Mass.: MIT Press, 1974).

Ozawa, T., *Multinationalism, Japanese Style: the political economy outward dependency* (Princeton, NJ: Princeton University Press, 1979).

Ozawa, T., "Japanese Multinationals and 1992," in B. Burgenmeier and J. L. Mucchielli (eds), *Multinationals and Europe 1992* (London: Routledge, 1991a).

Ozawa, T., "The dynamics of Pacific Rim industrialization: how Mexico can join the Asian flock of flying geese," in Riordan Roett (ed.), *Mexico's External Relations in the 1990s* (Boulder, Col. and London: Lynne Rienner, 1991b).

Ozawa, T., "Japan in a new phase of multinationalism and industrial upgrading: functional integration of trade, growth, and FDI," *Journal of World Trade*, 25 (February, 1991c), pp. 43–60.

Ozawa, T., "Foreign direct investment and economic development," *Transnational Corporations*, 1 (February, 1992a), pp. 27–54.

Ozawa, T., "Images, economies of concatenation, and animal spirits: dependency vs. emulation paradigms," paper presented at the conference on

"Perspectives on International Business: Theory, Research and Institutional Arrangements" held at the University of South Carolina (May 21–23, 1992), and to be published in Brian Toyne and Doug Nigh (eds), *The Institutional Status of International Business* (Westport, Conn.: Quorum, forthcoming).

Ozawa, T., "Foreign direct investment and structural transformation: Japan as a recycler of market and industry," *Business & the Contemporary World*, 5 (Summer, 1993).

Pitelis, C., *Market and Non-market Hierarchies: theory of institutional failure* (Oxford: Blackwell, 1991).

Porter, M., *Competitive Strategy: techniques for analyzing industries and competitors* (New York: Free Press, 1980).

Porter, M., *The Competitive Advantage of Nations* (New York: Free Press, 1990).

Rhee, Y. W., B. R. Larson and G. Pursell, *Korea's Competitive Edge: managing the entry into world markets* (Baltimore, Md.: Johns Hopkins University Press, 1984).

Ricardo, D., *On the Principles of Political Economy and Taxation* (London: J. Murray, 1817).

Schive, C., "Strategic responses of Taiwan firms to globalization," paper presented at the Global Business Seminar on "The Impact of Globalization and Regionalization on Corporate Strategy and Structure Among Pacific Rim Firms," Sapporo, Japan (August 3–7, 1992).

Shimada, H., "Structural policies in Japan," in Samuel Kernell (ed.), *Parallel Politics: economic policymaking in the United States and Japan*, (Tokyo: Japan Center for International Exchange; Washington: Brookings Institution, 1991), pp. 211–29.

Simon, Denis Fred, *The Emerging Technological Trajectory of the Pacific Rim* (Armonk, New York: M. E. Sharpe, 1995).

Smith, A., *An Inquiry into the Nature and Causes of the Wealth of Nations* (Chicago, Ill.: University of Chicago Press, 1976; London: Routledge, 1776).

Smith, T. C., *Political Change and Industrial Development in Japan: government enterprise, 1868–1880* (Stanford: Stanford University Press, 1955).

Stolper, W. F. and P. A. Samuelson, "Protection and real wages," *Review of Economic Studies*, 9 (November, 1941), pp. 58–73.

Thompson, W. R. and L. Vescera, "Growth waves, systemic openness, and protectionism" *International Organization*, 46 (Spring, 1992), pp. 493–532.

Vernon, R., "International investment and international trade in the product life cycle," *Quarterly Journal of Economics* (May, 1966), pp. 190–207.

Wade, R., *Governing the Market: Economic Theory and the Role of Government in East Asian Industrialization* (Princeton, NJ: Princeton University Press, 1990).

Womack, J. P., D. T. Jones and D. Roos, *The Machine that Changed the World* (New York: Maxwell Macmillan, 1990).

Yamazawa, I., *Economic Development and International Trade: the Japanese model* (Honolulu, Hawaii: Resource System Institute, East–West Center, 1990).

Part IV

Case studies

10 Globalization of a Korean firm

The case of Samsung

Chol Lee

INTRODUCTION

The world economy during the last decade has undergone several remarkable transformations. Perhaps one of the greatest and most profound changes is the globalization of markets and firms (Drucker, 1986; Keegan, 1989). In other words, the world is being rapidly driven toward the creation of a so-called borderless world by the globalization of firms and markets (Ohmae, 1990). Firms are increasingly becoming involved in foreign markets and diversifying their overseas ventures through direct investment or strategic alliances. They are becoming more and more globalized and see the entire world as their playground with the maximization of global profits being their decisive criteria concerning marketing, sourcing and R&D activities.

The trend toward firms' globalization has been accelerated by several forces. First, it is the result of the homogenization of consumer tastes around the world (Levitt, 1983). This is being driven by the rapid progress of information technologies and the transportation industry which enable consumers in Asia, Europe and America to respond to the same product similarly. Second, firms are more engaged in competition in more liberalized markets across the globe as a result of the break down of many trade barriers. Firms should compete against foreign ventures within domestic as well as overseas markets. Third, most products are in the maturity stage where price is the most influential factor in determining a consumer's brand choice. Intense price competition has driven firms to seek out economies of scale on a global scale (Levitt, 1983).

Recently, however, there also appears to be a strong movement toward regionalization. The trend toward regionalization is most clearly manifested in the formation of such economic integration as the EU or NAFTA. In general, regionalization is being fed by a number of forces, the foremost being the shift away from comparative advantage and toward a new emphasis on competitive advantage. Despite the growing attention to globalization at the level of the corporation, industrial policy and technology targeting are the forces that are driving the behavior of nation-states (Porter, 1990). Growing economic interdependence, which has left nation-states more vulnerable to the economic policies of other nations, and intense competition to develop state-of-the-art technology as an important source of global competitiveness are gaining strength to support the idea of economic nationalism at the regional level.

The impacts of globalization and regionalization of world markets on Korean firms can be seen in their expanding global activities. Recently foreign direct investment increased sharply by those Korean firms which seek to gain closer proximity to their foreign customers, which utilize cheap labor cost in developing countries and which circumvent the potential trade barriers of developed countries (Lee, 1990). Big Korean conglomerates are actively integrating their overseas activities and pooling their resources on a global scale through transnational networks with the aim of becoming truly globalized firms by the twenty-first century. Given the extent and speed at which they are moving to pursue the global path, multinationals from developing countries with similar external environments will need to learn from Korean firms' experience. In other words, Korean firm's experience of globalization can provide the basis for a framework which can explain the globalization process for multinational corporations from developing countries. Past research has found that the internationalization of the so called Third World multinationals is explained differently from the counterparts in developed countries (Wells, 1983; Lall, 1983; Kumar and Kim, 1984; Lecraw, 1981).

Viewed from this perspective, the aims of this chapter are threefold. First, it is my aim to identify the process by which Korean firms are trying to become globalized using the Samsung group as the case study. Specifically, historical developments, motives, general directions, and obstacles to globalization of the Samsung group will be described. Second, globalization of such functional areas as marketing, sourcing, R&D, financing, and human resource management are highlighted. Third, the process and performances of the globalization of Samsung are evaluated and future directions are suggested.

Table 10.1 Industry composition of Samsung Group

Industry	*Sales (%)**	*Investment (%)*
Electronics	21.6	35.1
Machinery	5.9	6.7
Chemical	4.2	39.1
Light industry	6.9	4.3
Construction	4.3	1.7
Trade/service	32.7	7.9
Financial service	24.3	5.1

Note: * The numbers in the table indicate each industry as a percentage of the total sales and total investments of Samsung Group

HISTORICAL DEVELOPMENTS OF THE GLOBALIZATION OF SAMSUNG

Samsung is one of the largest *chaebol* (which means a highly diversified business group) in Korea; its total sales reached US$37 billion in 1990. Samsung's businesses are so diversified that they include electronics, heavy industry, insurance, chemical, trading, construction, and financial services (see Table 10.1). Because Samsung Electronics and Samsung Corporation are the two core companies, the globalization process of Samsung will be described centering around these two companies.

The globalization process of Samsung can be divided into five different stages. During the first period of 1970 to 1975 globalization began when Samsung Corporation, working as the holding company of the Samsung Group, acquired the status of General Trading Company approved formally by the Korean government and expanded its foreign branches in New York, Tokyo and Frankfurt to the status of local corporations in order to develop export markets aggressively. The main motivation for globalization then was to acquire export markets by entering into major overseas markets such as the US, Japan and Germany.

The second period of globalization started between 1976 and 1980. During this period Samsung's global policy shift emphasized overseas resources development in order to acquire a stable supply of resources such as oil, coal and wool against rising nationalism in the Third World. Another area of globalization of Samsung started in the construction business, which entered in the Middle East to work on housing and harbor construction projects.

The third period of the globalization of Samsung occurred in the first half of the 1980s. Samsung Electronics started foreign direct investment for building production facilities in such developed countries as the US in 1984, Great Britain in 1987 and Portugal in 1982. The main motivation for starting foreign production was to overcome the trade barriers of developed countries and to respond to foreign consumers' needs more actively.

Later, however, foreign production sites were established in developing countries and foreign investments were rapidly expanded to other business such as textiles, consumer electronics and garments in the second half of the 1980s, the fourth period of the globalization of Samsung. During this period Korea's trade balance changed from a long-time deficit to a surplus, and Korean currency was overvalued and labor costs rose up rapidly. This resulted in the deterioration of Korean firms' international competitiveness. In response to these worsening conditions of domestic production and export to overseas markets, Samsung sought foreign production sites to utilize cheap labor costs in the developing countries of South East Asia and Latin America.

In the fifth period of the 1990s, Samsung has expanded its globalization to socialist countries such as China, Vietnam and to East European countries including Russia as the Korean government adopted an open-door policy with socialist countries and socialist and formerly socialist countries liberalized their economic systems by moving toward market economies. Also, Samsung is actively exploring the possibilities of joint ventures with North Korea and that will be realized in the near future. Up to now Samsung has sought to globalize its operations by expanding its export markets, establishing first distribution networks and then production facilities in overseas markets in order to overcome trade barriers and to raise production efficiency. From the historical developments of Samsung's globalization it can be seen that government policies play significant roles in defining the objectives and goals of the Korean firms' globalization.

The current status of globalization of Samsung is described in Table 10.2. At the end of 1991, Samsung's total foreign investment reached approximately US$1.2 billion and total export volume reached US$7.8 billion. Samsung owns thirty-eight overseas production subsidiaries, forty-seven sales subsidiaries, nineteen R&D facilities and 167 branches. Also, the total number of employees working overseas is about 12,000; one-tenth are expatriates and the rest are local employees. Most of these overseas facilities and employees are employed by Samsung Electronics and Samsung Corporation, who have played the major roles in the globalization of Samsung in the past.

Table 10.2 The current status of globalization of Samsung, 1991

Exports	US$ 7,800 million
Total foreign investment	US$ 1,181 million
Number of countries entered	56
Number of foreign sales subsidiaries	47
Number of foreign production subsidiaries	38
Number of foreign R&D subsidiaries	19
Number of foreign branches	167
Number of expatriate employees	926
Number of local employees	11,043

MOTIVATIONS OF SAMSUNG FOR GLOBALIZATION

The internationalization of Korean firms can be categorized into the following six motivational factors: local market development; saving labor cost and quota circumvention; securing natural resources; R& D outlet; local market protection; and supporting plant export (Min, 1985). Samsung's globalization fits into these categories.

Samsung has sought a globalization policy continuously as a survival strategy. The environmental changes in both domestic and overseas markets have forced Samsung to globalize its operations in order to maintain continuous growth. First, Samsung seeks its globalization in order to respond actively to the strengthening of trade barriers of developed countries. Regionalization and the protectionst trade policies of certain principal export markets have forced Samsung to establish local production subsidiaries in several developed countries such as Britain, France and the US. For example, Samsung Electronics built its first overseas production facilities in Lisbon in 1982 to avoid the trade barriers of European countries. Its second overseas investments was the building of a local production subsidiary in New Jersey in 1984 to circumvent US anti-dumping regulations.

Second, in responding to growing competition from local and overseas suppliers, Samsung has set up local sales subsidiaries or production facilities to provide better customer services and to coordinate local marketing activities more effectively. Being closer to customers, local subsidiaries better reflect local customer needs or preferences and compete with other suppliers more effectively.

Third, rapidly rising labor costs, high interest rates, and currency upgrading in the domestic market has caused Samsung to move production facilities of low-priced products to less developed countries in South East Asian countries, such as Malaysia, Thailand, and Indonesia, and in Latin America. Samsung Electronic's first overseas investment for this purpose was done as a joint venture with Thailand to produce color televisions and video tape recorders. Recently Samsung has tried to move overseas production sites to socialist countries such as China and Vietnam, or to formerly socialist countries such as Hungary, or Russia. In July 1992 Samsung announced its plan to enter a joint venture with a Chinese firm in Tien Jin to produce video tape recorders.

Fourth, Samsung has globalized its operations in response to the liberalization of domestic markets. The Korean government's policy of opening domestic markets to foreign firms in almost every field has forced Samsung to compete with foreign competitors, even in the domestic market. In terms of competition there is not much distinction between domestic and overseas markets: the domestic market is part of the global market. In response to this situation Samsung is actively seeking to globalize its operations in production, R&D, marketing and financing to compete more effectively with other competitors in and out of the domestic market. Specifically rivalistic behavior in globalization, so called follow-the-leader pattern is very apparent in the oligopolistic electronics industry. Knickerbocker (1973) found that there is a strong tendency for firms to follow each other in foreign production investments in oligopolistic industries. Thus, threatened by the establishment in 1981 of a foreign manufacturing subsidiary in the US by Goldstar, who is Samsung's archrival in the domestic electronic industry, Samsung made its first foreign direct investment in Portugal a few months later.

Fifth, Samsung has made direct foreign investments in resource-rich countries to develop and import critical resources such as oil, coal, wool and strategic minerals. As in Japan, some natural resources needed in industrial development are scarce in Korea. A major role of Samsung General Trading Company is to acquire a stable supply of scarce resources by developing local resources and importing them on a long-term basis. For example, Samsung made a direct investment in Malaysia with American and Taiwanese firms to produce and import crude oil on an output-sharing basis.

Sixth, Samsung has actively sought globalization to secure access to the advanced technology that foreign firms control. Samsung has established research facilities in such developed countries as the US to take advantage of available trained personnel in order to acquire advanced technology in product development and marketing know-how. For example, Samsung Electronics built a local research center in Silicon Valley in the US in 1983 to acquire high technology for

Table 10.3 Overseas investments of Samsung Group by motivations and geography

	Sales subsidiary	*Production subsidiary*	*R&D*	*Resource development*	*Others*	*Total*
North America	12*	2	9	–	4	27
South America	2	8	–	1	–	11
Europe	13	7	1	–	3	24
South East Asia	12	18	8	1	3	42
Africa and Middle Asia	2	–	–	1	–	3

Note: * The numbers in the table indicate cases of foreign direct investment undertaken by Samsung Group

producing semi-conductors. The overseas investments of Samsung according to these motivations is described in Table 10.3.

GLOBALIZATION OF SAMSUNG

There are six basic functional areas which Samsung has been seeking to globalize. These areas are R&D, marketing, management, organization, production, and human resources management.

Globalization of research and development (R&D)

Samsung has been trying to establish its local R&D facilities in developed countries, especially in the US and some European countries, in order to enhance the international competitiveness of Samsung's own technology (see Table 10.4). Through these facilities Samsung can acquire the advanced technology and know-how of the developed countries and use this as a basis for developing Samsung's own creative technology or product development. Also, it is trying to utilize local engineers and scientists fully by employing them through local education centers or by inviting expatriate engineers and scientists to Korea to educate engineers at its headquarters. In recent years Samsung has used merger and acquisition (M&A) activities for this purpose (see Table 10.5). When the timing of entry into business is very critical and the product life cycle gets shorter, M&A is a very effective strategy for acquiring foreign advanced technology. By purchasing high-tech firms in developed countries, Samsung can not only quicken access to the new technologies, but also catch up the forerunners in terms of technological capabilities.

Table 10.4 Overseas R&D centers of Samsung Electronics

Country	*Local name*	*Activity*
US	Samsung Information System	200 MB hard disk drive, Notebook, Notepad Computer
US	Samsung Semiconductor	Semiconductor technology
US	Samsung Software	Workstation related technology
Japan	Samsung Electronics	LCD Drive IC

Table 10.5 Overseas M&A by Samsung Electronics

Year	*Foreign firm*	*Technology*	*Investment (US$1,000)*
1986	Microntech	Semiconductor	5,000
1987	Micro Electronics	Semiconductor	3,950
1988	Gelco (Japan)	Computer	805
	Micro Five	Computer	2,400
1989	Norpak (Canada)	New media	N/A
1990	Skydata	Research center	2,100

This explains Samsung's recent acquisition of a significant number of shares in AST, the personal computer firm.

Globalization of production and sourcing

Samsung has globalized its operations by diversifying overseas networks and strengthening management of local subsidiaries. It has been trying to expand its overseas network of local subsidiaries, whether in sales or production, by active foreign direct investments. In particular Samsung Electronics has recently increased foreign investments in production in both developed and developing countries (see Table 10.6). The investments in developed countries were made to overcome the trade barriers which were already imposed on Korean firms or in the expectation of future barriers; in other words, most of Samsung's direct investments in development countries have been made in response to regionalization forces. The way Samsung tried to overcome the locational disadvantage in the developed countries was to build screwdriver-type plant which was mostly fed by inputs from the headquarters in Korea. However, the local content requirement and the imposition of dumping suits on parts nullified the effectiveness of those screwdriver plants. Recently Samsung closed its US plant and moved to the Mexican free trade area.

Table 10.6 Overseas direct investments of Samsung Electronics

Classification	*Country*	*Year*	*Ownership (%)*	*Product*
Developed countries	Portugal	1982	55	C-TV
	US	1984	55	C-TV
	UK	1987	100	MWO, C-TV
	Spain	1990	90	VCR
Less developed countries	Mexico	1988	–	C-TV
	Thailand	1989	51	C-TV, VCR
	Indonesia	1989	49	Refrigerator
	Turkey	1989	20	C-TV
	Hungary	1990	50	C-TV
	CIS	1990	–	VCR
	Czech Republic	1991	–	Refrigerator
	CIS	1992	–	VCR

Note: C-TV = color television

Another outcome of these difficulties is that Samsung recently has tried to bring its affiliated parts makers overseas. This will help Samsung assemblers achieve a higher local content ratio. A good example for this is the recent investment by Samsung Electric in Portugal to supply TV tuners and FBTs for Samsung Electronics' three plants in the UK, Spain and Portugal.

Also, Samsung have made increasing investments in the developing countries of South East Asian countries such as Malaysia and Thailand to utilize production efficiency in the face of rising domestic production costs and the threats from the low cost suppliers of South East Asian countries and China (see Table 10.6). Another objective for this movement is to circumvent the trade barriers imposed on Korean products by developed countries. Thus, the investments of Samsung in South East Asian countries seem to be the response to both globalization and regionalization forces.

Samsung has also tried to integrate its production network globally. Of prime importance in international networking are regional headquarters; Samsung is focussing on establishing regional headquarters to control local subsidiaries in the area. A good example of international networking is the operation of an international purchasing office (IPO) of regional headquarters which orders local production units to manufacture specific parts and components appropriate to local conditions and to collect them in an assembly site.

Also, for the improvement of performance of the existing local subsidiaries Samsung takes small and medium-sized manufacturers of parts and components to overseas production units to acquire the supply of parts or components on a stable basis.

Globalization of management and organization structures

Samsung has sought to fully adapt the management of local operations to local conditions and culture. It is trying actively to localize the management of overseas subsidiaries by delegating management authority to local managers, utilizing local employees fully and adopting local management styles. The main role of headquarters in relation to local subsidiaries is to evaluate the performance of local operations and to determine their managerial goals and long-term plans by joint discussions.

The specific criteria of performance evaluations of overseas subsidiaries are determined to reflect local conditions fully by shared opinions between headquarters and local managers. However, the headquarter provides a universal general direction for evaluation. Overseas subsidiaries can work as profit centers to implement business policy or strategy determined by sharing opinions with the headquarters.

However, there is differentiation in the role of local subsidiaries depending on the stage of economic development of the host country. Subsidiaries in developed countries are managed more autonomously by local employees as a focal group. However, in less developed countries, expatriates have a stronger voice in the managerial operations of subsidiaries. The ultimate goal of this direction is to fully localize management style, personnel, and systems to fit with the local conditions and culture and have local subsidiaries as autonomously managed profit centers but integrated as a whole by the global network.

Samsung's organizational structure has been also changed according to its globalization process. At first, international business was dealt with at the export section under manufacturing division, and then an international division was established separately to control functional activities in overseas markets and to design regional strategy. Recently Samsung established a US regional headquarters directly under the chairman and enhanced its position to be the same rank with other companies such as Samsung Electronics. The US regional headquarters is directly controlled by the chairman of the Samsung Group; it functions as an independent entity controlling all the business activities of Samsung in North America.

Another infrastructure to globalize is information flow. Samsung established its global VAN (Value Added Network) named

"TOPICS" to facilitate information exchanges not only between overseas subsidiaries but also between subsidiaries and headquarters for more effective coordination of global activities. However, up to now local subsidiaries are not prepared to use this network system and exchange information with other subsidiaries or headquarters.

Globalization of marketing

Most of Samsung's exports have been (original equipment manufacturer) brands, rather than own private brands. This OEM strategy has helped Samsung to achieve economy of scale in production and to enhance the quality control level in a relatively short time. However, the effectiveness of the OEM strategy has been decreasing in recent years in the face of rising domestic labor costs and the threats of cheap products from South East Asian countries. However, Samsung's major weakness in shifting from an OEM-based marketing strategy to true global marketing is the low brand recognition among overseas consumers. Recently Samsung realized that to become a true global firm it should establish its own brand name in the global market by investing heavily in overseas advertising and promotion programs. Samsung has been increasing its budget for global brand advertising and using more diverse ways of advertising, including sponsoring major events, in order to appeal to end users. Also it has actively tried to develop its own brand names or to acquire well-known brand names in developed countries. For example, Samsung Electric recently developed a new brand name, "SAMTRON," for its computer monitor which has a good reputation for its quality.

Samsung has sought to globalize marketing activities by localizing the implementation of its marketing policy and by integrating local marketing activities through the headquarters' coordination. Marketing managers of local subsidiaries are responsible for specific details of the marketing mix decisions for pricing, distribution network, advertising copy and sales promotion tools. However, the main directions of marketing policy are determined by coordination between local managers and directors from headquarters. For example, regional headquarters provide a unified advertising theme and local managers determine specific copy, message, and illustration on the basis of the guideline of headquarters.

Also, Samsung has been trying to recruit as many local marketing experts as possible to handle marketing activities and to manage local distribution networks, advertising, sales promotion and sales personnel. Samsung will raise the proportion of own brand up to

60 percent of total sales as a basic condition to fulfill in order to globalize marketing activities through the integration of localization through headquarter coordination.

Globalization of human resources

The goal of Samsung's human resource management in terms of globalization has been to raise and acquire human resources with a global view. To fulfill this goal Samsung has put a great emphasis on educating and training existing employees in adopting a global view.

The main curriculum of Samsung's education and training center emphasizes general international orientation and also operates many separate courses focussing on cross-cultural understanding of consumer behavior and business customs, etc. The cross-cultural training courses are not only for employees working on international dimensions or for expatriates in overseas subsidiaries but also for ordinary employees working in the domestic market.

Recently Samsung took a great step forward in globalizing human resources by adopting a program of dispatching over 200 unmarried employees to various countries for two years. The company pays all the expenses of staying in these foreign countries and provides all compensation deserved for normal work. There are no requirements as to what to do for two years; people can study, work or travel in the chosen country. The only assignment for them is to become familiarized with business customs, politics, economics and the cultural enviornment or local consumer behavior. In short, the aim is to become a specialist on the country which he resides in. This is a very ambitious program for raising globally-minded human resources who can be dispatched to overseas subsidiaries as area specialists. It requires a huge investment the outcome of which is only realized in the long term, and thus cannot be initiated without top management's strong commitment to the globalization of Samsung.

Another method of globalizing human resources is to use as many local employees as possible and provide them with the chance to work at the headquarters on a regular basis. This rotation work program enables foreign locals to mingle with other nationals, nourishes an international mind, and enhances the understanding of cross-cultural differences.

EVALUATION OF THE GLOBALIZATION OF SAMSUNG

There have been many criticisms of the globalization process of Samsung in the past. First, contemporary theory on multinational enterprises is based on the assumption that they operate and thrive under the conditions of imperfect competition. The focus of past research on the globalization of firms has been on the identification of those monopolistic advantages that enable a firm to establish overseas business operations despite the additional costs involved in crossing national boundaries and the incentives to make investments abroad. These advantages are often known as "ownership- or firm-specific advantages." The often cited types of monopolistic advantages are production technologies protected by patents, marketing technologies supported by well-known brand names, management technologies, and preferential access to production inputs including financial resources. However, foreign investments in developed countries by Samsung Electronics have not possessed such firm-specific advantages as advanced technology, marketing know-how, brand name or scale merit which can offset inherent disadvantages. This results in the gradual deterioration of profitability of subsidiaries in developed countries such as in the US. Samsung Electronics is considering whether to close its manufacturing facilities in the US and to move to a free trade zone in Mexico.

Second, the globalization of Samsung is at an elementary stage, focussing mainly on exporting. In the past, Samsung's main strategy of globalization has been focussed on exporting products mainly manufactured at headquarters. Also, the main motive for globalization is to circumvent trade barriers of developed countries and increase export volume. Thus, the past globalization of Samsung cannot be considered to be the globalization in the true sense of the word, since it has meant more emphasis on local marketing and production, and coordination of these local operations by global networks of human resource, money and information.

Specifically, Samsung Corporation as a general trading company is too dependent on the group-affiliated manufacturers for sourcing and has neglected to develop foreign supplies. Also the manufacturing companies of Samsung Group, such as Samsung Electronics, have not made much effort to develop overseas markets and establish local distribution networks through active local marketing activities since most of their international marketing has been done through Samsung Corporation. Also their international business has been through exporting based on OEM (original equipment manufacturer) which does not require local marketing activities.

Third, Samsung has not fully utilized the collective effects of globalization. In other words, the globalization of Samsung's companies have been sought individually rather than under a unified globalization strategy of Samsung Group. For example, international marketing know-how or experiences of international business operations accumulated by Samsung Corporation through its earlier globalization has not been shared among other affiliated companies. Thus, mistakes are repeated without utilizing past cases of failed investment in local production or marketing. Another reason that experience or know-how of global business activities are not being shared among managers is the insufficient support of information systems.

Fourth, the globalization of Samsung has been sought for defensive rather than offensive motives. Most of Samsung's companies have focussed on the domestic market to maintain a dominant market share and have taken a passive attitude toward risky international operations. Also, their main motivation for foreign direct investment in developed countries is defensive, that is to circumvent trade restrictions such as quotas. So, they have not accumulated the experience or know-how needed for globalizing their operations nor have they fully utilized the benefit of local production. As a result, several cases have been reported where companies have failed in fulfilling the goal of entering a foreign market and have divestment instead.

Fifth, affiliated companies of the Samsung Group are in different stages of the globalization process; Samsung Electronics is in the most advanced stage and is building overseas manufacturing facilities in eleven countries. Samsung Corporation as a general trading company is just behind Samsung Electronics; it owns eight manufacturing subsidiaries and has sixteen sales subsidiaries. However, other affiliated companies in textiles or electricity are in the early stages of the process (e.g. exporting), so they cannot utilize the experience or know-how of the leading companies in the Samsung Group.

Sixth, Samsung lacks a global mentality among its employees. Most of the employees are accustomed to the thinking of exporting, but have not been given enough education and training to raise their global orientation or attitude. Also, expatriate managers of local subsidiaries lack active initiative to proceed with globalization. They tend to look more to the headquarters for direction rather than using their own judgment.

FUTURE DIRECTIONS OF THE GLOBALIZATION OF SAMSUNG

Samsung's goal for the year 2000 is that it will be an excellent corporation with a global network of local marketing, R&D and production which will be managed by globally-minded employees. To this end Samsung will proceed in the globalization process gradually and systematically. As a conclusion, five basic directions are presented which Samsung will take in future globalization: the development of human resources with a global mentality; the creation of a global corporate identity; the globalization of management; the establishment of a global network of R&D and production; and the strengthening of global marketing (Simon et al., forthcoming).

Developing human resources with a global mentality

Future globalization of human resources at Samsung will proceed in two directions; first, the development of human resources with a global mentality and attitude; and second, the localization of human resource management at overseas subsidiaries. In order to train employees at headquarters and expatriates at overseas subsidiaries in globalization issues, Samsung will adopt a system of international management development for senior employees and send functional experts to overseas education institutes. It will also expand its "unmarried area specialists development program" where unmarried employees are dispatched abroad for two years to become area specialists; the plan will produce 1000 area specialists in five years.

The education and training program in international orientation will be strengthened by the increased courses in foreign languages and cross-cultural studies. Samsung will also strengthen education and training for expatriate employees in overseas subsidiaries by the establishment of overseas regional study institutes and cross-cultural training centers.

The localization of human resources at overseas subsidiaries will be achieved in several ways. Samsung will increase its use of local employees and install a career development plan for them. In this plan, qualified local employees will be able to become managers and work at headquarters on a rotating work system.

Creating a global corporate identity

To develop a global corporate identity Samsung will strengthen the global mentality of its employees and change its corporate philosophy to become more globally-oriented. For example, one of Samsung's missions is currently to contribute to national development; this will be changed to be to contribute to the development of global welfare. Also, Samsung will establish a new corporate culture which reflects a more global orientation and will design a new corporate identity.

Globalization of management

Samsung will actively seek the localization of management styles and the structure of overseas subsidiaries. It will delegate most of headquarters' functions to local managers and will re-establish the organization structure of overseas subsidiaries to fit local conditions. Also, the performances of overseas subsidiaries will be evaluated on the basis of criteria which fully reflect local conditions. However, the future globalization of Samsung will proceed centering around regional headquarters. Thus, regional headquarters will emphasize greater coordination of the local activities of subsidiaries in its regions. In other words, Samsung will develop a "globalization" which will integrate more globalization activities at the headquarter level and more localization at the subsidiary level.

Strengthening global marketing activities

The future globalization of Samsung will shift its focus from exporting to local marketing activities in overseas markets and finally to global marketing activities incorporating local marketing activities under universal global guidelines (for example, global product policy or global advertising strategy). For the globalization of marketing, first, it will strengthen the local marketing activities of overseas subsidiaries by transforming overseas branches to sales subsidiaries and establishing local distribution networks. Also, marketing managers of overseas subsidiaries will be given decision-making power to design their marketing activities in order to fully reflect local market conditions.

These strengthened local marketing activities will be accomplished centering around regional headquarters in the US, the EU and Japan. Samsung will differentiate overseas market strategies in the future depending on regional characteristics. In developed regions the focus will be on penetrating local distribution networks and establishing its own sales network. Also, much delegation of authority will be done in this region. However, in developing countries, more emphasis will be given to acquiring a stable source of supply at a reasonable price. Thus, relatively speaking, headquarters' control will be stronger in that region. Investment in socialist countries such as China or formerly socialist such as Russia will be treated case by case.

Second, for fully-fledged global marketing Samsung will develop a global product which is basically universal, but can be differentiated to adapt to local consumers' tastes and needs. Samsung's globalization of product policy as a means of obtaining international competitiveness and scale merit is well reflected in the global approach to new product development, which is called the "prototype approach" or the "think globally, act locally" approach. In this approach basic product type or major features are determined universally on the basis of a global concept, but the specific design or minor features are changed to adapt to local consumers' tastes or needs. Also, Samsung will focus its globalization process on three major businesses – electronics, heavy industry, and the service industry, especially insurance. It will specialize and concentrate on these core strategic businesses in order to develop them into global industries with international reputations.

Third, it will develop a common global theme which can be used in local advertising with illustrations adapted to local conditions.

Establishing global R&D and production systems

The objective of the future globalization of Samsung with regard to production is to establish a global network of production systems. To fulfill this goal Samsung will expand its overseas production facilities by direct foreign investment and will rationalize production systems to become fully automatic systems. It will also accompany small and medium-sized manufacturers to overseas production facilities to acquire a stable supply of quality parts and components. In the short run, Samsung will establish a network of international purchasing offices (IPOs) and specialize in the manufacturing of parts and components in overseas facilities depending on the condition of the host country. For example, Samsung Electronics will produce tuners in Thailand, speakers in China, and will assemble these components in Indonesia.

Finally, for successful globalization a firm should possess advanced technology as a firm-specific advantage in order to compete with foreign local competitors. Samsung will invest greatly in R&D activities to develop new technologies and products with international competitiveness. It will utilize merger and acquisition of foreign venture capital of high technologies and establish overseas R&D centers in developed countries in order to receive advanced technology directly and easily. On a long-term basis, Samsung plans to build a global network of R&D and production systems in which low-priced products are manufactured in developing countries with cheap labor costs, such as in South East Asia, to enjoy scale merit; however, high-technology products will be produced in developed countries on a small scale but with diversified items.

REFERENCES

Drucker, P. F., "The changed world economy," *Foreign Affairs* (Spring, 1986).

Keegan, W. J., *Global Marketing Management*, 4th edn (Englewood Cliffs, NJ: Prentice-Hall, 1989).

Knickerbocker, F. T., *Oligopolistic Reaction and Multinational Enterprise* (Boston: Division of Research, Graduate School of Business Administration, Harvard University, 1973).

Kumar, K. and K. Y. Kim, "The Korean manufacturing multinationals," *Journal of International Business Studies* (Spring/Summer, 1984) pp. 45–62.

Lall, S., *The New Multinationals: the spread of Third World enterprises* (New York: John Wiley & Sons, 1983).

Lecraw, D. J., "Internationalization of firms from LDCs: evidence from the Asia region," in K. Kumar and M. G. McLeod (eds), *Multinationals From Developing Countries* (New York: Lexington Books, 1981).

Lee, C., "The characteristics and performances of Korean joint ventures," presented at 1990 Academy of International Business (AIB) Conference, Toronto, Canada (1990).

Levitt, T., "The globalization of markets," *Harvard Business Review* (March–June, 1983), pp. 92–102.

Min, S. K., "Korean manufacturing FDIs," in Byungjune Hwang (ed.), *Korean Business Management* (Seoul: Hanwool Books, 1985).

Ohmae, K., *The Borderless World* (New York: Harper & Row, 1990).

Porter, M., *The Competitive Advantage of Nations* (New York: The Free Press, 1990).

Simon, D. F. et al., *Globalization, Korean Style: Samsung's Emergence as a World Class Corporation* (Boston: Harvard Business School Press, forthcoming 1995).

Wells, L. T., "Foreign investors from the Third World," in K. Kumar and M. G. McLeod (eds), *Multinationals From Developing Countries* (New York: Lexington Books, 1983).

11 The globalization of Fujitsu

Katsuto Kondo

HISTORY OF FUJITSU LIMITED

Origin

Fujitsu Limited was founded on June 20, 1935. Looking back over its almost six decades of business, its growth and aggressive entrance into new markets have been remarkable. Fujitsu ranked sixty-third in the Fortune Global 500 in 1990. Due to purchase of an equity share of International Computers Ltd. (ICL), a British computer company, Fujitsu has become the second largest manufacturer in the world computer industry, with only IBM ahead of it. Fujitsu originally started as the Fuji Electric Corporation's telecommunications division. Fuji Electric itself was a joint venture with Furukawa Industrial Electric Co. and Siemens, the German electronics giant. Fuji Electric decided to separate its telecom business in 1935 because of the growth of the telephone market and the difference between the nature of the heavy electrical business and that of the telephone business. Fujitsu, when established, called itself Fuji Telecommunications Equipment Manufacturing Limited (Fuji Tsushiki Seizo Kabushiki Gaisha). Fujitsu's case study is interesting, not only because of the fact that it is among the largest firms in the Pacific Rim, but also because it is a company operating in an industry characterized by dynamic technological innovation.

Chronology

The firm's historical development basically followed four stages according to its business foci. The first phase was from 1935 to 1953, during which it aimed to become a total telecommunications equipment vendor for Japan's telecommunications operating organizations such as the Ministry of Telecommunications (later to become the Ministry of Post and Telecommunications) and Nippon Telegram and Telephone (NTT, public until 1985), the national telephone operating company founded in 1952. Makers who served NTT used to be called the NTT family, and Fujitsu was part of that. Fujitsu's relationship with Siemens played an important role in upgrading its technology and the quality of its products.

The second phase was from 1954 to 1975. During this period the big issue was entrance into the computer business, and Fujitsu successfully established itself in the leading position in the Japanese market. In 1954, Fujitsu shipped its first computer-using relay technology. Transistor-based computers were introduced in 1961. However, the technological gap between the West and Japan was so large that the Japanese government protected and promoted Japan's computer industry through various programs. In 1967, when the computer business was recognized as an important industrial field, the company officially renamed itself Fujitsu Limited (Fujitsu Kabushiki Gaisha). Regarding its overseas business, Fujitsu started to export from the 1950s.

The third phase, between 1976 and 1990, was the period during which Fujitsu became a total information equipment vendor, from semi-conductors to computers and telecommunications equipment. Computing and telecommunications had melted into one area, combined by digital technology and microelectronics. Moreover, it was the period during which Fujitsu boosted its brand name and prestige both in Japan and overseas. A crucial point in Fujitsu's history was when it surpassed IBM in the domestic computer market in 1979 and became the number one computer manufacturer in the Japanese market. Fujitsu's overseas presence increased in all three product areas during the 1970s as well.

Today, in the 1990s, Fujitsu endeavors to become a total information equipment vendor for telecommunications equipment, computers, semi-conductors and services. It understands that the future of the firm will not simply lie in remaining a high-tech manufacturing company.

ORGANIZATION STRUCTURE IN FUJITSU

Business fields

Currently, the company operates in three main areas of business, namely computers and information processing, telecommunications and electronic devices, including semi-conductors. These areas accounted for 69 percent, 15 percent, and 12 percent respectively of consolidated revenues in the fiscal year 1990. The remaining 4 percent came from consumer electronics operations, such as car audio systems. Each unit is subdivided into product groups and independently managed.

Fujitsu's computer division was created in 1961. In 1962, the company's name in English was fixed as Fujitsu Limited. Until 1977, when the semi-conductor group became independent, it assisted the telecommunications division and the computer division by providing digital integrated circuits. Moreover, it used to sell analog ICs for outside customers. But in 1966, external sales were ceased in order to concentrate on the development of digital ICs for mainframe computers. NEC and Hitachi continued to supply analog ICs for both internal and external users. That is the primary factor which differentiates Fujitsu's semi-conductor business from other domestic rivals in terms of positioning and product lines. The rivals had more capacity to serve huge capital investment and manpower resources than Fujitsu. Therefore, the firm had to concentrate on R&D for computer digital ICs. Fujitsu is not a volume producer in commodity chips; rather the firm is doing well in its ASICs business.

Domestic operations

Fujitsu's organizational structure is a mixture of product lines and functions (see Figure 11.1). Product line structure appears in development and manufacturing activities. Development and manufacturing operations are composed of three units: telecommunications, computers and electronics devices. In terms of marketing, Fujitsu has a separate staff for each product line. Functional structure appears in the separation of manufacturing, sales, and service operations. Fujitsu's sales force is organized by region, and systems engineers are organized according to the industry sector of Fujitsu's customers for which they are responsible. Basic research functions are separately incorporated as a subsidiary, Fujitsu Laboratories Ltd.

However, the electronic devices operations, which have their own sales forces for domestic and foreign markets, are an exception to this rule. Although these groups are managed independently, coordination among sales, systems engineers, and manufacturing functions are maintained through communications in daily operations.

The rationale for the product-function mixture is to serve the

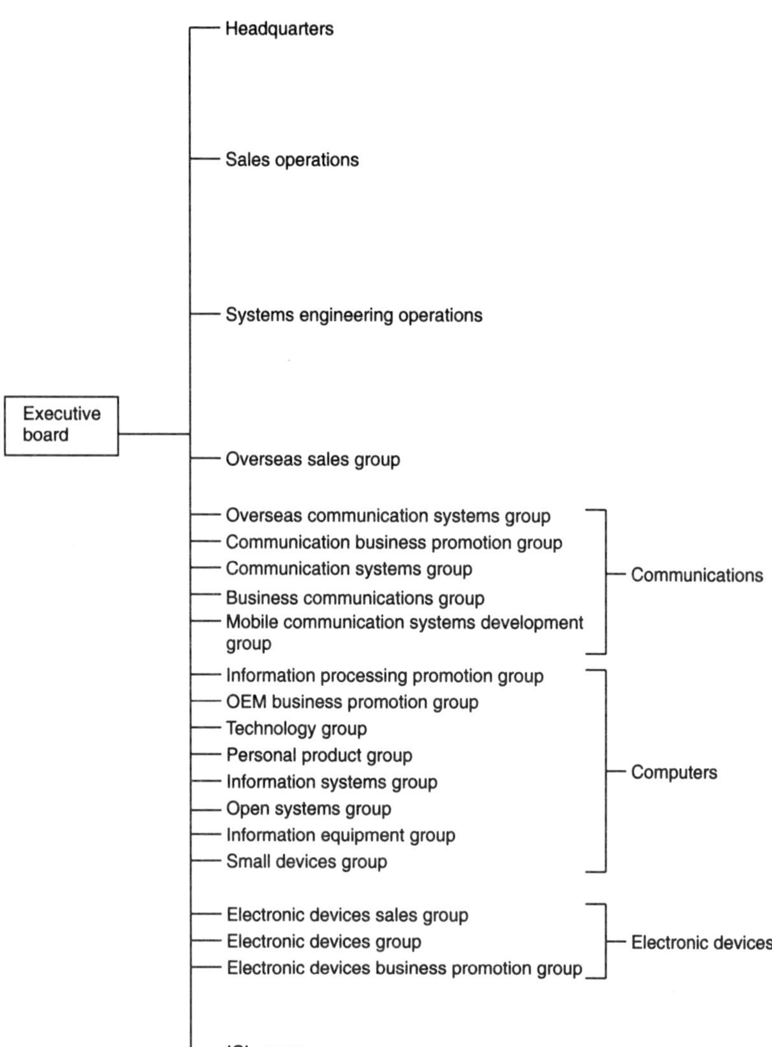

Figure 11.1 Fujitsu's organigram

Source: Fujitsu. Chart as of June 26, 1992

demand for systems business ranging from hardware to software, as well as to prove the integrated application of computers and telecommunications. The separation of the semi-conductor operations from this rule lies in the difference in nature of the business and its history. Semi-conductors, as industrial material products, are sold through different distribution channels to customers different from those of the two other product lines. Furthermore, until the late 1970s, there were no sales of semi-conductors to outside customers. Therefore, the sales force for chips was formed relatively late.

Overseas operations

Fujitsu's foreign and domestic operations are managed independently by each group. Thus the degree of development in overseas activities varies among the groups.

Fujitsu has an international division called the International Operations Group, which is mainly in charge of overseas sales and has administrative control of overseas subsidiaries. But the international division is designed to sell only products of the Computer and the Telecommunications Groups abroad, because the Electronic Devices Group has its own separate sales force. Each manufacturing product group has several overseas subsidiaries for production. For example, the Electronic Devices Group oversees a subsidiary in the US called Fujitsu Microelectronics Inc. (FMI) with plant facilities and development capability. The Electronic Devices Group also has its own overseas sales personnel. The Telecommunications Group has customers ranging from government to industry to consumers.

Fujitsu currently operates twenty liaison offices, twenty-five sales and service companies, twelve manufacturing companies, three R& D companies, and two finance companies. If ICL's 109 subsidiaries are added, the number of overseas subsidiaries becomes 151. Local sales forces are employed in overseas markets. The Computers Group depends on Siemens in Europe, and Amdahl Corp. in the US as its sales force for large-scale systems based on OEM agreements. In the US market, however, Fujitsu has also begun direct sales of mainframes to customers due to the increase in the number of Japanese firms which operate in the US and the resulting demand for Fujitsu products.[1] In addition, Fujitsu has deepened its tie with ICL, from technological cooperation to sales and manufacturing alliances worldwide.

OVERALL STRATEGY

Revenue maximization is Fujitsu's main strategic concern. Over the thirty years since 1960, its revenue has increased 170 times. During the same period, IBM and NEC increased their sales thirty-eight and eighty times respectively.[2] Fujitsu's impressive growth was achieved through its effort to focus on systems business of high value-added, high-tech products. Not only R&D and manufacturing but also systems engineering capability to meet the requirements of customers for made-to-order information systems is critical.

Fujitsu is not a niche player in any sense. It has been in the mainstream of what the microelectronics and information revolution offers to the market. Fujitsu's R&D expenditure is larger than that of any of its competitors. In 1991, the Fujitsu parent company alone spent 16 percent of total revenue on R&D. Moreover, the company has a strong desire to become a full-range information equipment maker. For instance, in the office computer market, although NEC and Toshiba were ahead, Fujitsu entered the market later and achieved a neck-and-neck position with the existing participants. Fujitsu's product lines vary from pocket-sized computers to super computers, from cellular phones to broad-band ISDN systems, from DRAMs to customized chips like ASICs and gate arrays.

Its production systems have strength in high value-added, high-quality, small-batch production. However, Fujitsu is weaker in high-volume, low-cost production in which firms like Matsushita Industrial Co. clearly have greater strength. Fujitsu tends to play high-end games even in high-volume consumer products.

The company's growth is remarkable, but there comes the next question: why was it possible? Porter's notion of "home base" helps us to understand where Fujitsu's competitiveness came from. Rivalry with domestic firms was fierce, but is not enough to explain the competition in the home base, because Fujitsu focusses on computers and information processing more than any other Japanese company. Fujitsu's true rival is a wholly-owned Japanese subsidiary of the world's largest computer maker: IBM Japan. Fujitsu differentiated its strategy from Hitachi and NEC by pursuing global competition with IBM within the domestic market. At country level, the size of the Japanese market and also various government programs to promote demands for computers helped Fujitsu to execute this strategy. At corporate level, Fujitsu focussed semi-conductor R&D on emitter-coupled logic (ECL) to serve the need for mainframe development. These technologies made Fujitsu enter the fast-speed computer development race with IBM, and also became bases from which it could associate wih foreign system houses like Amdahl, and ICL. "Reliability first" is the philosophy of Fujitsu's product development. Thus, Fujitsu provides better products than competitors with relatively low prices. Fujitsu created Japanese Extended Feature (JEF) to support the use of Kanji (Japanese characters) in computing. Moreover, the company put more focus on custom software development through systems engineering services. When the firm outpaced IBM Japan and became the leader in the Japanese mainframe market, Fujitsu had established an advantage on which to compete in the world market.

PERIOD OF INTERNATIONALIZATION

Export sales

Internationalization of Fujitsu's business refers to seeking overseas markets mainly through export. Fujitsu's internationalization process started in the 1950s. The first products to be sold in overseas markets were automatic telephone switching machines, exported in 1951. However, the telecommunications business abroad was not strong due to a licensing agreement with Siemens which limited market expansion outside of Japan.[3]

In the 1960s, the export of computer-related products began. Fujitsu shipped the first made-in-Japan computer to the Philippines Custom Bureau in 1963. The export of computers paralleled domestic market development because foreign competitors were strong in the Japanese market. FACOM M-series mainframe computers, which adopted IBM software compatibility, were developed to promote overseas sales. M-series computers were strategic products designed to attract IBM customers in both domestic and overseas market. This policy was the refusal of MITI's national computer development policy to consolidate Japanese computer makers. Fujitsu collaborated with Hitachi to develop IBM-compatible large-scale mainframes. Fujitsu was a "lone ranger" in its computer development, while other Japanese computer makers turned to Western firms for technology. For instance, Hitachi joined RCA, which made IBM-compatible computers. Therefore, collaboration with Hitachi encouraged Fujitsu to adopt IBM compatibility despite internal reservations and disagreement.

In the 1970s, transmitters were exported for the first time into overseas markets such as Papua New Guinea, New Zealand, Thailand, and Chile.

In order to promote exports, the international division was created in 1971, integrating the Overseas Division and the Trade Division. The International Operations Group worked on the expansion of overseas business through export and the creation of overseas facilities. Liaison offices were created in Vienna, London, Singapore, and Manila. Prior to that, there had been a single liaison office in New

York. Thereafter, export sales dramatically increased from ¥6 billion in 1971 to ¥16 billion in 1975.

Overseas investment

In the 1960s, Fujitsu started overseas direct investment to establish overseas facilities for the following two main purposes: technology acquisition and sales promotion. Its first overseas subsidiary was created to collect information on advanced technology. In 1968, the Fujitsu California Laboratory was established on Amdahl Corp.'s property in the Silicon Valley to pursue collaborative research. This laboratory later became Fujitsu America Inc. (FAI) in 1976. Fujitsu's tie with Amdahl Corp. began with the friendship between the pioneering engineers of both companies: Dr. Gene Amdahl, who was one of the chief engineers participating in IBM's 360 mainframe project, and Toshio Ikeda, Fujitsu's leading computer engineer. Dr. Amdahl left IBM due to an argument regarding IBM 370 System development, and formed his own company to build new mainframes. Fujitsu showed an interest in his new venture as a possible source of advanced technology. The fact that the company's first overseas facility was aimed at the acquisition of foreign technology shows the importance of Fujitsu's focus on technology.

Another purpose of setting up facilities abroad was to promote sales. In the early 1970s, overseas sales companies were created. The computer group was active because of keen competition in the domestic market. Fujitsu established sales arms in Australia, Brazil, Spain, Taiwan and Korea for mainframes. Facom Australia Ltd. (later renamed Fujitsu Australia Ltd. (FAL)) was established in 1972. From 1976, FAL promoted the sale of FACOM M-series mainframes. M-series were also welcomed in Brazil.

Moreover, in order to enter the local market, offshore manufacturing began. However, the strategy behind this development was a country-by-country (multi-domestic) approach. Overseas factories covered the local market and neighboring countries. Fujitsu's telecom business went overseas to carry out national projects for other governments. In 1973, Fujitsu Singapore Pte Ltd. (FSL) was established after signing a contract with Singapore Telecom to install crossbar switching machines. Although there were some business opportunities in Hong Kong, unfortunately orders from Singapore did not increase. Therefore, FSL had to concentrate on volume manufacturing of parts and components such as relay.[4]

Offshore manufacturing was also a way for Fujitsu to learn foreign business practice such as cross-cultural management of employees, technology transfer, and negotiation with host govenments. Fujitsu responded to host governments' policies for import substitutions. Fujitsu Espana S.A. (FESA), established in 1973, was Fujitsu's answer to the Spanish government's request to protect its national computer industry from IBM dominance. FESA started operations from the sales and maintenance of mainframes. Then, in 1975, Telefonica, the Spanish telecom company, and Fujitsu formed a joint venture, Secoinsa, to produce communications and information processing equipment. Secoinsa's factory was the first overseas factory for Fujitsu's computer business. In 1986 FESA merged with Secoinsa due to the Spanish government's request to make FESA a joint venture between Fujitsu and Telefonica. FESA is now one of Fujitsu's largest foreign operations with R&D functions. A former executive recalls that the Spanish venture helped Fujitsu to show commitment to European countries and enabled alliances with Siemens and ICL.[5]

At first, however, Fujitsu was reluctant to get involved in foreign operations. When Amdahl faced trouble in launching its first IBM compatible mainframe, a majority on the board of Fujitsu shied away from it despite its successful collaborative research project. Most executives thought that a foreign company's management was not Fujitsu's affair.[6] In the end, Fujitsu decided to support Amdahl through the purchase of a 23 percent equity share, assisting management and the supply of parts. Moreover, Fujitsu took on the role of sub-assembly of Amdahl's mainframes based on a manufacturing contract. The first final product was successfully shipped to NASA in 1975. Collaboration with Amdahl was Fujitsu's first big overseas project, in terms of both the scale and the technology involved. Thereafter, Fujitsu and Amdahl ran collaborative R&D projects of CPUs, peripherals, and communication softwares. Currently, Fujitsu owns approximately 44 percent of Amdahl's equity. The two firms sell each other's mainframe computers.

Fujitsu was gradually showing a presence in the North American market by the late 1970s. The Electronic Devices and Parts Group established an office in Fujitsu America Inc. in 1976. Then, in 1979, the Semi-conductors and Electronic Devices Group formed their own overseas subsidiary, Fujitsu Microelectronics Inc., and separated from FAI. FAI became a sales company for products, from computer-related equipment to telecommunications equipment. The Telecommunications Group formed a joint venture, American Telecomm Inc. (ATI) with American Telecommunications Corp. in

California. ATC sold OEM-based digital PBX under its own brand. The venture later became Fujitsu Business Communication Systems Inc.

THE PATH TO GLOBALIZATION

Awakening

The 1980s presented a crossroad for Fujitsu's overseas business. It was not only the period of establishing a worldwide manufacturing network, but also a step toward big change in its management of overseas operations. A steadily increasing presence in the US market forced Fujitsu to encounter quite a different business environment from any other in the world. Declining competitiveness and fear of dependence on the US multinationals might help the technology houses from the Pacific Rim, like Fujitsu, to enter Europe. But in the US, Fujitsu had to learn that a technologically excellent company may not always be the winner in international competition. Politics and legislature really played a role in this case. Fujitsu experienced three big incidents which became symbolic of deteriorating US–Japan relations. Every product category suffered as a result of these incidents. That was enough to change Fujitsu's management of its overseas businesses.

First, the AT&T bidding incident occurred in 1981. Fujitsu's Telecommunications Group won the bidding for AT&T's 900 km optical fiber network from Washington to Boston. However, the Pentagon vetoed this deal due to national defense concerns. The Pentagon justified its fear according to the belief that the telecommunications network is the lifeline of the nation and should not be dependent on foreign technology. Although Fujitsu lost a big business opportunity, it gained a reputation as a company of high-technology. MCI corporation, a long distance telephone operating company, is Fujitsu's primary customer in the US. Export to MCI started in 1980. Business with MCI continued to grow, and Fujitsu opened a factory in Texas, where MCI has a base, to supply transmitters.

Second, Fujitsu faced trouble with IBM regarding the intellectual property rights for mainframe operating systems. In 1982, FBI investigations revealed espionage activities by Hitachi and Mitsubishi for IBM's OS architecture. The following year, Hitachi and Fujitsu also had to agree with IBM not to use its software technology without receiving permission from IBM. However, in 1985, IBM sued Fujitsu for violation of the 1983 agreement. An arbitration agreement was achieved by the American Arbitration Association in 1988.

Third, Fujitsu failed to acquire Fairchild Semi-conductors in 1987. Initially, talks with Fairchild's parent, Shulumberger Ltd. went positively. However, the Pentagon and the US Department of Commerce ultimately vetoed the merger due to national security concerns. Although separated as a subsidiary, Fairchild ran a military-use semi-conductor business. The merger would have made Fujitsu one of the largest semi-conductor manufacturers in the world. Fairchild was eventually sold to National Semi-conductor. Ironically, National Semi-conductor sold the former Fairchild's military semi-conductor plant to Matsushita Electronic Industrial.

The lesson to be learned from these incidents was that Fujitsu would not grow bigger in the overseas market by just providing high-quality, high-tech products. These incidents forced Fujitsu to reconsider the management of its overseas business. An "overseas sales meeting" was held in December 1985, and former President Yamamoto (currently chairman) announced the new slogan of "Cooperation and Co-prosperity," and Fujitsu as a "Cross-cultural Company." In concrete terms, the slogans aim at: (1) harmony with local communities; (2) partnership with customers; (3) cooperation and co-prosperity with competitors through industry promotion.

Trade friction is, of course, not only a problem for Fujitsu but is a common managerial issue for Japanese manufacturing companies. In the late 1980s, the corporate environment was getting tougher for Japanese companies due to the appreciation of the yen, growing protectionism not only in the US, but also in Europe, which completed the formation of an integrated market by 1992. The response to the severe world political and economic environment was the formation of an overseas manufacturing network. Fujitsu continued on its path to globalization through its management philosophy and manufacturing strategy.

Formation of global network

Fujitsu's three main product groups respectively responded to competitive pressures and the market environment, and they created offshore production bases in the 1980s, embracing a strategic mission of promoting globalization for each product line.

The Electronic Devices Unit promoted a global production network by pursuing an international division of labor (see Figure 11.2). Although ASIC design function is spread across the US, the UK,

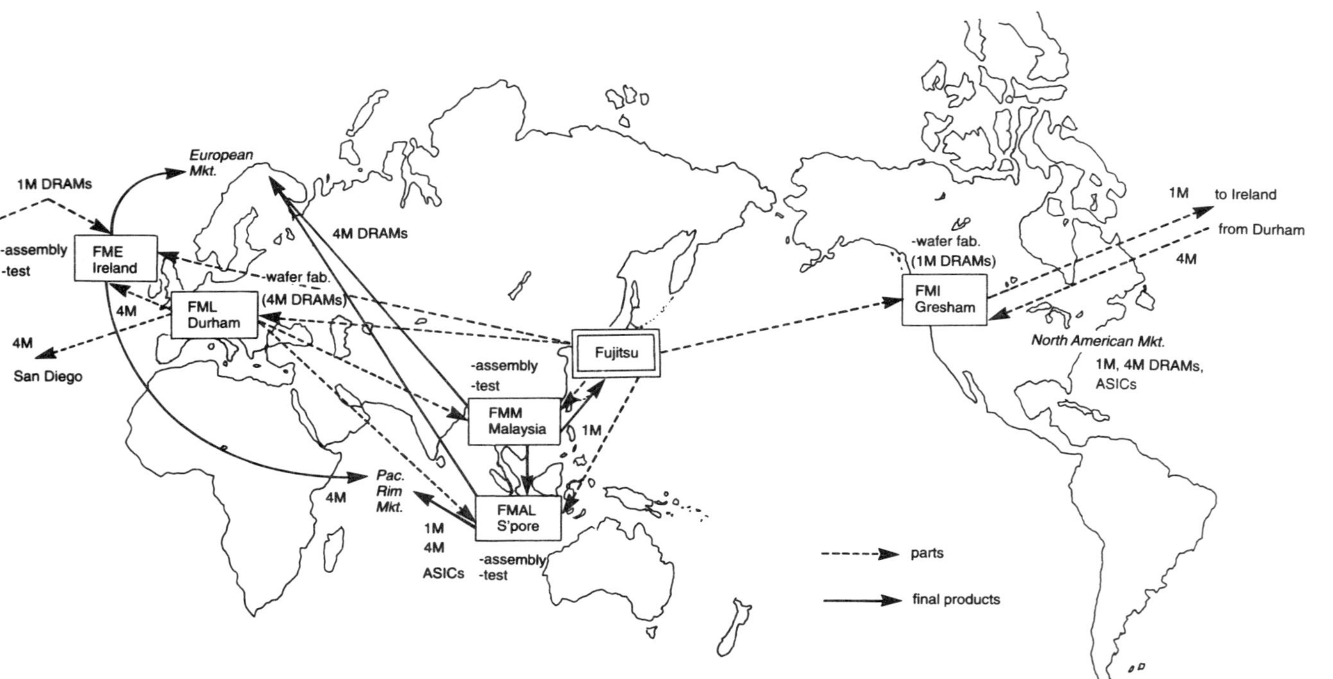

Figure 11.2 Global manufacturing network of semi-conductors

Sources: Press releases and interviews carried out by author

Hong Kong, and Singapore, R&D for new generation chips and new materials for semi-conductors is carried out in Japan. For semi-conductor chips, technological and cost advantage in Japan makes it unnecessary to always have overseas production. Before the trade conflict in semi-conductors occurred, there was less incentive to pursue overseas production. Therefore, market factors, especially trade restrictions, affected globalization in the semi-conductors business.

In the telecommunications business, Fujitsu focusses basically on a multi-domestic strategy and has increased the number of its manufacturing bases. The main reason for this is that the telecom business is based on national specifications. Switching machines for telephone operating companies have price tags of millions and even billions of yen, and last for ten to twenty years. In this business, a multi-domestic approach still makes sense. In 1990, Fujitsu began to provide manufacturing technology for digital PBX to Supersonic Radio Manufacturing, a Zimbabwe audio and radio equipment maker. The deal gave Fujitsu the first manufacturing base in Africa for Japanese telecommunications equipment makers. British Telecom and Fujitsu formed a joint venture for the manufacture of transmitters, Fulcrum Communications Ltd. (FCL) in 1991. The European Telecommunications Center, an R&D base established in London in 1990, will provide technical assistance to FCL.

The Telecom Group advances globalization according to market factors because the business is mainly in the governmental procurement market. But the group faces growing needs for the globalization of the software development process and the importance of the non-governmental market. Software development for telecommunications equipment has gone global due to a tight demand for domestic engineers. Fujitsu Singapore Pte Ltd. opened an R&D laboratory to perform software development for Integrated Systems of Digital Networks (ISDN). In the transmitters and wireless communications business, a global development and production network is under development (see Figure 11.3). Operations in Richardson, Texas, involve R&D functions for mobile telecommunications equipment. Cellular mobile telephones belong to a type of business that can become global. A global parts procurement network is under development.

In the computers and information processing field, Fujitsu advances the globalization of its manufacturing and development network among its overseas subsidiaries and local companies (see Figure 11.4). Fujitsu has aggressively promoted ties with foreign

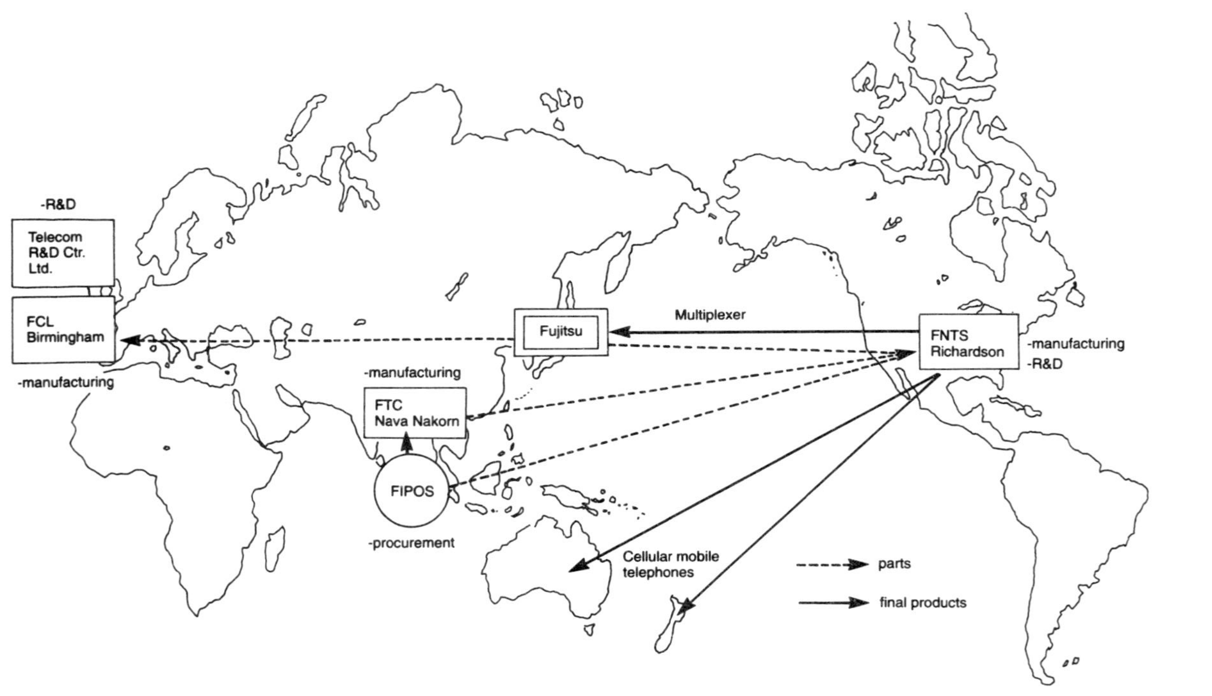

Figure 11.3 Global manufacturing network of transmission and wireless communication products

Source: Press releases and interviews carried out by author

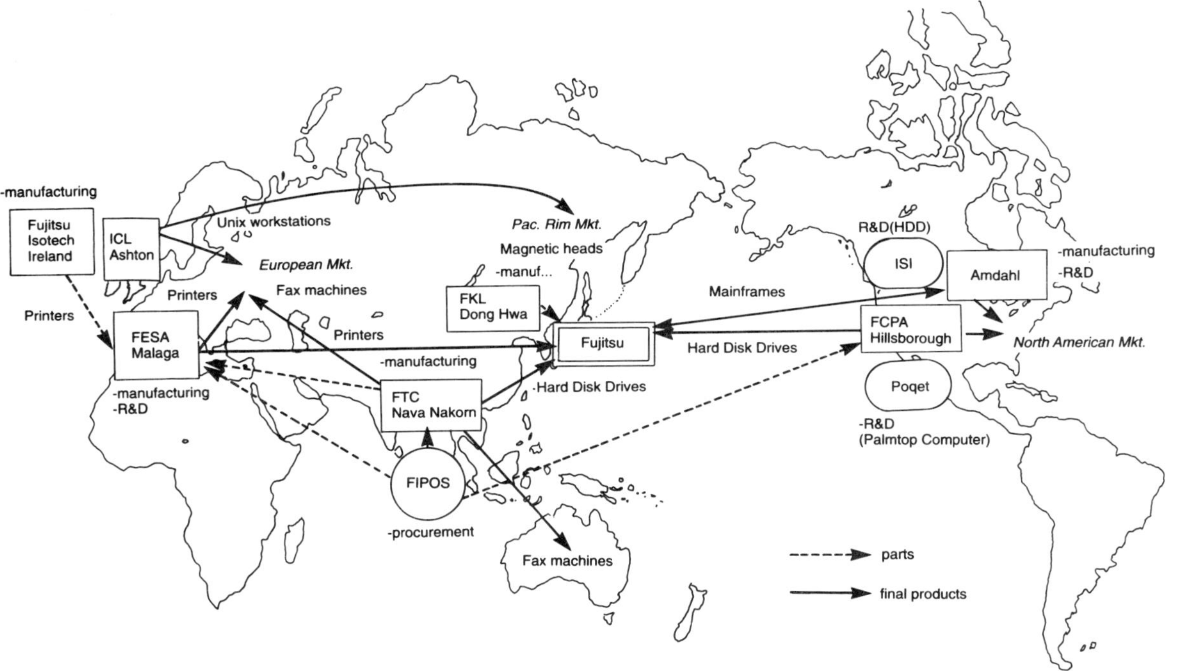

Figure 11.4 Global manufacturing network of computers and information processing equipments

Source: Press releases and interviews carried out by author

companies, forming alliances and making equity investments in the 1980s. Among them investment in ICL was the most important and strategic. In terms of a global manufacturing and development network, ICL is more advanced than Fujitsu.

ICL is the number two mainframe maker in the UK, and also has a proprietary operating system like Fujitsu. Therefore, the two companies face the same issue of how to preserve customers with their software assets and enhance them into UNIX based systems. ICL is an active member of international UNIX promotion organizations, such as X/Open, UI, and Sparc International. Fujitsu invested in Hal Computer System Inc., a UNIX system development company, to develop jointly a Sparc architecture based CMOS RISC processor. Open Systems Solutions Inc. (OSSI) was established for UNIX software development in 1991.

Fujitsu's behavior in the computer business is highly characterized by the formation of global alliances and foreign corporate acquisition. Although there have been changes in the nature of technology, the computer industry has not matured. The industry is driven by new technology development. Therefore, competition for technology development determines Fujitsu's behavior in this business.

Between 1980 and 1989, Fujitsu's percentage of overseas sales to total consolidated sales rose from 10 percent to 24 percent. The proportion for international revenue reached 31 percent in 1991, primarily due to consolidation of 80 percent of earnings of the newly-acquired ICL.[7] Over the last eight years, the export ratio to consolidated revenue declined from 24 percent to 14 percent (see Figure 11.5). This is due to an increase in overseas production facilities. Promotion of offshore production and alliances with overseas partners helped Fujitsu to become a global company.

Comparison with NEC's approach

NEC's offshore production ratio to total output has reached 20 percent, compared with approximately 5 percent for Fujitsu and Hitachi Ltd.[8]

High presence in foreign markets was a consequence of the fact that NEC started its overseas operations earlier than its Japanese competitors. Its overseas expansion began with a move into Taiwan in 1958. NEC has twenty-six marketing, service and research firms in eighteen countries, and more than 170 offices around the world.

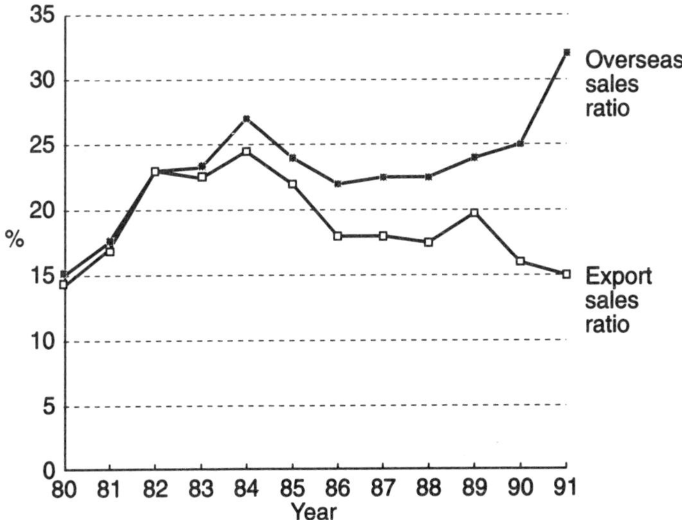

Figure 11.5 Export sales ratio and overseas sales ratio
Source: PR Department, *Data Book* (Tokyo, Fujitsu Ltd., September 1991)

NEC established a basic research laboratory, NEC Research Institute, in New Jersey in June 1988.

Offshore manufacturing is one of the most important features of NEC's overseas expansion. In 1990, NEC operated seventy-eight plants worldwide, among which about one-third, or twenty-five, are overseas plants in twelve different countries.[9] There are five NEC factories in the US. In Europe, three factories have already started operations.

The telecommunications business is the most internationalized because of the fact that NEC's overseas production has traditionally been characterized by joint ventures with host governments, because developing countries needed systems as a key component of economic progress. Earlier joint ventures include projects with Brazil, Argentina and South East Asian countries, all of which were responses to requests from the host government.[10] In terms of its computer business, NEC depends on export to Bull in France for OEM of mainframe computers.

NEC advocates the strategy of "mesh globalization" to manufacture in "optimum locations" worldwide. The International Procurement Division is in charge of studying NEC's globalization strategy. "To produce where the markets are" used to be NEC's production policy. However, a difficult business environment, including appreciation of the yen and trade frictions with Western countries has forced NEC to shift its strategy to embrace a new goal of "producing in the world's optimum locations." More recently, NEC is considering "cooperated globalization" to facilitate overseas factories as a common platform for the entire NEC group, and not just as properties of individual divisions.[11]

NEC's strategy is a global "production" strategy rather than a grand design for worldwide corporate organization. NEC has not exercised organizational changes for overseas operations yet. Its organizational structure is divided into sales lines and operational lines. Sales lines have international divisions, which are divided into regions. Therefore, the issue of effective usage of information technology is one of the most important tools of its globalization, in order to support manufacturing efficiency by coping with a decreasing economy of scale in domestic mass productions. NEC's procurement value-added network (VAN) supports its global strategy by allowing access to necessary information regarding the logistics of resource allocation. The network connects the international purchasing offices (IPOs) in Tokyo, Boston, London, Taiwan and Singapore. IPOs were established to serve as distribution bases. This network allows not only the procurement of materials and parts, but also production at optimum locations and distribution to all production bases. Each IPO provides information on the quality, price and inventory of parts and materials locally available.

NEC advances its globalization pragmatically through focussing on logistics and its information network. The firm prefers proprietary technology and is cautious about the acquisition of foreign companies. Fujitsu, on the other hand, promotes equity investment in foreign firms and corporate acquisitions to secure technological leadership.

MAJOR FUNCTIONAL CHALLENGES

Shift in organizational structure

The company's presence abroad, with diversified activities and partnerships with foreign companies, has resulted in a unique organizational response. First, organizational structure has been the major challenge for Fujitsu's overseas business management, resembling what some have called an "organizational merry-go-round". In Fujitsu's case, it required many attempts to shift away from the international division structure. Between the 1970s and today, the firm has reorganized its international operations structure four times. Fujitsu keeps sales functions separate from product groups in domestic activities. In terms of international business, however, sales arms are now put under each product group.

Initially, the Overseas Sales Divisions were formed in the Electronic Industry Division and in the Industry Division in 1971, through integration of the Trade Division and the Overseas Divisions. The Overseas Sales Division was put under the Product Division structure. Each division had its own overseas sales force. However, in 1979, the international division, called the International Operations Group, was established through the merger of four overseas sales groups for product lines. The aim of the reorganization was to integrate know-how and information like sales skills, business customs, information on country risk, political and economic situations, and customer information.[12]

In the late 1980s, when offshore production was stressed, the role of the international division began to be questioned. Finally, Fujitsu moved away from the international division structure to a product division structure. Between March and June 1991, the former International Operations Group was divided into an OEM Business Group under Computer Units, an Overseas Communications Business Group under Communications Units, and an Overseas Sales Group which became a support group for the processing of export orders. There was growing concern over the rationale behind the split. First, increasing overseas manufacturing reduces the effectiveness of the firm's international division, because overseas activities are no longer the export of finished products from Japan to foreign markets. Technology transfer and the procurement network have become the main concern between domestic product divisions and local subsidiaries. Second, the more that Japanese customers establish overseas business facilities, the more complex become the roles developed by the International Operations Group and Domestic Sales Group in order to respond to them. For example, the two sales forces for computers tended to compete in overseas markets for the same business propositions. Although coordination of both parties' activities was clearly required, technically a problem of how to draw a boundary between domestic sales and overseas sales emerged. Moreover, although the international divisions have expertise in overseas business customs, their knowledge of domestic customers' requirements are less than that of the domestic group.

Operations in the US were reorganized in December 1991. Fujitsu America Inc.'s operations were divided along product lines: Fujitsu

Network Transmission Systems and Fujitsu Computer Products of America, with FAI the holding company for the two. This parallels the reshuffle of the International Operations Group in June 1991.

Moreover, the international marketing function was also absorbed into the product division structure through a back and forth process. At first, abandonment of the overseas–domestic split occurred in marketing functions. Fujitsu established the Global Marketing Group in March 1991. Prior to that, marketing organizations were divided into domestic (Marketing Group) and international (International Operations Group, General Marketing Division). The Global Marketing Group was primarily in charge of marketing activities for computer-related products.[13] However, a corporate reorganization in June 1992 abolished the Global Marketing Group, and overseas marketing functions were absorbed into related product lines. The domestic marketing functions remained as the Sales Promotion Group.[14]

Creating a worldwide structure

Second, the acquisition of ICL stimulated a change in organizational structure. In order to manage ICL, Fujitsu incorporated an ICL Group in its headquarters structure in 1991. The Group is regarded as Fujitsu's fourth main business field along with computers, telecommunications, and electronic devices.[15] Therefore, the ICL Group is expected to provide coordination between Fujitsu's domestic computer unit and ICL's computer unit. Without coordination between the two companies' activities and a definition of their roles, conflicts and duplication between domestic operations and ICL operations may occur in the future. This is due to the fact that ICL has product lines ranging from PCs to mainframe computers, and that the two companies operate in the same countries. On the other hand, however, ICL has attractive features in its regions of operation and its technology offering. ICL has a greater presence in Europe than Fujitsu. It also has factories and a marketing structure in Eastern Europe. Moreover, ICL merged with Nokia Data, a software subsidiary of a Finnish electronics firm. In terms of business fields, ICL is strong in retail industry systems like point of sale (POS), in which it is number three in the world.

As Fujitsu–ICL cooperation has deepened from technological assistance to development and marketing activities, they have started to combine their assets in overseas markets and have restructured operations worldwide. In the US, Fujitsu merged ICL's design and manufacturing company for ISDN communication systems into Fujitsu Network Industry Inc. in December 1991. In April 1992, operations in North America, Australia, and Europe were reorganized, and three new entities were formed. First, a joint venture, Fujitsu–ICL Systems was established by merging ICl's US retail business subsidiaries, Fujitsu systems of America, and Fujitsu Customer Service of America. ICL has an 80 percent share and Fujitsu owns the rest. Second, Fujitsu Australia Ltd. merged with two ICL subsidiaries in Australia, and became a joint venture, in which Fujitsu has an 80 percent share and ICL has the rest. Third, a wholly-owned ICL company, Fujitsu Systems Business Europe, was formed to sell Fujitsu mainframes and provide systems engineering service mainly to Japanese companies operating in Europe. In order to draw synergy from ICL and Fujitsu assets, restructuring of world operations became necessary.

Autonomy in overseas facilities

Third, communications among overseas facilities became important. Given differences in business customs, telecommunications and computing environments between Japan and overseas markets, the parent in Japan is no longer the exclusive source of technology and know-how. Moreover, globalization of the customer base has accelerated the process of overseas facilities communicating with each other.

The case of Fujitsu Korea Ltd. (FKL) is a good example. One of FKL's customers, a specialized steel maker, acquired a Canadian company. The Korean steel maker had a better information system which would be appropriate in the merged Canadian firm. Installation of the system was performed by FKL systems engineers. This project became the first project for a systems engineering subsidiary, or Fujitsu Systems Business Canada, established in 1990. In FKL, teaching of the Japanese language used to be one of the important educational issues. However, English is now becoming strategically important. ICL's UNIX machines have gained attention in Korean market. FKL needs more communication with Fujitsu Australia and ICL. The globalization of customers forces Fujitsu overseas sales facilities to become independent from Japan and more interdependent with each other. In order to promote interaction among its overseas subsidiaries, Fujitsu has created the interaction among its overseas subsidiaries, Fujitsu has created the International Systems Business Committee to study various key issues.

STRATEGIC ISSUES

In the final analysis, it is inevitable that Fujitsu will pursue its path toward globalization, because the firm operates in industries where technological progress rapidly takes on global implications. So far, its globalization action through corporate acquisition has been effective inasfar as the firm has caught up with worldwide technological competition. However, a tough political and economic environment in the 1980s added more parameters on the management of worldwide operations. Fujitsu is now facing the following managerial issues in its course of globalization. When they are successfully coped with, Fujitsu's approach toward globalization will have quite unique features.

First, Fujitsu regards partnership with foreign companies as a strategic means of achieving globalization. Executives in Fujitsu call the relationship with ICL a "strategic alliance," although it is actually a relationship with a large equity investment. STC, the former owner of ICL, offered a deal of 100 percent ownership. However, Fujitsu insisted on 80 percent ownership. STC's shares will be sold on the stock market, eventually making ICL a listed company on the London stock exchange. The strategy here is that Fujitsu preserves ICL's independence, so that ICL will have some impact on Fujitsu's management style, corporate culture, and technology development process. Moreover, ICL provides Fujitsu with complementary assets for operations in foreign countries. The head of the ICL Group commented in an interview that as far as the systems business is concerned, the Japanese can not succeed in the overseas environment because the "capability to integrate systems is deeply rooted in a nation's culture."[16] In order to run the systems business globally, Fujitsu acknowledges the importance of partnerships with local companies. ICL, Amdahl, Siemens, and Nokia Data are partners who enable Fujitsu to supply corporate, industry and social information systems regardless of nationality. An already-loosened alliance with Siemens, which has started to sell mainframes made by Hitachi, has been refined. Siemens and Fujitsu expanded their alliance in the supercomputer field from April 1992. Fujitsu provides supercomputers on an OEM basis, and licenses UNIX software. These relationships are an integral part of Fujitsu's global network.

Second, Fujitsu expects globalization to be a catalyst in altering its management style and culture. Fujitsu does not place first priority on its own style of management for its overseas operations. Rather, it aims at cross-cultural management. ICL is ahead of Fujitsu in terms of experience in overseas operations, so it may become a catalyst for impacting on Fujitsu's culture and organization. For instance, a personnel exchange between ICL and Fujitsu has begun. Furthermore, Fujitsu has announced a plan to introduce an annual contracted salary system for managers. Details of the new salary system will be fixed according to ICL and Amdahl's cases.[17] Adherence to rules that can be accepted as the world standard are becoming important.

Third, R&D activities also have to become globalized. For electronics companies, there is the issue of how to respond to time-based competition of high-technology development. The formation of strategic alliance to secure complementary assets has become one of the important sources of competitiveness. Fujitsu's conception of technology trends in the future is based on four key words: downsizing, networking, open systems, and multimedia. UNIX is considered to provide the key computing architecture in the future with its strength in communications and inter-operability. Computer usage is shifting drastically from mainframes to personal computers and workstations. IBM's recent crisis demonstrates the strategic importance of collaboration with ICL and other UNIX companies. In line with this trend, Fujitsu also acquired Poqet Computer Inc. in order to obtain palm-sized computer technology. Regarding multimedia, Fujitsu's PC, FM Towns, is known for having better audio and visual capability than its rivals. However, its proprietary operating system limits the market for IBM and NEC PC users. So far Fujitsu has not responded to the worldwide consortium for multimedia technology led by Apple Computers, IBM, and Sony. Fujitsu cooperates with Intel and AMD for flash memory development.

Fourth, regionalization is becoming a new option for overseas strategy. Utilization of Asian technological capability has become important both for sharing the burden of R&D activities and for access to the opening market. As discussed already, ISDN software development has started in an R&D center established in the Singapore Science Park in 1989. In Taiwan, Fujitsu has a contract with Mosel Vitelic, a Taiwan semi-conductor manufacturer, to supply wafers by providing manufacturing technology, and has an OEM agreement with Acer for PCs. Fujitsu's response to opening markets like China and India has accelerated. Fujitsu worked with Mitsui Trading Co. to market Chinese word processors in China, and, in 1991, they formed a design and manufacturing joint venture for printers in Shenzhen. Beijing Fujitsu Software (BFS) has been in operation since April 1992 for UNIX Software development. A printer company was started in Fijian, and a telecommunications equipment manufacturing venture was started in Nanjing. Software development in India will begin.

Fujitsu's process for globalization is different from the multinational model represented by IBM. IBM's overseas strategy is based on the establishment of wholly-owned subsidiaries controlled by headquarters. It is also different from other Japanese rivals in that the globalization of Fujitsu goes beyond worldwide production strategies. So far, no other Japanese electronics company has undertaken the same kind of approach for globalization as Fujitsu. Therefore, Fujitsu certainly provides an interesting case for the study of international business.

NOTES

1 "Super/Hanyo Densanki, Fujitsu Oubeide Chokusetsu Hanbai," (Fujitsu begins direct sales of super and mainframe computers in the US and Europe), *Nihon Keizai Shimbun* (August 30, 1990), p. 11.
2 Fujitsu Limited, PR Department, *Data Book 1991* (September, 1991), p. 17.
3 Fujitsu Limited, *Shashi III*, (Corporate History III) (Tokyo, 1986), p. 43.
4 Ibid., p. 87.
5 Ibid., p. 85.
6 Norioki Kobayashi, *Fujitsu Ga IBM Ni Osorerareru Riyuu* (The reasons why IBM is threatened by Fujitsu) (Tokyo: Kobunsha, 1985), p. 54.
7 Fujitsu Limited, PR Department, op. cit., p. 81.
8 Robert Neff, "Why NEC has US companies shaking in their boots," *Business Week* (March 26, 1990), p. 90.
9 Makoto Yuasa, "NEC's global production strategy," *Tokyo Business Today* (May, 1989), p. 28.
10 Ibid., p. 28.
11 Junro Sato, "Kokusaika No Kenkyu, NEC Kenkyuu Kaihatsu Zaimu No Global-ka De Senkou," (A study of globalization: NEC leads globalization in R&D and finance), *Nikkei Sangyo Shimbun* (January 6, 1989), p. 24.
12 Fujitsu Limited, op. cit., p. 79.
13 "Fujitsu Global Marketing Honbu Setsuritsu," (Fujitsu creates Global Marketing Group), *Nikkei Sangyo Shimbun* (March 1, 1991), p. 31.
14 Fujitsu Limited, *Fujitsu News No. 427* (August 1, 1992), p. 22.
15 "Fujitsu ICL Honbu Shinsetsu" (Fujitsu newly establishes ICL group), *Nikkei Sangyo Shimbun* (December 21, 1990), p. 27.
16 Kinichi Shimizu, *Fujitsu: Atalashii Choryu Ni Idomu Excting Shudan No Zenbo* (Fujitsu: profile of the exciting organization to tackle on new trend) (Tokyo: TBS Britanica, 1991), p. 212.
17 "Fujitsu also adopts annual contracted salary system," *Nihon Keizai Shimbun* (July 21, 1992), p. 9.

12 Joint ventures between US and Pacific Rim firms

Problems and prospects

*David C. Mowery**

INTRODUCTION

International collaborative ventures between US firms and firms located throughout the Pacific Rim region have increased in number during the past fifteen years. US firms formerly employed joint ventures within the Pacific Rim and elsewhere primarily to support either production in specific foreign markets or the exploitation of natural resources in foreign economies. Now, however, these ventures are an important component of global production and product development strategies. Reflecting their new function, the activities pursued within these joint ventures now involve higher levels of joint R&D, product manufacture, and technology transfer than was formerly the case. International collaborative ventures highlight the opposing trends in the global economy discussed in Simon and Koppel (1992). Although these ventures have increased technological and economic interdependence, they are in part a response to the increased presence of governments in the management of international trade, investment, and technology flows. Indeed, the role of international collaborative ventures in such industries as telecommunications equipment or commercial aircraft suggests that governments retain substantial influence over the strategic decisions of global firms (Mowery, 1987).

This chapter reviews the data on growth in joint ventures between US and Pacific Rim firms, and presents some preliminary data on international collaborations involving Japanese firms. I also discuss some of the current and potential tensions created by international joint ventures among the firms and (in many cases) governments of

* I am grateful to Jim Sharp of Itsunami Inc. for data and to Tom Cottrell for valuable research assistance. The comments of the participants in the Sapporo conference and Denis Simon also contributed to this chapter. Research and preparation of this chapter were supported by the Alfred P. Sloan Foundation.

the nations within the Pacific Rim region. The joint venture activities of US firms within the Pacific Rim have been influenced by the rising technological strengths of Japan, and more recently, of South Korea, Taiwan, and other East Asian economies. The growing competitive strength of these economies also has affected US trade policy, creating incentives for trans-Pacific joint ventures. Most of the discussion below focusses on international joint ventures that are a component of firms' technology strategies. Technology-oriented joint ventures account for a large share of the international collaborative ventures formed during the past decade.

INTERNATIONAL COLLABORATIVE VENTURES: DEFINITION AND GROWTH

Joint ventures have long been common in extractive industries such as mining and petroleum production (see Stuckey, 1983) and account for a significant share of the foreign investment of US manufacturing firms since World War II.[1] Several features of recent collaborative ventures, however, differentiate them from earlier cases. The number of collaborations has grown.[2] Joint ventures now also appear in a wider range of industries.[3]

Most of the ventures of the pre-1975 era focussed primarily on production and marketing for the domestic market of a partner firm. The central activities of the newer forms of international collaboration, however, now focus more intensively on joint R&D, product development, and manufacture. These ventures are also more frequently aimed at global markets. Teaming allows firms to pool their technological capabilities in a single product without merging all of their activities into a single corporate entity.

International collaboration offers important advantages over such alternatives as direct foreign investment or licensing for the exploitation of firm-specific technological or other competitive assets. Many of the contractual limitations, transactions costs, and opportunistic behavior that are associated with licensing can be avoided within a collaborative venture. Partner firms make financial commitments to a collaborative venture that back their claims for the value of the assets they contribute; such financial commitments can substitute for the complete revelation of the value and characteristics of the asset that may be necessary to complete a licensing agreement.[4]

The noncodified, "inseparable"[5] character of many firm-specific assets that precludes their exploitation through licensing need not prevent the pooling of such assets by several firms within a joint venture, or the effective sale of such assets by one firm to another within a joint venture. Joint ventures enable partner firms to "unbundle" a portfolio of technological assets and transfer components of this portfolio to a partner. The difficulties of unbundling a firm's technological portfolio for arm's-length transfer may prevent the capture of these returns through licensing.

Collaborative ventures offer an alternative to the complete merger of firms as a means of pooling assets in a limited range of products. Partner firms may be competitors in other product areas, making mergers an impractical alternative to a joint venture. Collaboration also provides established firms with a (potentially) faster and less costly means than internal development to gain access to new technologies that are not easily licensed. This "technology access" has been an important motive for collaboration between established and young firms in industries based on new technologies, such as biotechnology and robotics.

By comparison with direct foreign investment, licensing, or export, collaborative ventures reduce the financial and political risks of innovation and foreign marketing. The products of a collaborative venture between a US and a foreign firm may encounter fewer political impediments to access to the domestic market of the foreign firm than would direct exports from the US firm.

Nevertheless, international collaborative ventures often complement other competitive strategies of global firms, such as direct foreign investment or licensing. The increased international economic interdependence that is measured by growing intra-firm and intra-industry trade, competition in "third markets" among the subsidiaries of global firms, and continued growth in international investment and technology flows (see Simon and Koppel, 1992) complements increased international collaboration. International collaboration can affect all of these measures of globalization, in part because these ventures are hybrids of market- and firm-based structures of governance. For example, the "strategic alliances" between US and Japanese auto firms (e.g. Ford and Mazda, General Motors and Toyota) have supported expanded investment by the Japanese partners in the United States.

This list of factors illuminates some of the key differences between joint ventures and other mechanisms for the exploitation or creation of firm-specific capabilities, but it sheds little light on the reasons for the recent growth in joint ventures among Pacific Rim firms. Explanations for recent growth trends, which are pursued below, must focus on the changes in the technological and policy environment.

CAUSES OF RECENT GROWTH IN PACIFIC RIM JOINT VENTURES

Changes in the technical capabilities of foreign firms and in the nature of product demand have intensified US firms' demand for foreign partners in collaborative ventures, especially within the Pacific Rim. The enhanced technological capabilities of many foreign firms have increased their potential contributions to joint ventures with US firms. Pacific Rim firms now are better able to absorb and exploit advanced technologies from US firms in industries characterized by a substantial technology gap between US and foreign firms. In other industries, foreign firms either are more advanced or are the technological equals of US firms and therefore can contribute managerial or technological expertise to joint ventures. US firms in the automotive and steel industries and some in the microelectronics industry now collaborate with Pacific Rim and other foreign firms to gain access to superior foreign technologies.

The risk- and cost-sharing features of international collaboration have become more attractive in recent years. The costs of the research and development necessary to bring a new product or process to market have risen considerably since 1960 in such high-technology industries as commercial aircraft, telecommunications equipment, computer systems, and microelectronics. Rising development costs strain the ability of firms to sustain ambitious R&D programs and increase the importance of penetration of foreign markets for commercial success. Firms in some industries require markets substantially larger than those provided by the huge US domestic economy. Moreover, high development costs raise the risks of new product development, since they increase the fixed costs incurred before introduction of the product.

Another source of cost pressure on R&D programs is a form of technological convergence. Technologies that formerly were peripheral to the commercial and research activities of a firm now have become central to competitive advantage in a number of technology-intensive industries. The increased interdependence of telecommunications and computer technologies is one well-known example; others include the growing importance of biotechnology within pharmaceuticals and food processing, or the greater salience of computer-based machine vision technologies within robotics equipment. Technological convergence requires firms to develop expertise quickly in unfamiliar technologies and scientific disciplines, straining R&D budgets and human resources. This factor has contributed to the growth of several types of R&D collaboration, including international collaborative ventures, domestic research collaboration among firms, and research collaboration between industry and universities.[6]

Shorter product cycles in many high-technology industries have made rapid penetration of global markets with new products more important to US firms. Rapid access to foreign markets may require joint production or other forms of collaboration with a foreign firm with an established marketing network in the target market. The importance of foreign markets reflects the decline in the share of global demand accounted for by the US market in many high-technology industries, and increased homogeneity in demand across the industrial economies.[7] Simultaneous introduction of a product in multiple industrial economies has become essential to commercial success.

The importance of technical standards for commercial success has also increased the importance of international collaboration in the electronics system and information technology industries. The establishment of a product as a de facto standard or dominant design may provide a profitable platform for the introduction of related products and subsequent generations of the product. In the global telecommunications equipment market, this dominant design motive is supplemented by the recognition that rapid penetration of many markets can contribute to a firm's influence within international standards negotiations.[8]

Still another factor underpinning the recent growth in both domestic and international collaboration involving US firms is the changing role of startup firms in the commercialization of new technologies within the US economy.[9] Small firms appear to have been more important sources of new commercial technologies in the US than in Japan and Western Europe, where established firms have played a more significant role in new electronics or biotechnology products. In the microelectronics and computer industries, the important role of small firms resulted in part from US government procurement demand, which created a substantial market with comparatively low marketing and distribution barriers to entry. The benefits of the military market were enhanced further by the substantial possibilities for technological "spillovers" from military to civilian applications. The US military market no longer plays such a strategic role in the computer and semi-conductor industries, and the possibilities for military–civilian technology spillovers appear to have declined in many areas of these technologies (see Mowery and Rosenberg, 1989 for further discussion of military–civilian technology spillovers). Biotechnology firms also face markets that are heavily regulated in the US and other nations.

These developments have raised the costs of new product introduction and the marketing-related entry barriers faced by startup firms in microelectronics, computers, and biotechnology. For this and other reasons, including the greater interest by foreign firms in the technological assets of US startup firms, collaborative ventures involving startup and established US and foreign firms have grown considerably in recent years.

The growth of non-tariff trade barriers[10] has also increased the incentives for US firms to seek foreign partners. Non-tariff barriers, especially government procurement policies and technology transfer requirements, favor the use of collaborative ventures that incorporate product research, development, and marketing, as well as manufacture. Public procurement policies create significant non-tariff barriers in export markets for such goods as commercial aircraft and telecommunications equipment, where public ownership or control of major purchasers is common. Government procurement decisions can be influenced by the production (or development and production) of components for the purchased product by domestic firms in the purchaser nation. Foreign governments also frequently provide development funding and risk capital to domestic firms as part of industrial development policies. Combined with high product development costs, foreign firms' access to capital from public sources has enhanced their attractiveness as partners in product development ventures with US firms in microelectronics, commercial aircraft, telecommunications equipment, and robotics.

Just as foreign government trade and industrial policies have created incentives for US firms to collaborate with foreign firms in export markets, non-tariff restrictions on foreign access to US markets have expanded collaboration between US firms and foreign firms wishing to sell in the United States. In several protected US industries, a foreign production presence has been achieved through a joint venture. Examples include the Toyota–General Motors and Ford–Mazda ventures.

Although the postwar growth of multinational firms and direct foreign investment raised the prospect in some assessments of "global firms" to whom national boundaries would mean little or nothing, much of the current wave of international joint venture activity reflects the opposite phenomenon. National governments are able to influence not only the production but, increasingly, the product development and technology transfer decisions of firms through the use of trade and other policies.

As was noted earlier, among the US industries that have recently been most active in forming international collaborative ventures are a number in which multinational organization, especially multinational production, has historically been rare. Commercial aircraft, telecommunications equipment, and steel are examples of these. The industries that have led in the formation of international collaborative ventures during the past fifteen years are characterized by: (1) heavy involvement by governments, as purchasers, providers of risk capital, or managers of international trade and investment flows; and (2) the competitive importance of technical standards in the establishment of "dominant designs," a feature common to telecommunications, semi-conductors, computer systems, and software.

RECENT TRENDS IN PACIFIC RIM JOINT VENTURE ACTIVITY

This section reviews data from Japanese and US sources on the international joint venture activities of US and Japanese firms within the Pacific Rim, discussing both US–Japanese joint ventures and those involving other Pacific Rim economies. Like the data discussed above, these data are flawed by biases in their sources that affect their coverage of industries, nations, and time periods. Individual observations are not weighted by size, making it difficult to reach strong conclusions about the "importance" of joint ventures in different industries or regions. The two databases differ significantly in their coverage and depth of detail on the collaborative ventures contained within each. Nonetheless, they present useful information on the industry mix and rate of formation of Pacific Rim joint ventures. The first body of data also includes limited information on joint venture failures for different industries and regions.

US and Japanese joint venture activity, 1984–91

Table 12.1 and Figures 12.1–12.13 are based on a recently assembled database on joint ventures in information technologies that is drawn from a broad sample of the US and global business press.[11] The database covers US and Japanese joint ventures within firms in

Europe and the Pacific Rim for 1984–91, employing a broad definition of a joint venture. These data are of interest primarily because of the light they shed on the mix of joint venture activity among regions and industries.

Table 12.1 US and Japanese international joint ventures in information technology, 1984–91

		Computer, robotics, office automation	*Electronics*	*Media*	*Satellite, telecommunications*	*Video*
	US w/ (Total)					
	Japan	542	182	115	209	232
	West Germany	143	32	27	75	27
1	France	21	5	18	26	8
	UK	275	53	126	228	64
	Taiwan	41	12	1	16	6
	Korea	45	39	5	15	13
	Japan w/ (Total)					
	US	542	182	115	209	232
	West Germany	39	15	4	13	12
2	France	8	4	7	4	8
	UK	69	22	25	39	38
	Taiwan	11	9	0	4	11
	Korea	13	8	2	1	5
	US w/ (Aborted)					
	Japan	25	10	7	4	10
	West Germany	4	1	2	1	0
3	France	3	2	5	2	1
	UK	12	4	5	12	1
	Taiwan	0	0	0	0	0
	Korea	0	2	0	1	0
	Japan w/ (Aborted)					
	US	25	10	7	4	10
	West Germany	3	1	0	0	0
4	France	1	0	1	0	1
	UK	5	3	0	0	1
	Taiwan	1	0	0	0	0
	Korea	1	0	0	0	0

Table 12.1 Continued

	US w/ (Non-Aborted)					
	Japan	517	172	108	205	222
	West Germany	139	31	25	74	27
5	France	18	3	13	24	7
	UK	263	49	121	216	63
	Taiwan	41	12	1	16	6
	Korea	45	37	5	14	13
	Japan w/ (Non-Aborted)					
	US	517	172	108	205	222
	West Germany	36	14	4	13	12
6	France	7	4	6	4	7
	UK	64	19	25	39	37
	Taiwan	10	9	0	4	11
	Korea	12	8	2	1	5

Source: Data from Itsunami Inc., Berkeley, California, *US–Japanese International Joint Ventures in Information Technology*

The data in the top two sections of Table 12.1 include joint ventures of US and Japanese firms that dissolved ("aborted") and suggest the dominance of US–Japanese collaboration. More than 40 percent (1,280) of the more than 2,900 international joint ventures in this sample involve US–Japanese corporate links. This dominance is unchanged when failed joint ventures are removed from the sample (US–Japanese joint ventures account for 1,224 of the total of 2,845 "non-aborted" joint ventures). Joint ventures involving US and Japanese firms (respectively, the first and second sections of Table 12.1) exhibit strong similarities in industry composition. The computer, office automation, and robotics sector dominates both nations' foreign joint venture activity. For US firms, the next most important sector for international collaboration is satellites and telecommunications, while video technologies (audio and video consumer electronics) are the second most important sector for Japanese international collaboration. Satellites and telecommunications ranks third among sectors for Japanese international collaboration, and video technologies occupy a similar position for US firms. Electronic component technologies (primarily semiconductors) is the fourth most important sector for joint ventures in both nations, and media ventures (print, broadcast, and cable communications) is the least important.

The first two sections of Table 12.1 suggest that the US and

Japan are the most important sources of international joint venture partners for firms from each nation. The next two most important national sources of joint venture partners for both US and Japanese firms are (in descending order by number of agreements) the UK and Germany. Among the economies included in Table 12.1's data, South Korean firms are the least important partners for Japanese firms. South Korea ranks behind Germany as a source of joint venture partners for US firms.

These data indicate that collaborative ventures linking either US or Japanese firms with firms from other Pacific Rim economies mainly involves firms from South Korea and Taiwan. Collaborative ventures with South Korean or Taiwanese firms are far less important than ventures linking Japanese or US firms with firms from two of the largest economies in Western Europe. French firms, however, are less prominent in ventures with US and Japanese firms than either German or British enterprises. Other analyses of data not included in Table 12.1 also indicate that few if any Pacific Rim joint ventures do not include a Japanese, European, or US firm.

The newly industrializing economies of this region do not yet appear to be forming international ventures with one another, in part because domestic markets are so much smaller than those of the "triad" economies, and also because the technological and other assets of firms in the Asian NIEs may not complement one another as well as those in ventures that link firms from the US, Europe, or Japan with firms from newly industrializing economies. These data also do not cover mainland China; as the PRC continues to expand its private sector, ventures linking PRC firms with those from newly industrializing economies (e.g. South Korea or Taiwan) could grow more rapidly.

These data do not suggest that international joint ventures are supporting the creation of a Japan-centered economic "bloc" that excludes US or European firms. Instead, Pacific Rim joint ventures appear to be linking the economies of the "triad" more closely. Firms from the developing economies of the Pacific Rim region are thus far less active in joint ventures with US, Japanese, NIE, or European firms. Indeed, some authors (e.g. Ernst and O'Connor, 1989) have argued that international collaborative ventures, combined with other forces in the global economy, may exclude developing-economy firms from high-technology industries in the future. (This point is made by Simon and Koppel (1992) as well.)

The four other sections of Table 12.1 allow for a crude comparison between surviving (sections 5 and 6) and discontinued (sections 3 and 4) joint ventures. Possibly because these data cover joint venture formation during a very recent period, the overall failure rate is low – only 4.4 percent of the US international joint ventures and 4.5 percent of the Japanese joint ventures formed during this period are classified as breaking up by late 1991. The least stable US international joint ventures, yielding a 6.5 percent failure rate, are in the media category, while the highest failure rate for Japanese joint ventures (5.8 percent) occurs in electronics, largely as a result of joint venture failures involving US firms. The nation providing the least stable joint venture partners for both Japanese and US firms during this period is France, whose firms exhibit failure rates more than twice as high as those for firms from other nations. The apparently low failure rates in US and Japanese joint ventures involving South Korean and Taiwanese firms may be an effect of the recent growth in ventures involving firms from these newly industrializing economies. These joint ventures are relatively "young" and therefore less susceptible to breakup.

Figures 12.1–12.13 display time trends in surviving Pacific Rim joint ventures involving Japanese, US, Taiwanese, German, British, French, and South Korean firms. US–Japanese joint ventures displayed a fairly steady upward growth trend during 1984–91, with a brief downturn in 1987. Computer and media joint ventures dominate the US–Japanese data (Figure 12.2), but electronics, video, and telecommunications joint ventures exhibited rapid growth late in the 1980s (the electronics joint ventures are in part a response to the 1986 US–Japan Semi-conductor Agreement; see below for further discussion).. Although the overall numbers are much smaller, US–South Korean and US–Taiwanese joint ventures (Figures 12.5–12.6) also grew during the 1980s. Taiwanese and South Korean firms pursue joint ventures with US firms in different industries, however, as electronics plays a more important role in US–South Korean joint venture activity than in Taiwan–US ventures throughout this period, which are dominated by computer-related undertakings.

The data on Japan–Taiwan and Japan–South Korea joint ventures (Figures 12.11–12.12) are sparse and therefore yield less reliable indications of time trends, but they suggest some decline during the 1980s in Japan–South Korea joint ventures, coupled with erratic and modest growth in links between Taiwanese and Japanese firms. The most prominent industries in Japanese joint ventures with Taiwanese and South Korean firms, computers and electronics, also dominate US firms' joint ventures with firms from these nations.

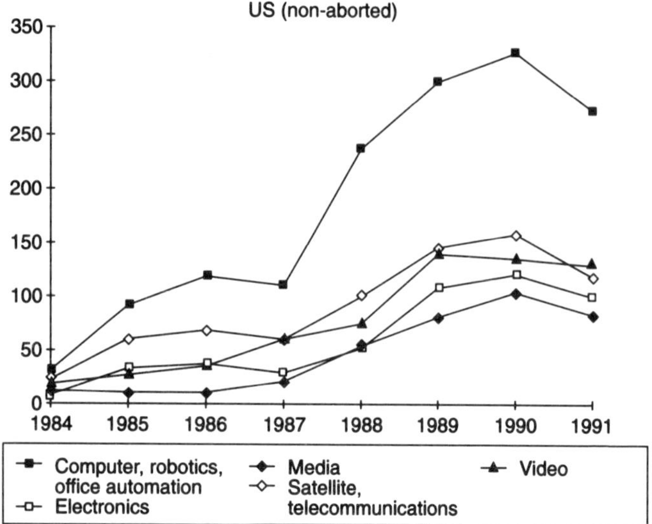

Figure 12.1 Surviving US international joint ventures in information technology, 1984–91

Source: ITsunami Inc.

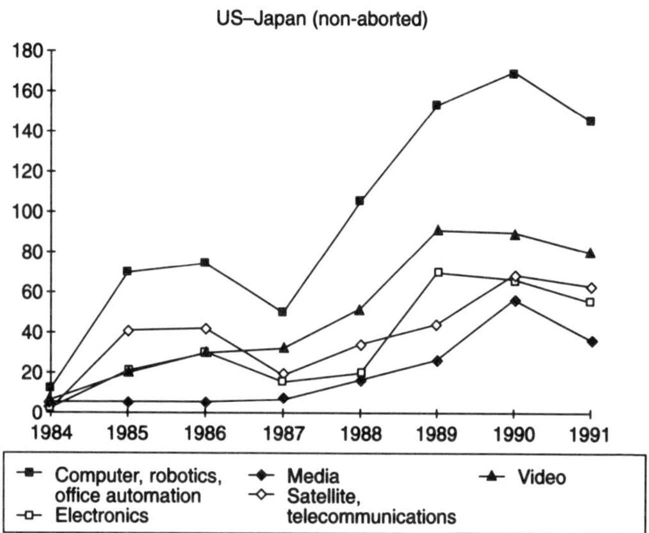

Figure 12.2 Surviving US–Japanese international joint ventures in information technology, 1984–91

Source: ITsunami Inc.

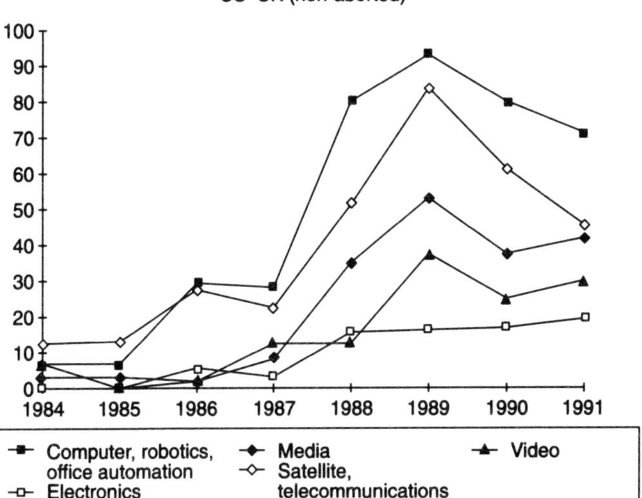

Figure 12.3 Surviving US–UK international joint ventures in information technology, 1984–91

Source: ITsunami Inc.

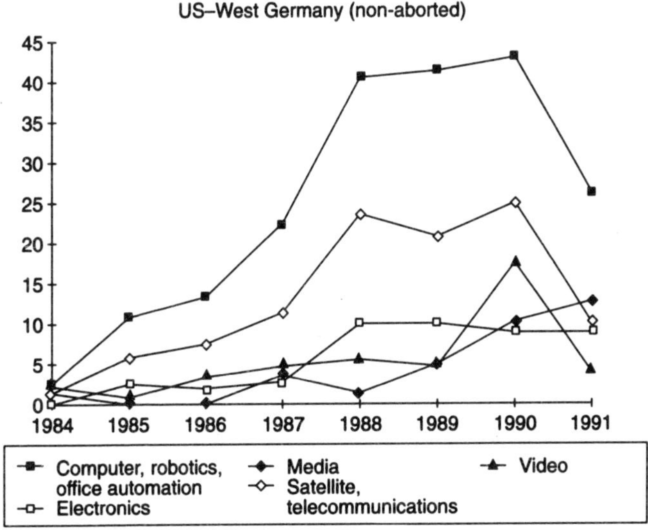

Figure 12.4 Surviving US–West German international joint ventures in information technology, 1984–91

Source: ITsunami Inc.

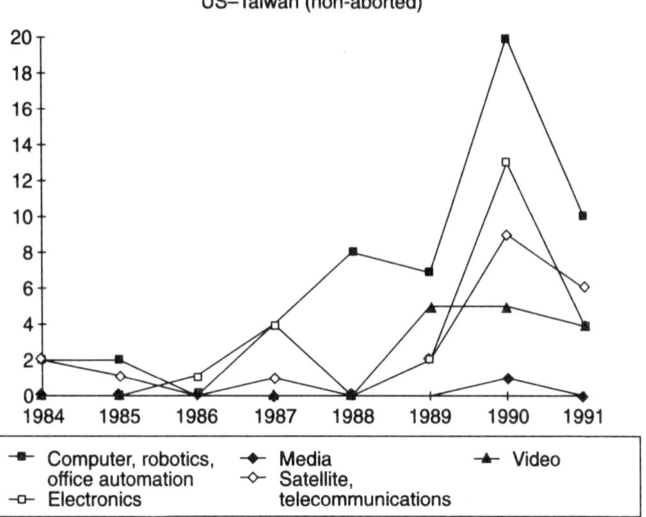

Figure 12.5 Surviving US–Taiwanese international joint ventures in information technology, 1984–91

Source: ITsunami Inc.

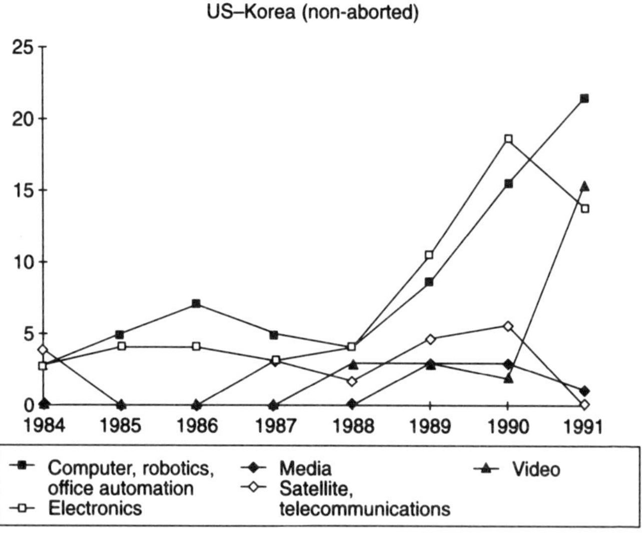

Figure 12.6 Surviving US–South Korean international joint ventures in information technology, 1984–91

Source: ITsunami Inc.

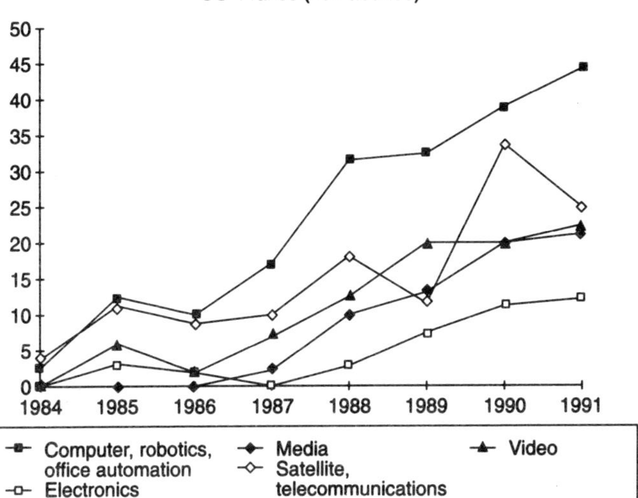

Figure 12.7 Surviving US–French international joint ventures in information technology, 1984–91

Source: ITsunami Inc.

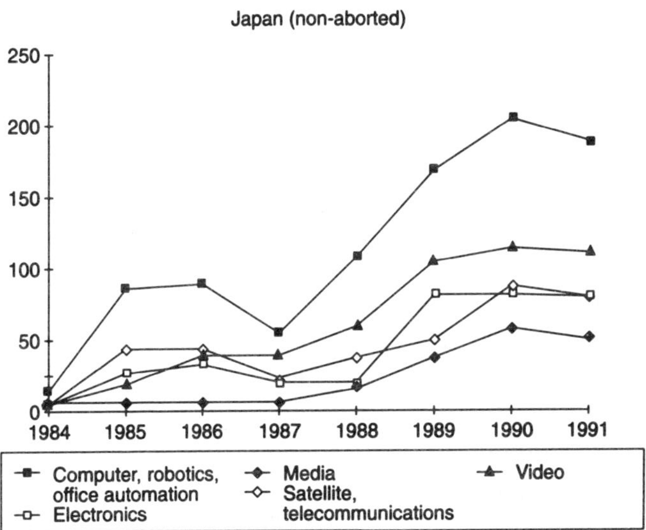

Figure 12.8 Surviving Japanese international joint ventures in information technology, 1984–91

Source: ITsunami Inc.

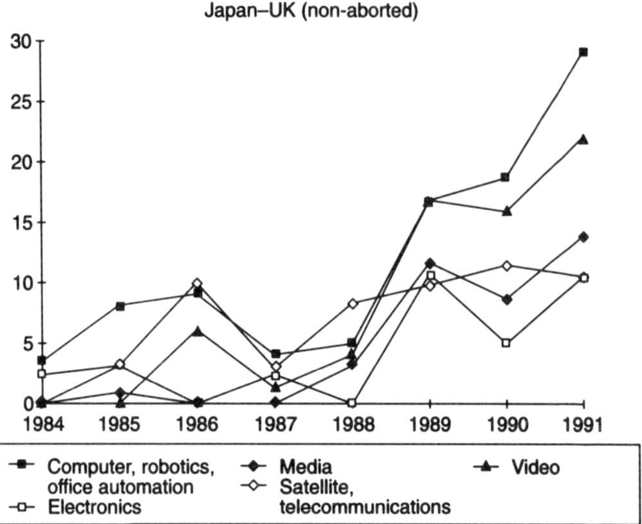

Figure 12.9 Surviving Japanese–UK international joint ventures in information technology, 1984–91

Source: ITsunami Inc.

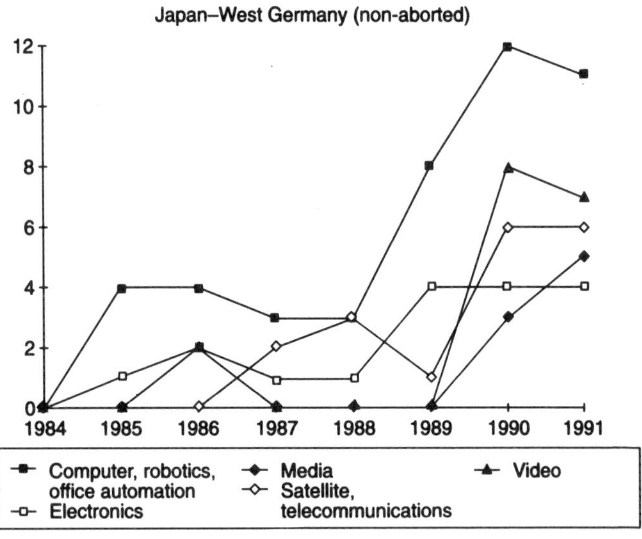

Figure 12.10 Surviving Japanese–West German international joint ventures in information technology, 1984–91

Source: ITsunami Inc.

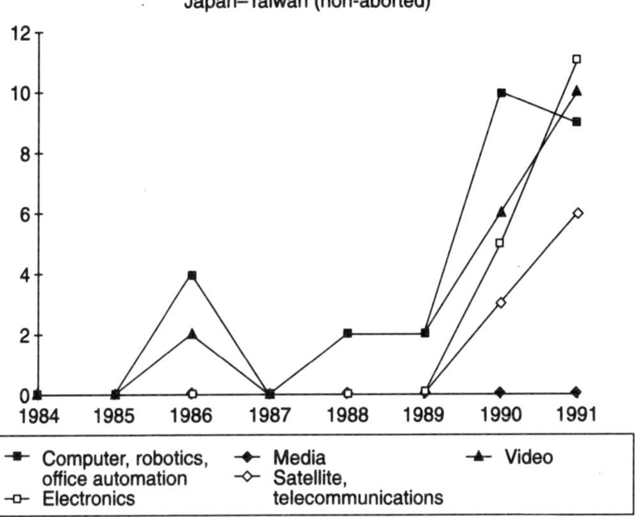

Figure 12.11 Surviving Japanese–Taiwanese international joint ventures in information technology, 1984–91

Source: ITsunami Inc.

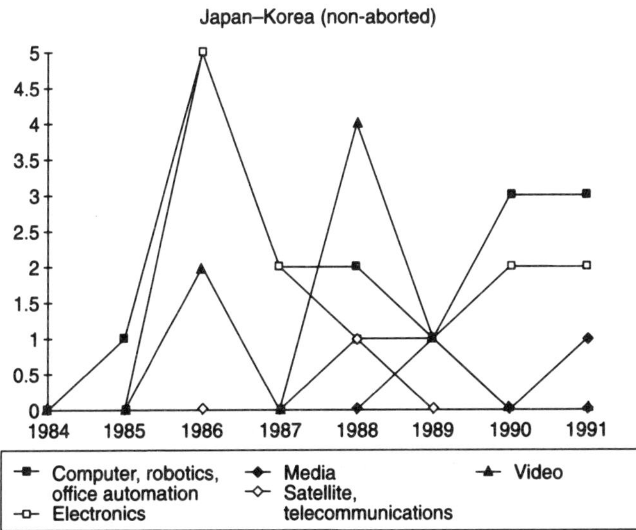

Figure 12.12 Surviving Japanese–South Korean international joint ventures in information technology, 1984–91

Source: ITsunami Inc.

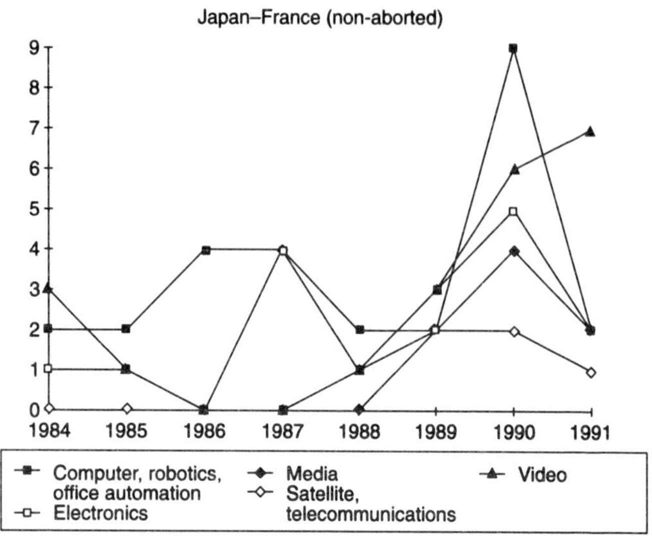

Figure 12.13 Surviving Japanese–French international joint ventures in information technology, 1984–91

Source: ITsunami Inc.

International joint ventures linking European firms with enterprises from the US and Japan (for the US, illustrated in Figures 12.3–12.4 and 12.7; for Japan, in Figures 12.9–12.10 and 12.13) exhibit broad similarities in time trends, although the rate of growth in Japanese ventures with firms from Western Europe accelerated in the latter portion of the 1984–91 period. This acceleration may be a response to the EC's tougher antidumping policy during the latter half of the 1980s, consistent with the earlier discussion of the role of non-tariff barriers in encouraging international joint ventures. Combined with the data on trends in Japanese joint ventures with other Asian firms, these data again suggest that the most significant geographic locus for Japan-based international joint ventures lies in other industrial economies, rather than in the East Asian littoral. Japanese economic links within East Asia may rely more heavily on direct investment than on joint ventures.

US–Japanese joint research ventures

Another body of data on Japanese firms' joint venture activities is displayed in Tables 12.2–12.4, drawn from a 1987 report by the Japanese Ministry of International Trade and Industry on Japanese participation in international research joint ventures (Ministry of International Trade and Industry, 1987). Although it covers a broader array of industries, this report appears to have employed a narrow definition of a joint venture, focussing on ventures devoted solely to joint R&D. As a result, the trends depicted in these tables differ from those drawn from other data sources. Table 12.2 displays trends in joint venture formation during 1982–7, revealing considerable growth in the formation of international research joint ventures, which increased from seven in 1982 to thirty-six in 1987.[12] The table's data also suggest a surprising concentration of Japanese international research joint ventures in the chemicals industry, which accounts for almost one-fifth of the total number of ventures formed during this period. Chemicals (not included in the data discussed in the previous section) ranks second only to electronics in the number of joint ventures formed during 1982–7. The importance of chemicals, which includes pharmaceuticals, as a focus of international collaboration between US and Japanese firms may reflect the importance of local links for drug testing and certification in foreign markets, a factor that has contributed to rapid internationalization of R&D activities in pharmaceuticals.

Table 12.3 contains information on the nationality of the foreign participants in the international joint ventures covered in the MITI study, and breaks down the joint ventures by technology field. US firms dominate both the "conventional" and "advanced" technology fields, accounting for 49 percent and 85 percent respectively of the international joint ventures in the two categories. US dominance in computers and communications, biotechnology, integrated circuits, and factory and office automation (all of which are included in the "advanced" technology category) is even more pronounced. These data again suggest that the international collaborative activities of Japanese firms focus on partner firms from other industrial economies, rather than being directed at other East Asian firms.

Table 12.4 disaggregates the international joint ventures by research activity. These data support the findings of other studies (e.g. Mowery, 1989) that international joint ventures rarely focus on basic or fundamental research. Instead, consistent with the blend of technology access and market access motives that underpin many

Table 12.2 Formation of new international research joint ventures involving Japanese firms, by year and industry, 1982–7

Japanese IRDJVs	*1982*	*1983*	*1984*	*1985*	*1986*	*1987*	*Cum. Total*
Total	7	7	23	37	25	36	135
%	100	100	100	100	100	100	100
Manufacturing:	6	7	19	29	18	30	109
%	85.7	100	82.6	78.4	72	83.3	80.7
food	0	0	1	2	1	1	5
%	0	0	4.3	5.4	4	2.8	3.7
textiles	0	0	0	2	0	3	5
%	0	0	0	5.4	0	8.3	3.7
chemicals	1	1	7	7	4	4	24
%	14.3	14.3	30.4	18.9	16	11.1	17.8
steel	1	1	4	0	0	2	8
%	14.3	14.3	17.4	0	0	5.6	5.9
gen. machinery	1	0	1	2	2	5	11
%	14.3	0	4.3	5.4	8	13.9	8.1
elec. machinery	3	4	4	9	6	6	32
%	42.9	57.1	17.4	24.3	24	16.7	23.7
heavy	3	1	0	4	3	0	11
%	42.9	14.3	0	10.8	12	0	8.1
household appl.	0	1	3	2	2	0	8
%	0	14.3	13	5.4	8	0	5.9
comm/computer	0	1	1	2	1	3	8
%	0	14.3	4.3	5.4	4	8.3	5.9
other	0	1	0	1	0	3	5
%	0	14.3	0	2.7	0	8.3	3.7
transport machinery	0	0	1	5	3	1	10
%	0	0	4.3	13.5	12	2.8	7.4
instruments	0	1	1	1	0	3	6
%	0	14.3	4.3	2.7	0	8.3	4.4
other manufacturing	0	0	0	1	2	5	8
%	0	0	0	2.7	8	13.9	5.9
Non-manufacturing:	1	0	4	8	7	6	26
%	14.3	0	17.4	21.6	26.9	17.1	19.3
construction	0	0	1	1	0	1	3
%	0	0	4.3	2.7	0	2.8	2.2
communications	0	0	1	2	1	0	4
%	0	0	4.3	5.4	4	0	3
finance	0	0	2	3	1	2	9
%	0	0	8.7	8.1	4	8.3	6.7
utilities	0	0	0	0	1	0	1
%	0	0	0	0	4	0	9
other services	1	0	0	2	4	2	9
%	14.3	0	0	5.4	16	5.6	6.7

Source: Ministry of International Trade and Industry, 1987

such undertakings, they are focussed on product development and/or modification for global markets ("market-specified" R&D in Table 12.4 refers to incremental product modifications for new markets).

Table 12.5 contains information from an analysis by the US Department of Commerce of US–Japanese collaboration in high-technology industries. The Commerce Department study examined a much broader array of linkages between US and Japanese firms, focussing on a "snapshot" of US–Japan corporate linkages in six high-technology industries during 1989–90. Joint ventures account for less than 40 percent of the number of inter-firm collaborative relationships in all of these industries, and in most instances are less frequent than are marketing collaborations and agreements. The importance of the market access motive for many current inter-firm alliances may be inferred from the substantial portion of collaborations in all of these industries that are focussed on marketing or marketing and development of new products. Consistent with the MITI data on the research content of international joint ventures, very few of these US–Japan joint ventures in Table 12.5 are concerned with research, as opposed to production and/or the development of products.

SOURCES OF TENSION IN PACIFIC RIM JOINT VENTURES

Any discussion of the prospects for collaborative activity among Pacific Rim firms must consider potential sources of tension within international joint ventures. These tensions stem from government-to-government conflict and conflicts among the objectives or strategies of partner firms. This discussion is complicated by interactions between these two sources of tension. In some cases, bilateral trade tensions mediated or negotiated by governments create conditions conducive to joint ventures. In other cases, however, joint ventures may contribute to intergovernmental trade frictions.

Firm-based sources of tension within joint ventures

Successful management of international joint ventures has proven to be extremely difficult. Joint product development ventures appear to be especially complex and costly, occasionally resulting in either failure or costs and development times that exceed those associated with independent development. Although a joint venture may reduce the dangers of opportunistic behavior, it does not

Table 12.3 Technology fields of international research joint ventures involving Japanese firms, 1982–7, by field of technology and nationality of foreign firm

IRJVs by nation 1982–7	*All tech fields*	*Conv. tech.*	*Advanced tech.**	*Communi-cations/ computers*	*Integrated circuits*	*Factory and office automation*	*Medical*	*Biotech.*	*New materials*	*Nuclear power*
US	93	30	63	16	15	9	4	13	4	2
Canada	4	2	2	0	0	0	0	0	2	0
UK	13	8	5	2	0	1	0	2	0	0
Germany	9	7	2	0	1	0	0	1	0	0
France	7	6	1	0	0	1	0	0	0	0
Italy	5	5	0	0	0	0	0	0	0	0
Other	4	3	1	0	0	0	0	1	0	0
Total	135	61	74	18	16	11	4	17	6	2

Source: Ministry of International Trade and Industry, 1987

Note: * Advanced technologies includes the seven columns to the right of this catetory, respectively communications and computers; integrated circuits; factory and office automation; medical technologies; biotechnology; new materials; and nuclear power

Table 12.4 International research joint ventures involving Japanese firms, 1982–7, by type of research and technology field

Japan IRJVs/type of research	*Conv. tech.*	*Advanced tech.*	*Communi-cations/ computers*	*Integrated circuits*	*Factory and office automation*	*Medical*	*Biotech.*	*Materials*	*Nuclear power*
Basic research	2	1	0	0	0	0	1	0	0
Applied research	7	18	3	0	0	0	11	3	1
Product oriented	23	38	9	10	3	3	7	4	2
Market specified	28	23	6	7	6	1	2	1	0
Other	1	0	0	0	0	0	0	0	0
Unspecified	4	3	0	0	2	0	1	0	0
Total	65	83	18	17	11	4	22	8	3

Source: Ministry of International Trade and Industry, 1987

Table 12.5 US–Japan "corporate linkages," 1989–90, in selected high-technology industries

US–Japan links 1989–90	*Aerospace*	*Computers*	*Software*	*Semi-conductors*	*SC equipment*	*Bio-technology*	*Total*
Marketing	19	36	38	33	11	22	159
Marketing/development	0	2	3	1	1	0	7
Joint venture:	15	18	27	34	10	28	134
R&D/product	7	10	12	18	8	10	
production	6	5	13	14	2	4	
research	2	3	2	2	0	14	
Licensing	6	3	11	11	3	10	44
Technology exchange	0	2	0	10	0	2	14
M&A	2	8	3	7	5	4	29
Direct investment	0	12	8	2	5	5	32
Consortia	1	1	0	0	0	1	3
Internal venture	0	0	0	4	2	4	10
Production	4	4	1	1	1	1	12
Other	0	1		2		1	4
Total	47	87	91	105	38	80	448

Source: US Department of Commerce, Japan Technology Program, 1991

eliminate them. In addition, the value of partners' contributions to a joint venture may not be easily established, and this difficulty is compounded by the severe uncertainties about technological and market developments that pervade any high-technology development project.[13]

These problems may be less serious in ventures that combine one firm's product development expertise with the production or marketing skills of another. Such ventures generally are closer to the market, reducing uncertainty about costs and prices, and volumes may be lower. Uncertainty over the value of partners' contributions nevertheless is possible in this situation as well, and changing assessments of the value of these contributions may force renegotiation or the demise of the venture. The Taiwanese government's decision not to pursue a joint venture with McDonnell Douglas in developing the MD-12, for example, reflected concerns that the value of the skills (especially in manufacturing) contributed to the proposed venture by McDonnell Douglas were substantially lower than originally perceived, even as the risks associated with the venture increased.

Another important source of conflict in Pacific Rim joint ventures is technology transfer. Especially in ventures that involve firms with different technological capabilities, the senior firm wishes to minimize, and the junior firm to maximize, the amount of technology transfer. Even if conflicts among the participants over the amount of technology transfer can be resolved, actions to control transfer may threaten the viability of the venture.

This problem is illustrated by the case of International Aero Engines, a consortium, founded in 1982 to develop the V2500 jet engine, that includes Pratt and Whitney, Rolls-Royce, Fiat, Motoren-Turbinen Union, Ishikawajima-Harima Heavy Industries, Kawasaki Heavy Industries, and Mitsubishi Heavy Industries. Pratt and Whitney and Rolls-Royce, the "senior partners" within the consortium, attempted to minimize the transfer of engine technology within the consortium by designing the engine in modular form and assigning the development of different modules to different participants. Serious problems in the integration of the engine components, however, delayed the delivery of the V2500 engine and led to a loss of orders (*Aviation Week and Space Technology*, 19/87b; Carley, 1988).

Similar concerns over technology transfer may explain the erratic growth trends in joint ventures between Japanese and South Korean firms in recent years, as the demands of South Korean firms for access to more sophisticated technologies of Japanese electronics and computer firms have blocked further expansion in collaborative ventures. The belief that joint ventures between US and foreign firms, especially Japanese firms, in industries such as electronics, commercial aerospace, or biotechnology result in considerable transfer of industrially valuable technology to Japanese firms (see Reich and Mankin, 1986) also has sparked opposition from US government officials to trans-Pacific joint ventures. Several members of the US Congress, for example, demanded that the US government block the proposed collaboration between Taiwan Aerospace and McDonnell Douglas.

Nevertheless, technology transfer often acts as a source of cohesion within product development ventures, especially those involving a dominant and a subordinate firm. These ventures often are more durable and successful than those between technological equals (Killing, 1983). Evidence from the commercial aircraft industry, in which international collaboration in development projects has been widespread for more than a decade, strongly supports this hypothesis. Product development ventures of technological equals, such as those between Rolls-Royce and Pratt and Whitney in the JT10D jet engine project, Fokker and McDonnell Douglas in the MDF100 commercial aircraft project, and Saab and Fairchild in the SF340 commuter aircraft project, often fail to bring a product to market or are unable to achieve commercial success with a product after its introduction. Product development ventures between technologically dominant and subordinate firms, however, such as the CFM International venture between General Electric and SNECMA of France and the collaborative ventures involving Boeing and the Japan Commercial Transport Development Corporation, appear to be more manageable.

Technology transfer has also acted as an adhesive rather than a solvent in US–Japanese joint ventures in microelectronics. In at least some such ventures spanning several products, monitoring of technology transfer and mutual assurances of reciprocity have been facilitated by the exchange of a firm's proprietary technology in one product for a partner's expertise in another. This form of reciprocity has aided the Motorola–Toshiba venture, in which Toshiba's CMOS process expertise has been exchanged for Motorola's microprocessor design capabilities in an enterprise that produces both microprocessors and DRAMs (Hamel et al., 1989; Armstrong, 1988).

Firms' motives for collaboration often center on knowledge or technology acquisition – once these processes are complete, partners may exit from the joint venture. The prominent role of technology and knowledge transfer within international joint ventures means that the assets contributed by each partner firm may lose their value to the other participants. As technology is transferred through a collaborative venture, learning by the other participants will reduce the value of the technological capabilities that originally were unique to one or another participant.

Depreciation is likely to be even more rapid in ventures to which one firm has contributed its marketing knowledge and network or other "country-specific" expertise – as the other participants improve their knowledge of the markets in which this partner has specialized, they may well choose to continue without it.[14] Depreciation in the value of US firms' contributions has contributed to the breakup of a number of joint ventures between Japanese and US producers of auto-parts. As the Japanese partners in these enterprises have gained knowledge about local markets and (particularly when selling to Japanese transplant operations in the US) local production conditions, they frequently have withdrawn from the joint venture to continue independently, as Phillips (1989) has noted.

Technological assets are likely to depreciate more slowly than such "country-based" knowledge assets, especially if technology transfer is closely managed. Even here, however, some types of technology-based assets may "leak out" more quickly. Hamel et al. (1989) suggest that process technologies are less transparent to other participant firms and therefore may depreciate more slowly than product technologies, which venture partners may learn more easily.[15] They assert that the strong manufacturing process skills of many Japanese firms create a fundamental imbalance in joint ventures with US firms, whose strength more often lies in (supposedly) more easily transferred, product-specific technologies. Of course, the reverse is also true – a key technological asset contributed by Boeing to its collaborative ventures with Japanese firms is the US firm's expertise in production technology and in the management of fluctuations in production volume for commercial airframes (Mowery, 1987).

Depreciation in the value of knowledge- or technology-based assets contributed to a joint venture is no less inevitable than depreciation of physical capital within a factory, and joint venture participants must take steps to reduce erosion in the value of their contribution. Investments in intra-firm technology development should complement the contribution of technologies to a joint venture; investment in manufacturing process technologies should underpin a joint venture in which one is involved in production. Where a firm is providing a "static" asset, such as market access, knowledge of local demand, or expertise in managing local workers, the collaborative venture may function most effectively as a means for exit from the industry or as a channel for learning process and product technologies.[16]

In addition to investments in improving or maintaining the value of the assets or skills contributed to a collaborative venture, participant firms must invest learning from partner firms. As Prahalad and Hamel (1990) note, NEC of Japan has been quite successful in managing its international joint ventures as "learning experiences," thereby supporting improvements in its technological capabilities. Similar investments must be made by firms from NIEs or developing economies, in order to maximize the positive effects of any technology transfer or learning opportunities within a joint venture.

A portion of the firm-based tensions in Pacific Rim joint ventures reflect differences in the ways many US and East Asian managers view these ventures. In Pacific Rim joint ventures, no less than in many other areas, US managers too often have ignored the need to maintain and improve corporate technological capabilities by drawing on external sources. Rather than entering into collaborative ventures as a vehicle for learning new skills or capturing new intellectual property, many US managers have approached joint ventures as a means of reducing costs, improving market access, or facilitating exit from a specific industry segment. In many cases, Japanese partners in these joint ventures have approached them as opportunities for learning and the enhancement or creation of a corporate "core competence."

The organizational structure of international collaborative ventures, especially those involving joint research and product development, raises additional challenges. There is no optimal management structure for a collaborative venture – its design will depend, among other things, on the character and magnitude of partner contributions. In collaborations of technological equals, an autonomous management structure in charge of a wide range of design, marketing, production, and product support may be preferable. Such a management structure is often costly since it duplicates some or all of the management structure of the member firms. Nevertheless, the experience of recent collaborative ventures clearly indicates the importance of strong links between the product development and design team and the organization responsible for marketing and product support. The organization managing the collaborative venture, be it the dominant firm or an autonomous management organization, must retain control of a number of downstream activities. On the other hand, in collaborations involving a senior and a junior firm, financial and organizational structure appears to be less important, so long as the technologically more advanced firm retains overall control of technology and management decisions.

Despite assertions to the contrary in much of the literature, this analysis suggests that within technology-centered collaborative ventures, complementary capabilities are a greater source of strength and stability than are strong similarities in the technological and other assets contributed by partner firms.[17] The enduring differences in firm-based process and product technologies within the Pacific Rim suggest that the possibilities for such complementary partnerships will remain abundant.[18] But the durability of such undertakings, as well as the distribution of benefits and costs of these ventures, will depend on actions by managers in all participating firms to enhance their contributions to and learning from these ventures.

"Managed trade," strategic technology policies and international joint ventures: the role of government

Change in the international trading system, much of which has been sparked by the shifting technology and trade policies of the United States, has transformed the trade policy environment during the past fifteen years in ways that create new incentives for and tensions within Pacific Rim joint ventures. As was noted earlier, the rise of non-tariff barriers is an important influence on growth in Pacific Rim joint ventures. US trade officials have created a number of these barriers to access to the US market and have responded to the growth of foreign non-tariff barriers. They have pressed foreign governments to change the structure of the domestic policy processes giving rise to such barriers, demanding "transparency" and "national treatment" for US firms.[19] Because this procedural focus often produces agreements that are difficult to enforce, an increasingly popular alternative is a "managed trade" agreement that stipulates outcomes rather than mandating improved processes. "Managed trade" policies provide an additional impetus to the formation of international joint ventures. One recent example of a managed trade agreement is the US–Japan Semi-conductor Agreement, which fixes a price floor for DRAMs and commits the Japanese government to ensuring a specific market share in Japan for US producers.

Although US firms have yet to reach the target market share, the US and Japanese governments have pressured Japanese firms to expand their use of US semi-conductor components. Increased use by Japanese firms of US components requires that US supplier firms meet these customers' stringent quality and delivery demands and will necessitate sustained interactions between suppliers and users of components during the development of a new chip or system. One way to meet these demands, the establishment by US components producers of wholly-owned Japanese production and design facilities, is too costly for many US merchant semi-conductor firms. As a result, US–Japanese joint ventures have become a popular strategy for meeting the demands of this government-to-government agreement and expanding the Japanese market share of US components firms.[20]

The bilateral talks that led to the US–Japan Semi-conductor Agreement of 1986 have been followed by negotiations in construction services and other industries. If these talks and the associated government monitoring of trade outcomes grow, joint ventures are likely to expand in the affected industries.[21] Since such bilateral "managed trade" agreements often cover trade among the industrial economies, the influence on Pacific Rim joint ventures is likely to have its greatest impact on US–Japanese joint ventures and Japanese–European joint ventures. Firms from the rapidly growing NIEs will nonetheless face increased pressure to use joint ventures to gain access to the US and European markets.

Changes in technology policy also have influenced growth in Pacific Rim joint ventures. Fears over the competitive consequences of international technology transfer have led US and Western European policymakers to restrict access by foreign firms to publicly funded programs in technology development. Paradoxically, the pursuit by the United States and other industrialized nations of nationalistic or technologically mercantilistic policies of support for domestic industries has encouraged the development of alliances that span national boundaries. The US government, of course, is far from alone in supporting "closed" technology development programs.[22] Many of the cooperative R&D programs that received public funds in Japan (e.g. the Very Large Scale Integrated circuits project, or the more recent and unsuccessful 5th Generation Computer project) have been closed to non-Japanese firms, although these restrictions have been relaxed in some recent projects (e.g. in high-temperature superconductivity). The ESPRIT (European Program for Research in Information Technologies) program of the

European Communities and the research projects sponsored by Eureka (including the Joint European Submicron Silicon Initiative, JESSI) also have been closed to most US firms, although IBM has been allowed to participate in portions of ESPRIT and JESSI.

National (and, in the EC, regional) R&D projects that exclude foreign firms provide incentives for firms to form international joint ventures, as firms participating in publicly sponsored programs within one nation or region develop links with foreign firms that exchange access to the "closed" research activities in the home country or each firm.[23] This tendency is most pronounced in microelectronics, where US firms participating in Sematech have formed joint ventures with Japanese and European firms that are currently barred from the US project (examples include the Motorola–Toshiba, Texas Instruments–Hitachi, and IBM–Siemens ventures). "Closed" national research programs in the US and Western Europe thus far are most significant in microelectronics and information technology. These sectors have been very active areas of Pacific Rim joint venture formation, and it seems likely that the expansion of neo-mercantilist commercial technology development programs has contributed to this growth.

Pacific Rim joint ventures based on managed trade or technological mercantilism most often link firms from the industrialized economies, and may exclude even technologically advanced firms from Asian NIEs. This tendency reflects the fact that a managed trade environment is one that rewards coercion, rather than adherence to rules – nations with greater coercive power and larger markets are more likely to fare better in such a world (although the living standards of their citizens may fare less well). The temptations of managed trade could create a cartelized regime in international technology development and exchange that would complement government-sanctioned international cartels for the management of trade in high-technology goods. Consumers throughout the world economy, and firms from the NIEs and developing nations in particular, would bear the costs of such a regime.

CONCLUSION

The factors that underpin the recent growth in international joint ventures within the Pacific Rim seem likely to support continued growth in the number of these ventures, which will link US and Japanese firms with one another and (to a lesser extent) with firms from the NIEs. Thus far, however, there is little evidence that these ventures are linking firms from the NIEs with one another. Nor does the current pattern of Pacific Rim joint venture growth suggest that this vehicle is supporting the creation of a Japan-centered East Asian trading "bloc" that excludes US firms.

Will conflict within Pacific Rim joint ventures, or among the governments of the nations from which the participants are drawn, ultimately choke off growth in these international ventures? Many of these tensions are inevitable products of the different goals of partner firms and the different strategies for the creation and maintenance of firm-specific technological capabilities. Other tensions are environmental, however, and reflect growth in the use of strategic trade and technology policies by Western European and the US governments. Some of these changes in the trade and technology policy environment create incentives for the formation of international joint ventures within the Pacific Rim that may exclude firms from the NIEs and from developing economies. On balance, a combination of technological, economic, and political forces seem likely to promote further growth in Pacific Rim joint ventures. The inter-firm sources of tension seem unlikely to disrupt growth in these joint ventures, and the intergovernmental tensions that contribute to their growth are likely to intensify.

Will these joint ventures "marginalize" firms from the NIEs and developing economies? Although they mainly link firms from the US Japan, and Western Europe, Pacific Rim joint ventures do not seem to have prevented NIE firms from gaining access to advanced technologies. Proliferation in the sources of new technologies has made it much more difficult for dominant firms to develop or enforce restrictive technology-sharing agreements similar to those among European and US firms during the interwar period. As a result, even in technologies like DRAMs, once dominated by a small group of Japanese firms, South Korean firms have been able to obtain critical technological assets and successfully enter the industry.[24] The expanding array of firms capable of supplying and exploiting advanced products and processes, which has motivated much of the international joint venture activity of the 1980s, thus may reduce somewhat the risk that these ventures will cartelize international markets for technology and goods. Unlike oil, technology moves too quickly within the world economy, and can be exploited by too many firms, for a small group of firms to establish a stable cartel.

International joint ventures among Pacific Rim economies also are likely to be of secondary importance to the prospects for the developing economies of this region. The critical preconditions for these nations to expand their roles in the global manufacturing economy are sufficient investment in domestic human and physical capital to support entry as a supplier of components and assemblies to the supply networks that bind together firms throughout the industrial and industrializing economies. The postwar records of such economies as Singapore, Taiwan, and South Korea strongly support the importance of these investments, and suggest that the risk of "marginalization" of the developing economies will be influenced by the actions of governments within these economies much more than by the growing links between firms from the industrial and industrializing economies of the Pacific Rim.

NOTES

1 Hladik's analysis (1985) of data from the Harvard Multinational Enterprise Project concluded that 39 percent of the number of foreign subsidiaries established by US manufacturing firms during 1951–75 were joint ventures.

2 Most of the data on which these analyses are based are drawn from the trade and financial press. The data suffer in varying degrees from at least two critical problems: (1) different research teams have utilized different definitions of international collaborative or technology-sharing agreements, and have employed different approaches to coding and categorizing the data; and (2) "mortality" data are rarely available, making it impossible to determine whether new agreements are replacing or supplementing earlier ones. This last problem means that some portion of the measured growth in the number of international joint ventures during the past decade may be spurious, and that any apparent levelling off in growth rates must be interpreted with great caution.

3 Harrigan (1984) concluded that domestic joint ventures involving US firms had grown during the previous decade. In the 1960s, joint ventures were concentrated in the chemical, primary metals, paper, and stone, clay, and glass industries, but now extend beyond these sectors (see also Harrigan, 1985). Hladik (1985) found significant growth from 1975 to 1982 in the number of international joint ventures involving US firms. Hladik and Linden (1989) found that between 1976 and 1987, the number of international R&D joint ventures entered into by US firms grew by more than 17 percent per year on average. By 1987, 47 percent of the ventures in their sample lay in the computer, electronics, semiconductor, or instrument industries. Analyzing domestic and international cooperative agreements by firms from the US, Europe, and Japan in biotechnology, information technologies, and new materials, Hagedoorn and Schaekenraad (1988:3) concluded that "although technology cooperation between companies probably goes back many decades, it has experienced a major boost during the eighties."

4 Brodley summarizes the advantage of joint ventures, defined as separate

corporate entities in which all partners hold equity shares, over mergers or market transactions as follows:

> By providing for shared profits and managerial control, joint ventures tend to protect the participants from opportunism and information imbalance. The problem of valuing the respective contributions of the participants is mitigated, because they can await an actual market judgment. The temptation to exploit a favored bargaining position by threatening to withhold infusions of capital or other contributions is reduced by the need for continuous cooperation if the joint venture is to be effective. Moreover, a firm supply capital to the joint venture can closely monitor the use of its contributed capital and thereby reduce its risk of loss. Common ownership also provides a means of spreading the costs of producing valuable information that could otherwise be protected from appropriation only by difficult-to-enforce contractual undertakings. Finally, joint ventures can effect economies of scale in research not achievable through single-firm action. Because of these advantages, joint ventures are especailly likely to provide an optimal enterprise form in undertakings involving high risks, technological innovations, or high information costs."
>
> (1982: 1528–9)

5 "Inseparability" refers to the fact that much of the firm's noncodified technological know-how may be embedded in the organization. Its transfer therefore will require the transfer of a large number of individuals. Separating and transferring a substantial portion of the parent firm's staff to another enterprise may not be feasible (see Teece, 1982 for further discussion).

6 Granstrand and Sjolander (1990) discuss this phenomenon of technological convergence in terms of the growth of "multi-technology corporations," firms that either have to significantly broaden or overhaul their technology base. As these authors note, one means to acquire new capabilities is through a domestic or international joint venture. A similar argument, emphasizing both the consequences of rising development costs and the demands of technological convergence, is made in Horwitch and Mazzone (1992), whose discussion covers both international and domestic joint ventures, as well as other methods to gain access to external sources of technology, such as mergers and acquisitions.

7 The "product cycle" model of direct foreign investment hypothesized that differences in local economic conditions gave rise to different firm-specific attributes that eventually were exploited in foreign markets through direct foreign investment. Economic development and faster international technology transfer mean that the characteristics of domestic markets within the industrial world differ less from one another, and the firm-specific assets and products that develop to serve these markets now are less "country-bound" (Vernon, 1979; Dunning, 1988).

8 See *Business Week*, which describes the licensing strategy of Sun Microsystems in workstations:

> Almost anyone can license Sun's basic software and Sparc, the superfast microprocessor that is the brain of its flagship workstation – a

> $9,000–and-up desktop machine that packs the power of a minicomputer. If enough manufacturers build Sun clones, the software companies will have to take notice. In the end, everyone will prosper. And Sun's Sparc workstation – it makes six other models – will become a desktop standard.
>
> (1989: 75; see also Khazam and Mowery, 1994)

9 This is not to deny the major role played by such large firms as IBM in computers and AT&T in microelectronics. In other instances, large firms have acquired smaller enterprises and applied their production or marketing expertise to expand markets for a new product technology. Nonetheless, it seems apparent that startup firms have been far more active in commercializing new technologies in the United States than in other industrial economies. Malerba's (1985) analysis of the evoluton of the microelectronics industry in Western Europe and in the US emphasizes the greater importance of startup firms in the US.

10 See the estimate by Tyson (1988) that 35 percent of US imports in 1983 were subject to non-tariff restrictions, an increase from an estimated 20 percent in 1980. Olechowski estimated that 17–19 percent of the imports of developed nations (by value) were covered by non-tariff barriers, and concluded that the use of non-tariff barriers increased significantly during 1981–5 (1987: 125).

11 These data, which extend through the third quarter of 1991, were provided by Itsunami Inc., of Berkeley, California. I am indebted to Mr. James Sharp for the use of the data.

12 The MITI data in Tables 12.3–12.5 contain no information on terminated joint ventures, and therefore may overstate the rate of growth in Japanese international research collaboration. The effects of any overstatement, however, almost certainly are more than offset by the effects of the MITI study's narrow definition of joint ventures.

13 Doz has pointed out the difficulties of measuring partner contributions in product development ventures that lie midway on a continuum between commercial production and fundamental research:

> When dealing with basic technology development – usually early in a partnership, much before a competitive stage – parity is maintained between the partners through balance in contribution; and the potential output is still so distant that precise valuation is not an issue. When dealing with well-developed technologies, a precise valuation of the outcome can be made, and the partners are almost at the stage of supply contracts, with precise product or system specifications, costs and prices, and some volume forecasts. Yet a "danger zone" often separates these stages in the evolution of a partnership, in the transition from precompetitive stages to competitive ones. During that transition one partner, but not the other, may shift from a valuation of the partnership based on contribution to one based on expected results, and show impatience with a divergence from the position of the other partner.
>
> (1988: 38)

14 Porter and Fuller have observed that collaborative ventures centered on marketing

> may be particularly unstable, however, because they frequently are formed because of the access motive on one or both sides. For example, one partner needs market access while the other needs access to product. As the foreign partner's market knowledge increases, there is less and less need for a local partner."
>
> (1986: 334)

15

> The type of skill a company contributes is an important factor in how easily its partner can internalize the skills. The potential for transfer is greatest when a partner's contribution is easily transported (in engineering drawings, on computer tapes, or in the heads of a few technical experts); easily interpreted (it can be reduced to commonly understood equations or symbols); and easily absorbed (the skill or competence is independent of any particular cultural context).
>
> Western companies face an inherent disadvantage because their skills are generally more vulnerable to transfer. The magnet that attracts so many companies to alliances with Asian competitors is their manufacturing excellence – a competence that is less transferable than most."
>
> (Hamel et al., 1989: 136)

16 Several US–Japanese joint ventures in the steel industry have been founded on the contributions by Japanese firms of technology and capital in exchange for the US partners' political protection (in the context of trade frictions and "voluntary" restrictions on Japanese steel exports to the US market), knowledge of the US domestic market, and (remarkably, in view of the history of labor–management relations in this industry) familiarity with the US labor force. Many of these ventures (e.g. Nippon Kokan–National Steel) have served as vehicles for the US firms to exit from segments of the domestic integrated steel industry (see Lynn, 1988).

17 Both Porter and Fuller (1986) and Hennart (1988) argue that partnerships based on similar assets are more durable, although Hennart applies his observation to a broader class of collaborative ventures than those centered on technology.

18 Simon, 1995.

19 "Transparency" refers to the ability of foreign enterprises to monitor and in some cases participate in the establishment of guidelines or standards within a specific policy area (e.g. through participating in hearings or commenting on proposed rules). "National treatment" means that policies and procedures are applied identically to domestic and foreign enterprises.

20 Schlesinger (1990: A6) notes that

> relationships between Japanese and American companies are developing in a variety of ways, prompted in part by the trade agreement. Companies in the two companies have started forming semiconductor

alliances, ranging from technology sharing to joint production. At the beginning of this year alone, a half dozen of these contracts were announced. American Telephone & Telegraph Co., for example, will start a new semiconductor product line with the help of NEC know-how.

But the ventures also help insulate the Japanese from lost sales – and from slighting long-time Japanese suppliers. When Toyota pulled some microprocessor business from Toshiba and threw it to Motorola, it wasn't a coincidence that the Motorola chips came from a 50–50 joint-venture plant the American company runs with Toshiba. Toyota clearly had Toshiba's well-being in mind, says Hiroshi Arai, a general manager with the company.

21 According to one account, the March 1988 agreement between the US and Japanese governments easing access by US firms to Japanese public construction projects has resulted in an extensive set of joint ventures between US and large Japanese construction firms (Rubinfien, 1988).

21 The public symposium on applications of high-temperature superconductivity (HTS) convened in 1987 by the White House Office of Science and Technology Policy and the National Science Foundation excluded foreign participants. The Reagan Administration's subsequent proposals for increased research funding (the Superconductivity Competitiveness Intiative, released in January 1988) for HTS development included provisions designed to prohibit or restrict foreign access to the results of publicly funded basic research in HTS. The US Sematech program and the National Center for Manufacturing Sciences (NCMS), which are funded in part with public monies, exclude foreign participation, and foreign firms' participation in many NSF-funded cooperative university–industry research programs is discouraged. Pentagon research intiatives in high-definition television (HDTV) also are likely to exclude foreign enterprises. Mowery and Rosenberg (1989a, 1989b) describe these and other examples of technological mercantilism in greater detail.

23 Chesnais (1988: 95) has noted the complementary relationship between relatively closed domestic research programs in the EC and the US, such as JESSI and Sematech, and international product development and technology exchange agreements in microelectronics:

> one finds a combination between *domestic* alliances in *pre-competitive* R&D (with all of the provisos attached to this notion), and a wide range of technology exchange and cross-licensing agreement among oligopolist rivals at the international level.
>
> (emphasis in original)

24 As the OECD noted in 1988 (Ernst and O'Connor, 1989: 8),

> A potentially radical change between past and future trends [of economic development] lies in the fact that the diffusion of technologies is becoming increasingly disconnected from the trade in products which embody the technologies. Such an evolution may open new opportunities for those NICs which are succeeding in the development of a technological infrastructure and an industrial organisation which

will allow them to respond quickly to the evolution of world demand, especially in the fast-growing sectors.

REFERENCES

Armstrong, L., "A chipmaking venture the gods smiled on," *Business Week* (July 4, 1988), p. 109.

Arrow, K. J., "Economic welfare and the allocation of resources for invention," in Universities-national Bureau Committee for Economic Research, *The Rate and Direction of Inventive Activity* (Princeton, NJ: Princeton University Press, 1962).

Arrow, K. J., "Classificatory notes on the production and transmission of technical knowledge," *American Economic Review* 59 (1969), pp. 29–35.

Aviation Week and Space Technology, "US, Europeans clash over Airbus subsidies" (February 9, 1987a), pp. 18–20.

Aviation Week and Space Technology, "Pratt and Whitney expands role in V2500 compressor work" (March 16, 1987), pp. 32–3.

Bhagwati, J., "Trade in services and the new multilateral trade negotiations," *The World Bank Economic Review* 1 (1897), pp. 549–69.

Borrus, M., *Competing for Control* (Cambridge, Mass.: Ballinger Publishers, 1988).

Bozeman, B., A. Link and A. Zardkoohi, "An economic analysis of R&D joint ventures," *Managerial and Decision Economics* 7 (1986), pp. 263–6.

Brodley, J., "Joint ventures and antitrust policy," *Harvard Law Review* 95 (1982), pp. 1523–90.

Brodsky, N. H., H. Kaufman and J. Tooker, *University/Industry Cooperation* (New York: Center for Science and Technology Policy, 1980).

Business Week, "Special report: the hollow corporation" (March 3, 1986), pp. 57–85.

Business Week, "AT&T: the making of a comeback" (January 18, 1988), pp. 56–62.

Business Week, "What's behind the Texas Instruments–Hitachi deal" (January 16, 1989), pp. 93–4.

Business Week, "Is the US selling its high-tech soul to Japan?" (June 26, 1989), pp. 117–18.

Business Week, "Clonemakers don't scare sun – It's sending them engraved invitations" (July 24, 1989), p. 75.

Carley, W. M., "Cancelled jet order is a setback for United Technologies Unit," *Wall Street Journal* (Febuary 9, 1988), p. 6.

Caves, R. E., *Multinational Enterprise and Economic Analysis* (Cambridge: Cambridge University Press, 1982).

Chesnais, F., "Technical co-operation agreements between firms," *STI Review* (1988), pp. 51–119.

COSEPUP (Committee on Science, Engineering, and Public Policy) Panel on the Impact of National Security Controls on International Technology Transfer, *Balancing the National Interest: US National Security Export Controls and Global Economic Competition* (Washington, DC: National Academy Press, 1987).

Dertouzos, M., R. Lester and R. M. Solow, *Made in America* (Cambridge, Mass.: MIT Press, 1989).

Donne, M., "Dunlop joins US group in Airbus contract bid," *Financial Times* (September 17, 1987), p. 6.

Doz, Y. L., "Technology partnerships between larger and smaller firms: some critical issues," *International Studies of Management & Organization* 17 (1988), pp. 31–57.

Dunning, J. H., *Multinationals, Technology, and Competitiveness* (London: Unwin Hyman, 1988).

Ernst, D. and D. O'Connor, *Technology and Global Competition: the challenge for newly industrialising economies* (Paris: OECD, 1989).

Farrell, J. and N. Gallini, "Second-sourcing as a commitment: monopoly incentives to attract competition," *Quarterly Journal of Economics* (1988), pp. 673–94.

Ferguson, C., "From the people Who brought you voodoo economics," *Harvard Business Review* 66, 3 (1988), pp. 55–62.

Florida, R. L. and M. Kenney, "Venture capital-financed innovation and technological change in the USA," *Research Policy* 17 (1988), pp. 119–37.

Ghemawat, P., M. E. Porter and R. A. Rawlinson, "Patterns of international coalition activity," in M. E. Porter (ed.) *Competition in Global Industries* (Boston, Mass.: Harvard Business School Press, 1986).

Gomes-Casseres, B., "Joint ventures in global competition," Harvard Business School Working Paper 89–023 (1988).

Gomes-Casseres, B., "Ownership structures of foreign subsidiaries: theory and evidence," *Journal of Economic Behavior and Organization* (1989).

Granstrand, O. and S. Sjolander, "Managing innovation in multi-technology corporations," *Research Policy* 19 (1990), pp. 35–60.

Gullander, S., "Joint ventures in Europe: determinants of entry," Working paper, Columbia University Graduate School of Business (1976).

Hagedoorn, J. and J. Schakenraad, "Strategic partnering and technological co-operation," presented at the EARIE conference, Rotterdam (August 31–September 2, 1988).

Hamel, G., Y. Doz and C. K. Prahalad, "Collaborate with your competitors – and win," *Harvard Business Review* (January–February, 1989), pp. 133–9.

Harrigan, K. R., "Joint ventures and competitive strategy," Working paper, Columbia University Graduate School of Business (1984).

Harrigan, K. R., *Strategies for Joint Ventures* (Lexington, Mass.: D. C. Heath, 1985).

Harris, J., "Spies who sparked the Industrial Revolution," *New Scientist* (May 22, 1986), pp. 42–7.

Hennart, J.-F., "A transactions cost theory of joint ventures," *Strategic Management Journal* (1988), pp. 361–74.

Hirsch, S., "An international trade and investment theory of the firm," *Oxford Economic Papers* 28 (1976), pp. 258–69.

Hladik, K., *International Joint Ventures* (Lexington, Mass.: D. C. Heath, 1985).

Hladik, K. and L. H. Linden, "Is an international joint venture in R&D for you?," *Research Technology Management* 32 (1989), pp. 11–13.

Hof, R. and N. Gross, "Silicon Valley is watching its worst nigthmare unfold," *Business Week* (September 4, 1989), pp. 63–7.

Hooper, L. and J. M. Schlesinger, "Memory chips' new frontier: intercontinental cooperation," *Wall Street Journal* (July 14, 1992), p. B1.

Horwitch, M. and T. Mazzone, "The rise of technology development networks and the creation of transformational capabilities," presented at the conference on "The Impact of Globalization and Regionalization on Corporate Strategy and Structure Among Pacific Rim Firms," Sapporo, Japan (August 3–7, 1992).

Hufbauer, G. C. and H. F. Rosen, *Trade Policy for Troubled Industries* (Washington, DC: Institute for International Economics, 1986).

Jorde, T. and D. J. Reece, "Innovation, strategic alliances, and antitrust," presented at the Conference on the Centennial Celebration of the Sherman Act, University of California, Berkeley (October 7–8, 1988).

Khazam, J. and D. Mowery, "The commercialization of RISC: strategies for the creation of dominant designs," Research Policy 23, 1 (1994), pp. 89–102.

Killing, J. P., *Strategies for Joint Venture Success* (New York: Praeger, 1983).

Klein, R., R. G. Crawford and A. A. Alchian, "Vertical integration, appropriable rents, and the competitive contracting process," *Journal of Law and Economics* 21 (1978), pp. 297–326.

Klepper, S., "Collaborations in robotics," in D. C. Mowery (ed.) *International Collaborative Ventures in U.S. Manufacturing* (Cambridge, Mass.: Ballinger Publishers, 1988).

Kogut, B., "Joint ventures: theoretical and empirical perspectives," *Strategic Management Journal* (1988), pp. 319–32.

Krugman, P. W., "(Import protection as export promotion: international competition in the presence of oligopoly and economies of scale," in H. Kierzkowski (ed.), *Monopolistic Competition and International Trade* (Oxford: Oxford University Press, 1984).

Lane, H. W., R. G. Beddows and P. R. Lawrence, *Managing Large Research and Development Programs* (Albany, NY: State University of New York Press, 1981).

Langlois, R. N., T. A. Pugel, C. S. Haklisch, R. R. Nelson and W. G. Egelhoff, *Microelectronics: An Industry in Transition* (Boston: Unwin Hyman, 1988).

Lardner, J., "The terrible truth about Japan," *Washington Post* (June 21, 1987), p. B19.

Leiberman, M. and D. Montgomery, "First-mover advantages," *Strategic Management Journal* 9 (special issue, summer, 1988), pp. 41–58.

Levin, R. C., A. K. Klevorick, R. R. Nelson and S. G. Winter, "Appropriating the returns from industrial research and development," *Brookings Papers on Economic Activity* (1987), pp. 783–820.

Lineback, J. R., "Can MCC survive the latest defections?," *Electronics* (January 22, 1987).

Lineback, J. R., "It's time for MCC to fish or cut bait," *Electronics* (June 25, 1987).

Lynn, L., "Joint ventures in the steel industry," in D. C. Mowery (ed.), *International Collaborative Ventures in US Manufacturing* (Washington, DC: American Enterprise Institute, 1988).

Malerba, F., *The Semiconductor Business: The Economics of Rapid Growth and Decline* (Madison, Wis.: University of Wisconsin Press, 1985).

Mansfield, E., "Industrial innovation in Japan and the United States," *Science* (September 30, 1988), 1769–74.

McCulloch, R., "International competition in high-technology industries: the consequences of alternative trade regimes for aircraft," presented at the National Science Foundation Workshop on the Economic Implications of Restrictions to Trade in High-Technology Goods, Washington, DC (October 3, 1984).

Ministry of International Trade and Industry (Japan), *Status Report on International Joint Research and Development of Japanese Private Enterprises* (Tokyo: MITI, 1987).

Mowery, D. C., *Alliance Politics and Economics: multinational joint ventures in commercial aircraft* (Cambridge, Mass.: Ballinger Publishers, 1987).

Mowery, D. C. (ed.), *International Collaborative Ventures in US Manufacturing* (Cambridge, Mass.: Ballinger Publishers, 1988).

Mowery, D. C., "Collaborative ventures between US and foreign manufacturing firms," *Research Policy* 18 (1989), pp. 19–32.

Mowery, D. C., "Public policy influences on the formation of international joint ventures," *International Trade Journal* (1991), pp. 29–62.

Mowery, D. C. and N. Rosenberg, "The influence of market demand upon innovation: a critical review of some recent empirical studies," *Research Policy* (1979), pp. 102–53.

Mowery, D. C. and N. Rosenberg, "Government policy and innovation in the commercial aircraft industry, 1925–75" in R. R. Nelson (ed.), *Government and Technical Change: A Cross-Industry Analysis* (New York: Pergamon Press, 1982).

Mowery, D. C. and N. Rosenberg, "Commercial aircraft: cooperation and competition between the US and Japan," *California Management Review* 27, 4 (1985), pp. 70–93.

Mowery, D. C. and N. Rosenberg, "New developments in U.S. technology policy: implications for competitiveness and trade policy," *California Management Review* 32 (1989a), pp. 107–24.

Mowery, D. C. and N. Rosenberg, *Technology and the Pursuit of Economic Growth* (New York: Cambridge University Press, 1989b).

Mytelka, L. K. and M. Delapierre, "The alliance strategies of European firms in the information technology industry and the role of ESPRIT," *Journal of Common Market Studies* (1987), pp. 231–53.

National Academy of Engineering, *The Competitive Status of the U.S. Civil Aircraft Manufacturing Industry* (Washington, DC: National Academy Press, 1985).

Nelson, R. R., *High-Technology Policies: a five-nation comparison* (Washington, DC: US Government Printing Office, 1987).

Office of Technology Assessment, *Commercializing High-Temperature Superconductivity* (Washington, DC: US Government Printing Office, 1988).

Okimoto, D., *Between MITI and the Market: Japanese industrial policy for high technology* (Stanford, Calif.: Stanford University Press, 1989).

Olechowski, A., "Nontariff barriers to trade," in J. M. Finger and A. Olechowski (eds), *The Uruguay Round: a handbook for negotiators* (Washington, DC: World Bank, 1987).

Perlmutter, H. V. and D. A. Hennan, "Cooperative to compete globally," *Harvard Business Review* (1986), pp. 136–52.

Phillips, S., "When US joint ventures with Japan go sour," *Business Week* (July 24, 1989), pp. 30–1.

Pisano, G. P., W. Shan and D. J. Teece, "Joint ventures and collaboration in the biotechnology industry," in D. C. Mowery (ed.), *International Collaborative Ventures in U.S. Manufacturing* (Cambridge, Mass.: Ballinger Publishing, 1988).

Porter, M. E. and M. B. Fuller, "Coalitions and global strategy," in M. E. Porter (ed.), *Competition in Global Industries* (Boston: Harvard Business School Press, 1986).

Prahalad, C. K. and G. Hamel, "The Core competence of the corporation," *Harvard Business Review* (May/June 1990), pp. 79–91.

Prestowitz, C., *Trading Places* (New York: Basic Books, 1987).

Reich, R. B. and E. D. Mankin, "Joint ventures with Japan give away our future," *Harvard Business Review* (March/April, 1986), pp. 79–86.

Rosenberg, N. and W. E. Steinmueller, "Why are Americans such poor imitators?," *American Economic Review* (1988), pp. 229–34.

Rosenbloom, R. S. and M. A. Cusumano, "Technological pioneering and competitive advantage: the birth of the VCR industry," *California Management Review* 29 (1987), pp. 51–79.

Rubinfien, E., "U.S. contractors forge alliances in Japan," *Wall Street Journal* (June 28, 1988), p. 28.

Sanger, D., "Computer consortium lags," *New York Times* (September 5, 1984), p. D1.

Sigurdson, J., *Industry and State Partnership in Japan – The Very Large Scale Integrated Circuits (VLSI) Project* (Lund, Sweden: Research Policy Institute, University of Lund, 1986).

Simon, D. F. (ed.) *The Emerging Technological Trajectory of the Pacific Rim* (Armonk, NY: M. E. Sharpe, 1995).

Simon, D. F. and B. Koppel, "Is globalization the 1990s version of interdependence? A look at some of the critical dimensions," presented at the conference on "The Impact of Globalization and Regionalization on Corporate Strategy and Structure Among Pacific Rim Firms," Sapporo, Japan (August 3–7, 1992).

Steinmueller, W. E., "Integrated circuits," in D. C. Mowery (ed.), *International Collaborative Ventures in U.S. Manufacturing* (Cambridge, Mass.: Ballinger Publishers, 1988).

Stuckey, J. S., *Vertical Integration and Joint Ventures in the Aluminum Industry* (Cambridge, Mass.: Harvard University Press, 1983).

Swann, G. M. P., "Industry standard microprocessors and the strategy of second-source production," in H. L. Gabel (ed.), *Product Standardization and Competitive Strategy* (Amsterdam: North-Holland, 1987).

Teece, D. J., "Economies of scope and the scope of the enterprise," *Journal of Economic Behavior and Organization* 1 (1980), pp. 223–47.

Teece, D. J., "Towards an economic theory of the multiproduct firm," *Journal of Economic Behavior and Organization* 3 (1982), pp. 39–63.

Teece, D. J., "Profiting from technological innovation: implications for integration, collaboration, licensing, and public policy," *Research Policy* 15 (1986), pp. 285–305.

Tyson, L., "Making policy for national competitiveness in a changing world," in A. Furina (ed.), *Cooperation and Competitiveness in the Global Economy* (Cambridge, Mass.: Ballinger Publishers, 1988).

US Department of Commerce Japan Technology Program, *The Role of Corporate Linkages in US–Japan Technology Transfer: 1991* (Washington, DC: NTIS, 1991).

Vernon, R. S., "The product cycle hypothesis in a new international environment," *Oxford Bulletin of Economics and Statistics* 41 (1979), pp. 255–67.

von Hippel, E., "The dominant role of users in the scientific instrument innovation process," *Research Policy* 5, 3 (1976), pp. 212–39.

Williamson, O. E.,, *Markets and Hierarchies* (New York: Free Press, 1975).

Williamson, O. E., "Transaction–cost economics: the governance of contractual relations," *Journal of Law and Economics* 22 (1979), pp. 233–62.

Williamson, O. E., "The economics of organization: the transaction cost approach," *American Journal of Sociology* 87 (1981), pp. 548–77.

Williamson, O. E., *The Economic Institutions of Capitalism* (New York: Free Press, 1985).

World Bank, *World Development Report* (New York: Oxford University Press, 1987).

13 Integration in the Asian Pacific Rim

Formation of networks by Japanese foreign direct investment as the driving force to integrate

Takeshi Aoki

CHARACTERISTICS OF THE THIRD WAVE OF JAPAN'S DFI

The G5 conference in September 1985 aligned the exchange rate of the major currencies, especially US dollar, vis-à-vis the Japanese yen. Since then, Japan's direct foreign investment (JDFI) has registered remarkable growth in terms of tempo and volume. This massive capital outflow can be described as the "third wave," preceded by the first wave from 1972 to 1974, in which the first oil crisis happened, and the second wave from the second oil crisis to around 1980.

According to the statistics published by Japan's Ministry of Finance, Japan's DFI surpassed US$10 billion in 1984 and continued to increase by US$10 billion almost every year and reached US$67.5 billion in March 1989, which recorded the highest ever level of outflow. In 1990, the rate became negative by 14.4 percent against the previous year. But the amount of outflow itself was US$56.9 billion which was the second highest after 1989 (Table 13.1).

The accumulative amount as at the end of March 1990 was US$310.8 billion, of which 73.1 percent was invested abroad in the five years between 1986 and 1990. The number of projects amounted to 26,309 in the same period, which was 41.6 percent of the accumulative at the end of March 1990.

The following changes were observed in the on-going process of Japan's DFI. The first is the increased ratio of the manufacturing sector. Its share in the total JDFI declined to 17.1 percent in 1986 from the peak of 31.8 percent in 1983 and then returned to 29.4 percent in 1988. In 1989, the ratio of manufacturing sector declined to 24.1 percent, but in 1990 it increased again to 27.2 percent, which

Table 13.1 The development of Japan's DFI and its regional composition (US$ million)

Region		*Regional composition (%)*					
Fiscal year	*World*	*N. America*	*Europe*	*Asia*	*NIEs*	*ASEAN*	*Sub-total*
1951–70	3,533	25.8	18.1	21.2	5.1	12.9	65.1
1971	858	26.8	9.8	27.6	11.2	16.1	64.2
1972	2,338	17.4	40.0	17.2	9.7	7.4	74.6
1973	3,494	26.1	9.6	28.6	12.9	15.6	64.3
1974	2,395	23.0	7.9	30.6	8.9	21.4	61.5
1975	3,280	27.6	10.2	33.6	8.4	24.5	71.4
1976	3,462	21.6	9.7	36.0	6.5	29.4	67.3
1977	2,806	26.2	7.8	30.8	10.3	20.3	64.8
1978	4,598	29.7	7.0	29.1	12.9	16.2	65.8
1979	4,995	28.8	9.9	19.5	12.3	6.8	58.2
1980	4,693	34.0	12.3	25.3	8.1	16.7	71.6
1981	8,931	28.2	8.9	37.4	8.1	28.8	74.5
1982	7,703	37.7	11.4	18.0	9.6	8.1	67.1
1983	8,145	33.2	12.2	22.7	13.7	8.0	68.1
1984	10,155	34.9	19.1	16.0	8.0	6.7	70.0
1985	12,217	45.0	15.8	11.7	5.9	4.9	72.5
1986	22,321	46.8	15.5	10.4	6.9	2.5	72.7
1987	33,364	46.0	19.7	14.6	7.7	3.1	80.3
1988	47,022	47.5	19.4	11.8	6.9	4.2	78.7
1989	67,540	50.2	21.9	12.2	7.3	4.1	84.3
1990	56,911	47.8	25.1	12.4	5.9	5.7	85.3

Source: Japan's MOF
Note: Fiscal year base

is the second highest rate after 1988. The second is the changes in the composition of the manufacturing sector. Throughout the 1970s, the material-processing industries have increased their share and in the 1980s the machinery-related sectors such as general machinery, electrical and electronics equipment, and transport equipment have increased their share. The total share of these three sectors has increased to 58.2 percent in 1990 from 47.6 percent in 1981.

The third characteristic was found in the regional changes of JDFI composition. The share of the developed countries has increased both in total amount and in manufacturing sectors. Its share in terms of accumulations by the end of the respective years had increased to 79 percent in 1989 from 46 percent in 1980 in all the sectors and in the manufacturing sectors the share has increased to 65.6 percent from 32.3 percent. The rest of the share is attributable to the developing countries, of which Asia holds 15.9 percent in all the sectors and 23.6 percent in the manufacturing sectors of the accumulative amount respectively as of the end of March 1990.

The fourth is the concentration of Japan's DFI to specific regions. A strong trend suggests that JDFI is going to concentrate in North America and Europe in the developed regions, and in Asia in the developing regions. During the 1980s in particular, this trend has been strongly observed in the manufacturing sectors. The combined share of the three regions in the manufacturing sectors reached 61.9 percent in 1970, 62.4 percent in 1980 and 87.6 percent in 1990 on the accumulative base as at the end of each fiscal year.

Finally, Japan's DFI has changed parallel with the comparative advantages of Japanese industries. As the economy has grown and matured, Japan's comparative advantage has shifted toward more capital and technology-intensive goods. Rising domestic wages and scarce land have driven Japanese manufacturers abroad to establish production bases for labor-intensive products in order to sell their products in the host countries and export to Japan and third countries. This is typically observed in the JDFI to Asia.

Until 1973, when the first oil crisis occurred, most of Japan's DFI was in the light industries, mainly textiles, followed by the raw-material based industries such as iron and steel and chemicals. The main motives for this were to restore export competitiveness threatened by wage increases and the sharp increase in costs brought on by two oil crises in the 1970s. In the latter half of the 1980s, particularly after 1985 when the yen appreciated tremendously, the processing and assembling industries such as the electrical and electronics industries and the transportation equipment industries have become the main component of JDFI. In the electrical and electronics industry the share jumped to 35.9 percent in 1988 from 8.3 percent in 1981.

In spite of the fact that the machinery-related industries as a whole have strengthened the international competitiveness of microelectronics, the reasons why they have promoted DFI at the same time have been the labor shortage, and the wage increase in Japan together with the increased import of parts and components. The latter has been accelerated by the yen appreciation and, in particular, small and medium enterprises who have lost price competitiveness have shifted their production bases abroad, outsourcing parts and/or products either totally or partially.[1] Japanese MNCs have also relocated their production facilities abroad, not only for outsourcing parts and components, but also as part of a worldwide marketing strategy. This can be observed in the DFI of the machinery-related industries.

The most remarkable change found in this process of DFI, particularly after 1985, is the formation of networks both inside and outside of a host country by Japanese companies and their affiliates, particularly in the machinery-related industries. These networks strengthen the interdependence or economic linkages between industries domestically and internationally through foreign trade involving Japan and third countries. In particular, constructing outside networks encourages the intensification and deepening of input and output relationships in the international scene through the restructuring of the international division of labor.

Japan is at present characterized as an economic giant in terms of the realization of economic dynamism. This economic dynamism is being supplied through various kinds of channels such as relocating production bases abroad, the export of capital and intermediate goods, the expansion of imports by providing a domestic market, financing, assisting and the international movement of people. Through these channels, Japanese economic dynamism has spread abroad and at the same time has included the dynamism of the other countries, and the parties concerned jointly constitute the mechanism of promoting competition and cooperation with each other. This movement is remarkable, especially in Asia. It shows the most dynamic factors penetrating deeply into the most stagnant parts of an economy, changing the latter and involving them in the international scene. In short all these developments contribute to the restructuring of industry and the international division of labor, increasing the possibility of growth.

In the section below, the structures of overseas production and export of the Japanese affiliates in the three main regions of North America, the Asian Pacific region and Europe are analyzed, comparing each in order to make clear the characteristics of Japan's DFI. In the third section their structures of procurement and sale are analyzed, and in the fourth section the structures of foreign trade are explored, focussing on the same group which becomes the hub of the networks.[2] Following this, the internal networks are analyzed using Malaysia as an example.

The networks formed by Japanese affiliates, particularly in the Asian Pacific Rim, function as a strong driving force, simultaneously inducing and integrating structural changes. The driving force for both functions is the Japanese economy. The mechanism of this – how the Japanese economy has two functions as the hub of the Asian

Pacific region – is then analyzed. In the final section the implications of the networks formed by the Japanese companies and their affiliates are explored, particularly in the Asian Pacific region.

OVERSEAS PRODUCTION AND EXPORT STRUCTURES OF THE JAPANESE AFFILIATES

The most remarkable characteristic of the third wave of Japan's DFI is that foreign affiliates have been strengthening their production activities. In fact, comparing the foreign affiliates of Japanese firms in North America, Europe, the NIEs and ASEAN, the production ratios of both mature products (the market growth rate is supposed to be below 5 percent per annum in the Japanese domestic market) and growth-expected products (above 5 percent) have been increasing faster in each region than at the time the respective overseas bases were established.[3]

The most important characteristic of the third wave as compared to the last two is relocation, namely Japanese companies shifting their production bases partially or totally to outside Japan. This has been enhanced by the sharp appreciation of the Japanese yen, particularly in the latter half of the 1980s.[4]

Relocating the production bases has the following effects. First, a new market emerges. For Japanese affiliates in general, the main purchasing target is usually the local market. As more and more production bases are shifted abroad, Japan becomes the overseas market for host countries. Second, foreign affiliates of Japanese companies must start production as soon as possible, so as not to lose Japanese and third-country markets. Therefore, as the foreign affliates cannot afford the time to find local firms who can supply suitable materials and components to meet their requirements, they must purchase them from the home country and/or third countries.

Furthermore, as technology systems are specific to the production of certain products, the production line is set up in the same way as it is in Japan. Even in industries such as transport and electronics – where many parts and components are involved – the processing lines that have been set up overseas still have an intimate number of links to the core operations of the parent firm at home. Therefore, a firm which has relocated its production base overseas, especially in the developing countries, often must still procure key components from the mother country. Most components are imported from Japan, especially from the parent company. In fact, this is the case for Japanese affiliates in Malaysia, where 70 percent of the materials are imported from Japan, of which an average of 70 percent is supplied by the parent companies. The products produced in the host country are mostly sold to the local market, the rest being exported to Japan and third countries.

These phenomena have been observed regardless of the particular industries or host countries. However, after 1985 a different pattern has emerged. The first is the increase of the ratio of local procurements. This ratio has increased from 34.1 percent in 1983 to 45.6 percent in 1990 worldwide. Second, the ratio of domestic sales has also increased from 73.2 percent to 79.6 percent in the same period. These two phenomena have both backwards and forwards effects for a host country, intensifying the economic linkages or networks among industries, and in turn involves making economic linkages between industries in the host countries. The reason why the two ratios have increased in terms of local requirements and local sales is that the Japanese affiliates have judged the yen appreciation to be a long-term trend and have also determined to reduce the cost of materials, diversifying the input sourcing, particularly from Japan to others.

The linkages between the industries made by the increase in the two ratios of local procurements and domestic sales have affected the structures of foreign trade and the restructuring of the international division of labor by making and reorganizing outside networks. This phenomenon is strongly observed in Asia where Japanese affiliates have strengthened the production-oriented direct foreign investments. This is the most remarkable characteristic of the third wave of Japan's DFI.

This trend has become particularly strong in the machinery-related industries which have increased the ratio of overseas production. With the increase in DFI by Japanese manufacturers, the overseas ratio of production has increased to an average of 5.7 percent in 1989 from 3.0 percent in 1985.[5] As to the overseas production ratio by industry, the machinery-related industries are comparatively high. The industry which has the highest overseas production ratio is the transport equipment industry at 14.3 percent followed by the electrical and electronics industry at 11.0 percent and the non-ferrous industry at 6.4 percent in 1989.

The structures of overseas production by region and industry is shown in Table 13.2. In 1987 the region which had the largest share (49.8 percent) of overseas production was Asia, followed by North America and Europe. The percentage share of these three regions alone was as high as 85.6 percent. By industry, the top share holder

Table 13.2 Regional and sectoral composition in production by the Japanese affiliates (per cent, 1987 and 1990 March)

Sector / *Region*	*Food*	*Textile*	*Wood and pulp*	*Chemicals*	*Iron and steel*	*Non-ferrous*	*General machinery*	*Electrical and electronics*	*Transport*	*Precision machinery*	*Petroleum and coal*	*Others*	*Total*
N. America	1.0	0.1	1.6	1.3	3.2	0.0	7.2	8.7	1.2	0.3	0.0	1.6	26.2
	1.4	0.2	1.7	3.7	4.0	1.2	2.1	9.0	13.4	0.9	0.0	8.7	46.2
Latin America	0.2	0.3	0.1	0.2	2.7	0.0	0.7	1.5	2.0	0.0	0.0	0.6	8.3
	0.0	0.2	0.1	0.4	0.1	0.5	0.2	0.4	1.4	0.1	0.0	0.0	3.6
Asia	0.6	8.2	0.2	2.8	1.7	2.1	1.5	19.4	7.3	2.7	0.0	3.1	49.8
	0.5	1.6	0.0	2.2	0.9	2.2	1.3	11.7	6.0	1.1	0.0	2.6	30.1
Middle East	0.0	0.0	0.0	0.3	0.0	0.0	0.0	0.0	0.0	0.0	0.0	0.0	2.9
	0.0	0.0	0.0	0.4	0.0	0.0	0.0	0.1	0.0	0.0	0.0	0.0	0.5
Europe	0.0	0.2	0.0	0.4	1.1	0.0	0.8	4.7	0.2	0.3	0.0	2.0	9.6
	0.0	0.0	0.0	1.3	0.0	0.0	0.2	4.7	3.5	0.6	0.0	3.0	14.9
Oceania	0.0	0.0	0.5	0.2	0.0	0.0	0.0	0.5	0.9	0.0	0.0	0.6	2.7
	0.3	0.0	0.0	0.0	0.0	0.0	0.0	0.4	3.1	0.0	0.0	0.3	4.4
Africa	0.1	0.0	0.0	0.0	0.1	0.0	0.0	0.1	0.3	0.0	0.0	0.1	0.6
	0.0	0.0	0.0	0.0	0.0	0.0	0.0	0.0	0.0	0.0	0.0	0.0	0.2
Total	1.9	8.8	2.4	5.0	8.6	2.2	10.2	34.9	11.9	3.4	2.6	8.0	100
	2.3	2.2	1.9	8.0	5.2	4.1	5.4	26.4	27.4	2.7	0.0	14.4	100
N. America	3.8	0.3	6.1	4.9	12.0	0.2	27.4	33.2	4.7	1.3	0.0	6.0	100
	3.0	0.4	3.7	8.0	8.6	2.6	4.6	19.4	29.0	1.8	0.0	18.8	100
Asia	1.3	16.4	0.5	5.6	3.5	4.3	3.0	39.0	14.7	5.4	0.1	6.3	100
	1.8	5.2	2.0	7.4	3.0	7.2	4.3	38.7	20.0	3.7	0.0	8.9	100
Europe	0.0	2.3	0.0	4.0	10.9	0.0	8.7	48.3	2.0	3.2	0.0	20.6	100
	0.6	0.4	0.0	8.6	0.5	0.5	11.3	31.7	23.4	3.8	0.0	19.0	100

Source: Ministry of International Trade and Industry, Tokyo, 1991, "Dai Sankai Oyobi Dai Yonkai Kaigai Toushi Toukei Souran" (The Third & Fourth Survey on Japan's DFI)

Note: Upper and lower figures are as March 1987 and March 1990 respectively

was the electrical and electronics industry, followed by the transport equipment industry and the general machinery industry. Including the precision equipment industry, four machinery-related industries held 60.4 percent share of the total. However, in 1990, the top position had changed both in terms of region and industry. By region, North America had the first rank, with a share of 46.2 percent, followed by Asia and then Europe. The combined share of these three regions was as high as 91.2 percent. By industry, transportation equipment had become top, followed by electrical and electronics equipment and then chemicals. With general machinery taking fourth position, the combined share of the four highest shareholders is 61.9 percent. The reason for this share shift can be attributed to North America. That is to say, the shares of transport equipment and chemicals have increased to 13.4 percent and 3.7 percent from 1.2 percent and 1.3 percent respectively.

Regarding outward networks, the regional export structures of the Japanese affiliates are shown in Table 13.3. From this matrix, by region and industry, the following characteristics are observed. First, the combined export share of Japanese affiliates in the three regions of North America, Europe and Asia has increased to 96.7 percent in 1990 from 86.9 percent in 1987. Second, Asia is the largest exporter of all the regions. However, its share decreased to 48 percent in 1990 from 56 percent in 1987. Third, of the Japanese affiliates in Asia, the export value in the NIEs has surpassed that in ASEAN countries. Fourth, especially from the standpoint of the export value between regions amounting over ¥100 billion, the regions which meet the above criteria are intra North America, exports from North America to Japan, exports from Asia to North America, Japan, Europe, intra Asia, exports from the Middle East to Japan and intra Europe. The above intra-regional exports occupy 86 percent of the total exports by all Japanese affiliates around the world, though in 1990 the share decreased to 74.1 percent. Fifth, on the basis of the abovementioned, it is becoming clear that exports destined for Japan have expanded. The share of exports to Japan out of total exports by Japanese affiliates operating all over the world had increased to 40 percent in 1990 from 35 percent in 1987, while the combined share from North America and Asia in total imports to Japan had also increased to 84 percent from 72 percent in the same period. This means that Japan has strengthened its reverse imports (i.e. Japan's imports from Japanese affiliates abroad), most of which are imported from the Pacific Rim countries.

Considering the changes analyzed above, the overseas activities

Table 13.3 Regional export structures of Japanese affiliates (billion yen, manufacturing)

Destination / *Exporting area*	*N. America*	*Latin America*	*Japan*	*Asia*	*Middle East*	*Europe*	*Oceania*	*Africa*	*World*
N. America	133	8	142	9	0[b]	17	0	0	310
	100[c]	7	311	16	117	34	3	1	589
Latin America	29	10	24	15	1	32	1	0	113
	19	10	46	4	0	6	1	0	86
Asia	328	9	506	409	31	146	13	8	1,451
	212	6	644	341	13	117	15	9	1,357
ASEAN	67	4	131	244	17	58	7	4	533
	53	0	160	124	4	22	3	1	367
Middle East	–[a]	–	136	5	–	2	–	–	142
	0	0	52	2	0	1	0	0	55
Europe	24	2	20	0	15	424	–	7	491
	20	1	35	10	10	610	1	4	691
Oceania	–	–	69	6	–	–	2	–	77
	1	0	46	4	0	0	8	0	59
Africa	–	–	–	–	–	8	–	–	8
	0	0	0	0	0	4	0	6	10
World	514	29	897	444	47	629	16	15	2,591
	352	24	1,134	376	24	772	26	20	2,847

Source: See Table 13.2

Note: [a] Bar means no trade flow
[b] Zero means the amounts below ¥1 billion
[c] Upper and lower figures are as of March 1987 and March 1990 respectively

of Japanese affiliates are shaped not only by industry factors but also by geography. That is to say, Japanese affiliates establishing machinery-related production bases mainly in North America, Asia and Europe, basically selling products intra-region, furthermore trade with specific regions such as the Pacific Rim, Japan and North America. The intra-regional export among the above Pacific Rimmers amounted to 45 percent in 1990, increasing from 42 percent in 1987. The following sections are analyses of the regional characteristics of the network patterns, particularly of North America (substantially the US, which has as much as 90.3 percent of North America's total exports), Europe (the EC has 81.8 percent of Europe's total exports) and Asia.

THE STRUCTURES OF PROCUREMENT AND SALES OF THE JAPANESE AFFILIATES IN THREE REGIONS

The structures of procurement and sales of Japanese affiliates operating abroad are shown in Table 13.4. From this table we see the following structural changes which happened between 1987 and 1990.

In terms of procurement structures, the import share from Japan, still being the largest, increased in the latter half in the 1980s. This is attributed to higher local procurement because of offsetting higher costs because of the yen appreciation. The region which has increased the local procurement ratio is North America. Asia has sharply decreased the import share from Japan while it has increased the local procurement ratio, surpassing the former in 1990. As to the sales structures, the local sales ratio is the highest in average. However, three regions have shown trends different from the world-wide trend. Almost all of the local productions of Japanese affiliates in North America have been sold to the local market, the ratio of the local sales in Asia and Europe being much lower than average. However, in the latter half in the 1980s, these two regions exhibited contrasting changes. That is to say, Asia increased the share of local sales while Europe's decreased. As to the export share for Japan, these regions have increased in common, Asia being the largest exporter. In terms of the export share to third countries, Europe has the largest, and it is increasing, 90 percent of which is destined for intra-region markets. The following is an analysis of the precise characteristics of Japanese affiliates in these regions in terms of procurement and sales structure by industry and by region at the end of March 1990.

The features of the procurement and sales structures of Japanese

Table 13.4 Regional composition of procurement and sales by Japanese affiliates (%, manufacturing)

		World				N. America				Asia				Europe			
		1981	*1983*	*1986*	*1990*	*1981*	*1983*	*1986*	*1990*	*1981*	*1983*	*1986*	*1990*	*1981*	*1983*	*1986*	*1990*
Procurement	Local procurement	42.5	34.1	36.9	45.6	39.9	62.8	32.3	47.1	42.2	38.5	42.2	49.8	39.3	34.8	33.1	35.1
	Import from Japan	42.8	43.4	53.0	45.7	49.1	28.2	62.3	49.2	41.5	33.0	45.3	38.9	44.5	39.1	51.2	41.9
	Japanese investor	36.5	31.0	–	–	48.5	17.4	–	–	–	31.4	21.8	–	–	43.8	26.9	–
	Import from third countries	14.7	8.6	10.2	8.7	11.0	2.4	5.4	3.7	16.3	14.5	12.6	11.4	16.1	14.4	15.6	23.0
	N. America	2.7	1.1	1.8	0.7	0.5	1.1	0.6	0.5	3.3	2.0	1.9	0.7	1.0	0.5	0.5	1.0
	Latin America	0.3	0.3	0.2	0.5	0.1	0.0	0.2	0.3	0.3	0.1	0.4	0.6	0.1	0.3	0.0	0.1
	Asia	5.4	1.4	3.3	3.2	4.1	0.0	4.3	2.6	8.7	2.4	5.6	4.8	0.6	0.8	1.1	3.9
	Middle America	0.0	0.1	0.1	0.1	0.0	–	0.0	0.0	0.0	0.1	0.1	0.3	0.0	–	0.1	0.0
	Europe	2.5	1.9	3.5	3.0	3.0	0.4	0.3	0.2	2.1	1.9	0.5	1.1	13.8	10.5	12.9	17.7
	Oceania	3.3	1.4	1.1	0.4	6.2	–	0.0	0.1	1.4	3.2	3.8	1.1	0.0	0.6	0.0	0.0
	Africa	0.1	0.2	0.3	0.1	0.0	–	0.0	0.0	0.1	0.2	0.3	0.4	0.6	1.5	0.9	0.0
	Total	100	100	100	100	100	100	100	100	100	100	100	100	100	100	100	100
Sales	Local procurement	72.9	73.2	77.1	79.6	84.9	72.0	92.8	93.1	63.9	66.9	54.7	63.9	74.6	68.9	70.3	66.5
	Export to Japan	10.9	11.6	7.8	7.9	7.8	12.2	3.3	4.5	9.8	10.8	15.8	15.8	0.3	3.3	1.2	1.7
	Japanese investor	7.4	9.7	–	–	7.1	11.7	–	–	8.7	8.1	–	–	0.1	3.3	–	–
	Export to third countries	16.2	15.2	15.1	12.4	7.3	15.8	3.9	2.5	26.4	22.3	29.5	20.3	25.1	27.8	28.5	31.8
	N. America	4.4	3.8	4.4	2.5	3.1	5.1	3.1	1.4	7.5	6.1	10.2	5.2	1.0	0.9	1.5	0.9
	Latin America	0.9	0.4	0.3	0.2	0.8	2.0	0.2	0.1	0.6	0.3	0.3	0.1	0.0	0.0	0.1	0.1
	Asia	5.4	3.3	3.0	2.6	0.5	1.0	0.2	0.2	12.8	6.1	12.8	8.4	1.3	0.1	0.0	0.5
	Middle America	1.1	0.9	0.4	0.2	0.1	0.1	0.0	0.0	1.5	1.1	1.0	0.3	0.4	0.4	0.9	0.5
	Europe	3.6	2.9	6.7	5.4	2.8	2.5	0.4	0.5	3.1	2.3	4.6	2.9	21.8	14.7	25.6	29.0
	Oceania	0.5	0.2	0.1	0.2	0.0	0.1	0.0	0.0	0.5	0.5	0.4	0.4	0.0	0.0	0.0	0.0
	Africa	0.2	0.2	0.1	0.1	0.0	0.2	0.0	0.0	0.3	0.2	0.2	0.2	0.6	0.3	0.4	0.2
	Total	100	100	100	100	100	100	100	100	100	100	100	100	100	100	100	100

Source: Ministry of International Trade and Industry, Tokyo, 1991, "Kaigai Toushi Toukei Souran", "Wagakuni Kigyouno Kaigai Jigyou Katsudou" Overseas Economic Activities of the Japanese Affiliates) various issues

Note: Figures are as of March of each year

affiliates in North America can be seen in Table 13.5. First, the features of procurement are observed as follows. (1) In the resource-based industries (from the food industry to the non-ferrous industry and coal and petroleum) the ratio of the local procurements is higher than the average in the manufacturing sectors. (2) As to the ratio of imports from Japan, they are very high particularly for the machinery-related industries. (3) The import ratio from third countries is very low through all industries. Asia's share in the import from third countries is over 70 percent, nearly 90 percent of which is occupied by the four machinery-related industries. By procurement source and industry, the electrical and electronics industry has the highest share in common in three different out-sourcings.

The characteristics of the sales structures are as follows. (1) The locally produced products are mostly sold to the domestic market. (2) The products with a comparatively high export share to Japan are woods/pulp, food and coal/petroleum. But the sales shares to Japan in respective total sales are comparatively high; as much as 36.6 percent in the wood/pulp industry and 23.9 percent in the food industry, while that of petroleum and coal is comparatively low, as little as 18.1 percent. (3) Of the export shares to third countries, North America is the biggest shareholder, with two-thirds of the total exports, followed by Europe and then Asia.

Judging from the above analysis, it can be concluded that Japanese affiliates in North America are importing components for machinery-related materials mainly from Japan, almost all of which are then sold to the domestic market.[6]

The basic structures of Japanese affiliates in Europe are almost same as those in North America, except for the following points. The largest difference relates to procurement. There are almost no imports from Japan and third countries, except in machineries.[7] Regarding the procurement of materials from outside of Europe, the ratio of Japanese affiliates in Asia is rather high. On the other hand, 95.6 percent of total sales is shared by locals and other European countries. That is to say, the activities of Japanese affiliates in Europe are concentrated almost entirely on intra-European markets, which is almost the same as those in North America.

The activity structures of Asian affiliates of the Japanese companies are different from those in North America and Europe. The most remarkable difference is that the ratio of the local sales is the lowest among the three regions. This is attributed to the fact that, as mentioned earlier, the Japanese companies have relocated their

Table 13.5 Sectoral composition of Japanese affiliates in North America (percent, March 1990)

	Sectors	*Composition of procurement and sales by sector*						*Sectoral composition by procurement and sales*					
					Regional composition of third countries						*Regional composition of the third countries*		
		Local	*Import (export) from (to) Japan*	*Import (export) from (to) third countries*	*N. America*	*Asia*	*Europe*	*Local*	*Import (export) from (to) Japan*	*Import (export) from (to) third countries*	*N. America*	*Asia*	*Europe*
Procurement	Manufacturer	47.1	49.2	3.7	13.6	70.6	5.7	100	100	100	100	100	100
	Food	94.8	1.6	3.6	17.5	8.0	6.4	3.0	0.1	3.0	3.9	0.3	3.4
	Textile	96.4	3.6	0.0	–	–	–	0.0	0.0	0.0	–	–	–
	Wood and pulp	95.3	1.7	3.0	75.5	5.7	18.8	2.8	0.1	2.8	15.9	0.2	9.5
	Chemicals	95.2	4.8	0.0	0.0	100.0	0.0	0.1	0.7	0.1	0.0	0.1	0.0
	Iron and steel	85.6	12.4	2.0	0.0	20.6	35.6	1.0	0.5	1.0	0.0	0.3	6.2
	Non-ferrous	76.9	21.6	1.5	0.0	1.8	4.8	1.1	1.2	1.1	0.0	0.0	1.0
	General machinery	34.9	63.8	1.3	26.9	6.7	66.4	1.6	5.8	1.6	3.1	0.1	18.4
	Electrical mach.	18.8	72.7	8.5	11.1	78.6	2.3	79.3	51.0	79.3	64.5	88.4	31.7
	Transport	53.0	46.8	0.2	87.0	1.7	0.2	1.4	31.3	1.4	9.2	0.0	0.0
	Precision	10.3	89.5	0.1	31.9	66.0	2.1	0.1	2.7	0.1	0.1	0.1	0.0
	Petroleum and coal	20.3	79.7	0.0	–	–	–	0.0	0.2	0.0	–	–	–
	Others	56.3	39.3	4.4	4.7	77.5	17.8	9.6	6.4	9.6	3.3	10.4	29.8
Sales	Manufacturer	93.1	4.5	2.5	62.9	9.7	21.1	100	100	100	100	100	100
	Food	74.5	23.9	1.6	2.8	16.1	76.7	2.1	17.5	2.1	0.1	3.8	8.2
	Textile	99.7	0.1	0.2	–	–	–	0.0	0.0	0.0	0.0	0.0	0.0
	Wood and pulp	40.3	36.6	23.0	72.9	10.6	10.9	36.9	32.1	36.9	45.6	42.8	20.2
	Chemicals	96.1	3.5	0.4	20.1	13.0	55.0	0.1	5.5	1.1	0.4	1.5	2.9
	Iron and steel	99.5	0.2	0.4	100.0	0.0	0.0	1.2	0.3	1.2	2.0	0.0	0.0
	Non-ferrous	88.8	6.6	4.6	16.8	19.3	62.3	5.0	4.0	5.0	1.4	10.7	15.8
	General machinery	96.2	1.3	2.5	12.9	3.4	63.2	4.4	1.3	4.4	1.0	1.6	13.9
	Electrical mach.	96.9	1.5	1.6	53.5	13.4	21.4	24.5	13.0	24.5	17.1	27.6	20.3
	Transport	94.1	4.0	1.9	86.1	0.4	13.6	17.4	19.7	17.4	25.4	0.7	11.9
	Precision	94.1	4.3	1.6	23.2	24.9	44.5	1.2	1.8	1.2	0.4	2.8	2.3
	Petroleum and coal	78.9	18.1	3.0	–	0.0	100.0	0.1	0.4	0.1	0.0	0.0	0.6
	Others	96.0	2.3	1.7	78.1	14.1	13.7	6.1	4.5	6.1	6.6	8.6	3.8

Source: See Table 13.4

production facilities in Asia, strengthening the production activities for more export. That is to say, Japan's DFI in the latter half of the 1980s can be characterized as export-oriented. In fact, out of 294 projects of DFI in Thailand, 193 projects (65.8 percent) were 100 percent export-oriented. The ratio whose export share was over 80 percent numbered 85 percent for Japan's DFI in Thailand in terms of the number of companies. In the case of Malaysia, the export share of Japanese affiliates who export over 80 percent is nearly 60 percent in terms of the number of the companies.

The structures of Japanese affiliates in Asia are analyzed in two groups – NIEs and ASEAN economies. The share of the two groups in the whole of Asia are 69.9 percent for NIEs and 26.6 percent in the local procurements, while that of imports from Japan are 67.4 percent for the former and 28.4 percent for the latter. As to the regional sales composition in Asia, NIEs constitute 63.6 percent, while the ASEAN countries' share is 34.2 percent. Accordingly, the two groups almost make up the total in the whole of Asia in terms of both local procurement and sales, while the share of the NIEs is much bigger in both than that of the ASEANs. Of imports from third countries, 99 percent is made up by two groups, and this is divided almost equally between them. Points of similarity and difference are as follows regarding the structures of sourcing and sales of NIEs and ASEANs (Table 13.6(1) and (2)). There are two big differences between the groups. First, the ratio of local procurements is much higher for NIEs. Second, the ratio of imports from third countries is much higher for ASEANs than for NIEs. Conversely, there are three similarities. First, the ratio of local procurements is comparatively high in the resources-based industries for both groups. Second, for imports from Japan, the ratio of imports for machinery-related industries as non-resource-based is very high. Third, as to imports from third countries, the share from intra-Asian countries is high. In terms of the structure by sourcing and industry, four machinery-related industries have a high share. However, it is noted that, as to imports from Japan, the share of transport equipment is more than that of the electrical and electronics industry.

The features of sales by Japanese affiliates are observed as follows. (1) The ratio of domestic sales is the lowest among the three regions. (2) Comparatively high is the export ratio to third countries. Exports to intra-Asian countries is rather high for both NIEs and ASEANs. For ASEANs, the share for intra-Asian is over 60 percent. Over 60 percent of intra-Asian trade is shared by the electrical and electronics industry. (3) The share of exports to Japan is 15.8 per-

Table 13.6(1) Sectoral production composition by Japanese affiliates in Asia (percent, March 1990)

	Sector	*Asia, total*			*NIEs*			*ASEANs*			*Regional structures of third countries*					
											NIEs			*ASEANs*		
		Local	*Import (export) from (to) Japan*	*Import (export) from (to) third countries*	*Local*	*Import (export) from (to) Japan*	*Import (export) from (to) third countries*	*Local*	*Import (export) from (to) Japan*	*Import (export) from (to) third countries*	*N. America*	*Asia*	*Europe*	*N. America*	*Asia*	*Europe*
Procurement	Manufacturing, total	49.8	38.9	11.4	52.9	37.0	10.1	45.5	40.9	13.6	5.6	64.2	17.1	9.7	40.2	6.6
	Foods	87.7	3.3	9.0	83.2	4.1	12.7	97.7	1.5	0.8	0.0	47.3	33.6	0.0	100.0	0.0
	Textile	43.1	22.4	34.5	60.0	6.0	34.1	24.7	39.9	35.5	0.0	25.6	34.9	15.0	10.1	11.0
	Wood and pulp	92.8	2.3	4.9	78.4	7.2	14.3	99.4	0.0	0.6	0.0	89.9	10.1	0.0	100.0	0.0
	Chemicals	56.3	34.7	9.0	48.9	46.0	5.1	64.6	20.5	14.9	31.1	25.1	20.2	23.3	18.8	20.3
	Iron and steel	36.0	56.1	7.9	42.3	49.1	8.6	30.3	62.4	7.3	17.0	45.2	19.0	0.0	56.7	0.0
	Non-ferrous	59.3	18.1	22.7	69.4	14.8	15.7	41.3	23.6	35.1	3.6	26.7	30.2	0.5	17.0	0.9
	General machinery	53.6	42.5	3.8	50.3	45.2	4.5	68.7	30.6	0.7	4.5	84.8	9.3	0.0	100.0	0.0
	Electrical and electronics	42.4	44.6	13.1	45.5	45.6	8.9	34.3	40.3	25.3	3.9	94.2	1.9	1.6	98.1	0.0
	Transport	57.7	41.8	0.5	70.6	28.1	1.3	53.3	46.6	0.1	4.0	19.4	72.7	0.0	5.4	94.6
	Precision machinery	42.1	45.2	12.7	52.6	34.2	13.3	15.8	72.5	11.7	0.3	99.7	0.0	49.4	48.7	0.0
	Petroleum and coal	89.5	10.5	0.0	93.0	7.0	0.0	58.0	42.0	0.0	–	–	–	–	–	–
	Others	36.0	48.4	15.6	39.0	45.5	15.5	29.6	54.6	15.8	17.1	45.2	29.5	15.3	44.8	7.9
Sales	Manufacturing, total	63.9	15.9	20.3	57.3	19.6	23.0	73.4	10.3	16.3	31.2	43.6	18.5	25.6	60.1	10.6
	Foods	66.9	16.1	17.0	78.4	12.8	8.8	26.7	28.1	45.2	9.5	44.2	24.1	19.3	66.2	10.2
	Textile	70.5	14.9	14.6	75.2	13.6	11.1	67.6	14.7	17.7	24.5	63.8	11.6	7.5	50.3	19.3
	Wood and pulp	34.4	35.9	29.7	67.1	2.6	30.3	14.4	56.4	29.3	59.0	41.0	0.0	20.7	79.3	0.0
	Chemicals	78.1	10.3	11.6	73.3	12.3	14.3	85.3	7.1	7.5	7.4	78.1	2.9	6.5	69.8	17.3
	Iron and steel	87.7	4.2	8.1	75.5	7.8	16.7	98.6	0.9	0.5	48.2	49.0	0.2	1.3	98.7	0.0
	Non-ferrous	73.3	12.1	14.6	87.5	0.9	11.6	41.6	37.0	21.3	0.0	99.0	0.1	19.1	75.7	8.0
	General machinery	56.9	18.2	24.9	44.3	23.5	32.2	98.0	0.7	1.3	16.3	23.0	53.4	0.0	100.0	0.0
	Electrical and electronics	37.4	26.9	35.7	37.1	30.4	32.6	34.9	17.5	47.6	39.7	42.2	13.2	30.7	61.6	7.3
	Transport	92.1	1.6	6.3	81.1	3.6	15.3	96.4	0.9	2.8	17.2	31.6	38.5	10.4	88.5	0.4
	Precision machinery	55.0	22.2	22.7	64.3	22.5	13.2	6.5	20.4	73.0	13.3	35.7	33.0	27.1	33.5	37.0
	Petroleum and coal	100.0	0.0	0.0	100.0	0.0	0.0	100.0	0.0	0.0	–	–	–	–	–	–
	Others	78.5	12.1	9.3	74.1	12.8	13.1	82.9	11.4	5.7	41.6	27.2	20.0	35.4	42.7	9.4

Source: See Table 13.4

Table 13.6(2) Sectoral composition of Japanese affiliates in Asia (percent)

	Sector	*Sectoral composition of procurement and sales*						*Sectoral compositions of the third countries*					
		NIEs			*ASEANs*			*NIEs*			*ASEANs*		
		Local	*Import (export) from (to) Japan*	*Import (export) from (to) third countries*	*Local*	*Import (export) from (to) Japan*	*Import (export) from (to) third countries*	*N. America*	*Asia*	*Europe*	*N. America*	*Asia*	*Europe*
	Manufacturing, total	100	100	100	100	100	100	100	100	100	100	100	100
P	Foods	4.5	0.3	3.6	3.7	0.1	0.1	0.0	3.1	8.2	0.0	0.1	0.0
r	Textile	5.7	0.8	17.1	3.4	6.2	16.5	0.0	7.8	39.9	30.2	4.9	32.7
o	Wood and pulp	0.3	0.0	0.3	1.2	0.0	0.0	0.0	0.4	0.2	0.0	0.1	0.0
c	Chemicals	8.5	11.5	4.7	12.9	4.5	10.0	24.1	1.8	5.2	32.3	6.3	41.5
u	Iron and steel	1.7	2.9	1.8	2.1	4.8	1.7	1.0	0.2	0.4	0.0	2.1	0.0
r	Non-ferrous	13.1	4.0	15.6	7.1	4.5	20.3	3.8	2.5	10.5	1.3	10.7	3.3
e	General machinery	7.1	9.1	3.3	3.5	1.7	0.1	3.1	5.1	2.1	0.0	0.4	0.0
m	Electrical and electronics	35.2	50.5	36.1	15.9	20.8	39.2	29.2	62.2	4.7	3.9	57.4	0.0
e	Transport	15.1	8.6	1.5	43.8	42.5	0.3	1.2	0.5	7.5	0.0	0.1	5.8
n	Precision machinery	3.2	3.0	4.2	0.6	3.2	1.5	0.3	7.7	0.0	10.6	2.5	0.0
t	Petroleum and coal	0.1	0.0	0.0	0.0	0.0	0.0	–	–	–	–	–	–
	Others	5.6	9.4	11.8	5.7	11.7	10.2	37.4	8.7	1.3	21.7	15.4	16.7
	Manufacturing	100	100	100	100	100	100	100	100	100	100	100	100
	Foods	4.0	1.9	1.1	0.5	3.7	3.7	0.4	1.3	0.1	3.4	5.0	4.4
	Textile	5.7	3.0	2.1	7.4	11.5	8.7	1.9	3.5	30.8	2.5	7.2	5.7
	Wood and pulp	0.2	0.0	0.3	0.1	2.8	0.9	0.4	0.2	–	1.0	1.5	–
S	Chemicals	11.7	5.7	5.7	9.6	5.7	3.8	1.5	11.3	2.3	1.1	5.3	0.7
a	Iron and steel	2.2	0.7	1.2	3.9	0.2	0.1	1.3	0.9	–	0.0	0.2	–
l	Non-ferrous	14.1	0.4	4.6	3.7	23.3	8.5	0.0	8.0	6.8	6.0	10.1	–
e	General machinery	4.7	7.2	8.4	3.7	0.2	0.2	5.0	5.1	7.5	0.0	0.4	–
s	Electrical and electronics	28.9	69.1	63.2	9.4	33.5	57.5	78.2	59.6	34.1	72.0	61.8	78.6
	Transport	13.7	1.8	6.4	48.0	3.0	6.2	4.0	5.3	6.7	0.4	1.3	0.6
	Precision machinery	5.1	5.2	2.6	0.1	2.7	6.1	1.0	2.0	1.1	7.9	4.2	4.3
	Petroleum and coal	0.0	0.0	0.0	0.0	0.0	0.0	–	–	–	–	–	–
	Others	9.8	4.9	4.3	13.6	13.3	4.2	6.3	3.0	9.4	5.7	2.9	0.8

Source: See Table 13.4

cent, which is the highest among the three regions. The electrical and electronics industry, which is the mainstream of JDFI, procures materials from Japan and other Asian countries and exports the locally produced products to intra-Asian countries. In terms of the export ratio for third countries, those of North America and Europe are considerably higher than those of Japanese affiliates in the said two regions.[8]

The most remarkable difference between Japanese affiliates in Asia and those in North America and Europe is that the latter two have the highest share in terms of local procurement, but the former is the lowest in terms of domestic sales. The reasons are as follows. (1) In Asia the supporting industries are less mature and therefore the production process cannot be completed in the country where Japanese affiliates are operating. The ratio of deals involving other Asian countries is consequently rather high. In fact, as is shown in Table 13.7, the number of Japanese affiliates in Asia producing parts and components in the electrical and electronics industry is considerably higher compared to that in other regions. (2) The reason why the ratio of deals with extra regions such as North America and Europe is comparatively high, is, together with the above mentioned point, that Japanese affiliates in Asia are playing the role of the suppliers of materials to American MNCs and to Japanese affiliates operating in Europe. For Japanese affiliates in Asia, Asian markets are not sufficient to absorb the locally produced product. Therefore, Japanese affiliates in Asia must develop an international division of labor.

THE STRUCTURES OF JAPANESE AFFILIATES IN THE SAME GROUP

The above analysis is based on the networks or "patterns of linkages" of Japanese affiliates in the three main regions of Japanese DFI in terms of procurement and sales. In the case of networks relating to import from Japan and export to Japan, Japan is considered as a whole and investors or financiers are not separated. The following analysis focusses on trade between the Japanese investors and the foreign affiliates of Japanese companies abroad, and the patterns of linkages in the same groups of industries.

Before analyzing foreign trade structures between Japanese parent companies and foreign affiliates, first those between Japan and the foreign affiliates of Japanese companies will be made clearer. Trade

Table 13.7 Sectoral and regional distribution of Japanese affiliates of electronics (Nos of firms)

	Year/month	*Asia*	*Europe*	*N. America*	*S. America*	*Africa*	*Oceania*	*Total*
Electronics for consumers	1990/6	112	45	45	15	4	3	224
	1991/6	128	47	44	15	4	3	241
	1991/1990 (%)	114.3	104.4	97.8	100.0	100.0	100.0	107.6
Electronics for industrial	1990/6	62	32	43	6	0	2	145
	1991/6	75	38	48	5	0	2	168
	1991/1990 (%)	121.0	118.8	111.6	83.3	–	100.0	115.9
Electronic components and devices	1990/6	304	53	77	17	0	1	452
	1991/6	332	59	94	16	0	1	502
	1991/1990 (%)	109.2	111.3	122.1	94.1	–	100.0	111.1
Total	1990/6	449	121	155	35	4	5	769
	1991/6	492	136	170	33	4	5	840
	1991/1990 (%)	109.6	112.4	109.7	94.3	100.0	100.0	109.2

Source: Nihon Denshi Kogyokai "List of the Japanese Affiliates (Tokyo: Japan External Trade Organization, 1991)

Note: Because of the double accounting by one firm, which has two more affiliates, total nos of firms do not coincide with the aggregate

ratios with the Japanese affiliates are computed as in Table 13.8 by industry and by region.

Export

(1) The ratio of the export from Japan to Japanese affiliates in the total export of manufactured goods by the respondents was 32 percent in 1987 and increased to 41.1 percent in 1990. (2) In the resource-based industries, except coal and petroleum products, the deal is almost nothing or the ratios are very low. (3) The industries which have rather high ratios, as detailed above, are four machinery-related industries. (4) By region, the above ratio as defined is the highest for exports to North America and rather high for exports to the developed countries of Oceania and Europe. (5) Combined with region and industry, the ratios are very high for exports to North America and Europe in four machinery-related industries.

Import

(1) In the manufacturing sector as a whole, the ratio of Japan's imports from Japanese affiliates is 23.4 percent which is much lower than the ratio of exports. In 1990, the ratio increased to 30.9 percent, as Japan had promoted imports from the Japanese affiliates. (2) The deal between Japan and its foreign affiliates is almost limited to the four machinery-related industries and to the three partners of North America, Asia and Europe. (3) The reason why the ratio of exports to Japan from Asia is very high in the machinery-related industries is that the trade is conducted through intra-firm transactions between parent companies and Japanese affiliates or between the affiliated companies.

Of the total export value from Japan to Japanese affiliates, the commercial sector shares 32.5 percent, while 67.2 percent is shared by the manufacturing sector. However, of exports from the manufacturing sector, 93.5 percent is exported by machinery-related industries, though the ratio decreased somewhat to 88.6 percent in 1990. The export and import structures of the four machinery-related industries by region is shown in Table 13.9.

From Table 13.9 the most remarkable characteristic is that exports from Japan to Japanese affiliates are concentrated in specific machinery and regions. That is to say, in the four machinery-related industries, the biggest shareholder is electrical and electronics, with a

Table 13.8 Japanese sectoral export and import to and from Japanese affiliates (percent, 1990 March)

	Region	Manufacturing total	Food	Textile	Wood and pulp	Chemicals	Iron and steel	Non-ferrous	General machinery	Electrical and electronics	Transport	Precision	Petroleum and coal	Others
	N. America	63.4	37.0	2.6	12.0	48.7	4.0	29.2	67.2	65.5	64.6	72.6	53.1	83.3
E	Latin America	17.2	3.6	19.7	0.0	12.6	2.8	0.0	14.1	34.4	4.7	3.8	0.0	12.9
x	Asia	17.8	10.4	5.3	1.3	9.3	0.8	15.2	21.4	25.4	22.1	32.5	6.9	12.9
p	Middle East	2.3	0.0	0.0	0.0	2.9	1.1	0.0	5.3	4.1	1.7	0.0	0.0	1.9
o	Europe	43.1	1.0	0.4	7.0	27.1	0.1	20.1	47.8	59.8	23.2	50.4	0.0	51.1
r	Oceania	48.9	37.9	0.0	0.0	1.6	0.2	10.3	63.8	57.8	54.1	13.9	0.0	46.3
t	Africa	2.0	0.0	0.0	0.0	4.0	0.0	33.6	3.9	0.0	0.0	0.0	0.0	2.9
	Total	41.1	18.6	3.3	5.2	21.9	1.4	19.2	43.8	50.9	41.1	52.8	36.5	43.8
	N. America	14.0	11.7	3.5	31.1	25.1	2.3	15.1	10.0	8.4	35.1	24.0	37.0	41.0
I	Latin America	110.0*	23.8	21.1	0.0	1.2	0.0	0.0	102.4*	8.4	0.0	0.0	244.8*	1.0
m	Asia	36.3	20.7	36.0	2.0	21.5	0.1	14.2	65.9	65.4	63.4	56.0	32.0	25.9
p	Middle East	27.5	0.0	0.0	0.0	0.0	0.0	0.0	0.0	0.0	0.0	0.0	21.6	0.0
o	Europe	49.1	14.3	0.0	0.0	4.0	0.0	0.2	2.2	16.0	13.1	8.6	327.2*	10.6
r	Oceania	7.4	16.7	16.5	23.9	6.5	0.0	0.0	0.0	125.4*	153.0*	0.0	43.1	31.7
t	Africa	3.9	0.0	0.0	0.0	8.2	0.0	0.0	0.0	0.0	0.0	0.0	25.9	0.0
	Total	30.9	14.8	14.8	22.9	9.9	0.5	5.7	34.2	35.8	36.0	38.1	51.8	25.1

Source: See Table 13.4

Note: * Lack of statistical consistency

Table 13.9 Japanese export and import structures to and from Japanese affiliates (Billion yen, March 1990)

		Value						Share (%)					
		Manufac-turing, total	Machinery, total	General machinery	Elec-tronics	Transport	Precision	Manufac-turing, total	Machinery, total	General machinery	Electrical and electronics	Transport	Precision
	N. America	5,828	5,241	298	2,048	2,598	297	58.7 100	59.6 89.9	49.8 5.1	51.1 35.1	71.5 44.6	54.4 5.1
E	Latin America	129	114	6	92	15	1	1.3 100	1.3 88.4	1.0 4.7	2.3 71.3	0.4 11.6	0.2 0.8
x	Asia	1,170	978	79	493	335	71	11.8 100	11.1 83.6	13.2 6.8	12.3 42.1	9.2 28.6	13.0 6.1
p	Middle East	20	17	2	8	7	0	0.2 100	0.2 85.0	0.3 10.0	0.2 40.0	0.2 35.0	0.0 0.0
o	Europe	2,329	2,005	171	1,267	393	174	23.5 100	22.8 86.1	28.6 7.3	31.6 54.5	10.8 16.9	31.9 7.5
r	Oceania	439	430	40	100	287	3	4.4 100	4.9 98.6	6.7 9.2	2.5 22.9	7.9 65.8	0.5 0.7
t	Africa	10	2	2	0	0	0	0.1 100	0.0 20.0	0.3 20.0	0.0 0.0	0.0 0.0	0.0 0.0
	Total	9,922	8,787	598	4,008	3,635	546	100 100	100 88.6	100 6.0	100 40.4	100 36.6	100 5.5
	N. America	383*	444	2	82	352	8	12.6 100	30.5 115.9	6.5 0.5	10.5 21.4	57.6 91.9	21.6 2.1
I	Latin America	744*	5	0	5	0	0	24.4 100	0.3 0.7	0.0 0.0	0.6 0.7	0.0 0.0	0.0 0.0
m	Asia	1,005	871	29	670	144	28	33.1 100	59.8 86.7	93.5 2.9	86.1 66.7	23.6 14.3	75.7 2.8
p	Middle East	443	0	0	0	0	0	14.6 100	0.0 0.0	0.0 0.0	0.0 0.0	0.0 0.0	0.0 0.0
o	Europe	377	59	0	16	42	1	12.4 100	4.0 15.6	0.0 0.0	2.1 4.2	6.9 11.1	2.7 0.3
r	Oceania	76*	78	0	5	73	0	2.5 100	5.4 102.6	0.0 0.0	0.6 6.6	11.9 96.1	0.0 0.0
t	Africa	9	0	0	0	0	0	0.3 100	0.0 0.0	0.0 0.0	0.0 0.0	0.0 0.0	0.0 0.0
	Total	3,037	1,457	31	778	610	37	100 100	100 48.0	100 1.0	100 25.6	100 20.1	100 1.2

Source: See Table 13.4

share of over 40 percent, followed by transport equipment. The combined share of the two industries is as high as 77 percent. By region, the export share for North America is 58.7 percent, followed by Europe, with a combine share of 82.2 percent. Exports of transport and electrical and electronics equipment from North America and Europe have a share of 63.6 percent of the total manufacturing export from Japan to Japanese affiliates. Including Asia, the combined share increases to as much as 71.9 percent.

The structures of imports to Japan from her affiliated companies abroad are almost the same as the export structures. Imports are mainly made up by the two industries of electrical and electronics *and* transport equipment and by three regions, the combined share of which is 43 percent of total manufactured goods. These imports are so called "inverse" imports, which means imports from foreign affiliates to Japan. However, it should be noted that the amount of imports is below one-third of the export amounts. But the "reverse" imports of manufactured goods have increased over four times between 1987 and 1990, the ratio of which has also increased to 17.8 percent from 7.5 percent. In particular, the amount "inverse" imports from Asia has increased by over 4 times, the ratio of which has sharply increased to 32.4 percent from 3.2 percent in the manufactured goods imported from Asia.

Another characteristic of the structure of Japanese affiliates with regard to sourcing and sales is a rather high ratio of the trading deal between the groups. This is shown in Table 13.10.

As to the importing patterns and relationships of Japanese firms, the most striking feature is that, of the three directions of sourcing and sales, the three regions of North America, Asia and Europe have commonly the biggest trading share with Japan in the same groups. Particularly in terms of procurement from Japan, the ratio of the electrical and electronics industry is over 90 percent worldwide. The average ratio of the four machinery-related industries is as high as 82.5 percent. By region, in the case of Asia, the ratios of procurement and sales are the lowest among the three regions. This is the reason that the Japanese Asian affiliates are now forming international production networks over this area, raising local procurement and selling products to third countries.

More features can be explored. First, regardless of industry and region, in Asia, the concentration ratio among the same group is very low both in terms of procurement and sales. Second, in dealing with Japan, the concentration ratios among the same group in the general machinery and the electrical and electronics industries are

Table 13.10 The concentration ratio among the same group (percent, March 1990)

		Procurement						Sales					
		Manufacturing, total	General machinery	Electricals and electronics	Transport	Precision	Total	Manufacturing, total	General machinery	Electricals and electronics	Transport	Precision	Total
World	Local sales (A)	5.1	0.5	13.3	4.7	3.3	6.4	8.1	22.5	9.1	9.0	4.7	4.5
	Export to Japan (B)	82.5	82.4	90.5	72.3	93.8	71.0	61.6	96.8	63.0	33.6	47.2	39.3
	Export to third countries (C)	38.3	62.4	49.6	17.4	93.3	10.4	44.2	59.7	55.0	46.2	44.0	18.0
	Total (A)+(B)+(C)	43.3	45.8	65.4	38.2	75.6	28.2	16.8	33.8	20.7	11.6	14.3	14.3
North America	Local sales (A)	4.7	13.1	13.1	6.5	3.6	5.5	7.0	15.0	3.8	13.7	1.0	4.5
	Export to Japan (B)	87.8	96.7	96.7	72.2	90.3	76.0	69.2	87.4	97.7	28.1	55.2	30.1
	Export to third countries (C)	34.8	33.2	33.2	70.1	18.1	4.7	24.1	56.8	42.7	5.5	16.5	4.2
	Total (A)+(B)+(C)	46.7	75.6	75.6	37.4	81.3	31.0	10.2	17.0	5.9	14.1	3.6	8.0
Asia	Local sales (A)	4.1	0.6	5.1	2.3	3.6	10.3	6.5	0.6	12.9	6.2	16.2	4.4
	Export to Japan (B)	62.6	79.1	65.3	48.9	96.1	63.2	58.9	98.5	60.3	35.7	50.8	34.3
	Export to third countries (C)	23.9	32.3	29.8	0.7	86.2	3.7	37.2	45.4	43.9	8.5	55.4	14.8
	Total (A)+(B)+(C)	29.1	35.3	35.1	21.8	55.9	18.0	21.0	29.6	36.7	6.8	32.8	16.1
Europe	Local sales (A)	10.7	0.0	35.6	0.0	0.0	8.7	19.7	60.0	24.2	1.0	0.8	5.4
	Export to Japan (B)	91.4	79.6	95.7	84.0	100.0	63.7	55.2	69.6	13.9	100.0	87.1	25.5
	Export to third countries (C)	56.9	94.8	74.8	0.0	98.6	19.6	62.6	67.2	78.9	92.2	51.0	28.3
	Total (A)+(B)+(C)	55.1	48.7	76.7	42.6	95.0	31.0	33.9	63.0	38.2	44.3	6.4	17.7

Source: See Table 13.4

comparatively high in the three regions. The fact that the concentration ratios among the same group in two industries of general machinery and electrical and electronics is comparatively high means that intra-industry trade is conducted in the form of product-differentiation and/or process-differentiation. As shown in Tables 13.14 and 13.15 we will go on to analyze the structures of intra-firm trade using the electrical and electronics industry as an example, which shows almost equal export and import amounts with Japan.

As an indicator to judge the degree of development of intra-firm trade, we can set the procurement ratio from Japan and the export ratio to Japan in a specific industry. In case of the electrical and electronics industry, the former is as high as 78.1 percent and the latter is as high as 73 percent. This means that between Japan (to be precise, the parent company and its affiliates in Japan) and its Asian affiliates, there is considerable intra-firm trade. Whether this intra-firm trade is horizontal or vertical can be explored.

As the indicator to judge if intra-firm trade is horizontal or vertical, the ratio of the components and parts in foreign trade can be used. According to this judgment, as to the imports to Japanese affiliates from Japan, the ratio of the components and parts reached 75 percent in 1987 while in 1990 its ratio has decreased to 72 percent, which is still very high. On the other hand, the export share of the components and parts to Japan from the Japanese affiliates had increased to 51 percent in 1990 from 29.4 percent in 1987.

Though there is very limited data available, we can infer some things about the structure of the international division of labor between Japan and its affiliates in Asia. The international division of labor in the electrical and electronics industry is basically vertical, Japanese parent firms supply components/parts and intermediate goods to the affiliated companies in Asia while importing and/or sourcing components with more value-added from them. But the general trend in Asia is that intra-firm trade is shifting sharply to the horizontal from the vertical. Using the specialization coefficient defined as the difference between export and import being divided by the sum of both in one country, if this figure should be –1 or +1, the structure is complete import or export specialization respectively. If the figure is around zero from both directions, we can say that the intra-industry trade is almost a horizontal international division of labor. If we examine the structural changes in the electrical and electronics industry between 1987 and 1990, the figure for this industry as a whole has decreased to –0.02 in 1990 from –0.07 in 1987 from the side of the affiliated companies. In terms of the products base, the products which increase the figure are components for electricals and telecommunications (from –0.56 to –0.31), while the products whose figures turn from positive to negative is computers (from +1 to –0.30). Comparing the production line of Japanese affiliates in Asia to the parent companies in Japan, 69.8 percent of the former are comparable to the latter, which implies that intra-firm trade has the potential to develop the horizontal international division of labor between them.

The above analysis is one side of the international production networks developed by Japanese companies and their affiliates abroad, focussing on foreign trade. The following section analyzes the other side of the international production network, that is to say the internal networks, using Malaysia as an example.

FORMATION OF INTERNAL AND EXTERNAL NETWORKS BY JAPANESE AFFILIATES IN MALAYSIA[9]

Internal networks

In general, industries tend to tighten their mutual linkages when the volume of intermediate input or the trade volume to meet the intermediate demand increases between the industries concerned. A well-balanced national economy has more potential to create such an industrial structure and to continuously increase the per capita income level through the prominent circulation of goods, services and money within the system.

While the economy of an industrialized country has this type of industrial structure with internal linkages, the Malaysian economy can be characterized as an independent or specialized type. An independent type means that few intermediate goods from other industries are procured and that each industry tends to operate in an independent manner with intermediate goods being produced within the same sector. A specialized type means that the sale of the products of one industry is limited to another specific industry (or industries). These characteristics originate from the fact that the Malaysian economy is still by and large dominated by primary industries which have strong features in common with extractive industries.

It is true that Malaysia has been rapidly achieving a more sophisticated industrial and export structure since the second half of the 1980s. However, close analysis immediately reveals the survival of the old structure described above. Two-thirds of Malaysia's exports of manufactured goods consist of electrical and electronics and textile goods, mainly manufactured and exported by foreign affiliates located in free trade zones (FTZs). Foreign affiliates in FTZs account for 90 percent of the production volume of these goods, of which 90 percent are exported by them. Almost all the raw materials and parts required for their manufacture are imported from abroad. Malaysia simply provides the land and labor for these companies in FTZs which seldom have any meaningful linkages with local firms. This is a typical example of an "export enclave" or a "tenant industry." In this context, industries in FTZs can be regarded as being similar to the independent type or specialized type industries described above.

The formation of a mutually interdependent industrial structure has long been the earnest wish of the Malaysian government. While the government also has high hopes for a significant contribution by small domestic companies, achievements have so far been inadequate. Instead, among Japanese companies which have moved their production bases to Malaysia since the mid-1980s have made their presence strongly felt. In the second half of the 1980s, there were signs of effective linkages (networks) being rapidly formed between both companies and industries with Japanese affiliates playing the role of a hub. The main reason for this was the shift of the procurement sources of raw materials, parts and components to local suppliers because of increased procurement costs from Japan, in turn brought about by the strong yen.

A questionnaire survey conducted in March, 1990 (by the author working at the JETRO Kuala Lumpur Centre) on ninety-five Japanese affiliates in the manufacturing sector clarified changes in the production value by industry and the procurement value as shown in Table 13.11. The table clearly shows that the procurement value of Japanese affiliates increased following an increase of the production value. The local procurement ratio showed an upward trend, increasing from 19.7 percent in 1987 to 21.9 percent in 1988 and further to 23.7 percent in 1989. Local procurement particularly increased in the electrical and electronics industry, accounting for nearly 80 percent of the local procurement value. Together with the transport equipment industry, which came second, the total ratio exceeded 90 percent of the local procurement value. This simply reflects the fact that electrical and electronics companies were the mainstay of foreign affiliates. Another important phenomenon is that local procurement has also been conducted since 1989 by

Table 13.11 Local procurement and production of Japanese affiliates*

	Production						Local procurement						Ratio of local procurement in production (%)			No. of Responses
	(M$ millions)			Composition (%)			(M$ millions)			Composition (%)						
	1987	1988	1989	1987	1988	1989	1987	1988	1989	1887	1988	1989	1987	1988	1989	
Food and agricultural and marine product processing	5	158	175	0.1	2.8	2.1	0	134	156	0.0	10.8	7.8	0	84.8	89.1	3
Textiles and textile products	307	375	486	8.6	6.7	5.8	12	14	21	1.7	1.1	1.0	3.9	3.7	4.3	3
Wood, pulp, and paper	92	103	126	2.6	1.8	1.5	7	11	20	1.0	0.9	1.0	7.6	10.7	15.9	4
Chemical and pharmaceutical products	116	222	277	3.3	3.9	3.3	24	28	14	3.4	2.2	0.7	20.7	12.6	5.1	13
Petroleum products	–	–	–	–	–	–	–	0	3	–	0	0.2	–	–	0	1
Ceramics	8	11	24	0.2	0.2	0.3	0	0	0	0	0	–	0	0	0	2
Iron, steel, and non-ferrous metals	536	793	968	15.0	14.1	11.6	21	26	35	3.0	2.1	1.7	3.9	3.3	3.6	11
Metal products	40	84	113	1.1	1.5	1.4	6	7	16	0.9	0.6	0.8	15	8.3	14.2	5
General machinery	1	7	12	0.0	0.1	0.1	0	1	2	0.0	0.1	0.1	0	14.3	16.7	1
Electronics and electrical equipment	1,835	2,982	4,671	51.5	52.9	55.8	546	901	1,519	78.0	72.8	76.7	29.8	30.2	32.5	35
Transport equipment	370	621	1,129	10.4	11.0	13.5	42	64	133	6.0	5.1	6.7	11.4	10.3	11.8	4
Precision equipment	–	–	–	–	–	–	–	–	–	–	–	–	–	–	–	–
Other sectors of the manufacturing industry	254	292	384	7.1	5.2	4.6	42	50	62	6.0	4.0	3.1	16.5	17.1	16.1	13
Total	3,562	5,637	8,365	100	100	100	700	1,236	1,981	100	100	100	19.7	21.9	23.7	95

Note: Questionnaires by JETRO Kuala Lumpur Centre, March 1990

foreign affiliates engaged in the manufacture of petroleum products or general machinery.

The increase in value of the local procurement does not necessarily mean that supplies came from local companies. There were many supply sources, with local companies having the largest share (47 percent in 1987 and 49.7 percent in 1989), followed by Japanese affiliates (20.4 percent and 23.1 percent), US and European affiliates (20 percent and 19.7 percent), ASEAN affiliates (8 percent and 5.4 percent) and NIEs affiliates (3.7 percent and 2.2 percent). By industry, the electrical and electronics industry accounted for an overwhelmingly large proportion in each supply group. However, its dominance was relatively low in the case of local companies as the procurement volume from resource-based industries was rather high.

In terms of the number of supply companies, the total number of suppliers steadily increased from 1,297 in 1987 to 1,915 in 1988 and 2,688 in 1989. Since the number of manufacturing companies in Malaysia was estimated to be some 20,000, Japanese affiliates had a trading relationship with more than 13 percent of local companies in 1989. (It must be noted, however, that this figure is rather exaggerated as there was an overlapping of subcontractors for Japanese affiliates.) Out of 2,688 subcontractors in 1989, 45 percent (1,214) was occupied by the electrical and electronics industry, followed by textiles and its products (9.8 percent, 264) then iron and steel and non-ferrous products (7.1 percent, 191) and last ceramics (6.2 percent, 167). If the number of source companies is broken down into nationality, such as local, Japanese, European/US, ASEAN and NIEs, the majority is shared by local (52.7 percent, 1,416), followed by Japanese (19.3 percent, 520), European/US (4.6 percent, 123), NIEs (3.8 percent, 101) and ASEANs (3.1 percent, 82). Each source company by nationality has the biggest number in electrical and electrorics industry, followed by textiles and its products.

Locally manufactured goods are either sold domestically or exported to Japan, as well as to third countries. On average, the domestic sales ratio is some 60 percent. While transport equipment (domestic sales ratio of almost 100 percent), chemical/pharmaceutical products (78 percent) and steel/non-ferous metal products (75 percent) have an above average domestic sales ratio, fibers/textile products (47 percent) and timber/pulp/paper products (30 percent) are examples of products with a less than average domestic sales ratio. Transport equipment enjoys the largest share in the domestic sales value of 33.5 percent, followed by ceramics (28.2 percent) and electrical and electronics products (23.3 percent).

In essence, Japanese affiliates in the manufacturing sector have been creating industrial networks using the effects of Hirschman's backward and forward linkage through the local procurement and domestic sale of mainly intermediate goods. This means the formation of internal networks. Malaysia has attempted to form such networks by means of policy guidance from above through the creation of an automobile industry which is the most representative assembly industry. In reality, however, it is no exaggeration to say that Japanese affiliates have been rather spontaneously creating networks through their own local procurement and sales efforts.

External networks

Raw materials and parts, and so on, which cannot be locally procured must be imported. Similarly, manufactured products which are not sold in the domestic market must be exported. Table 13.12 shows the import and export structure of Japanese affiliates. The table illustrates the following characteristics of the manufacturing activities of Japanese affiliates. With regard to imports: (1) 70 percent of imports come from Japan; (2) some 80 percent of imports from Japan come from parent companies; (3) the second largest source of imports is Singapore – together with Japan, the combined share is as high as 85 percent; and (4) by industrial sector, the electrical and electronics industry leads imports, followed by the chemical and pharmaceutical industry and the transport industry with the total import share of these top three industries as high as 85 percent. With regard to exports: (1) the export ratio is approximately 60 percent (remaining 40 percent for domestic sales); (2) a high export ratio is recorded by the food industry, the electrical and electronics industry and the ceramics industry; (3) the largest export industry is the electrical and electronics industry with an export share of 78 percent; and (4) the largest importer is Japan which accounts for 20 percent, followed by Singapore, and the electrical and electronics industry is the largest exporter in both cases.

The following characteristics of an external network, which is formed through external trade, can be pointed out. In the case of imports, a dominant position of parent companies is typical. In the case of exports, the export ratio to related firms in Japan is rather low compared to the same ratio to third countries, particularly those in Asia. It must be noted, however, that these exports to Asia still represent intra-firm trade. In fact, the questionnaire survey referred to earlier revealed that forty-eight (fifteen manufacturing parts and

Table 13.12 Export and import of Japanese affiliates by industry

	Export						Import		
	Composition (%)			*Export ratio (%)*			*% ratio from parent company*		
	1987	*1988*	*1989*	*1987*	*1988*	*1989*	*1987*	*1988*	*1989*
Food and agricultural marine product processing	0	4.1	3.2	0	91.8	90.9	100	90	91.7
Textiles and textile products	11.3	8.3	5.1	77.9	77.6	53.3	44.2	44.1	47.2
Wood, pulp, and paper	2.9	2.0	1.8	66.3	68.0	69.8			0
Chemical and pharmaceutical products	1.7	1.3	1.2	31.0	20.7	21.7	95.1	98.1	90.9
Petroleum products	–	–	–	–	–	–			
Ceramics	0.2	0.2	0.4	62.5	63.6	79.2		100	100
Iron, steel, and non-ferrous metals	7.1	7.4	4.9	28.2	32.8	25.2	68.9	88.8	92.7
Metal products	1.2	1.9	1.6	62.5	77.4	72.6	76.9	67.9	57.1
General machinery	0	0	0	0	0	0	100	100	100
Electronics and electrical equipment	69.2	70.4	77.7	79.7	82.6	83.1	84.2	80.8	82.8
Transport equipment	0	0	0	0	0	0	36.8	34.1	31.1
Precision equipment	–	–	–	–	–	–			
Other sectors of the manufacturing industry	6.3	4.4	4	52.4	52.4	52.3	93.3	87.4	81.1
Total	100	100	100	59.3	62.1	59.7	83.3	85.6	79.8

intermediate good and thirty-three manufacturing final products) of the 139 respondents mentioned the horizontal division of labor within the same group as the main motive for direct investment. Of these forty-eight companies, twenty-six are in the machinery sector, with electrical and electronics being the main field of operation. The favourite area for this practice of a horizontal division of labor is the Asian Pacific region, with the ASEAN region given prominence. Another qustionnaire survey which was simultaneously conducted with the above-mentioned found that forty-six of the 118 respondents chose the Asian Pacific region (twenty opted for ASEAN countries and forty-six opted for other parts of the Asian Pacific region, including Japan) for their horizontal division of labor. The Asian Pacific region is, in fact, the favorite area not only for an intra-firm division of labor but also for exports. The leading area for exports of the 240 respondents is Japan (65), followed by the ASEAN region (53) and NIEs (33). Together with other export destinations in Asia, 165 companies export their goods to Asia.

Japanese affiliates which have advanced into the ASEAN region are increasing their exports to Asia, particularly Japan. Table 13.13 shows Japan's imports from overseas production bases. The most noticeable change in the table is the rapid increase of the ASEAN region's share, from 6.9 in 1987 to 16.2 in 1989. Imports from the ASEAN region by overseas production type indicate a growing share of manufactured goods from overseas production bases. In the case of the imports from the Japanese affiliates operating in host countries, the share of electrical goods sharply increased and new items suddenly appeared on the export lists of Thailand and Malaysia around 1988 (Table 13.14). These items are presumably manufactured by newly-established Japanese affiliates in these countries.

Networking patterns

In accordance with the increase of the local procurement, the average number of suppliers for a manufacturing company also increased from nineteen in 1987 to twenty-nine in 1989 while the number of local suppliers increased from twelve to fifteen. Through this process, Japanese affiliates have formed their own networks, gradually integrating local companies into it. There are three typical patterns for the establishment of a network (Figure 13.1).

Pattern 1 is the most primitive way of establishing a network. In the case of pattern 1, a production base is moved to Malaysia for the

Table 13.13 Manufacturers' imports from overseas production bases

(Unit: %)

	Fiscal year	*Total value (US$ mil)*	*Import ratio*	*By region*					*By industry*						
				US	*EC*	*NIEs*	*ASEANs*	*Others*	*Auto-mobile*	*Elec-trical*	*Elec-tronic*	*Machine*	*Metal*	*Chemical*	*Others*
Manufactured goods imports	1987	1,910.7	100	11.5	1.0	56.7	6.9	23.9	3.5	40.2	2.0	11.7	0.2	18.9	23.5
	1988	2,896.9	100	18.7	1.3	45.9	13.6	20.5	9.8	31.0	6.4	10.8	1.6	19.4	20.9
	1989	3,450.0	100	14.7	2.0	45.7	16.2	17.7	7.4	33.2	10.7	10.5	1.2	17.1	19.9
From overseas production bases	1987	1,181.3	61.8	17.5	0.7	59.9	6.7	15.2	5.4	49.8	1.7	10.9	0.1	4.1	28.0
	1988	1,691.5	58.4	25.7	1.2	46.1	15.8	11.1	15.5	40.4	5.0	11.2	0.8	4.2	22.9
	1989	2,059.2	59.7	21.8	1.9	46.6	18.5	11.3	11.1	42.4	8.0	12.0	0.8	5.0	20.7
Through commissioned OEM production	1987	387.6	20.4	2.0	1.7	90.1	0.3	0.6	0.6	45.5	4.4	22.2	0.0	13.4	13.8
	1988	611.5	21.1	8.8	2.0	82.0	2.7	4.5	1.5	34.9	16.4	15.8	0.1	18.5	12.9
	1989	810.3	23.5	16.8	3.2	68.5	5.7	5.7	1.3	33.0	25.4	10.4	0.1	19.6	10.2
From companies in which capital participation is made (except OEM)	1987	339.7	17.8	1.2	1.4	7.2	15.3	74.9	0.1	0.6	–	2.5	0.6	77.0	19.2
	1988	594.2	20.5	9.2	0.8	8.3	18.2	63.5	2.2	0.4	–	4.7	5.5	63.6	23.6
	1989	580.5	16.8	9.1	0.8	10.6	22.5	56.9	2.0	0.6	–	5.3	3.9	56.9	30.4

Source: Import Office, MITI (based on survey conducted in June, 1989)

Notes: Figures for fiscal 1989 are planned figures
No direct comparison is possible as the number of companies in each subject year differs. Figures for 1988 and 1989 relate to the same number of companies

processing and assembly of final products, all the raw materials and parts of which are imported from Japan, for export. When a factory is located in an FTZ, it has virtually no connection with the local economy and is a typical example of an "export enclave." Pattern 2 is basically the same as pattern 1 except that Japan is no longer the sole supply source and raw materials and parts can be procured from other countries where costs are lower. Pattern 3 has a pyramidal structure with the parent company using a large number of subcontractors (affiliates) in Japan and abroad, further involving local firms.

JAPAN'S ROLE AND MECHANISM OF NETWORKING IN THE ASIAN PACIFIC REGION[10]

Through direct investment from Japan, a gigantic network called a core strategic network[11] is currently being built in the Asian Pacific region involving local firms and companies in third countries as shown in the above study of Malaysia. How are the Japanese companies at home going to commit themselves in such core strategic networks as Malaysia and what is the process and mechanism of the building networks? In this section, this is analyzed in the context of the structural changes both in Japan's economy and in the Asian Pacific region.

Continuous sophistication of Japanese industries

The first oil crisis forced a fundamental transformation of the heavy and chemical industries which had provided the development basis for the Japanese economy up until the early 1970s. The new course adopted by Japan was to opt for micro-electronics (ME) to rapidly advance the mechanization of industries and to introduce high technologies.

The structural change of the manufacturing industry had two noticeable features. One was the declining production share of the basic materials industries (chemicals, ceramics, earth and stone products, primary metals and metal parts) which had formed the backbone of the previous high growth and which were replaced by processing and assembly-type industries (machine industries). The share of the former steadily declined from 33.6 percent in 1970 to 29.5 percent in 1980 and further to 26.7 percent in 1988. In contrast, the share of the latter increased from 27.9 percent in 1970 to 36.6 percent in 1988 and further to 43.5 percent in 1988. Another notice-

Table 13.14 Import trends of electrical goods from Malaysia

(Unit: million US dollars)

	Item	*1988*	*1989*	*1990*	*1991*
Malaysia	DC generators/motors				29
	Memory devices				24
	Refrigerators/freezers				17
	Color televisions			5	61
	Audio equipment			9	40
	Resistors			8	15
	computer parts		9	38	52
	Radio equipment parts		14	25	41
	AV equipment parts		3	21	36
	Silicon rectifiers		6	20	35
	Pocket calculators (without external power supply function)		5	24	34
	Diodes		5	10	15
	Air-conditioners	14	19	14	138
	Radio receivers	19	25	34	102
	Transformers (and others)	3	12	22	30
	Insulated power cable and other cable	3	8	12	21
	Relays	4	7	13	11
	Transistors	5	7	6	8
Thailand	Refrigerators (household use)				43
	Radio equipment parts				23
	Pocket calculators (without external power supply function)				22
	Condensors				16
	Air-conditioners (fully assembled)			15	43
	Refrigerators/freezers (fully assembled)			12	35
	Telephones			12	16
	Computer parts	14	36	98	149
	AV equipment parts	10	35	55	71
	Memory devices	12	46	36	43
	Insulated power cable	7	16	27	42
	DC generators/motors	14	22	24	28

Source: "Japan's Manufactured Goods Imports: 1991" (Tokyo: Japan External Trade Organization, 1991)

able feature was the decline of the input ratio of intermediate goods (the ratio of input of raw materials and others from various industrial sectors to produce a unit product) in the manufacturing

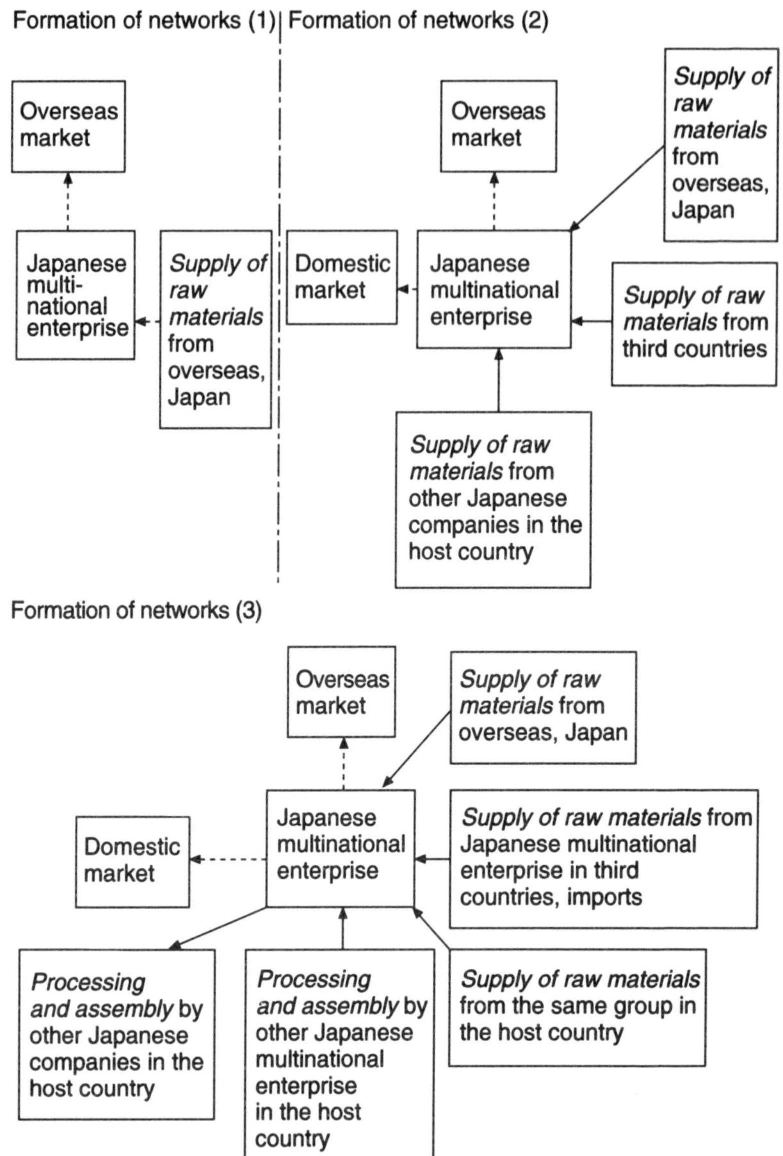

Figure 13.1 Formation of networks

industry. The ratio actually declined by 14.4 percent in the period between 1970 and 1983, having continued to decline in subsequent years.

These two changes within the manufacturing sector were not separate phenomena but were interrelated. The driving force was the electrical and electronics machine industry, producing ICs and semi-conductors which replaced steel, described as "the staple of industry," in the high growth period of the 1960s. In effect, this electrical and electronic machine industry has been playing a dual function of disintegrating the old industrial structure and integrating industries to create a new structure. In other words, two forces, i.e. disintegration and integration, are operating within the overall industrial structure, together forming a new structure.

Diversification and sophistication of import structure

The changes of the production composition within the manufacturing sector determine the input-and-output structures among industries, inevitably having a strong influence on the external trade structure. Industries which become more sophisticated, with strong competitiveness through the restructuring process, generally further increase their export volume while less comparative advantage industries either increase their imports of manufactured goods or move their production bases overseas.

One of the most conspicuous changes in Japan's exports has been the continuously increasing importance of heavy and chemical industries, particularly the machine industry. The export share of heavy and chemical industries increased from 72.4 percent in 1970 to 84.4 percent in 1980 and further to 87.5 percent in 1991. Similarly, the share of machinery in the exports of heavy and chemical industries increased from 64 percent in 1970 to 74.4 percent in 1980 and further to 86 percent in 1991. The ratio of high-tech goods in manufactured exports also increased from 29.8 percent in 1980 to 39.5 percent in 1987.

Significant changes have also taken place with regard to Japan's imports in the form of an increasing import share of manufactured goods and changing import items. The import share of manufactured goods was 30.3 percent in 1970, which declined to 20.3 percent in 1975 due to the high oil price level after the first oil crisis, but which showed an upward trend throughout the 1980s with minor fluctuations, reaching 50.8 percent in 1991, its highest level since 1960. Changes in import items were first observed with the replacement of raw materials by intermediate goods, followed by the emergence of goods manufactured abroad to replace domestically manufactured capital as well as consumer goods. Japan's increased manufactured goods imports are particularly evident vis-à–vis developing countries, particularly those in South East Asia, ie. NIEs and ASEAN countries.

Growing linkage between imports and exports

The above-described sophistication of Japan's industrial structure and exports, as well as the diversification and sophistication of imports, are not isolated movements but are closely related to each other. In the context of the present interest, the most important structural change is the growing linkage between imports and exports through intermediate sectors.

$$O = f(x) \;\ldots\ldots\; (1)$$
$$M = g(o) \;\ldots\ldots\; (2)$$
$$M = h(x) \;\ldots\ldots\; (3)$$

Equation (1) shows the impact of exports on production, while equation (2) shows the impact of production on imports. The insertion of equation (1) in equation (2) achieves equation (3), which indicates the direct and indirect impacts of exports via production on imports. The sophistication of exports (growing share of machine exports) and the diversification (growing share of manufactured goods) and sophistication (growing share of capital goods) of imports are achieved. As assumed by equation (3), the more sophisticated exports are, the more sophisticated the diversification and sophistication of imports. This process is further examined below using the input-and-output analysis method.

1 The ratio of exports in the final demand has shown a growing tendency, reaching 14.2 percent in 1987 from 8.4 percent in 1970 (Table 13.15(1)).
2 The import inducement coefficent of exports has shown the heaviest decline of all items. A similar trend is observed in the case of the import inducement although the decline for exports was not as large as that of the import inducement coefficient due to the increased export size (Table 13.15(2)).
3 Despite the changes described above, the import inducement coefficient and the import inducement dependency of exports by industry has shown a higher import inducement effect of exports by such industries as electrical machinery, transport machinery

*Table 13.15(2)*Import inducement coefficent and import inducement dependency by final demand item

Final demand item	*Import inducement coefficient*				*Import inducement dependency*			
FY	*1970*	*1975*	*1980*	*1987*	*1970*	*1975*	*1980*	*1987*
Consumption outside household expenditure	0.112	0.116	0.123	0.081	2.2	3.3	3.3	0.0
Consumption by private sector	0.134	0.134	0.136	0.138	46.6	49.4	50.7	54.3
General consumption by government	0.054	0.060	0.062	0.064	3.2	3.8	3.9	4.2
Domestic capital formation (government)	0.137	0.135	0.138	0.123	8.7	8.2	8.4	6.7
Domestic capital formation (private sector)	0.144	0.139	0.139	0.122	22.4	20.3	19.1	21.9
Net inventory increase	0.272	0.022	0.145	0.017	4.5	0.0	0.7	0.0
Exports	0.187	0.194	0.154	0.108	11.4	15.0	13.9	12.5
Final demand total	0.137	0.134	0.133	0.123	100	100	100	100

Source: See Table 13.15(1)

Note: Figures are based on 1980 prices

Table 13.15(3) Import inducement coefficient and import inducement dependency by export sector

Sector	*Import inducement coefficient*			*Import inducement dependency*		
Year	*1970*	*1980*	*1987*	*1970*	*1980*	*1987*
1 Agriculture, forestry and fisheries	0.009	0.004	0.004	0.043	0.040	0.054
2 Mining	0.118	0.082	0.032	0.148	0.173	0.147
3 Food	0.001	–	0.001	0.011	0.012	0.024
4 Textile products	0.001	0.002	0.001	0.105	0.120	0.098
5 Pulp, paper and timber	0.002	0.002	0.001	0.071	0.090	0.134
6 Chemical products	0.006	0.006	0.006	0.148	0.149	0.144
7 Petroleum and coal products	0.014	0.009	0.006	0.131	0.151	0.109
8 Ceramics, earth and stone products	–	–	–	0.044	0.069	0.071
9 Primary metal products	0.014	0.017	0.022	0.215	0.329	0.309
10 Metal products	–	–	–	0.042	0.073	0.084
11 General machinery	0.002	0.002	0.002	0.068	0.161	0.182
12 Electrical machinery	0.001	0.003	0.004	0.071	0.146	0.169
13 Transport machinery	0.001	0.003	0.003	0.077	0.172	0.180
14 Precision machinery	0.001	0.001	0.001	0.102	0.128	0.124
15 Other manufactuing goods	0.001	0.003	0.006	0.074	0.110	0.115
16 Construction	–	–	–	–	–	–
17 Electricity, gas and water	–	–	–	0.101	0.135	0.111
18 Commerce	–	0.001	0.001	0.044	0.062	0.073
19 Finance and insurance	0.001	0.001	0.001	0.088	0.117	0.124
20 Real estate	–	–	–	0.020	0.026	–
21 Transport and telecommunications	0.003	0.004	0.002	0.063	0.092	0.094
22 Services	–	–	0.005	0.023	0.040	0.077
23 Waste disposal and sewerage	–	–	–	–	–	–
24 Education, research, medical and health care	–	–	–	–	0.115	–
25 Public administration	–	–	–	–	–	–
26 Office supplies	–	–	–	–	–	–
27 Packaging	–	–	–	–	–	–
28 Others	0.004	0.005	–	0.099	0.175	–
Total	0.187	0.154	0.108	0.114	0.139	0.125

Notes: Based on 1980 price
Blank means either no trade or negligible

Table 13.15(1) Composition of final demand

(Unit %)

Final demand item FY	*1970*	*1975*	*1980*	*1987*
Consumption outside household expenditure	3.9	3.9	3.5	0.6
Consumption by private sector	47.5	49.3	49.3	48.1
General consumption by government	8.0	8.4	8.3	8.0
Domestic capital formation (government)	8.8	8.1	8.1	6.7
Domestic capital formation (private sector)	21.2	19.6	18.3	22.1
Net inventory increase	2.3	0.3	0.7	0.3
Exports	8.4	10.4	12.0	14.2
Final demand total	100	100	100	100

Source: Administrative Management Agency, *Tables of Industrial Linkage*, Annual Editions

Note: Figures are based on 1980 price

and those belonging to the so-called metal bloc. Both the import inducement cofficient and import inducement dependency have shown steep increases for industries in the metal bloc. The import inducement dependency for the electrical machinery industry increased from 0.071 in the 1970s to 0.169 in the 1980s, while the figure for the general machinery industry also increased from 0.068 to 0.182. The main reason for these increases was the structural changes in the machine industries where changes in the input of intermediate goods included imports from a wide range of other industries (Table 13.15(3)).

Formation of loop consisting of imports, exports and foreign direct investment

The internal structure of Japan's manufacturing industry, particularly machine industries, has been changing to stimulate imports as witnessed by the rapid growth of manufactured goods imports. Nevertheless, the import inducement effect of Japan's industrial activities, particularly exports, has generally declined due to the lowering of the raw material input ratio. Such a decline of the import inducement effect of exports indicates one mechanism generating Japan's trade surplus.

The surplus in the current balance inevitably flows out externally, taking the form of a deficit in the capital account balance. This notion is upheld within the framework of an open macroeconomy and is always true regardless of economic size or the stage of economic development. Japan's trade balance went into the black in the mid-1960s and has continuously been in the black since then, despite set-backs immediately after the two oil crises in the 1970s. In 1991, the surplus was as large as US$103.3 billion, the largest surplus ever recorded in the history of world trade. A surplus has also been recorded in the current balance, except for short periods (2–3 years) after the two oil crises, with the largest surplus of US$87 billion recorded in 1987.

This huge trade or current balance surplus necessitated an outflow of capital, mainly in the form of direct investment, as shown in Table 13.1. The importance of Japanese foreign direct investment lies not ony with its size, but also with its impact on the formation of internal networks through stimulated local production and also external networks through trade, particularly machine trade within the same groups of companies, reinforcing the relationship between Japan and the recipients of Japanese direct investment.

A gigantic network called a core strategic network is currently in the process of formation in the Asian Pacific region through direct investment, involving Japanese companies, their affiliates and local companies. The equation, i.e. current balance (*X-m*) + capital balance (*DFI*) = 0 (*X* and *M* stand for exports and imports respectively in the current balance, and further DFI is foreign direct investment in the capital balance because outflow of capital is much more than inflow in case of Japanese economy), is not a simple expression of an international balance of payment. Exports, imports and direct foreign investment form a kind of trinity, creating a single loop through their ever increasing mutual influence. The Japanese economy exports its dynamism in this manner and forms solid networks covering home and abroad, particularly in the Asian Pacific region.

IMPLICATIONS OF THE ECONOMIC LOOP

As to the domestic and international networks constructed by Japanese affiliates, especially in the three main regions of North America, Asia and Europe, the following implications are extracted. First, the pipeline taking economic dynamism from Japan abroad is contributing to the revitalization of the economies of the countries enforcing the inflow of Japanese capital. In short, at present Japan, as a super economic giant, is transmitting its economic dynamism abroad through such channels as DFI, export, import, technology, finance, assistance and the international movement of people, of which DFI is playing the most important role. To promote further transmission of economic dynamism, Japanese affiliates must procure more materials from local firms and build networks together with expanding local sales, intensifying economic linkages between industries. Furthermore, in its attempt to build networks, the Japanese affiliate must transfer the so-called "managerial resources" as much as possible to upgrade the technological levels of the local firms.

Second, regarding the above three regions, Japanese affiliates are playing a more important role in Asia than in the other two regions of North America and Europe, especially in terms of transferring "managerial resources."

Third, relating to the above items, in the development of the international division of labor in the Asian Pacific region, together with the industrialization, Japanese affiliates are playing the central role of promoting intra-firm trade. Through these develpments, for the first time in this area the principle of comparative advantage is functioning much more. And, furthermore, based on the technology, this principle intensifies the interlinkages between economies and promotes international production networks.

Fourth, mutual interdependences all over the world are intensifying, in constructing inward and outward networks with Japanese affiliates as their hub and involving local and third countries firms. This enables Japanese affiliates to play a very important role in checking the increasing trend of regionalism. That is to say, the international production networks built by Japanese companies and their affiliates are functioning as the infrastructure needed to deepen the interdependence of the world economy.[12]

Regionalism is defined as a group of specific countries in a certain region trying to make each other interdependent by forming a special framework. On the other hand, in contrast to regionalism, regionalization is defined, in the author's sense, as a group of countries in a certain region integrating each other by market forces and not through any form of institution and/or intentional framework such as NAFTA or the EC. In this context, the present situation in Asia can be classed as regionalization.

Economic integration is being developed in the Asian Pacific region in the most intensive form through international (or regional) production networks built by both Japanese companies and their affiliates.

The establishment of internal and external networks has caused continual changes in the economic structure throughout the Asian

Pacific region. All these changes point to the integration of regional markets, i.e. the formation of an "Asian economic zone." The movement to establish networks involving all countries in the Asian Pacific region, with changes in the Japanese economic structure and overseas investment by Japanese companies as turning points, has strengthened the linkages and simultaneously caused structural changes across the region, and has unified the results of these changes. The dynamism of the Japanese economy has most vividly manifested itself in the region in the formation of Asian Pacific networks and in the emergence of movements for structural changes and market integration, both being stimulated by the very process of networking.

As is clear from the above analysis, the Asian Pacific region is, de facto, integrated or unified by the formation of networks, particularly by Japanese direct foreign investment as the driving force to integrate with the trade channels of exports and imports. We can say that through the international production networks as analyzed in the above sections, Japanese companies and their foreign affiliates are now building region-wide infrastructures in the Asian Pacific region to promote intra-regional trade, the horizontal international division of labor and integration in the Asian Pacific region. Networks are also said to be just the mechanism to connect DFI with exports and the interlinkages of the economies in the Asia Pacific region which expand the potential economic frontier through the horizontal international division of labor. The intensity of the market integration is symbolized by the increasing share of the intra-regional trade both in terms of export and import in spite of the lower shares compared to those of the EU, which is the most integrated market in the world. The intra-regional share of the Asian Pacific region increased from 34.8 percent in 1980 to 38.1 percent in 1989 for exports, while imports increased from 32.9 percent to 42.6 percent in the same period. Also, in the trade of industrial goods, the intra-regional shares have increased both in total exports and in total imports. In the former, the intra-regional share increased to 29.1 percent in 1987 from 26.6 percent in 1980, while the latter increased from 52.5 percent to 56.1 percent in the same period (Table 13.16).

In observing the increasing share of the intra-regional trade in the Asian Pacific, it should be noted that this move is not made institutionally but by market forces. This region was once considered to be the furthest from the market mechanism, the so-called Asian stagnant way of production. Nowadays, however, it is no exagger-

Table 13.16 Intra-regional trade shares by goods and by country (percent)

Good	Year	*Export*						*Import*					
		Asia Pacific	*Japan*	*NIEs*	*ASEANs*	*China*	*EC*	*Asia Pacific*	*Japan*	*NIEs*	*ASEANs*	*China*	*EC*
Non-durable consumers	1980	16.0	22.3	10.3	14.8	43.9	61.8	75.1	74.9	75.7	71.5	80.3	65.2
	1987	22.0	34.4	15.3	11.6	47.8	61.1	85.0	88.7	81.3	77.4	91.9	67.1
Durable consumers	1980	14.7	12.7	18.1	34.6	48.6	56.2	64.3	32.8	67.4	73.5	78.3	71.2
	1987	14.8	11.0	17.6	30.9	53.7	59.7	65.8	36.8	73.9	74.4	84.3	71.7
Intermediates, labor-	1980	40.4	37.3	42.1	39.0	48.3	53.8	64.9	35.1	73.8	79.6	72.0	72.8
intensive	1987	51.2	45.3	49.1	38.1	76.8	58.6	72.4	42.9	76.2	81.1	89.5	74.9
Intermediate, capital-	1980	40.2	37.7	48.7	36.0	51.5	56.8	47.1	22.5	60.3	56.2	49.2	69.7
intensive	1987	49.8	45.5	57.0	54.2	60.7	59.9	43.0	22.4	58.0	58.1	58.6	73.0
Capital	1980	30.5	29.1	32.2	42.1	54.9	44.9	44.8	12.4	51.9	51.0	56.5	64.0
	1987	30.4	28.8	31.3	42.6	59.0	50.8	52.2	21.1	61.4	54.7	53.1	62.5
Hi-tech	1980	28.7	26.1	31.0	43.2	52.0	53.3	46.0	18.2	56.6	53.3	48.8	64.5
	1987	29.0	25.7	30.8	33.1	65.1	57.3	54.3	22.6	65.4	58.6	63.4	62.5
Industrial	1980	26.6	25.3	25.8	34.7	47.6	49.2	52.5	27.2	61.2	59.6	57.3	61.9
	1987	29.1	24.4	29.5	40.7	56.7	56.6	56.1	33.5	66.0	60.8	58.6	66.0
All commodities	1980	34.8	25.7	32.6	56.0	52.9	55.8	32.9	20.0	65.1	50.1	36.0	70.9
	1989	38.1	28.2	39.7	50.8	64.1	59.7	42.6	27.3	50.7	52.7	39.9	71.9

Source: AIDXT of Institute of Developing Economies, Tokyo, 1990

ation to say that this region is the most effective in terms of the operation of the market.

Furthermore, the Asia Pacific region now has two functions. First, it has a spillover effect of economic dynamism to the world. Second, it has magnetic effects. The US is increasing shares within the Asia Pacific region in terms of both export and import, strengthening itself as a Pacific country. Its export share was as high as 26.8 percent in 1989, having increased from 16.2 percent in 1970, while its import share increased from 24.9 percent to 37.9 percent in the same period. The EU has also increased its trade shares with the Asia Pacific region, in spite of the lower shares compared to those of the US. At the present stage, the Asia Pacific region is the only area to have two such functions. The Asia Pacific region has been strengthening the integration of the Asian Pacific area and also leveling up the interdependence with the rest of the world. Considering the present trend of the world economy toward regionalism in the midst of globalization, the dynamism of the Asian Pacific region should not be used to form any kinds of blocs. On the contrary, the economic dynamism of the Asia Pacific region should be used to restore and revitalize free trade and the world economy using the two functions mentioned above. This is the historic role of the Asia Pacific region, and in particular of Japan.

NOTES

1 As for the other reasons why Japan's machinery-related industries have shifted their production bases abroad so rapidly, especially in the second half of the 1980s, they are as follows: (1) There are so many trade frictions in the above industries. The expansion of local production and the maintenance of local markets are considered one of the few ways of mitigating these trade frictions through the direct foreign investments. (2) As the electrical and electronics industry has various kinds of product, for this industry it is comparatively easy not only to differentiate the product but also develop the international division of labor to produce different products in different countries.

2 Please see also the author's paper "Japanese DFI and forming networks in the Asia-Pacific Region: experience in Malaysia and its implications" in S. Tokunaga (ed.) *Japan's Foreign Investment and Asian Economic Interdependence* (Tokyo: University of Tokyo Press, 1991).

3 *Chusho Kigyo Hakusho* ("White Paper on Small & Medium Sized Firms"), MITI, Tokyo, 1989, pp. 46–9.

4 Regarding the motives behind DFI of firms who go abroad, half of the respondents cited the expectation of the growing markets for the developed countries; while for the NIEs, which are the prime recipients of DFI from the developing countries, the respondents cited as motives

the growing and rich market as the first and abundant and low cost labor as the second, the ratio being each one-third respectively. For ASEANs the prime motive is looking for cheap labor; about 60 percent of the respondents cited this.

5 The ratio of overseas production compared to those of American and European countries is relatively low. For example, the ratio of American firms was 24.9 percent in 1989 and the German ratio was 17.3 percent in 1986 (excluding intra-EC, this is lowered to 10.3 percent).

6 One of the problems which Japanese affiliates in North America face is the necessity to increase the local contents of the materials and components. This is a problem not only in North America, but also in other regions where it is requested by local governments.

According to the survey done by JETRO in 1989, the situation regarding the local content for Japanese affiliates in the US is as follows: (1) Japanese affiliates in the US answer that local procurement is the most important problem for 11.9 percent out of 670 respondents. By industry those which have a relatively higher share of the local content are textile products, furniture and wooden products, followed by machinery-related industries; (2) looking at the local content by industry, local contents are 100 percent in those industries such as furniture and wooden products and the pulp, paper, printing and publishing industries; those of foods and tobacco and chemical industries are 93.8 percent and 91.0 percent respectively. Those five industries with high local content ratio are all material-processed. Compared to the previous survey, made in 1987, one-third of the respondents have increased local content ratios. Those industries which have significantly raised the ratios of local contents include rubber products, metal industries and machinery-related industries centering in transportation equipment. This means that Japanese affiliates in America do not undertake the types of procurements of materials and components undertaken by their counterparts operating in the developing countries; (3) as to the numbers of subcontractors from which materials are supplied, 70 percent of the respondents answered that American subcontractors number over ten and 60 percent of the respondents answered that the number of Japanese subcontractors in the US is under two; (4) as an export destination, Japan is not of much interest to the respondents. The respondents interested in exporting to Japan and other countries is only 22.4 percent (those interested in exporting only to Japan being 6.7 percent); 24.6 percent of the respondents are interested in exporting except to Japan and 23 percent of the respondents answered that they are considering export in the future (JETRO, "Zaibei Nikkei Kigyo no Keiei Jittai" ("The current situation of Japanese affiliates in America) (March, 1990), pp. 43–7).

The gross product of foreign affiliates in the US increased from US$35.2 billion to US$151.9 billion in the period 1977 to 1987. The share of the total US GPD increased to 3.1 percent from 1.8 percent in the same period. The largest producer among foreign affiliates in the US is manufacturing, whose share increased from 47 percent in 1977 to 49 percent in 1987. In terms of regional composition, Europe, although its share decreased from 69 percent to 60 percent, is the largest producer, while the joint share of Asia, Africa and the Pacific countries increased from 9 percent to 16 percent, of which Japan's share increased from 7 percent to 11 percent. The average local content ratio of foreign affiliates in the US is very high. The ratio as the whole increased from 79 percent in 1977 to 81 percent in 1987 and in the manufacturing sector it also slightly increased from 90 percent to 91 percent (S. Bezirganian, "US affiliates of foreign companies," *Survey of Current Business*, p. 89).

7 JETRO, "Zaiou Nikkei Kigyo no Keiei Jittal" ("Current situation of Japanese affiliates in Europe") (March, 1990), pp. 38–46. The ratios of local contents, particularly of transportation equipment and general machineries, are very high (60.4 percent and 59.2 percent respectively) at the starting point of the operation and increased to 64.1 percent and 67.2 percent respectively. Within the category of general machinery, the number of the parts and components of the construction machinery is becoming lower. Accordingly, it is estimated that construction machinery is exported at lower cost.

8 Regarding procurement and sales of Japanese affiliates in Asia, the concentration on the electrical and electronics sector is due to so many firms having shifted their production bases. In terms of number of products, of the total number of 770 produced worldwide by Japanese affiliates, the Asian share is 53 percent (408). Of durable consumer goods (for example, TVs, VCRs, taperecorders, stereos) 99 out of 224 items worldwide are produced in Asia (Nihon Denshi Kogyokai, *Kaigai Seisan Hojin List* (List of the Japanese Affiliates) Oct. (Tokyo, 1990).

9 This section is summary of the author's book of *Malaysia Keizai Nyumon* (*Economic Development is Malaysia*) Tokyo: Hihon Hyoronsha (1990).

10 This is also summary of the author's book *Asia Keizai no Seijuku* (*Maturing of the Asian economies*) Tokyo: Keiso Shobou (1991). In this book, details are analyzed with relation to the mechanism mentioned in this section. That is to say, the three factors of exports, imports and direct foreign investment, which form a kind of trinity, create a single loop and grow linkages with each other.

11 UN, *World Investment Report 1991* (July 19, 1991), p. 45, p. 428. As to the networks built by the American MNCs, the author has already analyzed in another paper.

12 OECD, *Recent Developments in Regional Trading Arrangements among OECD Countries* (TD/TC/WP(90)81) (Paris: OECD, 1990), p. 3.

14 Economic integration in the Pacific Rim

Implications for the global business environment

Richard Drobnick

INTRODUCTION

This chapter attempts to provide perspective on the ongoing economic integration in the Pacific Rim, with the goal of trying to better understand how this process might affect the global business environment in the future. It discusses the Pacific Rim in the context of the changing world economy because its economy will be influenced by changing global trends and, in turn, Pacific Rim trends will influence the way the world economy evolves. And, of course, corporate intentions and capabilities to create cross-national strategic alliances are affected by the ongoing structural changes of the global and regional economy.

The economic integration of the Pacific region – which includes the United States, Canada and Mexico – is occurring rapidly, primarily as a result of intra-regional capital flows, increased trade liberalization, and privatization trends. Private-sector business opportunities between the west and east coasts and the northern and southern rims of the Pacific region are stimulating ever-larger flows of goods, services, capital, technology, and people among these economies.

To enhance this process, Pacific Rim leaders met in San Francisco in September, 1992 for the ninth general meeting of the Pacific Economic Cooperation Council (PECC) to promote their concept of "Open Regionalism: A Pacific Model for Global Economic Cooperation".[1] This open regionalism model imposes the following requirements on PECC members: (1) to become increasingly open to goods, services, and investment flows; (2) to comply with GATT disciplines, principles, and practices; (3) to accommodate subregional trade agreements that are in compliance with GATT principles; (4) to engage in commerce with non-PECC members that are committed to outward-oriented policies; and (5) to promote the further strengthening of "openness" in the Pacific Rim and in the rest of the world.

This chapter is organized as follows: the second section describes seven ongoing changes in the world economy which will influence the viability of the PECC's open regionalism model and affect the shape and structure of economic integration in the Pacific Rim. In the third section, the current patterns of Pacific Rim regionalization are described in terms of economic trends, policies, and institutions that have stimulated this process. Three possible scenarios of Pacific Rim regionalization are sketched in the fourth section: (1) Policy Paralysis: Business as Usual; (2) Policy Coordination: The US and Japan as Co-Conductors of a Pacific Rim Orchestra; and (3) Policy Conflict: The US and Japan Conduct Separate Orchestras. The fifth section provides policy recommendations for American and Asian leaders on how to increase the probability of the occurrence of the Policy Coordination Scenario, which reflects many of the goals of the PECC's open regionalism model.

THE CHANGING GLOBAL ECONOMY

A number of trends that gathered strength in the late 1980s will shape the international economic environment of the 1990s. Seven of these, which will shape the context for Pacific Rim integration, are described below: (1) the evolution of US–Russian relations from conflict to cooperation; (2) the collapse of communism in the Soviet Union and Eastern Europe; (3) the reversal of America's "locomotive" role; (4) the ascendancy of Japan as the world's banker; (5) the economic integration of Europe; (6) the economic integration of North America; and (7) the declining relevance of the GATT. All of these changes are likely to combine to strengthen economic integration in the Pacific Rim.

Evolution of US–Russian relations from conflict to cooperation

This trend will lead to increased competitiveness of America's manufacturing sector as defense cutbacks shift hundreds of thousands of talented people from the defense labor force to the civilian labor force. The Department of Defense (DoD) is scrapping almost all weapons procurement plans and substantially reducing the size of the armed forces. As a result, the American economy will become much less militarized.

Some of the "peace dividend" will be used for public investments, some for the reduction of taxes and government debt, and some for the reduction of government spending. On balance, the peace dividend will put downward pressure on the cost of capital and increase the skills and technology base of the commercial sector of the US economy. In turn, each of these factors will accelerate the ongoing trend of the reversal of the US trade deficit.

In addition to these economic impacts, the change in US–Russian relations reduces the primacy of military–security issues in the management of US foreign policy. As a result, the relative importance of US commercial interests and trade policy are increasing, as economic rivalry between the US, Japan, and the European Union (EU) becomes less constrained by the mutual security glue that has bound them together for the past forty years.

In the 1990s, the United States will also reduce its troop deployments in Asia, as well as in Europe. This process of disengagement will enhance the security presence of Japan in the Western Pacific and of Germany in central Europe at the same time as Japan's and Germany's economic and financial influence are substantially expanding.

Collapse of communism in Eastern Europe and the former Soviet Union

The collapse of communism and the rise of reform-minded movements throughout Eastern Europe and the former Soviet Union has gradually led to the integration of these nations into the world trading system. These nations are already attracting public and private sector capital that will be used to "connect" their inexpensive labor forces with the world market. They will become a new source of demand for consumer and capital goods and are likely, in the medium-term, to become a competitive source of supply of many labor-intensive manufactured goods which are presently supplied by Pacific Rim nations. It is almost certain that these goods will receive "infant industry" protection from a politically-responsive European Union.

As a result of the collapse of communist regimes and EU integration, the attention of European business and government leaders – as well as American and Asian leaders – has become more Europe-focussed. An increasingly Eurocentric attitude in politics and business will keep European academicians, businessmen, and government policy makers closer to home in the future. Consequently, Japan's regional influence in Asia is likely to increase (as is America's regional influence in Latin America). In a futile attempt to counter this trend, in February, 1990, Prime Minister Lee Kwan Yew of Singapore made a request to 1,000 business leaders attending the World Economic Forum in Davos, Switzerland.

> Western Europe should not concentrate on Eastern Europe to the exclusion of Asia. . . . Europe can find good partners amongst the NIEs and ASEAN in the unavoidable global competition with Japan, because they [NIEs and ASEAN] are keen on an economic order which is not dominated by Japan.[2]

An important strategic issue in terms of how open the new European economic space will be is whether or not a Russo–German economic cooperation pact can be designed that will intertwine Russian and German economic and security interests in a way that will promote peace and stability in the former Soviet Union and Eastern Europe. In other words, can the Franco–German rapprochement that created the EU be repeated and thus result in a reuinified Germany that is committed to economic development at both ends of Europe and a Russia that becomes economically integrated into the European community? If so, then the EU is likely to develop a long-term preferential trade and industrial strategy to promote development in the nations of Eastern Europe and the former Soviet Union. And the Pacific Rim region will have to become more cohesive in order to develop countervailing bargaining power on international economic issues against this expanded EU.

The reversal of America's "locomotive" role

US demand for imports and the stagnation of American exports between 1981 and 1985 created huge trade deficits and a strong stimulus to the world's export-oriented economies. As Americans increased personal consumption and reduced personal savings (without any substantial change in business savings and investment rates), the financing needs of a deficit-ridden American government had to be met by foreign creditors.[3] The US substantially changed the nature of its economic relations with the world. It joined the world's capital importing countries, running current account deficits from 1982 to 1992 of US$11 billion, US$44 billion, US$99 billion, US$122 billion, US$148 billion, US$164 billion, US$127 billion, US$101 billion, US$90 billion, US$4 billion (due to Gulf War receipts), and about US$35 billion. This produced the anomalous situation of the world's richest nation borrowing and attracting investment capital from poorer nations to such an extent that in ten years the US transformed itself from a net US$141 billion capital export position to a net US$533 billion capital import position. Unfortunately, this inflow of foreign capital did not increase America's investment rate as a share of GNP.

By 1986, the competitive effects of the dollar depreciation had started to work and merchandise exports from the US began a phenomenal expansion from US$227 billion to US$413 billion in 1991. The merchandise trade deficit declined from US$170 billion in 1987 to US$87 billion in 1991, and turned back up to about US$100 billion in 1992. In volume terms, between 1987 and 1992, exports of US goods and services grew at an annual average rate of about 10 percent while imports only rose one-quarter as fast.

In part this improvement in the trade balance was due to the steadily improving competitiveness of the US manufacturing sector, where unit labor costs declined from 1982 to 1990 by 3.5 percent, as compared to a 2.5 percent decline for Japan, a 17 percent increase for Germany, and a 22 percent increase for France. In terms of US dollars, unit labor costs in Japan increased by 67 percent, in Germany by 76 percent, and in France by 48 percent. For Taiwan, and Korea – between 1986 and 1990 – these costs rose by about 60 and 100 percent respectively (Table 14.1).[4]

If this change of America's trade pattern continues, then the Pacific Rim economies will need to find new export markets, as well as increase the role for domestic demand in their economic growth patterns. Given the likelihood of an increasingly inward-oriented European Union – in order to support reforms in Eastern Europe

Table 14.1 Manufacturing unit labor costs in US dollars

Year	*US*	*Japan*	*Korea*	*Taiwan*	*Germany*	*UK*	*France*	*Canada*	*Sweden*	*Italy*
1980	87	107	104	87	124	118	125	83	130	117
1981	94	114	100	97	104	112	109	89	120	103
1982	100	100	100	100	100	100	100	100	100	100
1983	98	103	94	97	95	86	93	99	84	99
1984	96	99	90	108	86	77	87	91	81	89
1985	97	97	88	112	85	77	88	88	85	88
1986	97	142	83	127	120	91	117	91	109	116
1987	94	157	91	160	156	103	138	99	130	138
1988	92	173	112	170	160	112	138	111	141	140
1989	93	161	153	192	150	106	128	123	146	143

Source: Monthly Labor Review, US Department of Labor and *Domestic and Foreign Express Report of Economic Statistics Indicators*, Ministry of Economic Affairs, Taiwan (various issues)

and the Soviet Union – the amount and shares of intra-Asian trade will have to increase. As part of this process, Japan will have to play a more substantial role as an "absorber" of Asian manufactured products.

Ascendancy of Japan as the world's banker

International financial power has shifted from the US to Japan (and to a lesser extent to Germany). The new reality is that Japan has replaced the US as the world's preeminent creditor nation, while at the same time the US has become the world's most heavily indebted nation. The rapidity and expected longevity of this epochal change of affairs can be seen by comparing the trends of the net external asset positions of the US and Japan, as well as of Germany. The US position has been steadily deteriorating since the mid-1980s, while the position of Japan has strengthened – even with the bursting of the Japanese economic bubble.

As a result of the continued growth of Japan's trade surpluses, its current account surplus reached US$131.45 billion in 1993 and approximately US$129.7 billion in 1994. Japan's cumulative current account surplus was about US$550 billion by the end of 1991 (more than three times as large as America's peak international creditor position of US$164 billion in 1984) and approached US$800 billion by the end of 1994.

The issue of recycling Japan's "export dollars" will continue to dominate tomorrow's financial and political headlines, much as the recycling of "petro-dollars" did in the 1970s. Clearly, Japanese capital will dominate Pacific Rim and worldwide flows of foreign direct investment, loans, and official development assistance for years to come. Along with this financial dominance, the business and political clout of Japan will increase substantially. German capital will remain closer to home. Because of Germany's political commitment to quickly rebuild Eastern Germany, strongly support reforms in Eastern Europe and the former Soviet Union, and play a leading role in EU integration, German capital will be fully utilized within Europe in the 1990s. In fact, Germany's current account balance had shifted from a US$60 billion surplus in 1989 to a US$20 billion deficit in 1992 and a US$25 billion deficit in 1994.

Economic integration of Europe with Germany as the conductor

The implementation of the Single European Act has caused the European Union to become a much more integrated economic and financial market. The most obvious consequences of reducing Europe's internal barriers to the flow of goods, labor, and capital are: (1) Europe will have more bargaining power; (2) Europe will become more efficient; and (3) income growth in Europe will accelerate. Also, huge internal aid and investment programs will push mountains of capital from the rich north to the poor south of the EU, as well as to Eastern Germany, Eastern Europe and the former Soviet Union. European industries are likely to concentrate more on their new pan-European "domestic" market than on overseas markets and the growth of European exports outside of Europe will slow, if not decline.

In effect, the Bundesbank sets monetary policy for the European Union, and increasingly it will do so for the nations of Eastern Europe as well. A reunified Germany will be the driving force of a new European Economic Space with a population of over 500 million. According to Helmut Haussmann, a former Economics Minister of Germany, it will be German capital, German technology, and German institutions that will invigorate Europe so that it can compete for world leadership against Japan and its Asian partners.[5]

Economic integration of North America with the US as a conductor

In 1990, the political momentum for creating a free trade zone throughout North America sharply accelerated. A contributing factor was that Mexico's President Salinas was unable to convince European industrialists to invest in the rapidly reforming economy of Mexico. In February, 1990, he had led a high level team of Mexican industrialists and cabinet secretaries to the World Economic Forum in Switzerland and went home convinced that European business leaders were so preoccupied with intra-European affairs that they had no time to pay attention to new opportunities in Mexico.[6] Going against Mexico's traditional fears of being dominated by the US, the Salinas team actively pursued the Bush Administration to quickly begin negotiations for a US–Mexico Free Trade Agreement.

As it evolves, the North American Free Trade Agreement (NAFTA) will lead to the creation of a large preferential trading bloc that could divert trade and manufacturing investment to

Mexico. Many US-based firms have already begun to locate some production facilities in Mexico in order to supply the North American market less expensively. Eventually, they might even relocate some of their Asian facilities that serve as low-cost "export platforms" to the US. In any case, they are unlikely to invest as much in new export platforms in Asia. Asian firms can also be expected to invest in manufacturing facilities in Mexico to service the US market from a "preferred" location. Also, Mexican investors will return flight capital to Mexico to take advantage of the guaranteed access to the US and Canadian markets, as well as to provide goods and services to what will become a rapidly growing domestic market in Mexico.

Preliminary macroeconomic evidence of such investment flows to Mexico is provided by a Ministry of Finance report which estimates foreign investment inflows rising to US$4.6 billion in 1990 and US$14.5 billion in 1991, compared to an average of US$3 billion in each of the prior two years. The formal establishment of NAFTA in late 1992 has now paved the way for an even steeper increase.[7]

The declining relevance of the GATT

Another important global trend which has affected the Asia–Pacific regionalization process is the outcome of the most recent multilateral GATT negotiations, including the formation of the World Trade Organization (WTO). The GATT negotiators were unable to achieve all the "ambitious" results hoped for in the Uruguay Round. This was partly due to the complexity and scale of the negotiations, partly due to the intractability of the agricultural subsidies issues, and partly due to the fact that the world's political leaders had more pressing issues to focus on during the critical 1990–3 closing phases of the GATT negotiations, i.e. the Gulf War, the dissolution of the Soviet Union, the Bosnia conflict, the Italian and Japanese corruption scandals, the loss at the polls by the French Socialists, etc. Nevertheless, some sort of compromise "victory" was achieved by the end of the Uruguay Round.

However, the relevance of the GATT (soon to be the World Trade Organization) is likely to decline as regional integration proceeds, as intra-firm trade continues to grow, and as trade among cross-national corporate alliance partners increases. This decline in the WTO will stimulate the codification and strengthening of regional rules for trade and investment. As this occurs, it will become even more important for Pacific Rim trading nations to organize themselves along the lines of an open regional trading system. A key requirement will be to develop new, non-WTO dispute settlement mechanisms that are perceived to be fair, effective and timely. The rapidly expanding Asia Pacific Economic Cooperation (APEC) process is likely to create mechanisms to implement such Pacific Rim settlement mechanisms.

PACIFIC RIM ECONOMIC INTEGRATION

Economic integration

The evolving Pacific Rim region is one in which economic and social relations among its members are rapidly intensifying. Between 1970 and 1990, intra-regional exports as a share of total regional exports increased from 56 to 68 percent among the seventeen member countries of the Pacific Economic Cooperation Council (PECC) – comprising the ASEAN countries, Asian's newly industrializing economies (NIEs), Australia, Canada, Chile, China, Japan, Mexico, New Zealand, Peru, and the US (Russian data not included).[8]

This intensification of trade relations is occurring as a result of greater flows of capital, technology, services, and people throughout the Pacific Rim. The capital movements include loans and aid, as well as portfolio and direct investments. The people movements include salesmen, workers, tourists, managers, students, and immigrants. All of these trends increase the interpersonal contact between the Pacific Rim nations in a variety of overlapping roles as competitors, customers, suppliers, partners, classmates, and neighbors.

Growth patterns

Economic growth in the Asia–Pacific region has been outstanding for the past twenty years and is expected to continue to be so during the next decade. A 1990 Rand Corporation study projected Japan's growth rate for the 1990s to be 50 percent faster than the rates projected for the leading European economies. Even taking into account the slowdown in the Japanese economy in the early 1990s, the overall trend still remains positive. During the 1990s, the growth rates of the other Asian economies are projected to continue to be twice as fast as European growth rates (Table 14.2).[9] In 1993 and 1994 growth rates of the Asian NIEs and ASEAN-4 were three to four times faster than that of OECD Europe. China's rapidly grow-

Table 14.2 GNP growth rates 1970–2000 (percent/year)

Area	*1970–80*	*1980–90**	*1990–2000*
US	2.8	2.8	2.6
Japan	4.7	3.9	3.0
Asian NIEs and ASEAN-4	7.9	6.2	5.3
China	5.5	9.1	4.6
West Germany	2.7	1.8	2.1
France	3.6	1.7	2.8

Source: Adapted from Yeh, Sze, and Levin, *The Changing Asian Economic Environment and US–Japan Trade Relations* (Santa Monica: Rand Corporation, R-3986–CUSCJR, September, 1990), p. 7

ing economy will further add dynamism to the Pacific Rim's economic trajectory.

Along with this rapid economic growth, integration of the Pacific Rim economy (as defined by the PECC) is substantially increasing. Three of the principal causes (as well as indicators) of this integration are intra-regional trade, intra-regional direct investment flows, and intra-regional tourist movements. By 1990, 68 percent of PECC exports went to PECC customers. Furthermore, the majority of foreign direct investments being made in PECC countries came from PECC investors and the majority of the tourists going to PECC destinations came from PECC countries.[10]

Export patterns

The Pacific Rim export relationships between North America (the US and Canada) and "Pacific Asia" (Japan, Australia/New Zealand, the Asian NIEs, the ASEAN-4, and China) have been changing significantly since the currency realignments of 1985–7. Intra-Pacific Asia trade has rapidly increased in importance and the North American market has become somewhat less important for Pacific Asia exporters.[11] Between 1986 and 1989, the share of intra-regional exports of Pacific Asia increased from 34 to 42 percent, while the share of Pacific Asia's exports to North America dropped from 35 to 30 percent.

As a result of the factors contributing to America's export expansion and import slowdown, it is likely that: (1) a larger share of America's exports will go to Pacific Asia, as Pacific Asian growth continues to dwarf European growth; and (2) a smaller share of Pacific-Asian exports will go to the United States. Indeed, in the 1986–9 period, the annual growth rate of North American exports to Pacific Asia was 22 percent, compared to the 10 percent annual growth rate of Pacific-Asian exports to North America.

The Asian-9 (NIEs, ASEAN-4, and China) will probably reduce the share of their exports to the US (given the projected slow growth of after-tax income in the US economy and rising trade frictions) and increase the share of their exports to Japan and to each other. In fact, in 1986–9, the annual growth rate of the NIEs' exports to Pacific Asia was 32 percent, compared to "only" a 23 percent annual rate of growth rate for their total world exports and "only" a 15 percent annual export growth rate to North America. The only real wild card is China, which ran about a $30 billion trade surplus with the US in 1994.

During the same 1986–9 period, there has also been a substantial acceleration of the annual growth rate of Asian exports to Japan: 32 percent by Asian NIEs; 15 percent by the ASEAN-4; and 17 percent by China. Japan's export growth to the Asian-9 has also been rapid, with annual growth rates of 20 percent to the NIEs and 30 percent to the ASEAN-4 in the 1986–9 period.

Foreign investment patterns

Intra-Asian investment, trade and aid are growing substantially and will continue to do so. Some of the principal driving forces for this change are: (1) the appreciation of the yen and the currencies of the NIEs and the depreciation of the US dollar; (2) the democratization, rising wage rates, and stricter pollution controls in Korea and Taiwan; (3) the 1989 elimination of the Generalized System of Preference (GSP) status of the NIEs by the US; (4) the liberalization of trade and investment regimes throughout the PECC; and (5) the political changes which have led to the re-opening of regional trade relations with China and the rapid economic growth of China.

These five forces have substantially changed national competitiveness, national asset values and the international purchasing power of the PECC countries. Between 1985 and 1989, the exchange rate and wage changes that occurred caused manufacturing unit labor costs, in US dollar terms, to rise by about 60 percent in Japan, 80 percent in Taiwan, 60 percent in Korea, 10 percent in Hong Kong, and 30 percent in Singapore. In combination, these forces are propelling waves of transnational direct investments and loans that are reshaping the Pacific Rim's industrial structure and trade patterns, as well as creating new webs of economic and political interdependencies.

In order to reduce production costs, Japanese, Taiwanese, Korean, Hong Kong, and Singaporean firms are investing heavily in manufacturing facilities in Thailand, Malaysia, Indonesia and China. Although US firms continue to invest in these countries also, the post-1985 investment flows are dominated by capital from Japan and the NIEs. The export-oriented nature of these post-1985 investments is demonstrated by the rapidly growing share of manufactured products in total exports. For example, between 1985 and 1989, the manufactured products export share increased from about 10 to 30 percent in Indonesia, from about 30 to 45 percent in Malaysia, and from about 40 to 55 percent in Thailand.[12] To a certain extent the ASEAN countries and China are rapidly becoming off-shore production centers for Japan and the NIEs.

The foreign investment boom in ASEAN since 1986 is obvious to all observers. However, it is difficult to quantify and compare the investment levels among countries because the recipient countries use different classifications for computing the value of investments and because actual investment data is difficult to obtain. Nevertheless, a review of foreign direct investment *approval* data (which is compiled by the recipient countries) provides an indication of the rapid overall growth and major sources of foreign investment in ASEAN. (FDI approvals will most always exceed actual investment, but can be utilized as a leading indicator.) These estimates show that foreign investment approvals between 1986 and 1990 increased by 80 percent for Indonesia, 122 percent for Thailand, 87 percent for the Philippines, 107 percent for Malaysia, and 26 percent for Singapore (Table 14.3). The numbers for China after 1991 reveal similarly impressive growth rates. These estimates also clearly show that Japanese investment plans dominate the totals, with Taiwanese, US and Hong Kong investors also being important sources.

Pacific Rim institutions

These regionalization trends are being facilitated by three different, but overlapping, institutions in the Pacific Rim. The Pacific Basin Economic Council (PBEC), which was founded in 1967, brings senior Pacific Rim business leaders together for annual discussions. The Pacific Economic Cooperation Council (PECC), which was founded in 1980, brings together an elite group of academicians, businessmen, and government policy makers from eighteen Asia–

Table 14.3 Trends of foreign investment approvals in ASEAN countries by major investing countries, 1986–90 (US$ millions and percent)

Recipient investor	*Thailand*	*Indonesia*	*Malaysia*	*Singapore*	*Philippines*
Japan	10,102 (33)	4,117 (20)	1,379 (29)	1,524 (36)	630 (26)
Taiwan	2,819 (9)	1,712 (8)	1,439 (30)	NA	422 (17)
US	2,526 (8)	1,399 (7)	243 (5)	1,627 (38)	402 (16)
Hong Kong	1,923 (6)	1,776 (9)	163 (3)	NA	403 (16)
Singapore	1,346 (4)	778 (4)	372 (8)	–	41 (2)
Korea	563 (2)	1,433 (7)	100 (2)	NA	41 (2)
NIEs Subtotal	6,651 (22)	5,699 (28)	2,075 (44)	NA	907 (37)
Total	30,903(100)	20,187(100)	4,749(100)	4,261(100)	2,462(100)

Source: Adapted from Junko Sekiguchi, "Transformation of the ASEAN manufacturing industry and its outlook," *RIM*, Vol. IV (Tokyo: Mitsui Taiyo Kobe Research Institute, 1991), p. 5. (Original investment approval statistics obtained from each recipient country.)

Pacific countries (Chile, Hong Kong, Mexico, Peru, and Russia became members in 1991). The purpose of the PECC is to anticipate economic developments, explore new opportunities for regional cooperation, and to act in concert to promote a more open global trading system. The PECC also advises and counsels its member governments as a result of the ongoing research undertaken by nine task forces on subjects ranging from agriculture to telecommunications.

The Asia Pacific Economic Cooperation (APEC) process, which was initiated in 1989, has created a regional inter-governmental forum for policy consultations among APEC trade, investment and foreign ministers. APECs's work program and agenda are supported by the research of the PECC task forces.

America's role

In general terms, America's critical role in promoting growth, development, and integration in the Asia–Pacific region can be summarized in terms of the following: providing markets for products made in Asia, providing capital to Asia, providing technology to Asia, providing training for Asian students, promoting the multilateral open trading system, providing aid, and providing a security umbrella, as well as massive infusions of war-related demand during the Korea and Vietnam conflicts. In this chapter, the discussion of

American stimuli to Pacific Rim growth is limited to the importance of the US market and US investments.

In the 1980s, the US market absorbed 30 to 40 percent of the ever-rising export production of most of the nations of the Western Pacific. This, of course, created jobs, business know-how, technology transfer, and massive foreign exchange earnings in Asia. US direct investment aid, technical assistance programs, and university education set the stage for Asian export growth in the 1980s. These exports to America provided high-quality industrial and consumer products and forced American firms to become more competitive. At the same time, these exports eliminated many US manufacturing jobs, led to an overblown US trade deficit and sowed the seeds for serious commercial and diplomatic confrontations between the US and Pacific Asia. However, since 1988, the trade imbalances have been shrinking as Asia's markets have become important sources of demand for American products, ranging from agriculture to aerospace (Table 14.4). For example, US exports to Japan increased by about 70 percent between 1987–91, from US$28 billion to US$48 billion. In these years, Japan's demand for American products grew at more than 20 percent per annum, while American demand for Japanese goods grew at only 5 percent. The pattern of America's export surge and import slowdown is similar with regard to other Asian nations, except China.

Table 14.4 Pacific Rim trade data (US$ millions – merchandise trade)

Country		*Exports (total)*	*Imports (total)*	*Exports to US*	*Imports from US*
China	1988	48,000	54,000	8,500	5,000
	1989	52,500	59,100	12,000	5,800
	1990	62,300	53,200	15,200	4,800
	1991	72,000	57,000	20,000	5,500
Hong Kong	1988	63,200	63,900	10,200	5,700
	1989	73,100	72,200	9,800	6,200
	1990	81,000	80,100	9,600	6,800
	1991	90,400	90,600	8,200	7,200
Taiwan	1988	60,600	46,800	24,700	12,100
	1989	66,200	52,200	24,000	11,300
	1990	67,200	54,700	22,700	11,100
	1991	72,400	60,800	22,200	12,600
Korea	1988	60,700	51,800	21,400	12,800
	1989	62,400	61,500	20,600	15,900
	1990	65,000	69,800	19,400	16,900
	1991	70,500	75,000	19,800	18,900

Table 14.4 Continued

Country		*Exports (total)*	*Imports (total)*	*Exports to US*	*Imports from US*
Japan	1988	264,900	187,300	89,500	37,700
	1989	275,400	211,100	93,600	44,500
	1990	286,900	234,800	89,700	48,000
	1991	305,400	243,600	90,200	47,700
ASEAN	1988	102,600	102,600	21,700	15,150
	1989	121,500	125,900	25,850	18,400
	1990	141,800	156,900	27,000	23,900
Indonesia	1988	19,800	14,300	3,200	1,100
	1989	23,800	17,400	3,500	2,200
	1990	28,100	23,000	3,300	2,500
	1991	29,300	25,500	3,500	2,600
Malaysia	1988	20,400	16,000	3,500	2,800
	1989	25,100	22,600	4,700	3,800
	1990	29,500	29,300	5,000	5,000
	1991	34,500	34,600	5,300	5,900
Philippines	1988	7,100	8,200	1,700	2,500
	1989	7,800	10,400	1,900	2,900
	1990	8,700	12,000	2,400	3,100
	1991	8,700	13,000	2,600	3,300
Singapore	1988	39,300	43,800	9,400	6,800
	1989	44,700	49,700	10,400	8,500
	1990	52,500	60,600	11,200	9,700
	1991	57,800	65,800	10,300	9,900
Thailand	1988	16,000	20,300	3,200	2,750
	1989	20,100	25,800	4,350	2,900
	1990	23,000	32,000	5,100	3,600

Source: US and Foreign Commercial Service, US Department of Commerce, *Country Marketing Plans – 1992* and *Survey of Current Business* (December, 1991), pp. 68–9

American capital flows to Asia have created jobs, transferred technology, provided access to the US market and generated export revenues for Asian economies. These investments have also provided low-cost, high-quality production bases for American firms. In the 1990s, the relative importance of American investments in Asia will continue declining as a result of the growth of intra-Asia capital exports from Japan, Taiwan, Korea, Hong Kong and Singapore. By 1990, the cumulative total of investments by American firms had reached US$14.9 billion in the NIEs, US$8.4 billion in the ASEAN-4, and US$21 billion in Japan. In 1990 alone, US firms invested

Table 14.5 American direct investment in Asia (US$ millions – annual flow historical cost basis)

Country	*1986*	*1987*	*1988*	*1989*	*1990*	*Cumulative historical total*
South Korea	39	396	323	354	241	2,096
Hong Kong	617	3,772	851	708	589	6,537
Taiwan	119	503	249	300	352	2,273
Singapore	382	128	73	7	1,653	3,971
Thailand	4	196	–142	139	244	1,515
Indonesia	–1,258	–147	–149	849	57	3,827
Malaysia	–119	–69	183	39	251	1,425
Philippines	–267	97	117	144	8	1,665
China	–144	40	100	63	NA	NA
Asian-9	–627	4,916	1,605	2,603	3,395*	23,309*
Japan	2,237	4,212	2,325	479	2,506	20,994
World	29,550	54,507	21,586	34,198	51,403	421,494

Source: US Department of Commerce, *Survey of Current Business* (August, 1987, 1988, 1989, and 1990), as reported in Ramstetter and James, "Inward and outward direct foreign investment among the United States and Pacific Basin economies," presented at PECC Structural Issues Conference, Osaka (September 4, 1991) and *Survey of Current Business* (August 1991), pp. 86–8

Note: * Excluding China in 1990

US$2.8 billion in the NIEs (compared to US$3.4 billion by Japanese firms) and US$0.6 billion in the ASEAN-4 (compared to US$3.2 billion by Japanese firms) (see Table 14.5).[13] US investment in China, while behind that of Hong Kong and Taiwan, has also begun to steadily increase.

Japan's role

Prior to the post-1985 yen appreciation, Japan's role in integrating the Asia–Pacific region was primarily in terms of purchasing raw materials, investing in import substitution industries, and providing foreign aid. Since 1985, Japan's direct investment in the Asia–Pacific region, its imports of manufactured products, and its foreign aid disbursements have been expanding rapidly. For example, the investment flow increased from US$1.4 billion in 1985 to a peak of US$7.8 billion in 1989 and continued to grow by another US$6.6 billion in 1990, resulting in a cumulative total in the Asian-9 of US$46.9 billion (see Table 14.6).[14] This has led to the transfer of technology and management practices, and has created jobs throughout the region. Japan's massive foreign aid and portfolio investments are

Table 14.6 Japanese direct investment in Asia (US$ millions – annual flow, notification basis)

Country	*1984*	*1985*	*1986*	*1987*	*1988*	*1989*	*1990*	*Cumulative historical total*
South Korea	107	134	436	647	483	606	250	4,104
Hong Kong	412	131	502	1,072	1,662	1,898	1,800	9,866
Taiwan	66	114	291	367	372	494	450	2,735
Singapore	225	339	302	494	747	1,902	850	6,565
Thailand	119	48	124	250	859	1,276	1,150	4,418
Indonesia	374	408	250	545	586	631	1,100	11,535
Malaysia	142	79	158	163	387	673	750	3,257
Philippines	46	61	21	72	134	202	200	1,522
China	114	100	226	1,226	296	438	NA	2,912
Asian-9	1,605	1,414	2,310	4,836	5,526	8,200	NA	46,914*
US	3,359	5,395	10,165	14,704	21,701	32,540	27,200	131,600
Europe	1,937	1,930	3,469	6,576	9,116	14,808	NA	44,972*
Latin America			4,700	4,800	6,400	5,200	3,600	40,500
World		12,000	22,300	33,400	47,000	67,500	56,800	310,800

Source: Ministry of Finance, *Okurasho Kokusai Kinyukoku Nenpo*, 14th edn (1990), pp. 443–4, as reported by Edward Lincoln, "Japan's rapidly emerging strategy toward Asia," (Paris: OECD Development Centre, Mimeo, October, 1992), Table 1; Japan Economic Institute, No. 31A and No. 39A; Mitsuru Taniuchi and Masatoshi Inouchi, "Foreign Direct Investment in the Asia Pacific Region," a paper presented at the PECC Structural Outlook Conference, Osaka (September 4, 1991)

Note: * Excluding China in 1990

financing a large portion of Asia's capital requirements, and Japanese direct investments are integrating the Asian economies into Japan's production systems. This surge of Japanese direct investment, accompanied by the anticipated increases in Japanese loan and foreign aid capital, is contributing to the economic and financial integration of Asia, with Japan as the "conductor" of the regional orchestra.

Although ASEAN leaders are concerned about the prospect of increased Japanese influence, they are resigned to their lack of alternatives. Nothing much is likely to come of their efforts to increase intra-ASEAN economic cooperation without capital, technology and guidance from Japan. However, unless this de facto regional integration is thoughtfully managed, many observers worry that it will unduly reduce the self-reliance and independence of the social-economic systems of the other Asian nations. As the chairman of a Japanese international management research institute notes:

> Many of these manufacturing operations are joint ventures between Japanese and local corporations, which means that industrial developments in Asian countries have been substantially influenced by the international business strategies of Japanese companies. In many respects, therefore, Asian countries have had to adjust their policies to the (Japanese) business strategies taking place in their countries.[15]

The new capital exporters: the Asian NIEs

Since 1987, Taiwan, Korea, Hong Kong, and Singapore have all become important suppliers of direct investments in the Western Pacific region. Capital exports from these countries are another powerful force for increasing the economic integration of the Pacific Rim economies and they provide some counterbalance to the flood of Japanese investments. The NIEs' investments also transfer technology and management practices, create jobs, and connect the ASEAN countries to a pre-established global distribution network.

Estimates of the cumulative current account balances of the NIEs, which provide the "ammunition" for their capital exports, are provided in Table 14.7. It can be anticipated that the importance of the NIE's direct foreign investments will continue to expand. This is particularly true regarding China, where all of the NIEs have become imporant sources of FDI.

Table 14.7 Cumulative current account balances of Asian newly industralizing economies (US$ billion)

	1986	*1987*	*1988*	*1989*	*1990*	*1991*	*1992*	*1993*
Taiwan (1972–)	+46	+64	+74	+85	+96	+108	+120	+132
Korea (1972–)	−23	−14	0	+5	+3.8	−5.0	−13.0	−20.0
(1986–93)	+4.5	+15	+29	+35	+32.8	+24.0	+16.0	+9.0
Hong Kong (1987–)		+2.5	+5.3	+10.6	+14.1	+16.6	+17.2	+19.4
Singapore (1987–)		+0.5	+1.2	+3.5	+5.7	+9.9	+14.2	+19.2

Source: The historical data for Taiwan are from Council for Economic Planning and Development, *Taiwan Statistical Yearbook 1988* and for Korea are from Bank of Korea, *Economic Statistics Yearbook 1987*. Estimates of subsequent years and estimates for Hong Kong and Singapore are computed from forecasts in OECD, *Economic Outlook* (June, 1992), p. 45

The growing friction between the United States and Japan

As US–Japan commercial relationships have expanded, pernicious emotions of anger, fear, distrust, and disdain seem to be growing even faster – especially in the past few years. Recent changes in American public opinion about Japan and the US are particularly striking.

For example, in 1989, CBS surveyed the American public about which country they thought would be the number one power in the world in the next century.[16] Forty seven percent thought it would be the United States and 38 percent thought it would be Japan. Less than two years later, in October 1991, a CBS–New York Times survey asked the same question and only 25 percent chose the United States; 58 percent selected Japan! Along with this perception of an impending role reversal – and perhaps because of it – there are growing reports of anti-Japanese (and anti-Asian) behavior and sentiments across the US.

Furthermore, a 1991 Yankelovich Clancy Shulman opinion poll of Americans reported the following results:[17] (1) 70 percent were highly suspicious of the intentions of Japanese business and government; (2) 90 percent considered the trade deficit to be a serious threat to the US economy; (3) 70 percent think that Japan denies American products the opportunity to compete fairly in the Japanese market; and (4) 60 percent favor federal legislation to severely limit the importation of Japanese products.

In Japan, in the meantime, growing numbers of Japanese have become increasingly disdainful of the values of American institutions, the quality and productivity of American managers, and the ineptitude of American macroeconomic policy. These attitudes have been highlighted and stimulated by erroneous comments from a number of Japanese political leaders during the past few years. Also, the increased frequency of US government requests that Japan harmonize its social, commercial, and business practices with those of the United States further angers many Japanese. Some recent American interference in what they perceive to be Japan's internal affairs. Others interpret the US requests as the disguised pleadings of a pitiful loser who is seeking an overly large "handicap."

A Rand Corporation study on US–Japan relations reports on the rising flood of mutual recriminations from both Japanese and Americans about the unfairness and inequity of the US–Japan relationship.[18] The study concludes that these antagonisms are leading to a negative policy spiral between the US and Japan and will probably result in a rise of patchwork protectionism which will further undermine the relationship. To prevent this, the report recommends immediate and serious action from American and Japanese leaders to manage and improve the relationship.

Since the evolution of the US–Japan relationship is uncertain, alternative outcomes have been presented in this chapter in the form of alternative Pacific Rim scenarios in the next section.

THREE SCENARIOS FOR ASIA–PACIFIC REGIONALIZATION

As described earlier, the Pacific Asia economies are high-growth and exported-oriented and increasingly trading with each other. Although their trade growth has substantially spurred their economic growth, their trade dependence on the United States and OECD Europe also presents potential vulnerabilities. The economic strength and openness of these markets is vital to the economic strategies of the Asia–Pacific countries. A prolonged period of slow growth in OECD nations (which could possibly result from the correction of the financial excesses of the late 1980s in the United States and Japan, as well as from unanticipated difficulties in re-integrating the former Soviet bloc economies into the European economic structure), a substantial increase in protectionism in the EU or the United States, unmanageable trade conflicts between the United States and Japan, or a collapse of the multilateral trading system would force changes in economic strategies throughout the Asia–Pacific region.

Thus, even though an open economic integration process has

rapidly occurred in the Pacific Rim during the 1980s, it is not certain that such patterns will continue throughout the last half of the 1990s. The speed and nature of the economic and social integration in the Pacific Rim in the 1990s will depend on the effects of ongoing changes in the global political–economic environment. To explore the types of Asia–Pacific integration that may occur in the latter 1990s, three scenarios are sketched below. Each of them is a product of different outcomes of the major factors in the changing global economy and of the US–Japan relationship discussed earlier.

Scenario # 1 policy paralysis: business as usual

The ongoing patterns of open economic integration in the Pacific Rim continue in the second half of the 1990s. Intra-PECC trade and investment shares continue to grow even though no formal trade or investment preferences are given to any actor. However, in fact, Japan, as the dominant investor and donor in the Asian-9, has access to insider information on government policy initiatives. Furthermore, Japanese firms often shape or influence government policies to make them comparable with their business strategies. The "weight" of Japanese capital allows Japanese firms to obtain de facto preferential treatment in terms of such things as achieving quasi-monopoly status for investments, setting technical standards, and obtaining government procurement contracts.

The Asian-9 continue to have bilateral deficits with Japan which are financed by their trade surpluses with the US. This triangular trade pattern continues because the US is unable to regain its competitiveness, Japan continues to develop superior technologies and remains as a major supplier of capital goods, technology, and management practices, the NIEs continue to follow export-led development strategies, and Japan does not replace the US as the major absorber of the trade surpluses of the NIEs.[19]

In this scenario, Japan continues to run a substantial bilateral trade surplus with the United States and a current account surplus with the world of US$70–100 billion per year. Many Japanese analysts argue that such a surplus is necessary in order for Japan to supply the necessary foreign aid and investments to a capital-hungry world. Japan's influence in Asia continues to grow and it becomes the "conductor" of the Asia–Pacific regionalization process and orchestrates national policy and business strategy of the other Pacific Rim nations (including the US). In this scenario, Japanese firms engage in ever larger amounts of intra-firm trade between their subsidiaries in the region, as well as exporting directly from these subsidiaries.

The improvements in the US trade and current accounts stall at deficits of about US$50–60 billion per year. By the year 2000, America's net foreign debt approaches US$1 trillion. This means that America would need to continue to follow monetary, fiscal, and trade policies that make America attractive for foreign investors and lenders.

In order for this "policy paralysis" scenario to occur, almost all of the global economic changes described above would have to be turned upside down. That is, one would have to assume that US foreign policy does not become more commercially-oriented; the EU does not try to protect new East European firms; the US does not become competitive enough to achieve trade surplus by the mid-1990s; the Mexican economy encounters serious difficulties.

This scenario is unstable. It implies ever-rising tension between the US and its Asian trade partners, as well as the unlikely reversal of the seven global economic trends discussed above. Such conditions would probably trigger a substantial US retreat from its commitment to an open multilateral trading system. It would slow the globalization of the world economy and lead to excess export capacity in most of Pacific Asia.

Scenario # 2 policy coordination: US and Japan as co-conductors of a Pacific Rim orchestra

The United States and Japan actually re-structure their economies in keeping with the themes of the Structural Impediments Initiative (SII) agreements of 1990. After slowly recovering from the recession of the early 1990s, the United States follows a restrictive fiscal path causing consumption growth to remain slow; the economy is pulled along by export-led growth. Japan follows a path of domestic demand-led growth and continues to open its economy to imports. The US–Japan bilateral trade deficit is eliminated by the later 1990s and Japan becomes a major absorber of imports from the Asian-9.

With the US and Japan reaching agreement that "harmony requires balance," it is relatively easy to strengthen the PECC and APEC processes from ones of ad hoc consultation to a regular exchange of views, coordination of policies, and adjudication of disputes. The NIEs also accelerate their policies of domestic demand-led growth and liberalization of their trade regimes. The PECC and APEC processes of policy analysis and policy coordination, and the balancing of US–Japan interests within the context of a regional framework, become important factors in achieving these outcomes.

No formal preferential privileges were given to PECC members, other than what was involved in the US–Mexico–Canada Free Trade Agreement. However, due to the enhanced consultation and policy coordination processes developed by the PECC and APEC, intra-PECC trade and investment shares grew rapidly and economic and social integration of the region was accelerated. Also, APEC used its bargaining power to countervail potential EU tendencies to develop overly restrictive preferential policies. As a consequence, a relatively open worldwide trading system was maintained.

The stimuli for this "policy coordination" scenario consist of the following factors. First, the United States becomes serious about eliminating its twin deficits. After taking the politically painful actions to reduce its federal deficit, the US needs to stimulate growth by promoting exports. Second, with the reduction of security concerns in the aftermath of communism's collapse in Europe, Americans realize that economic rivalries will dominate its relations with the EU and Japan. This realization helped America do two things: (1) to take micro and macroeconomic measures to promote its long-term competitiveness; and (2) to seriously negotiate trade issues with the objective being to improve commercial results, rather than to improve the processes of the multilateral trade system. These new perspectives cause the US to: (1) develop a national economic strategy that makes the nation more producer-oriented and less consumer-oriented; and (2) makes credible threats to limit the access of Japan and the NIEs to the US market, unless they stimulate domestic growth and open their economies. The continued specter of a protectionist US–Mexico FTA and a potentially more protectionist EU motivate Japan and the NIEs to respond in a way to strengthen a more open and dynamic Asia–Pacific region.

Scenario # 3 policy conflict: the US and Japan conduct separate orchestras

A tri-polar world of relatively protectionist trading blocs in Europe, North America, and the Western Pacific emerges. Slow growth in the United States, frustration at the failure to shrink the budget deficit, resentment over Japan's reluctance to balance its trade account, the failure of the GATT negotiations, and the emergence of an even more protectionist EU combined to motivate the United

States to follow a "hardball" strategy in its trade and economic policy negotiations with the EU, Japan, and the NIEs.

The "unreasonable" American negotiation posture, rising nationalism in Japan, and the "revealed superiority" of Japan's model of managed economic and trade policies encouraged Japan to develop a Pacific Asia Economic Region. Building upon the substantial foundation of Japanese trade, investment, and aid relations throughout Asia, more foreign aid funds are channelled to the Asian-9. This was done in order to accelerate the infrastructure development needed to support the continued expansion of Japanese private sector investments. Japanese subsidiaries in the Asian-9 increased their exports to Japan, but were limited in their ability to substantially expand their exports to the EU and the US, as a result of the new preferential access given by the EU to production sourced in Eastern Europe and given by the US to production sourced in Mexico.

Japan's financial flows, its supply of capital goods, technology, and management expertise, and it ability to bargain for access to the North American and EU markets are critical factors that compel the Asian-9 to subsume some of their latent fears and distrust of Japan's leadership. Political and business leaders in the Asian-9 came to reluctantly accept the idea that preferential relations with Japan are necessary in order for their nations to prosper in the more protectionist world of the 1990s.

Since Japan no longer needs to follow American security policies in Asia, it rapidly expands its commercial relations with China, North Korea and Vietnam. To some extent, these nations became competitors with Japan's other Asian-9 partners for capital and markets. However, the integration of these nations into the Pacific Asia region also creates new markets and new destinations for low cost foreign investments for other members.

Inter-regional trade and investment between North America, Europe, and Asia still continue to grow, but at a slower pace than in the 1980s. The American, German, and Japanese regional "conductors" focus most of their new initiative and capital on developing "their" regions. Whether or not these regional groups become "stumbling blocs" or "building blocs" for a more open world trading system depends on how discriminatory and how acrimonious relations became between the three regions.[20] Theoretically, regional integration processes that lower internal barriers could be consistent with a progressively liberalized world trading system. The outcome depends on the vision, courage and trust of business and government leaders in the three regions.

POLICY IMPLICATIONS FOR GOVERNMENT AND BUSINESS

The world economic order is changing. A potentially disruptive question facing the world economy is how to reduce global trade and financial imbalances, as the United States returns to trade and financial balance by the later 1990s, and as the nations of Eastern Europe and the former Soviet Union attempt to become integrated into the global capitalist network. American leaders need to continue to reduce America's need for foreign capital and make certain that American products continue to become more competitive. American and foreign leaders need to make certain that the markets of America's trading partners become open enough and strong enough to absorb US$600 billion worth of US merchandise exports per year by the later 1990s. And, of course, the recent dramatic expansion of Japan's external surplus needs to be reserved.

In the final analysis, the stabilization of the international economic system and the developmnt of the PECC's Open Regionalism Model (which is consistent with the policy coordination scenario) requires an expansion of exports from America and a slowing – if not an actual reduction – of imports into America. America's domestic demand needs to grow more slowly than its production of GNP for the rest of this century. Such a reversal of American consumption and trade patterns will profoundly shape the economic structure of the Pacific Rim and the world in the years to come. It will also shape the business environment and cause more American firms to look overseas for growing markets.

An American approach

What are some actions that American leaders can take to manage this inevitable process of adjustment? American leaders need to rid themselves of the self-crippling mindset that says America does not have enough resources to influence and shape international events. America is a rich, productive nation that can make a number of choices to release resources in order to shape the international economic environment. This is a matter of commercial and political choice – not destiny.

American leaders in business and government should never again talk themselves into decline with self-fulfilling political rhetoric about America's weaknesses, nor should America's leaders be continuously begging Japan to finance America's domestic capital needs and the world's international capital needs. There is no need for America to be a spectator of, or a mere respondent to, the dynamic changes occurring in the global marketplace. America can and should – along with its allies – shape the international economic environment. It is in America's self-interest to pursue an activist policy in international economic affairs, especially with regard to the Pacific Rim.

If America demonstrates its seriousness about being a leader in international business competition, its Pacific Rim partners, in particular, will pay more attention to America's requests for fair play and reciprocity in international business transactions. This could be effectively negotiated in the Asia Pacific Economic Cooperation (APEC) structure. APEC has created an intergovernmental regional forum for policy consultations among its trade, finance, and foreign ministers. However, in order for APEC to evolve into a dynamic and effective structure for promoting Asia–Pacific prosperity, APEC needs the visionary leadership and support from both the US and Japan.

Such cooperative leadership could evolve from the concepts of the US–Japan Global Partnership Declaration.[21] This partnership is intended to produce bilateral US–Japan cooperation on a broad range of issues, such as promoting world peace, enhancing security cooperation, cooperating on science and technology, enhancing mutual understanding, reinvigorating the SII talks, enhancing bilateral trade and investment cooperation, etc.

If the US and Japan cannot become partners, then there is a possibility that current trends could eventually make them enemies. Thus, it is imperative for Americans and Japanese to modify their economic and commercial fundamentals to accomplish a quick balancing of US–Japan trade flows. Simply stated, this requires a substantial expansion of US exports to Japan, or a substantial reduction of Japanese exports to the US, or some combination thereof.

An Asian response

Asian leaders should inform themselves and their key constituents of the far-reaching implications of the major changes in the international economy described earlier. First, the leaders of Asian capital exporting nations should accelerate their efforts to restructure their economies from export-led growth patterns toward patterns of more sustainable domestic demand-led growth. Second, Asian leaders should accelerate their efforts to diversify export markets away from the United States. Third, Asian leaders should prepare themselves for much more difficult bargaining with American trade negotiators regarding "fair" trade, reciprocity, intellectual property rights, trade-related investment measures, and currency exchange rates. Fourth, Asian leaders should expand their efforts within the PECC and APEC process to foster policy consultation and coordination to improve balance and harmony in the Pacific Rim.

CONCLUSION

This chapter asserts that ongoing economic integration in the Pacific Rim will continue in the years ahead. It identifies several changing trends in the world economy that will shape the speed and nature of this Asia–Pacific integration process. Although three scenarios have been described – policy paralysis, policy coordination, and policy conflict – only the last two seem plausible. The policy paralysis scenario appears inconsistent with the direction of change in terms of global trends. It was included, however, because it happens to be the scenario that seems to reflect much of today's conventional wisdom. Of the remaining two scenarios, policy coordination and policy conflict, wich is more likely? The answer, of course, depends on the policy actions taken by key actors over the next few years. The growing phenomena of strategic business alliances between American and Japanese firms, between American and Korean firms, and between American and Taiwanese firms, should help promote regional integration, as should the trend toward the institutionalization of governmental policy coordination that is rapidly evolving in the APEC process. The emergence of China as a major economic force in the region should also facilitate greater regional linkages.

In the final analysis, there is a great deal at stake for all parties – private and public – if they choose to delay confronting the trends described in this chapter. In many respects, the corporate sector remains ahead of the government in responding to opportunities. Accordingly, it will be incumbent upon all participating economies in the Pacific Rim to pay closer attention to their common interests (at firm level) rather than political rivalries so that foreign investment and economic cooperation can be harnessed as a force for greater global prosperity.

NOTES

1 For a summary of the conference, see Mark Earle Jr., *PECC IX: Executive Summary* (Washington, DC: US National Committee for Pacific Economic Cooperation, 1992).
2 Lee Kwan Yew, "The Asian/Pacific region in the new geopolitical context," *World Economic Forum*, Davos, Switzerland (February 4, 1990).
3 An analysis of the macroeconomic causes and consequences of America's excess spending is provided by M. A. Akhtar, "Adjustment of US external imbalances," *74th Annual Report of the Federal Reserve Bank of New York* (April, 1989). For a discussion of policy implications of the deficit, see Francis M. Bator, "Must we retrench?" *Foreign Affairs*, Vol. 68, No. 2 (Spring, 1989), pp. 93–123.
4 US Department of Labor, *Monthly Labor Review* (November, 1991), p. 152; data on Taiwan and Korea from Taiwan's Ministry of Economic Affairs (see Table 14.1).
5 Dr. Helmut Haussman, "Remarks at the World Economic Forum", Davos, Switzerland (February 3, 1990).
6 For information on the progress of Mexico's economic reforms and its historic policy reversal to pursue a Free Trade Agreement with the United States, see Wilson Perez Nunez, "From globalization to regionalization: the Mexican case" (Paris: OECD Development Centre Technical Paper No. 24, August, 1990).
7 Jose Angel Gurria, "The road to the virtuous circle: Mexico's efforts and achievements since 1982," a paper presented at the OECD Development Centre (November 25–6, 1991), by Mexico's Undersecretary for International Financial Affairs.
8 Pacific Economic Cooperation Council, *Pacific Economic Outlook 1992–1993* (Washington, DC: US National Committee for Pacific Economic Cooperation, June, 1992), p. 66.
9 K. C. Yeh, Man-bing Sze, Norman Levin, "The changing Asian economic environment and US–Japan trade relations," (Santa Monica: Rand Corporation, R-3986–CUSJR, September, 1990), pp. 7 and 50.
10 US National Committee on Pacific Economic Cooperation (June, 1992), pp. 66–8.
11 Kiichiro Fukasaku, "Economic regionalization and intra-industry trade: Pacific–Asian perspectives" (Paris: OECD Development Centre Technical Paper No. 53, February, 1992), pp. 54–7, Appendix Tables 1 and 2.
12 Junko Sekiguchi, "Transformation of the ASEAN manufacturing industry and its outlook," *RIM*, Vol. IV (Tokyo: Mitsui Taiyo Kobe Research Institute, 1991), p. 8.
13 Eric Ramstetter and William James, "Inward and outward direct foreign investment amongst the United States and Pacific Basin economies," a paper presented at the PECC Structural Outlook Conference, Osaka (September 4, 1992). The data is from the *Survey of Current Business* (August, 1991), pp. 86–8 (historical cost basis).
14 Mitsuru Taniuchi and Masatoshi Inouchi, "Foreign direct investment in the Asia Pacific Region," a paper presented at the PECC Structural Outlook Conference, Osaka (September 4, 1991) and Edward J. Lincoln, "Japan's rapidly emerging strategy toward Asia" (Paris: OECD Devel-

opment Centre Technical Paper No. 58, April, 1992). The data are from the Ministry of Finance (notification basis).

15 Kennosuke Katayama, "The role of Japanese companies in Asia's economic development," *RIM*, Vol. IV (Tokyo: Mitsui Taiyo Kobe Research Institute, 1991), p. 3.

16 Reported by David Gergen, "America's missed opportunities," *Foreign Affairs* (Winter, 1992), p. 16.

17 Reported in "America and Japan in conflict: an emotional and cultural explanation" (Los Angeles: Saatchi & Saatchi DFS/Pacific (Mimeo), 1992).

18 See R. Benjamin et al., "The fairness debate in US–Japan economic relations" (Santa Monica: RAND Corporation # R-4100–CUSJR, 1992).

19 For these viewpoints, see Yung Chul Park and Won Am Park, "Changing Japanese trade patterns and the East Asian NICs" (Seoul: Korea Development Institute, WP # 9003, March, 1990).

20 For a discussion of four global trade scenarios – (1) More of GATT, (2) Regional Blocs, (3) Managed Trade, and (4) Super GATT – see Robert Z. Lawrence, "Scenarios for the world trading system and their implications for developing countries" (Paris: OECD Development Centre Technical Paper No. 47, November, 1991).

21 "The Tokyo Declaration on the US–Japan global partnership" (Tokyo: Ministry of Foreign Affairs (mimeo), January 10, 1992) and Takashi Hatagawa and Reizo Utagawa, "Beyond the action plan: a new US–Japan alliance" (Tokyo: IIGP Policy Paper 77E, February, 1992); Yasuhiro Nakasone, "Beyond Kenbei and Japan bashing" (Tokyo: IIGP, June, 1992).

Index